Constructive Concepts

Willy Rotzler

A History of Constructive Art
from Cubism to the Present

Published in the United States of America in 1989 by:

Rizzoli International Publications, Inc.

597 Fifth Avenue / New York 10017

© 1977/1989 by ABC Edition, Zurich

The publication of this book
was sponsored by
Pro Helvetia,
Arts Council of Switzerland

English translation by Stanley Mason
Layout Hans Rudolf Ziegler
Color separations Cliché + Litho Ltd., Zurich
Produced by Jean Frey Druck, Zurich

Library of Congress Catalog Card Number: 77-89937
ISBN: 0-8478-1024-0

Printed in Switzerland

Contents

The highest life is mathematics —
The life of the gods is mathematics —
Pure mathematics is religion.

Novalis (1772–1801), Fragments

Special circumstances were involved in the appearance of the first edition of this book in 1977. From the early sixties onward a collection had been taking shape in New York which grouped the productions of constructive art, from its beginnings to the present, in the form of a history of the development of constructive trends. It restricted itself closely to displaying developments and changes in the greatest possible clarity and breadth and to documenting the persistence of constructive concepts up to the very latest departures.

Once this collection had been rounded off, it seemed an obvious step to compile a history of constructive art on the basis of its exhibits. The first edition of this book thus relied for its illustrations on the items in the McCrory Collection, New York, though it mentioned in the text works and artists not included therein. The collection, no doubt the most comprehensive of its kind, was initially the personal concern of Meshulam Riklis, who says "that art should be an integral part of the human environment. It should not just be experienced by a privileged few but should be made available to all levels of society. A modern corporation should play a significant role in the cultural endeavors of the community and thereby improve the quality of life in our society. Art should excite the individual, so that he or she will have the opportunity to look, to study, to appreciate and to grow in the process of observation."

The assembling of the collection goes to the personal credit of Mrs. Celia Ascher. Entrusted with the gathering of a "McCrory Collection", she pursued a clear program in many years of persevering work: the development of Constructivism. She comments: "My attention was not entirely directed to the pioneers of this style. My interest was also drawn to the younger contemporary artists who try through their constructive concepts to recognize the basic structures of our life and our time and make them visual."

This statement furnished the title of the book: "Constructive Concepts". If the word "concept" is taken in its literal sense to mean the form in which an idea is first conceived, it implies that behind works of a constructive character there are ideas which may only be partly contained in the finished work itself or which may point beyond it. The concepts of constructive artists may be formal and aesthetic, social and Utopian, philosophic or epistemological. They have only a limited kinship with the so-called Concept Art of the sixties and seventies.

From 1976 onward parts of the McCrory Collection were to be seen in many traveling exhibitions that were shown in museums in Europe, the United States and Japan. In view of the vigorous response and the wide publicity evoked by these exhibitions, Mr. M. Riklis decided in 1985/86 to donate about one third of the McCrory Collection to each of three major museums: the Museum of Modern Art in New York, the Museum Louisiana in Humlebaek near Copenhagen, and the Tel Aviv Museum.

There is no other movement in the art of the twentieth century which has remained so tenaciously alive and has diffused into so many creative areas as constructive art. In retrospect it can be seen as a logical consequence of the endeavors made since 1900 to find a non-objective art language. The advance into non-objectivity—the most revolutionary achievement of modern art in the West— took place on three fronts which can be classed under the headings of emotional, sensuous, and rational, corresponding in the creative pictorial sphere to the expressive, organic and constructive approaches. Constructive art has mobilized the faculties of painters and sculptors of widely differing temperaments since the beginning of this century, in ever new waves, in many places, and with a continually changing emphasis.

Max Bill presented the phenomenon of constructive art in its entirety for the first time in Zurich in 1960, when he staged the exhibition "Concrete Art, Fifty Years of Development", and compared it with other, freer forms of concrete presentation. The book "Constructivism, Origins and Evolution" by George Rickey, published in 1965, reviewed the more recent expressions of Constructivism against the background of the achievements of the pioneers.

Both the German and the English editions of "Constructive Concepts" have long been out of print. It therefore seemed desirable to reprint a work that is still useful as a handbook. Mr. M. Riklis and the McCrory Collection with Mrs. Celia Ascher kindly gave their consent to the preparation of a revised version.

In this new edition the illustrations have been extended to include important works from all phases of constructive art, and in some cases examples from the McCrory Collection have been replaced. The text has been worked over and now takes account of the more recent literature on individual aspects of constructive art.

The closing chapter on the present-day situation has been rewritten and furnished with new illustrations. The annex is also new, with a select bibliography and a comprehensive chronological chart. Both are intended, in view of the reawakening of interest in geometric art, to stimulate the reader to undertake his own investigations.

W.R.

Tectiforms, paleolithic rock painting, El Castillo Cave, Santander, Northern Spain

Geometric Form as a Fundamental Experience

In 1910 Wassily Kandinsky, then living in the village of Murnau in Upper Bavaria, painted a watercolor that differed not so much in degree as in kind from his previous "Improvisations". While in the latter—greatly simplified pictures in expressive forms and colors—rudimentary landscape and figurative elements can be discerned, the new watercolor, which was left untitled in the artist's estate, is completely devoid of any suggestion of an objective or figurative starting point. It is a free non-objective or non-representational composition of improvised lines and patches of color. This watercolor does not stand alone either in Kandinsky's work or in the art of the time.

All over Europe, from Paris to Moscow, artists of the most diverse origins were busied in 1910 on pictures which cannot be regarded as representations or interpretations of visible reality. All these pictures are characterized by the arrangement—sometimes strictly controlled, sometimes free—of color and form elements that do not "mean" anything either alone or in the framework of the composition as a whole. This advance into complete abstraction or into the "non-objective world", as another Russian, Kasimir Malevich, was later to call it, is one of the greatest and perhaps the most daring achievements of twentieth-century art.

What was it all about? The confrontation with visible reality which had been the artist's business, with certain variations of purpose, for hundreds of years had suddenly forfeited its compulsive power. The visible world had lost interest, it could no longer draw and hold the artist's attention. Instead, he freed himself deliberately, and often with express intent, from ties to the phenomena revealed by sight. And he turned resolutely to new and quite different problems: to the visualization of inward images, inward realities, and at the same time to the problems, immanent in all art, of a conscious coming-to-grips with the pictorial media of form and color.

This forward thrust into integral abstraction and non-objectivity—long prepared on the intellectual plane—was undertaken in practice at the beginning of the second decade of this century. The audacious venture, embarked on at about the same time by many artists in many places, often without previous contacts, has fundamentally changed the face of art. For the rejection of any kind of representation or reproduction of aspects of the visible world results in the extraordinary phenomenon of the complete correspondence of form and content in the work of art. The artist's media are freed from their subservient function. The work of art no longer "means" anything, but is exactly what it is. It refers to no objective world outside of itself. Its reality and its autonomy are absolute. All the art produced since, whatever its style, would be unthinkable without this radical advance into the non-objective world.

Obviously, art is an abstraction at all times and in all forms. Even the most objective, reality-mirroring art is an abstraction: the transference of the three-dimensional reality of plastic and spatial phenomena to a two-dimensional surface is clearly an abstraction, however "naturalistic" or illusionistic a painting may be. Even in sculpture that attempts to reproduce a corporeal form with complete truth to nature, the translation of the original material qualities and consistence of the model into the plastic substance used by the artist—stone, bronze, wood or plastics—is as much a form of abstraction as the change of scale. Perhaps the highest degree of abstraction is involved in drawing, in which a thin, surfaceless, bodiless outline must somehow capture the surfaces and corporeal forms of the model.

Abstraction, or the renunciation of truth to nature, can be understood as a continuous process: motifs or complexes thereof taken from visible reality are simplified to an increasing extent, are stylized and reduced to their essentials. This gradual elimination of the fortuitous details of an objective complex, or in other words the substitution of the typical or generally valid for the individual appearance, can be observed in the development of numerous artists who have sought liberation from visible reality in our own century.

Abstraction can also be understood, however, as a voluntary and as it were unique act, a spontaneous decision to renounce from the first the use of any element of visible reality as a starting point for the creative process. This resolve to produce "pure art" or "absolute art" can also be observed in many artists in the years following 1910. Kandinsky's watercolor of 1910, unquestionably non-objective, can be seen either as a final stage in a process of abstraction experimentally pursued from work to work or as a voluntary act consisting in the conversion of "inward images" into the reality of the work of art. The painter and sculptor Jean Arp was the first to term this translation of mental concepts into real works "concretion", meaning the material rendering of a vision which is in principle completely free of any reference to the form-world of visible phenomena. The continuous process of abstraction which finally leads to non-objectivity contains the logic and consistency of every evolutionary system. Free and unconditional creation from the artist's own form-conceptions is, by comparison, a much bolder undertaking: an adventurous step into a completely new art world, a revolutionary act of liberation.

The concept of "concretion" chosen by Arp for the visible rendering of mental images—as opposed to the concept

Geometric face painting of a Nuba tribesman, Sudan

of "abstraction" as the final stage of a process — was later taken up and refined by Theo van Doesburg. In his "Manifeste de l'art concret" published in Paris in 1930 he endeavored to distinguish this "concrete art" clearly from "abstract art". He speaks of a "time of concretization of the creative spirit" and contrasts the "natural form", which is still the basis even of an abstraction, with the pure "mental form". Doesburg's idea of concrete art was again seized upon in 1944 by Max Bill: "We call Concrete Art works of art which are created according to techniques and laws entirely appropriate to them, without taking external support from experiential nature or from its transformation, that is to say, without the intervention of a process of abstraction."

From the outset, or in other words from soon after 1910, it became clear that this new non-representational art was moving in two opposite directions, between which there are many transitional forms. These two directions of non-objective art may be qualified, by way of simplification, as free, organic or expressive non-objectivity on the one hand and geometric, constructive non-objectivity on the other. The former may be taken to belong more to the emotional and irrational, the latter to the rational realm. There is no need to point out here that in the shaping process of art the intellect and the emotions are not mutually exclusive, but are both involved, even though their proportions will continually differ. The manifold aspects of non-objective art in the last eighty years, as well

as the personal lifeworks of the artists who have contributed to it, bear witness to this fact.

The polarization of organic and geometric forms is not an invention of the new art that has arisen since 1910. It is first distinctly manifested in the applied arts and particularly in the ornament of the "Art Nouveau" or "Jugendstil" of the turn of the century, in which the undulating "floral" style of the French movement (Hector Guimard and others) contrasts sharply with the strictly geometric style of the Scottish school (Charles Rennie Mackintosh in Glasgow) or the "small squares style" of the Viennese workshop (Kolo Moser, Josef Hoffmann and others). It has therefore been rightly pointed out that the immediate sources of geometric and non-objective art, as represented throughout Europe since the second decade of this century, must be sought in the form-language of the geometric "Jugendstil" and in the closely related early functional architecture. It is quite legitimate to ask, however, whether the division of "organic" and "geometric" art does not correspond to a fundamental antinomy of creative concepts and processes which would accordingly also be present in the art of other epochs and cultures.

The theoretical study "Concerning the Spiritual in Art" by Wassily Kandinsky offers direct access to the artistic thought of 1910. Written in 1908—1911 and published in Munich in 1912, this little book, which appeared first in German but has since been brought out repeatedly and in various other languages, has retained its importance as the earliest expression of a new conception of art in our century. In spite of some high-flown and effusive writing, it enables us to follow the genesis of an idea of art which differs fundamentally from all previous theories. An important element is the realization — more accurately formulated by Kandinsky in 1930 in his essay "L'Art concret" — that "it will never be possible to practice painting without colors and lines, but that painting without objects has long existed in our own times". This pure painting, according to Kandinsky, can be either organic or geometric (or, as he terms it as early as 1912, constructive). Both branches of non-objective art, the organic type, which often becomes expressionistic, and the geometric, have since played a prominent role in all domains of artistic endeavor. The development of geometric or constructive art since the second decade of this century, however, has been steadier and more consistent than that of its organic counterpart.

It goes without saying that the protagonists of this new art, conscious as they are of having fathered something radically new, have looked around in the art of other periods and of foreign cultures for analogous artistic trends. In this need to establish some sort of "tradition" for the school of thought they represent they do not differ from the generation immediately preceding them, the Fauves and Expressionists, who had discovered fascinating parallels to their own expressive utterance in the wooden sculpture of African Negroes and of the South Sea peoples, and who also thought they recognized a kindred spirit in the primitive pre-Romanesque art of the Middle Ages and above all in popular art.

For the representatives of non-objective art the question of historical parallels took a different form. They had to look to those epochs and cultures in which art, for whatever reason, had forgone the reproduction of figural or material reality, or in other words for a more or less pronounced leaning to abstraction. This feeling for the quality of abstraction, for the non-representational basis of art, had been awakened and stimulated by a publication which may be regarded as having really initiated the development of abstract art in the twentieth century: Wilhelm Worringer's theoretical study "Abstraktion und Einfühlung" (Abstraction and Empathy), which appeared in Munich in 1908.

Worringer sets out from the premise that in man there is not only an "empathic urge" but an "urge to abstraction", which plays a leading part in artistic creation among certain peoples and at certain times. Arguments drawn from the psychology of art even lead Worringer to see in the urge to abstraction the beginning of all art. According to this theory art is a medium, in fact the only medium, by which man can hold his own against the confusing diversity and domination of visible phenomena. "All transcendental art is therefore directed toward a disorganization of the organic, that is, a translation of changing and conditional elements into the unconditional values of necessity. Man, however, can perceive such necessity only in the great realm beyond living things, in the inorganic world. This leads him to the rigid line, to the dead crystalline form. He has converted all life into the language of these imperishable and unconditional values. For these abstract forms, liberated from all finiteness, are the highest and the only ones in which man can rest from the confusion of his picture of the world. On the other hand, the laws of this inorganic world are mirrored in the law of that organ with which we overcome our sensuous dependence, namely our human intellect."

No sooner had Worringer's defense and justification of the ideas and impulses of abstract art appeared than they became for the artists concerned an aesthetically and psychologically founded argument for their own rejection of natural models. The art theorist's sharp attack on the "banal imitation theories which . . . have made us blind to the truly psychic values" had the full support of the generation which, around 1910, was attempting to free itself from all forms of imitative art.

Worringer's epoch-making statement that abstraction is not a late phase or even an aberration of artistic evolution but a primary expression of the shaping will and perhaps the beginning of all art supplied the young art of his day with the substantiation it needed. It also contributed considerably to the downfall of the materialistic outlook of the nineteenth century, and above all of the traditional view of an art based on a "classical" canon of beauty. The eyes of contemporaries were opened to qualities of art and to the artistic productions of periods and cultures that had previously been disregarded or held in low esteem. Of course, modern art since Impressionism had also contributed considerably to this reorientation through the growing interest of artists in the media of art. Today, when we can look back over eighty-odd years of non-objective art, we have no difficulty in recognizing in the artistic productions of other eras the phenomena in which some of Worringer's "urge to abstraction" is embodied. We are therefore in a position to distill from the whole heritage of art the evidence for the "antecedents of abstract art" and to cite some eloquent examples. The collection of such material, however, involves a risk of al-

Pyxis with horses on the lid, Attic-geometric style, c. 750 B.C., private collection

Floor mosaic in the House of the Trident, Isle of Delos, 8th century B.C.

Basket, split bamboo, Indonesia, Zurich, Museum of Ethnology

"Celosia", lattice from the Mosque in Cordoba, Hispano-Islamic, 9th century

Astronomical instruments, Observatory of Jaipur, India, 17/18th century

lowing mere formal analogies to the phenomena of twentieth-century art to masquerade as actual models and forerunners. The new departure that began in Western art about 1910—the exploitation of all artistic media without any representational or illusionistic intent—evolved out of itself when certain preliminary conditions were satisfied. It certainly did not result from a knowledge of earlier models or from any desire to imitate them.

The preliminary conditions were of a very complex nature. They are reflected first of all in the concentration of artists from the middle of the nineteenth century onward upon the basic prerequisites of art: on the systematic study and conscious application of the media of art: color and form. The sociological requirements of art also played their part. With the rise of a bourgeoisie in the nineteenth century, with the democratization of the structures of state and society, the artist had lost his established position of supplier of works of art to the church, the nobility and the wealthy classes. This social alienation was accompanied by another of an artistic character: forced into the role of an outsider, the artist tended more and more to set his own assignments. Liberation from social duties was in fact accompanied by a parallel artistic liberation. The material difficulty of selling art productions to contemporaries who were increasingly at a loss to understand them was counterbalanced by the ideal and personal advantage of being free to seek solutions to self-appointed artistic problems. To solve these problems involving forms and colors the artist had less and less need of motifs drawn from visible reality; he could abstract from them and finally do without them altogether. These are the conditions for the increasingly elitist position of progressive art: the artist turns with his new message to his colleagues and to a limited circle of open-minded art-lovers. This narrow circle of initiates has been extended in the last eighty years by widely varying forms of art publicity, by an art trade pledged to contemporary production and by the activities of art institutions widely dispersed at first, but later becoming more numerous.

Non-objective geometric or constructive art in particular was felt on its emergence to be something new and revolutionary and was acclaimed or rejected as such. It soon proved, however, that it had many historical parallels. While they differ considerably in character, they reveal one thing very clearly: that the intuitive or conscious use of rationally accessible geometric and, in the extreme case, exact mathematical compositional means have fascinated the artistically inclined throughout man's history. The promoters and champions of geometric and constructive art have for years been drawing attention to such forerunners, analogies and parallels.

It is well enough known that since Neolithic times, during the transition from the hunter and gatherer cultures to those of herdsmen and tillers of the soil, a tendency to abstraction and even to geometry can be observed in man's artistic utterances. A so-called "geometric style" opens all the great early cultures (ill. p 11 top). This primitive proclivity for geometric forms, exemplified particularly in New Stone and Bronze Age pottery of the fifth to the second millennium B.C. in Egypt, Mesopotamia and above all Persia, has sometimes been associated by researchers with the development of sedentary habits and of feudal agrarian societies, with the change from a magic to a cultic conception of existence, with the evolution of exact measurement of time and thus with historical thinking. Mathematicians call this geometric ornament of the Neolithic era "mathematical ornament" and see it as early evidence of a preoccupation with mathematics.

Whatever the reasons may be for this preference for geometric ornament and the translation of figural motifs (man, animals) into abstract ciphers, it is striking that throughout the Old World—in the Mediterranean area, in the Near, Middle and Far East and in the ancient American cultures—there is a complete or nearly complete absence of figuration at corresponding stages of development, while the picture-making urge finds its outlet in geometric designs. Although their exact meaning may still be disputed, geometric patterns predominate in pottery, in early textile art, in wickerwork and in the decoration of Bronze-Age tools and weapons. There can be no doubt that the seemingly ornamental patterns contain symbolic meanings (ill. p. 11). We may assume that they have to do with the great issues of life and with relations to higher powers.

It so happens that systematic investigation of the art of the Old Stone Age and thus of the last Ice Age has also brought to light examples of geometric art that are thousands of years older than the Neolithic and Bronze-Age styles. We are dealing here with the clearly geometric line patterns found in the cave art of the Old Stone Age in southwestern France and Spain, within the confines of the Franco-Cantabrian culture (ill. p. 8). Researchers cannot yet agree on the signification of these "tectiforms". The more obvious interpretation is that they are the shapes of houses, roofs or tents, whence the name given them (Latin: tectum = roof); but others see in them schematic traps and nets, which would bring the geometric signs into relation with the magic practices of paleolithic hunters and fishermen. The grids and frames delineated on cave walls and ceilings have even been classed as a rudimentary sex symbolism. Whatever they may have meant, they show that even in prehistoric art the "abstract" straight line and the line systems constructed with it were a valid form of pictorial utterance and understandable to contemporaries, perhaps in direct contiguity to the astonishing "naturalistic" drawings and paintings of animals.

Compared with these prehistoric signs, the geometric style of the early cultures is easier for us to understand. In Neolithic pottery in particular, the development of the decorative patterns on the necks or shoulders of vessels can be directly related to the potter's technical resources. The decorative function of these patterns, however, should not mislead us into regarding them merely as a craftsman's routine for embellishing certain objects, without any real artistic relevance (ill. p. 11). A systematic study of this primary ornamentation shows instead that the basic repertoire of linear surface treatment is put to use: straight lines, wavy lines, zigzags, angular lines, dotted lines, dot structures, parallel lines, advancing and returning line movements and so forth. In many instances there is no clear dividing line between geometric ornament and elementary symbolism. In any case basic symbolic shapes, such as circle, triangle, cross, swastika, spiral, spoked wheel and whirling disk, are often combined with pure line systems to form complex geometric surface structures. They are the expression both of aesthetic pleasure in geometric patterns and of hidden, or perhaps we should say coded, sign-messages. Even today, certain African tribes use geometric patterns for body-painting and tattooing (ill. p. 10). The development of writing from pictogram to ideogram and finally to syllable or letter signs shows that these geometric signs also bear a certain relationship to language and its fixation in writing.

If we assume, then, that pure geometric configurations are one of the original channels for man's pictorial utterance—and the evidence cited supports the assumption—it is justifiable to ask what happened to this elementary shaping urge, apart from mere representational purposes, in the great cultures of antiquity, in which—as art history shows—the evolution of figurative art moved from primitive or stylized presentation toward ever greater truth to nature. There could be no better example of this evolution than Greek art as it passes from Hellenic archaism to the classical period of the fifth century and to final decline in the Hellenism of the third century B.C.

Provided that we accept the existence of a latent geometric shaping urge, we can argue that in antiquity, as a result of a dominant esteem for anthropomorphism, of the ideal of human beauty, this urge withdrew into the realm of ornament, but retained its importance there. Perhaps we can go further and say that the "innate" need of the human being to express himself in abstract and preferably geometric forms was displaced in antiquity to the domain of architecture. In this sphere of activity the faculty of thinking in abstract forms and form complexes was able to find particularly clear expression. For the object here was to translate abstract concepts into the reality of three-dimensional stereometric bodies while making ever greater use of basic mathematical principles. The cubic content of these bodies was the result of rationally related line systems representing length, breadth, depth and

Maze, from a series of woodcuts by G.A. Boeckler, 1664

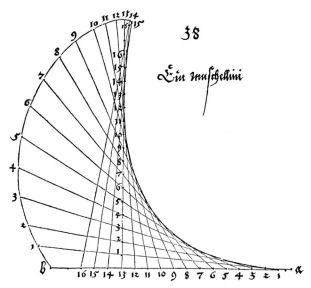

38

Albrecht Dürer, "Shell-Line", woodcut from "Unterweisung der Messung", 1525

height. Greek temples are based on purely mathematical principles of proportion, progression, division and so forth. And what more eloquent evidence could there be for the compulsion to express oneself in rationally comprehensible mathematical — or in this case stereometric — forms than the Egyptian pyramid, which as the tomb of the king embodies the gradual compression of the sprawling earthly surface into one highest and sublimest point, into the apex of the pyramid, in which all directions are cancelled or contained. Archeologists have revealed to us in concrete examples the extent to which both Egyptian and Greek monuments, as well as the exact divisions of their plastic adornment, are based on accurate mathematical constructions. Even Greek statues have been found to incorporate structural principles, for instance for bodily postures, in which geometric rules derived from the proportions of the human body are applied.

The great importance of geometric ornament shows that thinking in the forms and structures of geometry was not eclipsed in Antiquity, but was only transferred to a secondary plane. A province in which the elementary delight in the marshaling of geometric shapes finds specially lively expression is the art of the mosaic. Apart from illusionistic scenes from mythology, from daily life or the animal world, there were many mosaics in the floors of Greek or more particularly Roman buildings that consisted of geometric patterns, often executed only in black and white. The patterns are created by the addition or combination of elementary geometric shapes — square, triangle, circle and segment, hexagon, octagon, rhombus, trapezium; the contrast of black/white is used to emphasize the composition. Specimens that have been preserved show that the possibilities of physiological optics were exploited, for in many cases a three-dimensional impression is created by the ingenious combination of black and white units — an expedient widely regarded as an invention of Op Art after 1950 (ill. p. 11). This use of purely optical effects to break out of the two-dimensional surface, a quite common feature of the mosaic floors of Ro-

man villas, was passed down from late Antiquity to the Middle Ages. The mosaic or tessellated pavements of many Romanesque or Gothic churches — such as the Cathedral of Siena — continue this ingenious art of lending structure to a flat surface. The delicate stone tarsias of the Cosmati also deserve to be mentioned in this connection, as do the geometrically structured marble facings of external and internal walls, often in black and white. The façades of Santa Maria Novella and San Miniato in Florence are good examples.

Geometric principles are of special importance in cultural circles in which representational and above all figurative art productions are rejected or forbidden for religious reasons. This explains why Islam has produced the most magnificent examples of geometric art. Geometric ornament of inexhaustible inventive variety is to be found on wall coverings and above all in screens and panels that form part of mosques, palaces and other monuments. We know that the Arab peoples, as the heirs of the Greeks, developed mathematics to astonishingly high levels and were among other things the inventors of algebra. Many Islamic ornaments which at first sight seem only complicated or at most ingenious interlacings of lines and bands are based on exact mathematical principles, the lattice system actually used often being only a small portion of a much larger geometric construction. These line patterns are far from being playful puzzles or charming decorations meant only to beguile the eye. The belief in a divine element that is contained in mathematical laws lends these geometric adornments, with their hidden numerical meanings, the quality of visual inducements to meditation. Within their visible order there is a mathematical and therefore a divine order (ill. p. 12). Even the things that remain invisible to the believer are a form of praise to Allah.

Much of what has just been said about Islam also applies to India. Perhaps the most superb of all combinations of mathematics with plastic forms is to be found in the monumental geometric sculptures of the old observatory in the palace of Jaipur, which in reality are exact instruments made of marble (ill. p. 12). A similar predominance of geometric forms is found in the productions of Tantric art, especially in its miniature painting, where purely geometric compositions are both instruments of astronomical calculation and aids to meditation.

This belief in a relationship between mathematics and the divine which colors the thinking of ancient and Islamic mathematicians and philosophers is not entirely absent from Western Christianity, even if the Christian faith curtails the autonomy of mathematical principles or clothes them in aspects of the doctrine of salvation. The most striking example of the latter procedure is no doubt the concept of the Trinity, which can be understood as an equilateral, upward-pointing triangle. In medieval Europe mathematical thought dominated architecture, as is shown by the plans of Gothic cathedrals that have come down to us and by the geometric tracery of their windows; but it also deeply influenced intellectual leaders, a fact clearly demonstrated in the drawings and texts of the book on building compiled in 1230/35 by Villard de Honnecourt, a French architect at the height of the Gothic era. The full effect of the theoretical writings of Leonardo Fibonacci, one of the great mathematicians of the Middle

Ages, on the art and thought of the thirteenth century has yet to be investigated. It is at any rate interesting to note that the numerical progressions of Fibonacci have recently been rediscovered by representatives of Concept Art such as Mario Merz.

The liberation of the individual from the patterns of thought imposed by ecclesiastical dogma in the fifteenth century marked the beginning not only of scientific reasoning but of technical activity. Mathematics became one of the chief instruments in the exploration of man's world. From this, art and artists also derived benefit. There is no more characteristic attribute of the artist of the Italian Renaissance than his passionate interest in mathematical problems. This goes so far that art and mathematics are often thought of as one, and the artist sees himself at the same time as a mathematician.

The Florentine architect and sculptor Filippo Brunelleschi may have started the ball rolling. He is said to have discovered the exact laws for the construction of perspective about 1420. Of even greater importance were the writings of the architect Leon Battista Alberti, particularly his treatise "Della pittura", composed about 1436, which deals with the mathematical principles of painting, and the building manual "De re aedificatoria" with which Alberti in 1452 or thereabouts, basing his approach on the Roman Vitruvius, combines the geometric construction of the various building elements with an architectural theory of proportions. The most powerful influence of all in the Italian Quattrocento, however, was exercised by the Franciscan monk Fra Luca Pacioli, who provided in his "Summa de arithmetica" a résumé of all mathematical discoveries since the ancients, but whose treatise "De divina proportione" had an even greater impact on the ar-

tists of his time and in fact on contemporary society in general. The painter Piero della Francesca was encouraged by his friend Luca Pacioli to write "De prospectiva pingendi", which made him one of the great theorists of Renaissance art. Leonardo da Vinci, another admirer of the mathematically obsessed monk, was not above making the illustrations for Pacioli's theory of proportion. The latter's preoccupation with the Golden Section finally led him to the preparation of a canon of the human form. This occupied Leonardo's mind, as his sketchbooks show, for the rest of his life. And from here an almost unbroken line can be drawn to modern thinking on the construction of the human figure.

About 1500 the movement in Italy sparked off the same developments in the art world of the rest of Europe. Albrecht Dürer was convinced that a thorough knowledge of mathematical laws was the foundation of all artistic activity. He set down the main principles in various theoretical discourses, for instance in his "Treatise on measurement with compasses and ruler" in 1525 and "Four books on human proportion" in 1528, and thus endeavored to disseminate his knowledge (ill. p. 14). These mathematical writings by artists of the Renaissance formed the basis of many subsequent inquiries into theories of art. Or perhaps it would be more correct to speak of the theories of artists, since theories of art were to be formulated later by philosophers as a branch of aesthetics.

In the artistic practice of the fifteenth and sixteenth centuries the mathematical problems — such as picture composition on the basis of proportions derived from the Golden Section or the construction of spatial perspectives — are often only veiled by the actual subject matter of paintings and sculptures. In many instances it is difficult

Private house in Takawashi near Osaka, Japan, 16/17th century

to avoid the impression that the artist was more interested in a certain construction system than in the contents of his work. Thus it is quite obvious that pictures of St. Jerome in his Study were frequently only a pretext for the design of an inner space in perspective and that the saint's furniture provided an opportunity for the projection of complicated stereometric bodies on to a two-dimensional surface. Even Raphael's "School of Athens" in the papal apartments of the Vatican, a glorification of science and philosophy, is imbued with this taste for spatial construction, for the correct rendering in perspective of figures and their proportions.

The fact that the use of mathematical principles from the Renaissance onward serves increasingly to permit a correct, i.e. a scientifically exact, representation of reality is another matter. It would be rewarding, however, to explore the hidden clues to a purely mathematical approach, or in other words the antecedents of modern abstract geometric art, in the productions of artists since the Renaissance. It can be clearly demonstrated — to give only one example — that complicated ground plans of Baroque churches with their "irrational" spatial distortions are nothing more or less than exactly plotted deformations of simple, interpenetrating geometrical forms. The plan of Francesco Borromini's church of San Carlino in Rome, for instance, is the result of an anamorphosis of a cross constructed of circles.

There can hardly be a more impressive instance of the continuity of geometric ideas over the millennia than the representation of labyrinths. From prehistoric times till the present day people of all cultures have been fascinated by the spirally curving or angular plans of a path that leads from the outside to the inside, past all sorts of wrong turns, to a center or sanctum. Magic, mythical and cultic significance attaches, with corresponding practices, to this geometric symbol (ill. p. 13). The gardens of the middle and late Baroque period, veritable wonders of intricate geometry, reveal to what a degree it occupied the human mind in the profane epochs following the Middle Ages. In our time Land Art and Arte Povera have taken a new interest in spirals and mazes.

The fact that the functionalism of buildings and their parts veils an underlying interest in basic stereometric forms such as cubes, pyramids, cones, cylinders and spheres which has existed at all times in architectural thought is sufficiently proven by individual buildings, from the Pyramids to the cylindrical towers of castles and forts and even to the spiral of Frank Lloyd Wright's Guggenheim Museum in New York. The purest expressions of this architectural interest — which, perhaps for that very reason, have remained projects only — can be found in the architecture of the French Revolution, which was strongly influenced by Newtonism. The spherical structures of Etienne-Louis Boullée and Claude-Nicolas Ledoux at the end of the eighteenth century are good examples of this type of building.

Examples from all cultures show that elementary symbolic forms played a central part in the geometric styles of early history. It is precisely in their use as symbols that geometric configurations persist most tenaciously over the centuries. The close connection of geometric art and symbolism is a clear proof of the high spiritual content of human utterances in geometric form. And this again shows that the shaping urge we are here dealing with is far more than a mere decorative impulse.

Man's relation to the powers that be, to supernatural beings and forces beyond his rational comprehension, has at all times found expression in simple and easily interpreted symbols. Such symbols are signs for the unspeakable and numinous which are made understandable within a closed society by their easily recognizable geometric characteristics. This applies as much to prehistoric sun symbols as to the Christian cross, the ancient Egyptian life-symbol Ankh or the monad of the Far East. In many cultures symbols are also among the ideograms in which writing originated.

No other people has developed such a great variety of symbols as the Japanese — a feature which reflects a highly differentiated formal culture. This evolution of a timeless range of "abstract" emblems has been governed by a feeling for geometric form just as has the austere secular architecture of Japanese dwellings, in which, over and above all functional considerations, the aesthetic permeation of the country's culture has found its most striking expression (ill. p. 15).

The original cultic meaning of symbols has often lost its pride of place as a result of secularization processes in the various societies. The divine symbol has become a worldly emblem, for instance in heraldry, and ultimately the easily understood cipher of spontaneous visual communication. Flags and banners, rail and shipping signals, modern traffic signs, the numerous scientific and technical sign languages and finally the trade marks of commercial enterprises are the latest profane categories of an initially sacred geometric symbolism.

In dealing with the abstract and, more particularly, the geometric non-objective art of the twentieth century, we can never overlook the immemorial heritage of joy in geometric shapes, the close and sometimes very clear-cut relations of art to mathematical thinking, even if we admit that many of the artistic pioneers of our own century have not been conscious, or at least not fully conscious, of the extent and significance of this multifold heritage. Even though the work of these artists is felt to be new and revolutionary by their contemporaries, they are in fact the upholders of a tradition that is clearly based on the fact that certain standards for the use of forms and colors underly all artistic endeavor. The form and color teachings and particularly the comprehensive theories of art which have appeared in such abundance in the course of this century do not merely offer systems for the use of the artist's means of expression, they also embody a standardizing trend in aesthetics that has dominated this century's art for long periods and often over a broad front. And constructive art in its widest sense is the domain in which a normative aesthetic most clearly determines the lines of artistic thought or the "pictorial thinking" spoken of by Paul Klee.

The Dismantling of Reality

Cubism and Futurism

Grave perturbations have shaken the cultural life of the European capitals and even of the smaller provincial centers since the dawn of this century. Revolts and new breakthroughs have succeeded each other in a general movement of liberation from the fetters of traditional values and from the academic models previously accepted for painting, sculpture, architecture, literature, music, drama and the dance. These new departures have brought with them forms of expression that are felt to be contemporary, "modern", even tailored to the requirements of the future, so that they are qualified, their exponents believe, to give us access to the thought, feelings and life of a "new man" inhabiting a new world.

As far back as 1900, pioneers of this revolutionary thinking, such as the Belgian painter, architect, designer and theorist Henry van de Velde, were talking of a "new style" that was to comprehend all aspects of life. The movement was not primarily a revolution in aesthetics; the Utopian goal was rather of a social and ethical nature: the vision of man as part of a new society. In the philosophical domain this new conception of human life was subtly delineated by the French thinker Henri Bergson, who set out to demonstrate that life can only be understood through direct experience. The universe, Bergson claimed, is in a state of creative development and evolves freely by virtue of its own "élan vital".

This great revival ran through all the fields of cultural endeavor, where it sometimes took parallel, but occasionally opposite courses. It included, for instance, an emotional and even irrational component on the one hand, on the other a rational and intellectual tendency closely bound up with science and technology. This may be the origin of a growing multiformity in the artistic movements of our century, an ever more pronounced pluralism of artistic attitudes. One thing that is common to the confusingly diversified trends that have been apparent since the beginning of the century is a strong individualist element. This may be due to a natural attempt to defend the private sphere of the individual against the growing danger of standardization and mass leveling exerted by our modern industrial society, particularly in the big urban agglomerations. In the arts this will to survive as an individual takes the form of highly personal creative idioms and objectives.

It is absolutely logical that the desire for liberation from the compulsions of tradition, in the early years of this century, should have expressed itself first of all in an outbreak of an emotional character, and that this emotional element should have taken the form of a violent explosion of color, with a deliberate neglect of all discipline in the matter of form. It should be remembered here that it had been one of the main aims of the Impressionists to see the world solely as a phenomenon of light. The Impressionists were not concerned with corporeal reality, with things as they are (and as we know that they are), but with their appearance. This led to the dissolution of form in a colorful vibration of light, an "atomization" of the object into patches of color which, being intermingled in accordance with the principle of complementary contrasts, recreate the complete picture in the eye of the beholder. The pseudoscientific claim of the Impressionists that they were producing by this method an "objective" picture of visible reality gained some systematic foundation only in the Neo-Impressionist phase with the Divisionism of Georges Seurat and Paul Signac. It was important for further developments, however, that Impressionism had for the first time in the history of painting given up the objective in favor of the apparent color and had destroyed the coherence of the object. The Impressionist painters had undertaken to prove that a destruction of objective relations is possible and for some creative purposes even necessary. This teaching has not been forgotten since.

The following generation of "wild" rebels, whom the critic Louis Vauxcelles for this reason disparagingly called the "Fauves" (the wild beasts), gave color absolute precedence in painting but refused all system as being a hindrance to spontaneous artistic expression. Color became the carrier of the artist's immediate emotional response, his unpremeditated utterance. "La joie de vivre" (The joy of life) is the title of a key picture by Henri Matisse dating from 1906. This dominance of powerful, unmixed color, combined with the reduction of all formal elements of the subject to rough, rudimentary terms, characterizes the whole of European Expressionism about the year 1905. It was not by accident that this was the generation that discovered "primitive art", the expressive wooden sculptures of African Negroes and of the peoples of the South Seas. This spontaneous, expressive art united the Fauves in France with their German contemporaries in the group known as "Die Brücke" (The Bridge) in Dresden.

Henri Matisse, spokesman of the Fauvist movement, was perhaps the first to recognize the fundamental novelty of the new art when he said that in viewing a picture one ought to forget completely what it represents. His remark heralds an art which is primarily or even exclusively occupied with problems of color and form and pays no attention to the visual reality of the objects portrayed. Here, a non-objective, "absolute" art takes on definition.

Hardly had the color explosion of Fauvism made its impact when, in keeping with the law of action and reaction, an alternative presented itself. The new artists came from another camp: their great teacher was Paul Cézanne, who in his years of maturity had stood aside from the general stream of developments. Cézanne had tirelessly tried to capture nature in his paintings by reducing it to basic geometric and stereometric forms. "Everything in nature is modelled on spheres, cones and cylinders; we must learn to paint on the basis of these simple forms," he said. A younger generation of painters took this statement as a cue for dissolving the cohesion of complex representational forms and breaking them down into their elements. What was here involved was formulated by the strongest personality in this new generation, Pablo Picasso, in the form of an aphorism: "Nature is a reality, but my canvas is a reality too." In other words, the autonomy of the work of art, its sufficiency unto itself, had won recognition.

The fact that all matter is built up from basic elements had been postulated by the atomistic philosophers of Antiquity from the time of Democritus. Serious experimental evidence, however, was only collected from the end of the nineteenth century onward. Various models of the atom were developed and this culminated in 1913 with the model of Niels Bohr on which modern atomic physics is founded. The claim of concrete organisms to absolute reality was also challenged in other domains: from 1905 onward Albert Einstein developed his theory of relativity, which was in its narrower sense a physical theory intended to explain contradictions in certain phenomena, such as the behavior of light, but was at once generalized by his contemporaries and extended to all spheres of life and thought. From now on it was impossible to give an objective answer to the question of what truth is in the world of creative art. The inner truth of the individual work was now fundamentally beyond question. Every truth, every realization, however, is now "relative", that is to say, it is valid only in a certain context and on certain conditions.

The rise of an art diametrically opposed to the expressive nature of Fauvism can be traced exactly. It was primarily due to the work of two men of quite different personalities, Georges Braque and Pablo Picasso. In the summer of 1908, during a stay in L'Estaque, Braque painted a number of landscapes and still lifes which were composed of angular, prismatic volumes in muted tones constituting a dynamic whole. Matisse, who saw these rigorously constructed paintings as a member of the jury of the "Salon des Indépendants", described them to the art critic Louis Vauxcelles as consisting of "petits cubes". Once more a disparaging name coined by Vauxcelles — "les peintres cubistes" — was to become a tag for a new movement.

Like his friend Braque, Picasso also endeavored, from 1908 onward, to arrange his pictorial elements independently of their significance as objects. In an earlier experiment he had represented heads and bodies with a few violent lines so as to translate inward into outward movement, which had led him to an expressive form-language. This phase of his work — known as the "époque nègre" — in fact displayed more than fortuitous resemblances to the African and Oceanian sculptures and masks that contemporary artists had just discovered. Picasso's main work in this period, the painting "Les Demoiselles d'Avignon", begun in 1907 and left unfinished

in 1908 — often regarded as the first of all modernist pictures — reflects the artist's transition from a purely expressive to a Cubist idiom.

The transition Braque's work had gone through in L'Estaque took place in Picasso's work during a stay in Horta de San Juan in Spain in the summer of 1909. The shapes of objects became the hard facets, outlined by clear angles and sharp edges, of almost crystalline structures. Neither the "real" relations of front and back nor a "real" source of light, falling from a definite direction, play any role in the new picture-space. The artist gives up his fixed standpoint relative to his subject and presents several views simultaneously. And in the same way the lighting of the angular volumes obeys only the laws of the picture organism itself.

Picasso's adoption of Cubism coincided with his change of address after his return from Spain in the fall of 1909. He had moved from his Bohemian studio in the "Bateau Lavoir" at Place Ravignan to a comfortable studio apartment on Boulevard Clichy. As a result of the support of Ambroise Vollard, who had exhibited the pictures brought back from Horta, and of Daniel-Henri Kahnweiler, who now became an ardent promoter of his work, he enjoyed a measure of economic security. The dissection and rearrangement of overall forms was now continued in still lifes, female nudes and portraits of seated women. The influence of Cézanne can still be felt in the reduction of the objects represented into simple volumes such as cubes, cylinders, cones and prisms, as well as in the dominant contrast of green and red-brown shades that are far removed from the intensity of the Fauvist palette. The "Seated Woman" of 1909 (ill. p. 19) is a typical example of this progressive and conscious dissection of represented form, combined with the renunciation of bright colors and of illusionistic pictorial space. In the next few portraits of Ambroise Vollard (1909), Wilhelm Uhde (1910) and Daniel-Henri Kahnweiler (1910) the transition from early Cubism to the analytic Cubism of the years 1910–1912 takes place: a complete geometrization of pictorial elements. Similar developments can be studied in Georges Braque's paintings of the same period. "Le Portugais" of 1911 is a good example (ill. p. 21).

The last vestiges of an interest in real space had thus vanished. Constructed of straight and curved lines, the pictures now consisted of a dynamic pattern of interpenetrating and superimposed geometric surfaces which, by virtue of the almost monochrome gradations of dark and light in an exclusively grey-brown palette, could either combine to form volumes or create spatial impressions. The arbitrary and wholly unrealistic handling of the light here plays an important role. It underlines the specifically Cubist logic of the picture: surfaces and illusionary volumes of great graphic force are combined in a "simultaneous" presentation that is incompatible with the traditional logic of three-dimensional bodies and space.

The "papiers collés" to which Picasso and Braque turned their attention from 1912 on played a decisive role in the clarification of geometric ordering principles on the surface. They had been preceded from 1910 by the inclusion in "analytical Cubism" of painted numbers, letters or fragments of words, mostly applied with stencils. By the end of 1911 the layering and intersection of the picture segments had been carried so far that — as Herta Wescher

Pablo Picasso: Femme assise dans un fauteuil, 1909

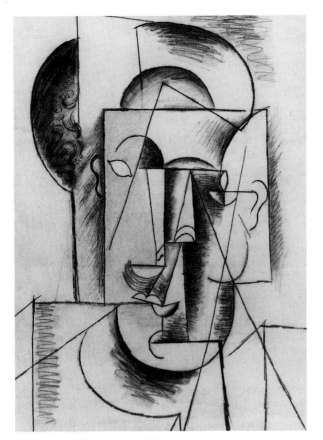

Pablo Picasso: Tête d'homme, 1912

points out in her book on collage — a marked organization of surfaces had replaced spatial clarification. The objective motif was no longer developed out of the depth of the picture but was deployed in clearly distinguishable surfaces in the foreground.

In early 1912 cut-out paper elements stuck on the picture ground were used for these surfaces. No doubt the attraction of the material, the sensuous quality of the real, extraneous element in the drawn or painted composition, here played an additional role (ill. pp. 22, 23). The collage technique with straight-edged paper surfaces does much to further the formal geometric structuration. The elements of the pictorial composition, often drawn, consist of clear, austere line systems relating to the collage surfaces, so that truss-like patterns result. The composition consequently has a high degree of transparency. The technique introduced by Braque and Picasso with their "papiers collés" became, in the space of a few years, a technical and compositional resource employed by a whole generation.

The "Cubist adventure" of the dismantling of objective reality and its reassembly into a new pictorial reality did not remain the intellectual preserve of Braque and Picasso. With an eagerness which reveals how much this new departure was awaited in 1910, other artists at once turned with active interest to the form fragmentation of the Cubists. This prompt acceptance of Cubist principles by a whole generation of artists is all the more astonishing because the works of Braque and Picasso were hardly on public view in Paris, except for a Braque exhibition mounted by Kahnweiler in 1909. The new idea spread as a result of a brisk exchange of studio visits rather than through the intermedium of public exhibitions. A good example of this is the picture "Les Demoiselles d'Avignon", which did not leave Picasso's studio until it was publicly exhibited in 1916, yet had exerted, since its execution, an immediate influence on the artist's contemporaries.

The Cubist paintings of Picasso and Braque were so little in the public eye that between 1910 and 1912 others who had hastily adopted the new form-language were able to give themselves out as the initiators of Cubism. Among them were Albert Gleizes and Jean Metzinger, who published their study "Du Cubisme" as early as 1912 — the first attempt at a theoretical explanation of the new painting and its methods. The two real founders of the movement offered no theoretical comment on it either then or later. They were so reserved toward all endeavors to explain their pictorial experiments that it seems questionable whether they in fact had any theoretical conception of their undertaking. Braque expressly confirmed in later statements that he had not, as for instance in his autobiographical "My Way" in 1954; and the same probably holds true to an even greater degree for Picasso, who was always opposed to theoretical interpretations. However, Braque remarks in retrospect: "We both lived in Montmartre, we saw each other every day, we talked together ... In those years with Picasso we said things that nobody will ever say again ... things that nobody would now understand ... things that filled us with so much joy and that will one day die with us ..."

This reveals that something in the nature of theoretical discussions of art must have gone on constantly in the "Bateau Lavoir". They also touched, we know, on mathematical questions. Among the regular visitors was Maurice Princet, an insurance mathematician, who was interested in non-Euclidean geometry and speculated on the fourth dimension and painting with his artist friends. Later, with Jean Metzinger and Juan Gris, he tried to grapple theoretically with this subject. In 1910 Metzinger stated in an essay that Picasso was formulating a free, mobile perspective from which Princet had derived an entirely new geometry. The abandonment of the traditional central perspective was of course a main factor in the dissolution of logical space in the Cubist composition. In Braque's words: "Traditional perspective did not satisfy me. Its mechanization never yields full possession of things ... I was particularly attracted by the visualization of the new space that I sensed; a fascination that became the guiding idea of Cubism." And elsewhere: "Cubism is an art which occupies itself primarily with form, and when a form has been realized it is there, and lives its own life. A mineral substance that is geometrically organized has nothing transient about it, it remains what it is and will always retain its form."

Among the artists who at once seized upon Cubist thinking and whom the writer and poet Guillaume Apollinaire presented in monographic chapters in his epoch-making work "Les peintres cubistes" in 1913, three are of special importance. In each of them, from the first, the principles of the Cubist dismantling of visible reality prompted unmistakably individual pictorial experiments.

To Fernand Léger, who like Braque began with Cubist landscapes about 1909, Cubism was a wonderful oppor-

Georges Braque: Le Portugais, 1911

Pablo Picasso: La Guitare, 1920

tunity to give expression to a new experience evoked by the dynamism of the machine. Neither Braque nor Picasso took any notice of the mechanization of life, or for that matter of modern life at all. A hymn of praise to the new machine world would have been utterly alien to them. But Léger was convinced, from the first, of what he said in 1924 in his "Aesthetic of the machine": "Modern man lives more and more in a mainly geometric order. All human creation, whether mechanical or industrial, is based on geometric intentions." Whether it was the female form or townscapes that Léger took apart, particularly between 1912 and 1914, and reconstructed in assemblies of tapered tubes, cylinders and sections of cones set at angles to each other, the result always displayed a dynamism in which the motorized rhythms of modern life are expressed. His "Contrast of Forms" (ill. p. 25) send shocks of movement through the picture from top to bottom, from front to back. "Contrasts produce dissonances, and therefore a maximum of effect. I take the visible impression of rounded masses of smoke rising between houses and convert this impression into plastic values. That is the best example of the application of the principle of cumulative, multiplex corporeal values. I use these curves eccentrically in as many forms as possible, but without the loss of unity. I box them up in the hard, dry structure of house walls, of dead surfaces, which become

mobile because they are in color contrast to the middle mass and in opposition to animated forms: that yields a maximum of effect."

The development of the work of Robert Delaunay was in a quite different direction. Starting out from a style in which Fauvist chromatic intensity was combined with a Divisionist brush technique similar to that of Seurat, he was overtaken by early Cubism about 1909. At first an Expressionist tendency was also present in his art, as is witnessed by the dynamic Gothic church interior of "Saint-Séverin". In 1910 he produced compositions on the subject of the town ("La Ville") in which a streetscape is broken down into a dramatic Cubist pattern, while a systematic Pointillistic coloring technique creates a mood of vibrant light. These Parisian visions are an overture to the themes which Delaunay was later to develop in his "window pictures". Here the dynamism has been replaced by a balance of straight lines and curves that lends an ordered grandeur to the picture surface.

The poetic mood of these window pictures led Guillaume Apollinaire to speak of an "Orphic Cubism" or "Orphism" in the work of his friend Delaunay. The painter himself said: "These windows open on a new reality. This new reality is merely the ABC of idioms that draw on the physical elements of color and so lead to a new form. There are still suggestions of nature in this painting, but only in

Georges Braque: Guéridon, 1913

a very general sense and not analytical and descriptive as in the previous Cubist phase. These pictures also mark the color reaction in the development of Cubism."

In 1912 Delaunay went still further with his "formes circulaires". These circular rhythms do without objective references altogether and are therefore, with the expressive color compositions of Francis Picabia, one of France's principal contributions to non-objective painting. Delaunay himself talks of "peinture inobjective". In place of representation color now comes to the fore with the use of the principles of simultaneous contrast — a marked antithesis to the near achromatism of early Cubism. In Delaunay's words: "Color is form and subject in one." In 1913, impelled by his interest in the modern metropolis and its life, Delaunay returned to figurative components. Visions of the Eiffel Tower and of football games occupied his mind. One of his principal works from this period is "L'Equipe de Cardiff", the subject of which is a pretext to assemble a vision of city life out of the most heterogeneous elements, including walls of advertising and a giant wheel. The oil study for a later version of this subject (ill. p. 27), however, shows clearly how close the form and color relations remain to the Orphic window pictures.

Yet another personal reaction to early Cubism was shown by Marcel Duchamp. He came from a group which had been working quite independently of Braque and Picasso to develop the double legacy of Cézanne and Seurat, and the Fauves' liberation of color, into a new creative language. The group met regularly in the studio of Duchamp's brother, Jacques Villon, in Puteaux. The painters Albert Gleizes, Jean Metzinger, Roger de la Fresnaye, Fernand Léger and Jean Crotti and the sculptor Raymond Duchamp-Villon belonged, together with Guillaume Apollinaire and Maurice Princet, to this Puteaux group, which also took a lively interest in mathematical problems. It presented its work to the Parisian public in 1912 in an important exhibition, using the significant title of "Section d'or". All the Cubists were represented with the exception of Braque and Picasso.

After some figurative compositions under Cubist influence — mainly chess-players — Duchamp painted his "Coffee mill" in 1911. It was the first painting to show nothing but a machine. The same year saw a first draft, and 1912 the definite version of the "Nude Descending a Staircase" (ill. p. 240). This picture, which developed from Duchamp's study of the motion photographs of Jules Etienne Marey, employs the Cubists' analytical breakdown of the human form to capture the element of movement in painting by the simultaneous portrayal of superimposed phases. The work so shocked contemporaries that it had to be withdrawn from the "Salon des Indépendants" in 1912. It aroused a similar storm of protest in

23

Gino Severini: Oval Composition, 1913

influenced by his own musicality. It should be added that Kandinsky was at the same time examining the relations between music and "pure" painting.

We have written evidence of the fact that Kupka had had at least a vision of such "absolute" non-objective painting much earlier, shortly after the turn of the century. He had written in a letter in 1905: "I do not believe that it is necessary to paint trees. For people can see better ones, real ones on the way to the exhibition. I paint of course, but I paint only the idea, the synthesis; if you will, the chords."

In Kupka's oil paintings and watercolors about 1912 there appear, in addition to circular forms, attempts to combine vertical surfaces in a balanced composition. At the same time he was studying the possibility of a confrontation of these vertical ribbon-like surfaces with diagonal forms. This led to compositions in which the two directions cut across each other, which involved complex mixtures and resolutions of colors. A further component that resulted, and certainly one that was consciously integrated in the general effect, was a spatial, architectonic impression: the interpenetrating vertical and diagonal bands form angles which the viewer at once interprets as an illusion of space. The picture "Vertical and Diagonal Planes" of 1913/14 (ill. p. 29), painted in several versions, is the central example of these space-creating surface rhythms. The version shown was first owned by Jacques Villon, then by Marcel Duchamp—a proof of the importance attached to this kind of painting by the Puteaux group.

The goal of Picasso and Braque in their analytical Cubism was to establish the autonomy of the work of art. Their efforts, even though they radiate into other domains, were restricted to art in its narrower sense. Other movements in this first decade of the century aimed at more radical and more extensive change. A few Italian painters and poets went to extremes, at least in their demands. They called themselves "Futurists", implying that to be merely modernist was not sufficient for them; they saw themselves as the trailblazers of things to come.

The crucial realization of the Cubists, more important than their return to the basics of form and color, had been, then, the autonomy of the work of art. This comes out clearly in many early statements of their protagonists, perhaps nowhere with such eloquence and self-assurance as in the essay "Du Cubisme" by Albert Gleizes and Jean Metzinger published in 1912:

"The picture bears the reason for its existence in itself. It can be moved with impunity from a church to a gallery, from a museum to a private room. Independent by its nature, necessarily complete, it need not satisfy the imagination immediately, but rather leads it gradually to the seeming depths in which coordinating life resides. The picture does not harmonize with this or that environment, it harmonizes with the sum of things; it is an organism...

"We must experience, through form and color, the plastic consciousness. Discerning a form involves, apart from the visual function and the ability to move, a certain development of the imagination: the outside world is amorphous in the eyes of the majority. To discern a form is to verify a preexistent idea, an act of which only the artist is capable without outside help. Faced by a natural spectacle, a child, wishing to coordinate his impressions and to bring them into line with his inner world, compares

the "Armory Show" in New York in 1913. This rendering of movement, painted almost entirely in Cubist ocher tones, marks a transition in the œuvre of Duchamp to a quite new category of work embodied for instance in the "Ready-mades", constructs of "objets trouvés" whose relation to art Duchamp started to investigate.

A neighbor of Duchamp's brother Jacques Villon in Puteaux in 1912 was the Czech painter Frank Kupka. He was likewise preoccupied with problems of motion. He had grown out of the Art Nouveau tradition of the turn of the century and had turned both to the expressive colors of Fauvism and to the possibility of composing pictures with purely geometric forms. As Kupka was primarily interested in movement and in rhythms—including those of music—round, rotating and interpenetrating forms monopolized his attention. In 1912 he exhibited one of his pictures in the "Salon d'Automne" in Paris for the first time—"Fugue pour deux couleurs"—and reaped general consternation. It was not Kupka's first non-objective work. It had been preceded by pure color rhythms such as those of "Nocturne" in 1910. At the same time as Kandinsky in Munich, and possibly even before him, Kupka had arrived at a type of painting which renounced every suggestion of objective reality and derived its effect solely from form and color. His were sound-pictures deeply

Fernand Léger: Contraste de Formes, 1913

Gino Severini: Danseuse, 1912

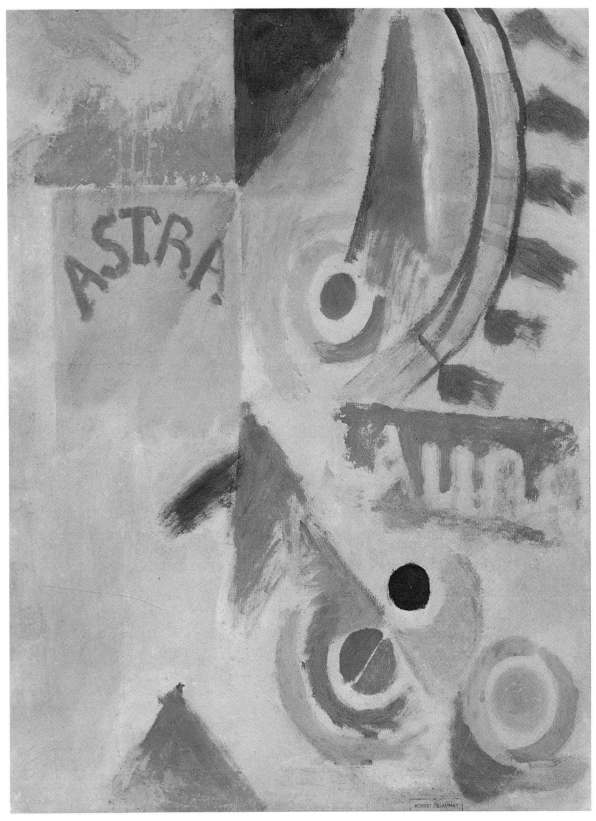

Robert Delaunay: Football. L'Equipe de Cardiff, 1916

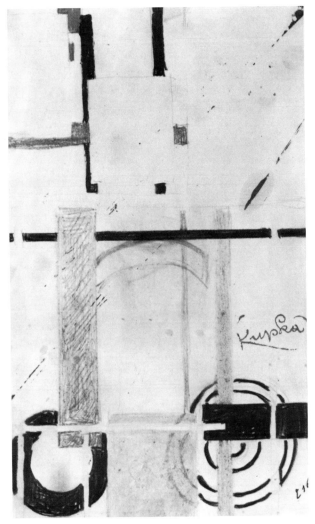

Frank Kupka: Crayon drawing, c. 1925/30

them with his picture book; the adult, culture intervening, thinks of works of art.

"The artist, having discerned a form that shows a marked similarity to the preexistent idea, prefers it to other forms and endeavors to compress the quality of this form (the incommensurable sum of affinities he perceives between the visible manifestation and the tendency of his mind) into a symbol that is qualified to affect others . . .

"Let the picture imitate nothing; let it present only its own motif. We should be ungrateful if we were to deplore the absence of all the things — flowers, landscape, faces — of which it can only be a reflection. Yet, let us admit that the reminiscence of natural forms cannot — for the present at least — be completely excluded. Art cannot be raised to the highest purity at one step.

"The Cubist painters who tirelessly study pictorial form and the space it engenders are aware of this. We have negligently got into the habit of confounding this space with pure visual space or with Euclidean space . . .

"If we wished to refer the space of painters to geometry, we should have to refer it to the non-Euclidean mathematicians; we should have to study carefully certain theorems of (Bernhard) Riemann's.

"As for visual space, we know that it results from the combination of sensations of convergence and accommodation. For the picture, a plane surface, accommodation is excluded. Convergence, which perspective teaches us to represent, cannot evoke the idea of depth. We know, moreover, that even very serious infractions of the rules of perspective do not compromise the spatial quality of a painting . . .

"To establish pictorial space, we must have recourse to tactile and motoric sensations, and in fact to all our faculties. Our whole personality transforms the picture plane. As this plane reflects the personality on the mind of the observer, pictorial space may be defined as a perceptible transition between two subjective spaces.

"The forms that are situated in this space have a dynamism which we must master. If our understanding is to grasp it, we must first exercise our sensibilities. Only nuances are here involved; the form has properties that are identical with those of color. In contact with another form, it is tempered or stimulated, it is destroyed or emphasized, it is multiplied or it vanishes. It may happen that an ellipse is changed into a circle because it is inscribed in a polygon. A form that is more strongly emphasized than its surroundings may dominate the whole picture, imprinting its own configuration on everything . . . The great masters were aware of this when they used pyramids, crosses, circles, semicircles, etc., in their compositions. Composing, constructing and designing can be reduced to this: controlling the dynamism of form by our own activity."

The idea of the dynamism of form already points beyond analytical and the later synthetic Cubism with their constructive surface qualities to experiments that are still related to Cubism but differ from it in their direction and aims. These other activities of the first decade of the century had as their goal a radical alteration of art. A few Italian painters and writers, as we have mentioned, here went to extreme lengths.

On February 20, 1909, the Milanese writer Filippo Tommaso Marinetti published his "Futurist Manifesto" in the Parisian daily "Le Figaro". The high-flown text was mainly concerned with a fundamental renewal of poetry, but it also contained references to essential elements of Futurist art, which were then set forth in more detail in later "technical manifestos": a confession of faith in the modern, motorized world, in the dynamic and dangerous aspects of life, a hymn to speed and to war, and a jeering rejection of past achievements and particularly of all traditional works and values. The beauty of the roaring racing-car is praised as leaving the Nike of Samothrace far behind. The destruction of all archives, libraries and museums is urged. All previous art is declared null and void.

Marinetti's "Manifesto of Futurism" of February 20, 1909, outlines the new attitude. It closes with a bouquet of provocative demands such as the art world had never heard before:

"We intend to glorify the love of danger, energy and daring. — The essential elements of our poetry will be courage, audacity and revolt. — While literature up to now has glorified pensive immobility, ecstasy, and slumber, we wish to extol the aggressive movement, the feverish insomnia, the nimble stride, the perilous leap, the buffet, and the blow. — We declare that the splendor of the

Frank Kupka: Plans Verticaux et Diagonaux, 1913/14

Fernand Léger: Composition, 1920

Fernand Léger: Eléments mécaniques, 1922

world has been enriched with a new beauty, the beauty of speed. A racing automobile whose chassis is adorned with great pipes like snakes of explosive breath . . . a howling automobile which seems to run on exploding munition is more beautiful than the Victory of Samothrace.

"We will sing the praises of man holding the steering wheel, whose imaginary axle traverses the earth, which is flung out of its orbit. — The poet must spend himself in warmth, brilliance, and prodigality to heighten the fervor of the primal elements. — There is no other beauty than that of struggle. No masterpiece without the stamp of aggressivity. Poetry must be a violent assault on unknown forces to compel them to lie down at the feet of man. — We stand on the extreme promontory of the ages! Why should we look back just when we are about to break down the mysterious gates of the impossible? Time and space died yesterday. We already live in the absolute, for we have created the eternal, omnipresent speed.

"We will glorify war — the only true hygiene of the world. — We will destroy museums and libraries and fight against moralism, feminism, and all opportunistic and utilitarian cowardice. — We will praise the great masses agitated by work, pleasure, revolt; the multicolored and polyphonic surging of revolutions in modern capitals; the nocturnal vibration of warehouses and building sites

beneath their glaring electric moons; the voracious stations full of smoking serpents; factories hanging from the clouds by threads of smoke; bridges hopping nimbly over the diabolical cutlery of rivers glinting in the sun; adventurous steamers scenting the horizon; broadbreasted locomotives stamping on the rails like huge steel steeds held together by long tubes; and the gliding flight of airplanes whose propellers flap like flags in the wind and clap applause like a raving crowd."

These visionary, pathos-laden aspirations are followed by remarks expressing the contempt of the Futurists for the past. At the same time they arrogantly announce their readiness to act as trailblazers for a new man who is to be really abreast of the times:

"It is in Italy that we publish this glowing and vehement manifesto with which we today found Futurism because we wish to free Italy from its canker, the professors, archeologists, ciceroni, and antiquaries. Italy has too long been the big market of the second-hand dealers. We wish to free it from its innumerable museums that cover it like countless cemeteries.

"Museums, cemeteries! . . . Truly identical in the gloomy promiscuity of bodies unknown to each other. Public dormitories, where one slumbers forever beside hated or unknown beings. Ferocity of painters and scultpors murdering each other with lines and colors in the same museum. — Let a yearly visit be paid to them, as one visits

Juan Gris: La Femme à la mandoline, 1916

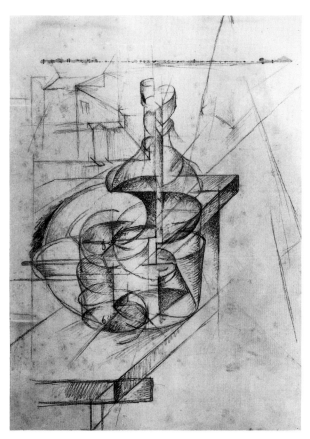

Umberto Boccioni: Tavola + bottiglia + caseggiato, 1912

the graves of dead relatives — that we agree to! . . . Let an annual offering of flowers be laid at the feet of the Gioconda — we can understand that! . . . But to take our sorrow, our failing courage, our restlessness for a daily walk through the museums — that is something we cannot tolerate! Do you want to be poisoned? Do you want to rot?

"What can one see in an old picture but the laborious contortions of an artist who struggles to surmount the insuperable barriers that foil his desire to express his dream? To admire an old picture is to pour our sentiment into a funeral urn instead of hurling it forth in violent throes of action and creativity. Will you waste your strength in useless admiration of the past, to end up exhausted, weakened, an object of pity?

"In reality this daily frequenting of museums, libraries, and academies (these graveyards of vain exertions, these Calvaries of crucified dreams, these registers of broken wings) is to the artist much like the endless regimentation imposed by parents on intelligent young people inebriated with their own talent and ambitions. — That may perhaps do for the dying, for invalids and prisoners. The admirable past may be a salve for the wounds of those who are debarred from the future . . . But we will have none of it, we who are young and strong, the living Futurists!"

"Welcome, therefore, to the kind incendiaries with the sooty fingers! Here they are! Here! Set fire to the bookshelves! Divert the canals, till they flood the vaults of the museums! . . . Oh, let the glorious old canvases float

adrift! Seize pickaxes and hammers! Sap the foundations of the time-honored towns! . . . The oldest among us are thirty, yet we have already squandered treasures, treasures of strength, love, daring, and determined will, hastily, in delirium, without reckoning, in a flash, breathtakingly. — Look at us! We are not out of breath. Our heart is not at all fatigued. For it has been nourished on fire, on hatred, on speed! You are astounded? It is because you do not even remember having lived! Aloft on the pinnacle of the world, we once more hurl forth our defiance to the stars."

In the following year, on April 11, 1910, a second pamphlet appeared in Milan, the "Technical Manifesto of Futurist Painting", signed by Umberto Boccioni, Carlo Carrà, Luigi Russolo, Giacomo Balla, and Gino Severini. The statements of this manifesto refer much more specifically to painting than Marinetti's manifesto:

"We declare: That all forms of imitation should be despised, and all forms of originality glorified. — That it is necessary to rebel against the tyranny of the terms 'harmony' and 'good taste' as being such elastic expressions that it would be easy to demolish the works of Rembrandt, of Goya and of Rodin with them. — That art critics are useless or harmful. — That all worn-out subjects must be flung aside in order to express our effervescent life of steel, of pride, of fever, and of speed. — That natural development in painting is an absolute necessity, just as free meter is in poetry and polyphony in music."

These declarations are followed by the war cry proper:

"We fight: 1. Against the bituminous tints with which an attempt is made to obtain the patina of time upon modern pictures.

"2. Against the superficial and elementary archaism of monotonous coloring, which, by imitating the linear technique of the Egyptians, reduces painting to a powerless synthesis that is childish and grotesque.

"3. Against the false claims to belong to the future made by the Secessionists and the Independents, who have erected new academies no less stereotyped and routine-ridden than those that preceded them.

"4. Against the nude in painting, which is as nauseous and as tedious as adultery in literature.

"Let us explain this last point. Nothing is immoral in our eyes; it is the monotony of the nude we fight against. We are told that the subject is nothing and its treatment everything. That is agreed; but this truism, unassailable and absolute fifty years ago, no longer applies to the nude today, since artists obsessed with the desire to exhibit the bodies of their mistresses have transformed the Salons into marketplaces of unwholesome flesh! We demand for the next ten years the total suppression of the nude in painting!"

A year later again, on May 11, 1911, there appeared a "Manifesto of Futurist Musicians" written by Balilla Pratella, followed on April 11, 1912, by the "Technical Manifesto of Futurist Sculpture" signed by Umberto Boccioni, "painter and sculptor". In this we find the demand: "Abolish in sculpture as in every other art the traditional supremacy of the subject." Speaking of the sculptor's materials, Boccioni says: "Destroy the alleged nobility, erudition and tradition of marble and of bronze. Deny the exclusivity of one material for a work of sculpture. Affirm that even twenty or more different materials may com-

Umberto Boccioni: Sviluppo di una bottiglia nello spazio, 1912

pete in a single work when the plastic expression requires it. Let us enumerate some: glass, wood, cardboard, iron, cement, horsehair, leather, cloth, mirrors, electric lights, etc."

The painters who rallied to this cause were at first able to satisfy its theoretical requirements only in part. Like many of their contemporaries in Paris, they had passed from the floral style of Art Nouveau through Divisionism and expressionist Fauvism to analytical Cubism, though they had admittedly done their best to introduce dynamism into this last movement. Their endeavor was to make motion—and thus the time element—visible in the picture, much as Duchamp had done in his "Nude Descending a Staircase". Painting was evidently feeling the challenge of the film, which had just become a medium in its own right, and was therefore seeking to master "forms in movement". In Boccioni's work this type of dynamization—of night traffic, for instance—appears only about 1911. Balla's attempts to portray consecutive phases of motion simultaneously date from 1912. In the same year the Futurists had a first exhibition in Paris. As Boccioni stated in the preface to the catalog, Futurism was divided from Cubism by an abyss. The Futurists in fact accused Cubism of static composition and of a lack of contact with the drama of life. They wanted to challenge this "surface art" with their own "interpretation in depth".

This Futurist attitude did not prevent Gino Severini from further developing the teaching of his friends Picasso and Braque in delicate Cubist still lifes, even though his compositional structure becomes increasingly dynamic (ill. pp. 24, 26). Giacomo Balla went quite a bit further. In a series of pictures painted in 1912/13 he sought to combine the Futurist demand for dynamic and vibrant life with geometric order. His "iridescent interpenetrations", purely constructive works done with ruler and compasses, already contain optical effects and stand isolated in Futurist painting and in the art of their time quite generally. It should, however, not be forgotten that Marinetti published a "Futurist Manifesto of Geometric and Mechanical Splendor and of Numerical Sensibility" in 1914. It sets off the accurate beauty of geometry and mechanics against the "chaos of the new sensibility". Balla himself, who was to carry over Futurist thinking in a modified form into the twenties, later returned repeatedly to his non-objective geometric compositions, which always contain forms in dynamic movement (ill. p. 35). Many of them recall the geometric black-and-white settings in Antonio Giulio Bragaglia's Futurist film "Perfido Incanto" of 1916.

Cubist form analysis soon led to what is known as "synthetic Cubism", which began to spread after 1912, a geometrically oriented art of brightly colored surfaces, upon

Félix del Marle: Looping, 1914

Mario Sironi: L'Aeroplano, 1916/17

which the later "painterly abstraction" was chiefly based. The dynamic element contained in the Cubist principle of fragmentation, and more still the Futurist demand for dynamism and movement in pictures that were now thought of not as an autonomous world opposed to reality but as the condensed essence of the beauty-in-ugliness of modern life, determined the character of European art in the second decade of this century far beyond the boundaries of Paris or France. A "dynamic Cubism" or "Cubistic Futurism" became a generally valid artistic language in which the lifestyle of the years leading up to and following the outbreak of World War I could evidently be most satisfactorily expressed. The dynamic drawings of the Frenchman Félix del Marle, mostly devoted to aviation, are good examples of this general trend (ill. p. 34). With his own Futurist manifesto of 1913 Del Marle became the spokesman of Parisian Futurism. From about 1920 he was influenced by Kupka, and later by Mondrian. We are quite justified in designating this international style, in which European Expressionism is also contained (we need only think of the late work of Franz Marc), as Futuro-Cubism. Contemporaries themselves occasionally spoke of "Cubo-Futurism". It was the starting point of many of the lines taken by later developments.

The geometrization of motifs and more particularly of the picture area, leading finally to abstraction, was evidently not enough for the many young artists in West and East who had been directly or indirectly influenced by Cubism. It is conceivable that this progressive generation was afraid that the aesthetic leanings inherent in Cubist painting might be the beginning of a new academicism. This would explain their ready acceptance of the Futurist demand for the "dynamization" of the picture area, or even for the "total" renewal of art as an expression of a truly "modern" feeling for life. The situation is reflected in the impetuous desire for change that was evident in many groups of artists in those years. We need only mention the "Blaue Reiter" with Kandinsky and Marc in Munich, the "Moderne Bund" in Switzerland and the "Moderne Kunstkring" in Holland.

It may be that the younger generation sensed the approaching end of the agonizing "Belle Epoque", in which case art once more showed seismographic sensibility. For the political and social tensions of those years were mostly local and sporadic and hardly presaged as yet the terrors of a world war that would be triggered by a seemingly accidental assassination. Nietzsche's "transvaluation of all values", as humanity was to experience it in 1914–1918 and the following years, was being in a sense rehearsed in the worldwide revolutionization of art around 1910. And the password was "Cubo-Futurism".

Important theoretical texts by Futurist artists appeared regularly in their magazine "Lacerba". One of the best is Carlo Carrà's article "From Cézanne to us, the Futurists", published in May 1913.

"Cézanne is the last exponent of the old epoch. Those who proclaim him the initiator of a new school of painting are fooling themselves and others. His realism has the character of an architectonic block. His works bring to mind Michelangelo. Although his compositions are erroneously considered dynamic, they are, instead, in their solidity and sobriety, absolutely static. The things

Giacomo Balla: Circolpiani, 1924

Cézanne chooses to represent are locked in an old type of design, even though he tries to render nature in terms of cones, spheres, and cylinders. So far as the field of plastic deformation goes and its use in the study of motion, Paul Cézanne's works have on many counts the air of museum pieces . . .

"We Futurists combat the Cézannesque objectivism of color, just as we reject his classical objectivity of form. For us, painting must express color the way one senses music even though the means are very different, that is, analogously. We stand for a use of color free from the imitation of objects and things as colored images; we stand for an aerial vision in which the material of color is expressed in all of the manifold possibilities our subjec-

tivity can create. For to us Futurists, form and color are related only in terms of subjective values. . .

"We Futurists have surpassed the simple construction of Cézanne's colored masses because we have gone beyond the 'melodic' type of construction in painting. Melodic construction is based, in its repetitions and its symmetrical equilibrium of rhythms and simple tones, on a pictorial feeling of calm. In this, Cézanne is not very far from Giotto . . .

"The rhythms and line forces give us the abstract weight of concrete plastic elements (machine, man, house, sea, etc.). If an object has its maximum emotive force in its formal construction, we shall give it in its architectonic essential. If on the other hand, the object has such force

Ardengo Soffici: Tipografia, 1914

in its harmony and disharmony of color, or in the refractions of light, we shall give it in terms of its tonal and luminous constructions. For our Futurist principles comprehend the three ways in which the plastic world is revealed to us: light, ambience, volume, and we intend to dramatize the coloristic formal and luminous masses in such a way as to assemble from these various entities a general pictorial dramatic unity.

"If we accuse the Cubists of creating not works but only fragments, as did earlier the Impressionists, it is because one feels in their works the need for a further and broader development. Further, it is because their canvases lack a center essential to the organism of the work as a whole, and those surrounding forces that flow towards such a center and gravitate around it. Finally, it is because one notes that the arabesque of their paintings is purely accidental, lacking the character of totality indispensable to the life of a work.

"Our paintings are no longer accidental and transitory sensations, limited to an hour of the day, or to a day, or to a season. We Futurists, destroying the unity of time and place, bring to the painting an integration of sensations that is the synthesis of the plastic universal . . .

"Guided hitherto by a static concept, painters have constructed dry and fixed forms and have not presented the motion of any given movement, the currents and centers of the forces which constitute the individuality and synthesis of the movement itself. They artificially limited and stopped movement.

"We are against the falsehood of the fixed law of the gravity of bodies: for Futurist painting, bodies will respond to the special center of gravity of the painting itself. Thus the centrifugal and centripetal will determine the weight, dimension, and gravity of bodies. In this way, objects will live in their plastic essence as part of the total life of the painting. If man were able to create a plastic measure capable of measuring the force that bodies express in lines, in the weight of their color-value, and in the direction of volumes, forces that our intuition leads us to apply in our works, all accusations of being arbitrary would be canceled. And the public would no longer be scandalized and shout, because they would no longer be afraid that they were being tricked and would understand the new truth that we have agitated for in Italy and elsewhere for four years, a truth that has thrown the camp of painting into revolution."

36

Liberation from the Object

From Rayonnism to Constructivism and Suprematism in Russia

Anyone who takes up Anatoly Lunacharsky's "Letters from Paris" and reads what the later Soviet People's Commissar for Culture had to say in 1913 about artistic developments in Paris is likely to be puzzled; for the very movement he condemns as an aberration that could lead nowhere — Cubism — was to prove the starting point of a unique evolution for Russia's young artists. Lunacharsky's comments read as follows: "This impression (of charlatanism) is justified by the deafening hue and cry that is raised around such monstrosities in the artistic development of our times as Cubism, Futurism and the new-born Orphism. The extravagance, the eye-insulting fatuity of these seekers, who have put the mad pranks of their predecessors wholly in the shade, bear witness to a profound decline of taste and of artistic technique . . ." In reproaches addressed to the "avant-garde", which today appear as a doubtful anticipation of Stalinist attitudes, Lunacharsky interpreted the endeavors of the young Parisian artists to create an autonomous reality for the work of art as mere striving for originality at all costs. Yet this was the goal toward which the bold aspirations of Russian artists of roughly the same age were to be increasingly directed.

A glance at the biographies of the Russian artists who played a part in later developments reveals that hardly one of them was prepared to forgo at least a short stay in Paris in the decisive years between 1909 and 1913. This holds good for Nathan Altman, Yuri Annenkov, Alexander Archipenko, D.W. Baranov-Rossiné, David Burliuk, Serge Charchoune, Alexandra Exter, Naum Gabo, Mikhail Larionov, Jacques Lipchitz, El Lissitzky, Antoine Pevsner, Liubov Popova, Ivan Puni, Vladimir Tatlin and Ossip Zadkine. Even in the case of Kasimir Malevich a stay in Paris around 1913/14 seems possible, though there is no evidence for it. Express evidence is forthcoming, however, for a visit paid by Vladimir Tatlin to Picasso, a visit that was to have its consequences. A few Russian artists decided at that time to stay in Paris. Annenkov, Archipenko, Charchoune, Zadkine, and others assumed French nationality and were later followed by Larionov, Goncharova and other compatriots, some of whom came as a direct result of the October Revolution.

The close contacts of St. Petersburg and Moscow with Paris, however, go even deeper than this would imply and reach further back into the past. It may be stated without exaggeration that, from the turn of the century onward, Russian artists and art-lovers were better informed about artistic happenings in Paris than the Parisians themselves. The reason for this was that two passionate Muscovite collectors, Sergei Shchukin and Ivan Morosov, had closely followed artistic developments and within a few years had amassed important collections of works by young French artists, to which they gave their countrymen liberal access. While Morosov concentrated chiefly on the Impressionists and Post-Impressionists with their contemporary followers, Shchukin kept up with the very latest developments. Among the two hundred odd French pictures done since the Impressionists which were in his possession in 1914, there were fifty works by Matisse and as many by Picasso, who was represented even by some of the most recent productions of analytical Cubism. Shchukin became acquainted with Picasso through Matisse, who had made a special trip to Moscow to hang his principal works of the Fauvist period. Picasso's development was convincingly presented in a special hall, where it was effectively supported by a number of African masks. This direct knowledge of contemporary French art in Moscow and St. Petersburg must not be overlooked if we are to do justice to the relationship of the Russian art of the time to developments in Western Europe. Although these developments were accessible to them, or perhaps precisely because this accessibility stimulated their interest, most young Russian artists decided to go to Paris and see things for themselves. It was this direct personal confrontation with the protagonists of the new era that gave Russian art the impetus needed for a new departure. The development of Marc Chagall shows how important the experience of Paris could be for a Russian: his early Expressionist work, hesitantly absorbing a few Cubist elements, continues until 1911; in 1912 he travels to Paris and undergoes a conversion to Cubism that culminates in the markedly geometrical picture "Hommage à Apollinaire" and then leads up to the Futuro-Cubist paintings of the years 1912 and 1913.

The explosive developments of Russian art can hardly be correctly understood without some reference to the conditions that prevailed at the end of the nineteenth century. After 1850, against the background of the popular liberation movements against Tsarism and serfdom, an art trend initiated by revolutionary intellectuals such as Nikolai Gavrilovich Chernyshevsky sprang up in opposition to the socially accepted academicism. It was nurtured partly by popular pan-Russian sentiments, but also contained elements of rebellion and anarchy. From this time onward all the strivings for more or less radical change in Russian art were to be influenced directly or indirectly by anarchist thinking. Mikhail Bakunin had set the stage for this evolution.

The highest goal of the grassroots realists of the late nineteenth century, who formed the group known as "Wanderers" (Peredvizhniki), was truth to unadorned everyday life. This markedly national realistic movement, whose most powerful exponents were Valentin Alexandrovich Serov and Ilya Repin, led about the turn of the century to a partly popular, partly aesthetically inclined Symbolism. It was manifested by one of the first groups of young exhibiting artists, known as the "Blue Rose", which made its public debut in 1908. Its tendency to underline the musical quality of color by attempting to blend painting and music is a foretaste of things to come. It was the Lithuanian painter and composer Mikolajus Chiurlionis who went furthest in this direction in his abstract symphonic compositions called "Sonata pictures". The strong drift of the day toward a "total" work of art is also exemplified by the attempts of the musician Alexander Scriabin to combine music and dance with abstract colored light patterns and even with scent compositions. Wassily Kandinsky, at that time working in Munich, was very much influenced by these currents. In his book "Concerning the Spiritual in Art" he postulates relationships between the world of forms and colors and that of sounds, he uses musical expressions such as "Improvisation" to designate his works and in 1913 gives a poetic picture-book the title "Klänge" (Sounds).

The musical element in art had already played an important part in the movement "World of Art" (Mir Iskusstva), which can best be understood as arising out of the spirit of Symbolism. The intellectual leader of this movement —which comprised a group of artists and an exhibition organization, but first and foremost a journal—was the versatile Alexander Benois: "The movement sought to influence society in various ways and to implant in it a definite relationship to art in its widest sense, including poetry and music." The "World of Art" found most convincing expression in the cooperation of Alexander Benois with the Symbolist painter Léon Bakst and the enterprising Sergei Diaghilev. From 1898 onward they turned their attention to the journal, but finally found the renewal and artistic permeation of ballet to be the best means of attaining their goal of a truly comprehensive art.

The abortive revolution of 1905 was not without its influence on artistic developments. It brought a division of opinion: on the one hand a retreat into realism mitigated by Impressionism, or into Symbolism of a merely aesthetic vintage; and on the other hand a radicalization of the endeavor to bring about artistic change. The rival groups of artists that now presented their "revolutionary" works to the public were a kind of surrogate for the social and political revolution that was not yet feasible but was already recognized as inevitable by progressive minds.

New magazines and new exhibition organizations now followed one another in swift succession. The first important group was the "Blue Rose", a reaction of young Muscovite artists to the attitude of the "World of Art", which they felt to be antiquated. The more prominent representatives of this group, which made its first appearance in 1908, were Pavel Kusnetsov, Georgy Yakulov, Natalia Goncharova and Mikhail Larionov. Their organ was the journal "Golden Fleece", first published in 1906. One of the aims of the magazine and the group's exhibitions was to bring about a confrontation between modern Russian and Western art. Their artistic line made a direct rapprochement possible with the Fauves, who had been led from 1905 onward by Henri Matisse. Some of Matisse's principal Fauvist works could be viewed in Shchukin's collection. The first original works by Natalia Goncharova and Mikhail Larionov are in the same Expressionist style with a leaning to Primitivism. This Russian Fauvism was a clear rejection of both realistic academicism and the all too literary Symbolism. Elements of popular art and of the expressive art of Old Russia are combined in it with the Expressionistic forms and colors of Fauvism. Picasso's Negro Period can be sensed in the background. There is no mistaking the search for "pure" and spontaneous painting without any strong ties to objective reality. Goncharova and Larionov are the most notable representatives of this trend. They owe a good deal, however, to their meeting in 1907 with the brothers David and Vladimir Burliuk, who were soon afterwards joined by Alexandra Exter from Kiev. With the appearance of the Burliuk brothers the changes taking place in the art world were accelerated. These two temperamental personalities stimulated the formation of several new groups among the young artists of Moscow and St. Petersburg. They all joined forces for the first time in the "Knave of Diamonds" exhibition in Moscow. The name was due to Larionov, and the geometric form of the card suit was just as important an element in it as playing-card symbolism per se. The ace of diamonds, as Leon Trotski recounts in his autobiography, was at that time sewn on to the clothing of political prisoners.

Among the Western influences then operative in Russia it was the emotional and expressive spirit of Fauvism and perhaps of the German Expressionists that predominated and not—though this would have been quite possible from 1908 onwards—the strict order, the discipline of color and form characteristic of analytical Cubism. Around 1910/11 a preoccupation with Cubism can be detected in the work of many Russians, for instance Vladimir Burliuk. Italian Futurism, however, at once gained a greater following, either directly or in the compounded form of the rapidly spreading Futuro-Cubism. The Futurist sense of exaltation, the call for a more dynamic treatment of picture content and for spontaneous expression of the speed and danger of modern life—all this fell upon fertile ground in Russia. A Futurist movement was consequently under way even before the spokesman of the new theories, F. T. Marinetti, visited Russia on one of his global publicity trips in early 1914. The exact date of Marinetti's first stay in Moscow and St. Petersburg is admittedly a matter of dispute; an alleged visit at the end of 1909 or the beginning of 1910 cannot be substantiated by any reliable evidence. A more important point is that the "Futurist Manifesto" was translated into Russian in 1909, shortly after its appearance, and had a powerful effect. However, fundamental differences of opinion soon arose between Marinetti and the Russian Futurists and evoked a statement from him to the effect that the Russians were false Futurists and had betrayed the true meaning of the movement.

The term "Futurism" appeared very early in Russia. It was used in the domains of art and literature and implied a rejection of past forms of life and art and the acceptance of a spontaneous, dynamic and forward-looking mode of self-expression. In addition to the brothers Burliuk, the poet Vladimir Mayakovsky may be cited as an eminent representative of "Futurist man". In both Russian art and poetry there were traits which anticipated the interest

Natalia Goncharova: Green Forest, Rayonnism, 1911

Olga Rozanova: The Factory and the Bridge, 1913

Liubov Popova: Early Morning, 1914

evinced by the Dadaists, in Zurich in 1916–1918, in the nonsensical and fortuitous. Among pre-Dadaist ventures we may mention the attempts of Larionov and David Burliuk to extend the sphere of art to the body of the artist by fantastic face-painting — a first essay in the Body Art of our own day. This type of assault on the public eye, which we know was also undertaken by Vladimir Mayakovsky, wholly in keeping with his attitude of protest, was meant to shock and disconcert the man in the street.

At about the same date, in 1910, Larionov was seeking a new personal style, drawing on the discoveries of Cubism and no doubt of Futurism but at the same time consistently continuing his withdrawal from the object. "The objects we see every day play no further part in the picture. On the contrary, the attention is attracted only by what is essential in painting: the combination of colors and their concentration, the relations of the color masses to each other, depth, brushwork — all things that interest the true connoisseur of art." If Larionov is here pointing to the possibility of a non-objective art, we must remember that Kandinsky published his essay "Concerning the Spiritual in Art" in Munich in the same year, and also painted his first non-objective "Improvisations". In Paris, moreover,

Robert Delaunay was at the same time conducting his studies of color contrasts on the basis of the color investigations of the American physicist Ogden N. Rood. These reflections on art were to lead Larionov to a form-language which, at the suggestion of his companion Goncharova, he was to call Rayonnism. In 1912 he wrote his "Manifesto of the Rayonnists and Futurists", which was later signed by ten of his fellow artists. The text, similar in tone to that of the manifestos of the Italian Futurists, but expressly disassociating its authors from them, defines Rayonnism in concise terms: "The style of Rayonnist painting which we practice is based on those spatial forms which are produced by the intersection of rays reflected by various objects chosen by the artist. For simplicity's sake the ray is represented on the surface by a colored line. The objects encountered in everyday life play no further role in the Rayonnist picture ... The picture has in a sense a flowing quality, it imparts a sensation of being outside of space and time, it creates a feeling of what is known as the 'fourth dimension'. The height and breadth of the picture, the thickness of the paint, are the only attributes of the surrounding material world. All other sensations evoked by the contemplation of a Rayonnist picture are on another plane. In this way painting approaches music, yet without losing its own individuality . . ." The manifesto closed by designating Rayonnism as the first step toward a "true liberation of painting". In 1912, the year of its formal proclamation, Goncharova and Larionov presented the first pictures complying with these theoretical requirements (ill. p. 39). This happened in the framework of an exhibition organized by an association with the rather unusual name of "The Donkey's Tail". The jocular allusion contained in this designation was understandable only to initiates even at the time: the two Parisian critics André Warnod and Roland Dorgelès had made fun of contemporary art trends by sending to the "Salon des Indépendants" in 1910 a picture entitled "Sunset on the Adria" by a fictitious artist, but in reality the work was painted by a donkey with a brush tied to its tail. The joke, which had amused the contemporary art world, thus provided the couple Goncharova-Larionov with a group name nicely imbued with Dadaist irony. Word-plays and railleries of this kind were then the order of the day for the names given by artists and writers in Moscow to their cliques and magazines. The poems and prose of Mayakovsky offer innumerable instances of this deliberate use of absurd designations, often employed to wonderfully poetic effect, an exercise in which he had no rival unless it were Velimir Khlebnikov, a friend of Larionov and the two Burliuks.

Both the protagonists of this style and attitude and the perplexed public classified such things under the general heading of Futurism. In reality the movement had little to do with Italian Futurism proper. Mayakovsky makes some clear statements about the intellectual and artistic atmosphere of 1912–1914 in a letter dated 1922: "Futurism as a unified, exactly defined movement did not exist in Russia before the October Revolution. The term was applied by critics to everything that was new and revolutionary. One ideologically well-cemented group was our own, rather infelicitously called 'Cubo-Futurists' (V. Khlebnikov, V. Mayakovsky, D. Burliuk, A. Kruchonikh, W. Kamenski, N. Asseyev, O. M. Brik, S. Tretyakov, B. Kushner). We had no time to devote to the theory of poetry, we offered only practice. The sole manifesto of this group was the preface to the collection entitled 'A Slap in the Face of Public Taste', which appeared in 1913. A poetic manifesto that expressed the aims of Futurism in emotional slogans . . ." In spite of such unequivocal declarations, Soviet literary criticism later attempted to deny Mayakovsky's role in the Russian Futurist movement and to belittle its significance in general.

The "Donkey's Tail" exhibition in March 1912 marked the breakthrough of the Rayonnist group. Along with Goncharova and Larionov, Kasimir Malevich and Vladimir Tatlin figured prominently in the group. These were regarded as the "big four" and were each represented by about fifty works, including not only their latest Rayonnist compositions, but older pieces of Primitive or Fauvist inspiration. As was to become clear in the exhibitions that now followed in quick succession, Rayonnism was to be only a passing phase: Natalia Goncharova was soon painting typically Futurist pictures such as the "Cyclist" of 1912/13; Vladimir Tatlin benefited from his meeting with Picasso and experimented from 1913 onward with Cubist collages which soon changed into colored three-dimen-

sional reliefs. Ivan Puni took a similar line that led him to exquisitely colored floating material montages (ill. p. 59). Prepared in preliminary studies, they combine plastic force with great chromatic sensitivity.

Under the influence of Matisse, but also of the formal power of Old Russian icon painting, Malevich attempted to monumentalize his expressive compositions of 1908–1911, mostly scenes from peasant life. In the pictures dating from 1911, the strong impact of Fernand Léger's current work is apparent: with ever more obvious intent Malevich transforms the figures and objects of his peasant motifs into highly plastic forms composed of tubular elements, cylinders and sections of cones. Dispensing with all objective and painterly details, he combines these tubular forms in compositions having the character of murals ("Taking in the Harvest", "The Woodcutter"). Such works, which can be clearly distinguished from similar productions of his comtemporaries, have been classed as "Cubo-Futurism". The same term was applied by Alxander Archipenko, likewise influenced by his friend Léger, to his three-dimensional "sculpto-paintings" produced about the same time and representing a special kind of colored sculpture.

The trait that distinguishes Malevich ever more clearly from his revolutionary colleagues is his gradual abandonment of expressive dynamism and his cultivation of a disciplined, formally severe picture composition. The year 1912 was to bring the decisive break. Whatever the truth may be about Malevich's possible visit to Paris about this time, his adoption of the synthetic Cubism of Paris can be followed quite clearly in his work. The transition is consummated in a "Head of a Peasant Girl", known also as the "Large Cubist Rose". From this point onward his compositions gradually lose their spatial and corporeal qualities. Motifs with much of the character of still lifes are built up from an agitated mass of chromatically articulated surfaces that overlap and mesh with each other, sometimes in a vertical-horizontal, sometimes in a diagonal pattern. Fragments of the kind familiar from Cubist painting — glasses, bottles, sheets of music, parts of guitars — are utilized, as are odd pieces of city architecture. Finally, bits of Russian letters and words make their appearance in compositions dating from 1914, as in "An Englishman in Moscow" and "Woman in front of a Poster Pillar". Occasionally Malevich also uses collage and object montage techniques borrowed from Cubism, fitting "objets trouvés" into his pictures — a thermometer, for instance, in "Soldier of the First Division". It is fascinating to observe in these works, dating from 1914, how Malevich becomes more and more interested in clear relationships between large monochrome surfaces and small-textured, vibrating centers of the composition which are enclosed as though they were jewels. No less striking is the almost complete emancipation from the represented object.

The Cubist composition "Samovar" (ill. p. 43), an analytical fragmentation of the still-life motif, was completed just before this phase. Probably painted in 1912/13, it figured in the exhibition of the "Union of Youth" at the end of 1913 and went from there to the "Salon des Indépendants" in Paris in 1914, as extant photographs prove. The work bears witness to the artist's taste for delicately colored paintings rich in skillfully handled details, a proclivi-

Kasimir Malevich: Samovar, c. 1913

Liubov Popova: Architectonic composition, 1921

Liubov Popova: Composition, 1920

ty that also expressed itself in Malevich's subsequent non-objective pictures.

A clear move toward synthetic Cubism is revealed at the same time by the work of other Russians. In most cases a basically Expressionistic attitude is retained and comes out either in the colors or in the dynamic nature of the forms; a preference for dramatic diagonals and spiral movements is also unmistakable. The Cubist still lifes of Liubov Popova (ill. p. 41), who, with her colleague Nadezhda Udaltsova, studied under Le Fauconnier and Jean Metzinger in Paris in 1912/13 and sent her pictures from there to Russian exhibitions, are distinctly synthetic and Futurist in character. Much the same holds true for Olga Rozanova, who progressed from highly expressive Futuro-Cubist industrial landscapes (ill. p. 40) to synthetic compositions incorporating fragments of French words. In a sense the first works of Alexander Rodchenko also belong to this grouping: Futuristically dissolved figural compositions consisting of a surging accumulation of curved or spiral forms.

The year 1913 brought the exhibition "The Target" organized by Larionov, which united almost all progressive forces and provided the occasion for the publication of the Rayonnist-Futurist Manifesto. It also brought an important experience for Malevich: he was able, after a Futurist congress in Finland, to design the settings and costumes for the Futurist operetta "Victory over the Sun" by the poet Alexei Kruchonikh, with music by Mikhail Matyushin, performed late in 1913 in St. Petersburg. The figurines reveal Cubist simplifications and exaggerations of the costume, while the drawings for the stage settings are non-objective dynamic Cubist compositions, and in one instance a simple geometric composition: a black-and-white square, divided diagonally.

Malevich later pointed out that this was the beginning of Suprematism. His remark, "In 1913, in my desperate endeavor to free art from the ballast of the objective world, I took refuge in the square," is disputed in its application to the dating of the famous black square on a white background. The fact is that in 1913 and 1914 Malevich did not exhibit a single Suprematist picture, but only Cubist works. Suprematism was even absent from the "first Futurist exhibition", which took place in Petrograd in February 1915 and was entitled "Tramway V".

It was only in a further exhibition in Petrograd, called the "Last Futurist Exhibition 0.10" by its organizer, Ivan Puni, that Malevich appeared as a Suprematist. This was toward the end of the year 1915. The fundamentally new departure led not only to artists' squabbles, that are not unusual at such exhibitions, but to some very basic differences of opinion. Witnesses reported that Malevich and Tatlin had come to bitter blows, with the result that a sharp dividing line ran through the exhibition. In the section which Malevich dominated with 36 non-objective works, the "Black square on a white background" hung in a corner just below the ceiling. The brochure "From Cubism and Futurism to Suprematism", the forerunner of other, more extensive publications by Malevich, was offered for sale. This theoretical review of the contemporary scene was backed by a "Suprematist Manifesto" by Ivan Puni and Xenia Bogoslavskaya, later to become his wife. Tatlin, who was represented by twelve painting-reliefs and corner-reliefs — so-called counter-reliefs — issued a state-

Liubov Popova: Pictorial-Tectonic, 1916/17

Kasimir Malevich: Suprematist drawing, c. 1916/17

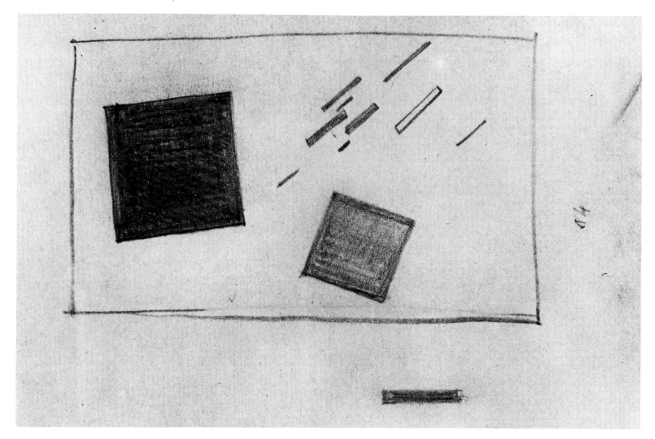

Kasimir Malevich: Suprematist drawing, c. 1916/17

Kasimir Malevich: Black and red Square, c. 1915

Kasimir Malevich: Suprematist drawing, c. 1915/17

Olga Rozanova: Abstract composition, 1916

Vladimir Tatlin: Model for the Monument to the Third International, 1920

Naum Gabo: Constructed head, 1916

ment of his own as a rejoinder. The violent quarrel about the priorities of the new creative advances need not interest us here, any more than the fact that the dating of the first Suprematist works by Malevich is still unclear. The issue is in any case confused because Malevich may well have gone on painting figurative pictures even after proclaiming the new doctrine of Suprematism.

What exactly did Malevich mean by Suprematism? The question is not easy to answer, for there are many contradictions in his own texts on Suprematism including the definitive formulations in a work entitled "On New Systems in Art, Static and Speed", published in Vitebsk in 1919. The same applies to his main theoretical work dating from 1922: "Suprematism, the World as Non-objectivity". When a German edition of the "Theory of the Additive Element" (1926) appeared in 1927, with the title "The Non-objective World", in the series of Bauhaus books, extracts from "Suprematism" were included in it. Finally, when Malevich visited Berlin in 1927, he left with his German friends much-revised manuscripts of the various texts on Suprematism. These were believed lost for many years, but they were found again in 1953 and were first published in 1962 in a German translation.

Malevich repeatedly makes it clear in his commentaries that Cubism was the first step in the liberation of painting from its adherence to the object, or as he puts it, from objective-practical realism. "Cubism destroyed the idea of the object. By constructing paintings, it created a new artistic consciousness. The first signs of non-objective painting were already contained in it. Cubism opened the door to independence, to liberation from the regimen of the commonplace, for the whole artistic world. In it the nature of painting was in fact made manifest." Malevich sees this intrinsic nature of painting as a complete liberation not only from all conditions but also from all aims. "The essential content of Suprematism is the totality of non-objective, natural excitations without any goal or purpose."

All the theoretical statements of Malevich are inspired by the conviction that art up to his time had been—like religion, science and technology—directed toward an end. Nature, however, to which he repeatedly appeals, is free of all logic, all striving toward a goal. "Nature is our teacher, but a teacher whose lessons, experiments and experience are not necessarily understood by her pupils . . . Her teaching is only non-objectivity, and it is to be assumed that in this non-objectivity true life is to be found."

Such observations show that Malevich was pursued by a vision of an art fundamentally different from anything that had gone before. "The new art has given priority to the principle that art can have no other content than itself. We accordingly do not find in it the idea of any particular thing, but only of art itself, of its own content. The intrinsic idea of art is non-objectivity."

Malevich calls this absolute purposelessness of art "Suprematism". He understands this as "liberated nothingness". The only thing that impels the artist is excitement, the "supremacy of pure sensation". The utterances of Malevich, usually instilled with passionate fervor, point beyond art proper. He is attempting to articulate a new conception of the world, a silent nothingness that lies beyond all experience. Suprematism in this sense is the finding of new signs to make visible on a canvas direct

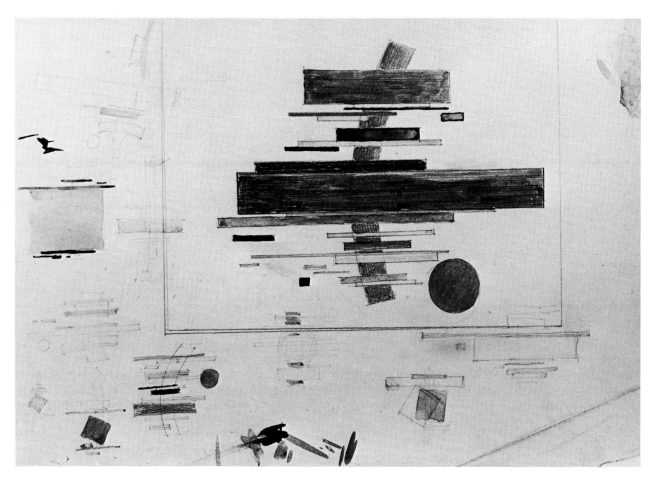

Ilya Grigorievich Chashnik: Suprematist composition, c. 1924

sensations, unconscious excitements and the cosmic interrelation of all such responses. Seen from this angle, all the Suprematist pictures painted by Malevich from 1915 onward must be regarded as the products of contemplative or even meditative thought, as "icons of a new way of perceiving the world", as Werner Haftmann called them in the foreword to the German edition of the texts. Malevich himself had already referred to his black square in 1915 as the "zero form", the "naked, unframed icon of my time".

One is inclined to conclude that in his vision of a non-objective art—he himself wonders whether it can still be considered as art in the conventional sense—Malevich was advancing into the realm of philosophy and religion. For some of the great mystics God has been a nothingness, and the German philosopher Georg Wilhelm Friedrich Hegel proclaimed: "Pure being and pure nothingness are the same thing." The thoughts of Malevich might be termed, after Immanuel Kant, "speculative metaphysics".

In his work he first made a radical return to the simplest forms, square, circle, cross, rectangle, which he set on a white background. This background is not to be understood as a surface on which the elementary forms are placed and pinned in position, but rather as an unlimited space in which they float freely. Very soon Malevich began to use his elementary forms not in isolation but in compositional relationships above and beside each other (ill. p. 47).

In his paintings, and more particularly in the numerous drawings for which no corresponding completed paintings are to be found (ill. pp. 46, 48), the static and silently hovering elements are replaced by movement, sometimes very vigorous, that as a rule gathers momentum in an upward direction or radiates in all directions. The individual form elements—bars, beams, rectangles, arcs, etc.—are set in an irrational yet geometrically exact relationship. They attract or repel each other as though they were invested with magnetic force. In some cases the movement seems to die out in the depths of the picture space, in others it thrusts forward from the depths. In certain pictures the solid forms—a yellow trapezoid, say—will dissolve gradually upward, toward the depths of the picture, fading into the white of the background. All fixation to palpable earthly things appears to be cancelled, most impressively when a white area is set off against a white background only by the structure of the brushstrokes and the faintest color modulation.

Like other progressive or "leftist" artists, Malevich was able to step into the limelight after the October Revolution of 1917. Perhaps because the "destruction of the object" in art was equated with the destruction of the Tsarist bourgeois society, the new art was identified with the hard-won victory of the new Socialist-proletarian society.

Ilya Grigorievich Chashnik: Suprematist Composition, C. 1924

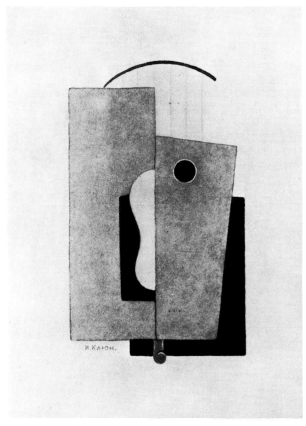

Ivan Kliun: Composition, c. 1920

Developments which had taken place underground and among outsiders in a few years of wild activity — supported only by a handful of progressive collectors — now received official recognition. The artists were quite willing to seize their opportunity, and Malevich even proudly announced that Cubism and Futurism had, as prerevolutionary art movements, anticipated the political, social and economic revolution.

This pioneering attitude, and possibly the fact that the party leadership was fully occupied with more vital problems of domestic and foreign politics, resulted in the official acceptance of the spokesmen of the new art, who through the efforts of Anatoly Lunacharsky were also given important posts. Malevich was made director of the art institutes of Moscow by the Narkompros, the People's Commissariat for Culture and Education, then in 1919, when art teaching was reorganized, professor at the Art Academy of Vitebsk. In 1922 he became director of Inchuk, the Leningrad branch of the Institute of artistic Culture in Moscow. Some members of "Unovis", a group of promotors of the new art founded in Vitebsk in 1920, here seconded his efforts.

In the meantime Suprematism had gained in popularity, partly as a result of Malevich's own example, partly through his theoretical writings. Artists from the Cubo-Futurist circle joined the Suprematist movement more or less on their own initiative. A personal credo that Malevich had preached out of passionate conviction thus became a style, the principles of which could also be applied by others. Yuri Annenkov (ill. p. 60), Liubov Popova (ill. pp. 44, 45), Olga Rozanova (ill. p. 49), Alexander Rodchenko (ill. pp. 62, 63), and Ivan Kliun (ill. p. 53) now became its principal exponents. Other artists gathered around this central group, for instance Vassily Ermilov (ill. p. 61), Ilya Chashnik (ill. p. 51), Nikolai Suetin (ill. p. 60), Ivan Kudriachov (ill. pp. 56, 57), and others. Suprematist principles could also be applied successfully on a practical level, as is proven by the Agit decorations designed in 1918 to embellish the streets for the May celebrations and the anniversary of the October Revolution. The use of Suprematist form elements on tableware made in the state factories reveals that they could also be utilized in the field of industrial design. The most important contributions to this applied Suprematism were made by Malevich and his pupils Chashnik and Suetin.

The further development of Cubo-Futurist principles in the direction of geometric abstraction did not take place exclusively along the lines proposed by Malevich in his proclamation of Suprematism in 1915. Even at that time there were differences of opinion that were to lead to divergent lines of development resulting in a fragmentation of the movement. Vladimir Tatlin in particular sought a rational basis for his work which was in contrast to the irrational and even mystic approach of Malevich. His relief and corner constructions are a continuation of the material assemblages of Picasso and mark the beginning of a Constructivist art proper. It is certainly no accident that Tatlin did not start out from painting but from architecture, and that he remained a close friend of the brothers Wesnin, who were among the leading architects and stage designers of the day.

Tatlin's work, however, is not solely determined by the rational use of form elements that can be assembled in log-

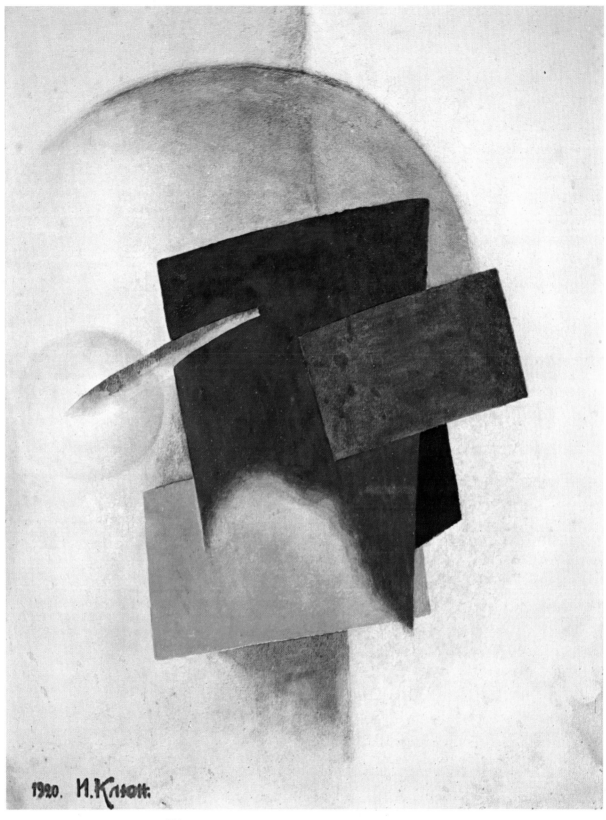

Ivan Kliun: Suprematist composition, 1920

Alexandra Exter: "Romeo and Juliet", stage design, c. 1921

Alexandra Exter: Composition, 1920

ical constructions. He did not believe in the autonomy of art but saw art as a means of solving socio-economic and even practical problems by the provision of models and examples. Despite their high value as art, his works are always functional and often utilitarian in conception. It was therefore quite logical that from 1918 onward he should hold various official posts in state cultural institutions. In 1919 Lunacharsky commissioned from Tatlin a monument to the spirit of the Revolution. It has since come to be known as the "Monument to the Third International": a project in which architectural, sculptural and painterly elements were to be combined in a symbolic glorification of the idea of the Revolution. Conceived as a huge, obliquely rising and unfurling ribbon-like spiral, this Utopian monu-

ment is known from plans and photographs of the model (ill. p. 50). There have also been some later attempts to reconstruct this rotating tower.

In the field of sculpture Tatlin's project for this dynamic spatial construction had no direct forerunner. Certain parallels can be found in the work from about 1900 of the Art Nouveau sculptor Hermann Obrist, and Johannes Itten designed a "Tower of Fire" as a monument to aviators, quite independently of Tatlin's project, at the Bauhaus in Weimar in 1919/20. But Tatlin's work — a consistent application of Constructivist principles of art to monumental sculpture — went far beyond anything before it both in its dimensions (it was to be some 400 meters or 1300 feet high) and in its bold synthesis of steel and glass. It was the first step in a sculptural development which was to replace solid volumes by spacial frameworks. Tatlin's later experiments were no less Utopian. Always functional in their motivation and therefore beyond the bounds of fine art, they were concerned with concrete problems of industrialization and stage design. Tatlin's theories found their purest expression in his studies for a Utopian glider, the "Letatlin". Like Malevich, but in a more concrete and technical vein, he here takes up the Futurist demand for the conquest of the universe by aeroplane and spaceship.

After the Revolution, other artists also turned, as Tatlin did, to practical tasks related to the realities of a workers' republic. Such attempts at functionalization may be seen either as a sign of weakness — a lack of creative potency — or of strength, an active acceptance of the new proletarian society. For many the first outlet was work in the theater, which went through a period of brilliant success, especially under Vsevolod Meyerhold, in the years immediately following the Revolution. Alexandra Exter, for instance, designed costumes and settings and was closely connected with the bold theatrical experiments of the time (ill. p. 54). Many others were likewise seized by enthusiasm for Meyerhold's "Biomechanics", the theatrical counterpart of Constructivism, and lent expression to the Constructivist spirit particularly in stage structures.

Other forms of contact with the new way of life were sought by Alexander Rodchenko. About 1915 he had come under the influence of Malevich, but before long he sided with Tatlin (ill. pp. 62, 63). When in 1918 Malevich proposed "white on white" painting, Rodchenko took up the challenge and answered with a painting in "black on black". He too was given official educational assignments from 1918 onward and turned in 1919 to three-dimensional constructions which are a radical continuation of Tatlin's sculptures. A similar line was taken by the brothers Georgy and Vladimir Stenberg, who with their "space constructions" of 1920/21 represented an "industrial Constructivism" directed against "pure art" (ill. p. 66). It is a remarkable fact that progressive artists in Russia, and for that matter in Western Europe at that time, liked to consider themselves as "fitters" and "constructors", as leaders in the building of a new world along industrial lines. As a professor at the Vkhutemas, Rodchenko expressly postulated the idea of the "artist-engineer". He himself turned more and more to photography and film. Working to a large extent with Mayakovsky, he developed a new style of poster and brochure layout embodying a Constructivist combination of photographic and typographic

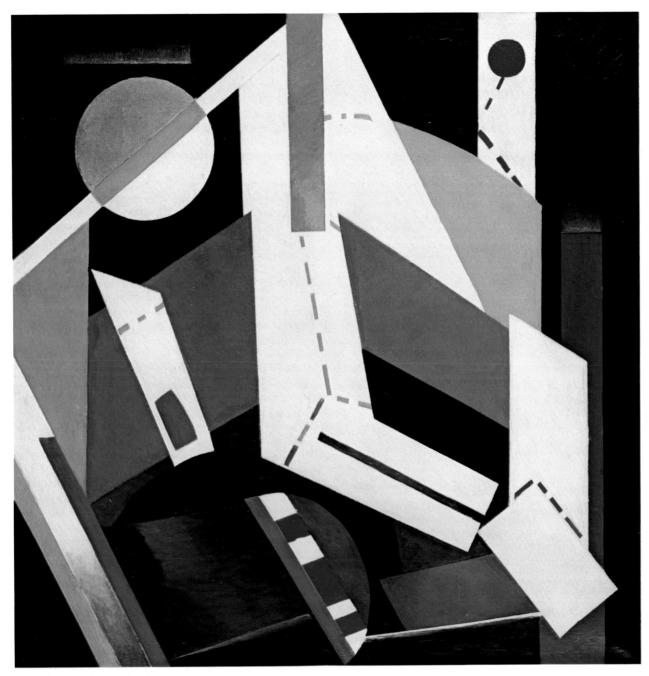

Alexandra Exter: Construction, 1922/23

elements. In compositions intended for exhibitions, posters and book illustrations he created a new style of Constructivist photomontage which had the full approval of
the party leaders and also set a model for Western Europe.
Around 1920 there was evidently a form of rational geometric design in Russia which contrasted with the Suprematism of Malevich and was known by its protagonists as
"Constructivism". The name "Constructivism" crops up in
1920 in the Productivist group to which Tatlin, Rodchenko and his wife Varvara Stepanova belonged. After a
number of manifestos in which this group had opposed a
free, aesthetically inspired art and had instead proposed

"tectonic" and "productionist" work, Alexei Gan formulated in 1922 the principles of Constructivism and the ac-
tivist political attitude on which it was based.
This proclamation of Constructivism had been immediately preceded by another statement about art theory:
the "Realist Manifesto" of the brothers Naum Gabo and
Antoine Pevsner, published in August 1920 by the state
printing office in Moscow. This manifesto — probably
written, as we now know, by Naum Gabo alone — likewise
grappled critically with Cubism and Futurism. But over
and above that it was an emphatic affirmation of life,
whose laws must determine the laws of art. The manifesto points to space and time as being the two determi-

Ivan Kudriachov: Suprematist drawing, 1923

Ivan Kudriachov: Suprematist composition, 1921

nants of life. "Space and time have been reborn for us today. Space and time are the only forms on which life is based, and they are the starting point from which art

must be constructed." The account given of what art should and should not be ends with the statement that a "new element of kinetic rhythms" must form the foundation of all approaches to space and time. The manifesto further proclaims the intention to create an art which will emerge from its isolation, which will meet every man in streets and squares as an integral component of the modern world.

From 1915 on, Naum Gabo had attempted to extend the Cubist tradition by constructing heads and busts from circular and segmented plane surfaces. This led to three-dimensional figure constructions without any solid volumes. The interconnected disk-like elements enclose compartments in which light is captured as if in a windowless building (ill. p. 50). From here, Gabo advanced about 1920, by way of niches, to free spatial constructions of the greatest dynamic intensity. The substitution of transparent celluloid for solid, opaque materials next brought about a dematerialization which permitted the stresses, the lines of force, to be even more clearly emphasized. While Tatlin was working on his monument to the Revolution, Gabo was designing gigantic radio stations whose transmission towers were like great feelers reaching out into space.

We know from the third of the brothers, Alexei Pevsner, that Antoine arrived at similar three-dimensional compositions — after giving up a loose, painterly Cubism — only in the early twenties and under the influence of Gabo. The major development of his work as a sculptor took place after 1923, the year in which he moved to Paris. The further work of both Gabo and Pevsner is in the nature of three-dimensional construction, the solid plastic form being resolved into a pattern of lines of force (ill. pp. 119, 253).

The group of the Constructivists proper — with Tatlin, Rodchenko, Puni, Pavel Mansurov, the brothers Stenberg — also included El Lissitzky. He had studied architecture in Germany before the war and had then traveled around Europe as a painter. Returning to Moscow, he worked as an architect and took part in art exhibitions. Immediately after the Revolution he accepted official commissions and functions, for instance designing the first Soviet flag. In 1919 Chagall appointed him to a post at the art academy of Vitebsk, where he worked with Malevich and evolved a geometric and initially Suprematist style. Probably during a process of detachment from Malevich — "not world visions, but world reality" — Lissitzky developed a Constructivist art of his own which he called "Proun", an abbreviation of "Pro Unowis", which stood for a movement to establish new forms of art. Apart from his practical duties and teaching work, Lissitzky devoted himself from 1919 on to a form of painting which, with its spatial constructions mostly on a white ground, belongs to the world of the imagination but expresses a rational and progressive philosophy akin to that of Tatlin (ill. p. 65). As organizer of the "First Russian Art Exhibition" in Berlin in 1922, Lissitzky achieved the wish of the Russian government to break, through cultural contacts, the long blockade of Russia by the Western nations. This exhibition in Berlin, to which we shall return later, familiarized Germany with the latest Russian art and led to the borrowing of Constructivist principles. Lissitzky took an active part in making known these principles, particularly through

Ivan Kudriachov: Suprematist composition, 1919

Ivan Puni: Study for relief sculpture, 1916

Ivan Puni: Suprematist relief sculpture, 1915

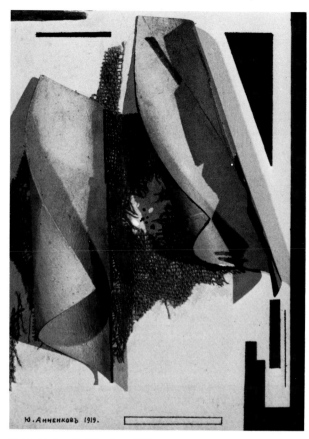

Yuri Annenkov: Relief collage, 1919

the graphic and typographic work he did in Germany (ill. p. 64) and in Switzerland.

The progressive artists of the West, most of whom were leftist in their political persuasions and therefore followed the establishment of a Socialist state in Russia with approval, tended to equate Constructivism with the new Russia. It was hardly noticed that rapid changes soon began to take place in Russia itself. Even the more and more frequent immigration of Russian artists to Western countries does not seem to have made much impression. The fact that the Constructivists turned their attention more and more to practical work was taken in the West as impressive proof that a union of art and life had been achieved in Russia, that the artist had been usefully integrated into the new Socialist society. Every Russian guest performance in Western theaters, every poster, every piece of printed matter was evidence of this fruitful union. And the Suprematist dishes out of which the proletariat spooned its soup were regarded with undivided admiration.

It was obviously not realized that the situation was in reality fraught with danger and that progressive artists were clutching at the proverbial straw. In retrospect it is clear that the transfer of creative work to the non-artistic sectors of Russian everyday life, in what was in the last analysis a merely decorative function, was a sign of a basic change in the assessment of progressive art movements

by the party leaders. At first there had been a readiness to accept the new form-world of art and the progressive attitude it sprang from as an expression of the new man and the new society. Then voices began to be raised in the responsible committees asserting that this progressive art was fundamentally foreign to the people. This attitude was probably as much due to a lack of understanding and to reactionary resistance on the part of the party bosses as to the unfavourable reactions of the working classes. The artists themselves were not oblivious of the danger. While most of them were certainly honest in their support of the new Socialist state, it was primarily out of self-defense that they made themselves available for practical tasks and presented their works as models for the solution of other problems. Those who did not anticipate grave developments and therefore leave the country for Western Europe thought it best to prove their usefulness as builders of the new proletarian state. This in part explains the translation of Suprematist principles into three dimensions on the part of Malevich and his pupils, and the expansion of their graphic compositions into architectural visions. Malevich calls these plastic constructions "Architectona" or "Planites" and sees them as mod-

Nikolai Suetin: Study for composition, 1920

Vassily Ermilov: Composition No. 3, 1923

Alexander M. Rodchenko: Constructive forms, 1918

The criticism directed by the authorities against the art of Malevich and his companions, and against an attitude which was labeled pointedly as "formalism", had really begun at an early stage. Lenin, whose tastes in art were very conservative, had been highly skeptical about the initial equation of revolutionary art and the Revolution. But the change of heart comes out most unmistakably in the attitude of the responsible commissar: Anatoly Lunacharsky, a fervid opponent of Cubism and its ramifications long before the Revolution, had been willing, in his first few years of office as head of the Narkompros, to allocate important functions in the official cultural elite to the artistic avant-garde. But as soon as the wind veered, he withdrew his support from the new art more and more categorically. As early as 1924, in a report on a German art exhibition in Moscow, he takes sides very energetically for the popular Realists and against the Abstractionists in Russia.

After the death of Lenin in January 1924, as Joseph Stalin moved gradually into power, cultural policy turned more and more strongly against progressive tendencies in art. A milestone in the new relationship of the party to art is the "Decree concerning party policy in the domain of artistic literature" of 1925. It goes far toward install-

els for an upcoming architecture. It is typical of his visionary attitude that he includes spaceships in his architectonic conceptions and in a manifesto dating from 1924 expressly mentions these "aeroplanes" as constituent features of a new age.

The difficulties began for Malevich with his appointment to the position of Director of the Institute for the Investigation of Artistic Culture (Inchuk): his criticism was directed more and more specifically against the new state, then against Socialism as such and finally against historical Marxism. To this opponent of "objective realism" the idea of Socialism became "the extreme limit of human objective-scientific realism". He can be even more explicit: "Historical materialism is an obvious example of the inadequacy of human thought. There is no other future for it than that of further inadequacies, especially if historical materialism has made its goal the culture of the production of objects . . . Historical materialism must be rejected just as definitely as the object in art." In 1927 Malevich was for the last time granted permission for a trip to Berlin, where he contacted representatives of the Bauhaus. When he returned, he left a collection of his works behind and, as a kind of legacy, important manuscripts. His Suprematist pictures were exhibited in Russia just once more in the same year. We know from the scanty flow of further information that he later reverted to figurative painting — possibly a last move to save his own life in the face of imminent danger. When he died in 1935, he had given up painting altogether.

Alexander M. Rodchenko: Line construction, 1920

Alexander M. Rodchenko: Composition, 1918

El Lissitzky: Proun I, lithograph, 1923

El Lissitzky: "Wendingen", cover of a magazine, 1921

ing "Socialist Realism" as the official form of art. The final curtailment of all free artistic development came with the "Decree concerning the reorganization of literary and artistic organizations" of 1932. Many of the leading thinkers in these fields had left the country years before. Others observed a studied silence or turned to practical tasks that could draw no suspicion. Stalin succeeded in suppressing completely the further development of Constructivist art in Russia. But it had already had a powerful influence in Western Europe and had touched off a spate of work whose initiators were frankly recognized as being the Russian Constructivists.

Following the Stalinist decree concerning the reorganization of art, issued in 1932, painting and sculpture in the Soviet Union were put completely under the centralized control of the Union of Artists. The abolition of the academicist conception of art — for years the common postulate of all leftist and progressive artists — was now considered an unacceptable criticism directed against the Soviet population. The old Academy was re-established under the direction of Isaak Brodsky, a fervent traditionalist who even before the Revolution had opposed the slightest renewal in art. His famous portrait of Lenin at the Smolny Institute, painted in 1930 and considered a highlight of the Tretyakov Gallery in Moscow, is a milestone along the new road Russian art was to take.

But Constructivist Russian art was not completely silenced. It was further developed by emigrated leading artists outside the Soviet Union, in Western Europe and in the United States. As a co-editor of the London magazine "Circle — International Survey of Constructive Art" the sculptor Naum Gabo published in 1937 the essay "The Constructive Idea in Art". Without referring to the Stalinist art policy the article gives a convincing summary of the ideas of the Russian Constructivists.

"Our own generation found in the world of art after the work of the Cubists only a conglomeration of ruins. The Cubistic analysis had left for us nothing of the old traditions on which we could base even the flimsiest foundation. We have been compelled to start from the beginning. We had a dilemma to resolve, whether to go further on the way of destruction or to search for new bases for the foundation of a new art. Our choice was not so difficult to make. The logic of life and the natural artistic instinct prompted us with its solution . . .

"The Constructive idea is not a programmatic one. It is not a technical scheme for an artistic manner, nor a rebellious demonstration of an artistic sect; it is a general concept of the world, or better, a spiritual state of a generation, an ideology caused by life, bound up with it and directed to influence its course. It is not concerned with only one discipline in art (painting, sculpture or architecture), it does not even remain solely in the sphere of art. This idea can be discerned in all domains of the new culture now in construction. This idea has not come with finished and dry formulas, it does not establish immutable laws or schemes, it grows organically along with the growth of our century. It is as young as our century and as old as the human desire to create.

"The basis of the Constructive idea in art lies in an entirely new approach to the nature of art and its functions in life. In it lies a complete reconstruction of the means in the different domains of art, in the relations

El Lissitzky: Study to Proun 30 T, 1920

between them, in their methods and in their aims. It embraces those two fundamental elements on which art is built up, namely, the content and the form. These two elements are from the Constructive point of view one and the same thing. It does not separate content from form — on the contrary, it does not see as possible their separated and independent existence. The thought that form could have one designation and content another cannot be incorporated in the concept of the Constructive idea. In a work of art they have to live and act as a unit, proceed in the same direction and produce the same effect. I say 'have to' because never before in art have they acted in such a way in spite of the obvious necessity of this condition. It has always been so in art that either one or the other predominated, conditioning and predetermining the other . . .

"This was the main obstacle to the rejuvenation of art, and it was at this point that the Constructive idea laid the cornerstone of its foundation. It has revealed an universal law that the elements of a visual art such as lines, colours, shapes, possess their own forces of expression independent of any association with the external aspects of the world; that their life and their action are self-conditioned psychological phenomena rooted in human nature; that those elements are not chosen by convention for any utilitarian or other reason as words and figures are, they are not merely abstract signs, but they are immediately and organically bound up with human emotions. The revelation of this fundamental law has opened up a vast new field in art giving the possibility of expression to those human impulses and emotions which have been neglected."

Vladimir Stenberg: Construction in Space KPS 6, 1919, reconstructed in 1973

Mathematical Aesthetics

De Stijl in the Netherlands

It was not only revolutionary Russia that was to become a leading center of geometric non-objective art — surprisingly enough, the bourgeois Netherlands were to play a comparable role. It is of course true that Holland and Belgium had had a great artistic past, but not very much was left of it in the nineteenth century. The Netherlands vegetated peaceably against a background of agriculture; anyone who wished to break away from the uneventful life of a law-abiding burgher could go to sea or into shipbuilding, or could try his hand in the lucrative and adventurous colonial trade on which the country's prosperity was founded. The Flemish part of Belgium still dreamed of its past glories under Spanish dominion, but had experienced industrialization in its harshest form — that of mining — and now followed the cultural lead of the nearby French capital.

Important changes, however, began to take place around the turn of the century. A movement of independence sprang up in Belgium, mobilizing Flemish culture as a counteraction to French influences. This movement was soon challenged by a similar Walloon movement. Symbolist poets such as Emile Verhaeren and painters of the Neo-Impressionist school, who had joined together to form the group known as "Les Vingt", sought a new idiom in art and poetry, and one no longer dictated by Paris. James Ensor, the fantastic forerunner of Flemish Expressionism, and the Pointillist Theo van Rysselberghe are typical representatives of this development.

The determination to build up a Flemish culture was concurrent with the universal renewal movements afoot at the beginning of the new century. Personalities such as Henry van de Velde, who started as a Pointillist painter and became a many-sided creative artist and cultural critic, or Victor Horta, who evolved a new architectural language with his iron constructions, are typical of a new form-consciousness in Belgium, accompanied by a Socialist political outlook, which soon began to spread to the rest of Europe. It was also in Brussels that the Viennese architect Josef Hoffmann erected the Stoclet Palace, a building which was to set new standards. In its differentiated cubic forms and the puritanic severity of its black-and-white ornament it is both a characteristic expression of the geometric branch of Art Nouveau and a forerunner of Functionalist architecture.

The situation in the Netherlands was rather different. Here too innovation sprang from the spirit of renewal that came with the end of a century. A militant rejection of historical styles and of the floral branch of Art Nouveau, emanating from Paris and exemplified by Hector Guimard, found particularly clear expression in the work and theories of the architect Hendrik Petrus Berlage. Berlage stood for very consistent rationalism based on the strict Calvinist persuasions of the Dutch bourgeoisie. This led, soon after 1900, to a geometrically inclined style. Ornament was here entirely subordinated to the functional logic of the individual elements of a building or a piece of furniture. In Berlage's way of thinking space came before the façade, and walls were used as form-creating factors. This severe style was based on a belief in the necessity of rationally determined proportions. The so-called Amsterdam school developed a mathematical aesthetic which had a stimulating effect far beyond the sphere of architecture proper. Its instigator was Jan Hessel de Groot, among whose numerous writings there was one — entitled "Form-Harmonie" and published in 1912 — that had a particularly powerful influence. A passage from the introduction reads in translation: "This book gives suggestions as to how a harmony of form can be achieved through formal relationships. I call a form harmonious when its inner relationships are so chosen that they form a single whole."

Like other European artists, the Dutch had close connections with Paris after about 1908. These connections first went by way of Brussels with its groups "Les Vingt" and "La Libre Esthétique". The central figure of Dutch Art Nouveau, the painter Jan Toorop, was soon joined by a younger generation that sought to obtain its impulses direct from Paris: Kees van Dongen, Jan Sluyters, Otto van Rees, Piet Mondrian and others. These artists, of differing origins and training, soon found their way to Cubism, mostly through direct contacts with the Fauves in Paris and with Picasso, Le Fauconnier, Léger, Gleizes and Metzinger. In 1910 the painter and critic Conrad Kickert founded "De Moderne Kunstkring" in Amsterdam, an association of young artists including Sluyters, Mondrian and Toorop. The group's first exhibition in 1911 brought works by Cézanne, Picasso, Braque, Herbin and others to Amsterdam. Among the Dutch artists Expressionist and Pointillist experiments led in many cases to a Fauvist style to which Kees van Dongen was to remain true. Sluyters, who had got to know Mondrian in 1907, espoused the cause of Cubism and soon began to incorporate dynamic elements in his work that show resemblances to the contemporary compositions of Kupka and Delaunay and that led around 1914 to a definitely Futurist style. Otto van Rees, who had come from South Germany, also gravitated by way of Cubism to Futuro-Cubist pictures, but then became the first artist in the Netherlands to adopt the collage technique. In 1916 he and his wife Adja van Rees, a textile artist, were among the founders of the Dada movement in Zurich.

Piet Mondrian, who had been a drawing teacher and had painted curiously conventional pictures in dark hues, was over thirty-five when he found his way into the new

Chris Beekman: Composition, 1920

movements. In 1908 he began to stylize simple motifs in clearly perceptible stages: a windmill or the church steeple at Dombourg. The gradual process of abstraction can best be followed, however, in his successive renderings of an apple tree: in 1910 an expressively Pointillist transposition of this everyday motif into intense reds and blues, with a clear debt to Van Gogh; in 1912 a Cubist-inspired composition translated into terms of pure vibration, in which the muted and broken colors also betray a preoccupation with the principles of analytical Cubism.

From 1911 onward Mondrian lived in Paris. Sequences showing the process of abstraction, such as the pictures of the apple tree, bear eloquent witness to the swift yet purposeful development of the Dutch artist in his new and stimulating environment. He later recalled: "I took a long time to discover that the peculiarities of form and natural color evoke subjective feelings that obscure the pure truth. The appearance of the natural forms changes, but the reality remains. To create pure plastic reality, one must reduce the natural forms to their constant form elements, the natural colors to primary colors. The aim is not to produce other, special colors and forms with all their limitations, but to strive for greater unity."

After moving to Paris, Mondrian succeeded in speeding up this process of reducing natural forms to their essentials. The view from his studio window in the Rue du Départ was often a source of inspiration: an anonymous, insignificant piece of the Parisian architectural landscape. His pictures were window and façade scenes in which the horizontals and verticals of windows, doors and sills grew more and more rigid and therefore independent of the real model. Only an occasional diagonal or arc recalled the slope of a roof or a portal. The coloring of analytic Cubism, with a predominance of ocher, was at first retained, as was also the concentration of the picture—typical of still lifes by Braque and Picasso—in an oval within the rectangular outline of the canvas. From 1913 onward Mondrian's palette became brighter, pale blues and pinks joining the ocher. The bar systems still suggested spatial relations: at the bottom of the composition the cubic forms were bigger and the colors stronger, toward the top everything became smaller and more delicate. This rearward movement was given up in 1914. Mondrian now renounced every illusion of space and began to rely on the surface. The horizontal-vertical line structure gained strength and dominated the composition. Mondrian was beginning to find his own style. In this determinant phase of his development he was surprised by the outbreak of war in July 1914 while on a visit to Holland. For the time being a return to Paris was out of the question.

At home Mondrian continued systematically the work he had begun in Paris. In 1914 he was already producing wholly non-objective horizontal-vertical compositions using no color but only short black bars that are assembled like plus and minus signs on the white ground in a dense, almost nervous rhythm. This was a consistent development of the compositional principles he derived from Cubism. It is more than daring to interpret these black-and-white works as references to war cemeteries, as has sometimes been done. Can we even claim to recognize the original models of these non-objective pictures—the church porch as sketched at Domburg or the pier against the background of the ocean?

As early as 1913 Guillaume Apollinaire had recognized the individuality of Mondrian's world: "This Mondrian is inspired by the Cubists, but he does not imitate them... This form of Cubism seems to me to take a line that differs greatly from that of Braque and Picasso..." Apollinaire was right. The "intellectualisme très sensitif" which he recognized in the Dutchman was to lead Mondrian in a few years to a form-language that had nothing to do with the Cubism of Paris even in its later forms of development.

Toward the end of 1914 Mondrian settled in Laren. In this old artists' colony not far from Amsterdam he met the people who were henceforth to be his companions. His first meeting was with the philosopher Dr. Jan Schoenmaekers, who had given up the Catholic priesthood and now professed a creed that he called "Christosophy". Mondrian made the acquaintance of Schoenmaekers on the occasion of a series of lectures in which the latter for the first time expounded his new conception of the world, a conception which was based on mathematical principles. The book "Het Nieuwe Wereldbeeld" (The New Cosmology) appeared in 1915. Like the work Schoenmaekers published the following year, "Beginselen der Beeldenden Wiskunde" (Principles of Formative Mathematics), it had a powerful influence on Dutch artists.

It is quite clear from the later statements of Mondrian and Van Doesburg on their work and goals that their approach to art was based on a kind of Neoplatonic philosophy. In a review of their joint beginnings written in 1929 Van Doesburg tells us: "We expressed this fundamental concept with the word 'beelding' in the sense of

Chris Beekman: Composition, 1916

creative shaping. The word took on a new connotation for us and meant the suprarational, the alogical and inexplicable, the depth rising to the surface, the equilibrium from within and without, what was achieved in a creative struggle with ourselves. A sort of new terminology came into being in which we expressed our collective ideas as a

Willem van Leusden: Abstraction of figure, 1920

Vilmos Huszar: Composition with female figure, 1918

Bart van der Leck: Study, c. 1916/17

motive force for joint action. All arts, acoustic or optic, are rooted in one and the same concept: beelding." In this connection Van Doesburg also points out, quite unpolemically, that Mondrian's phraseology is mainly based on the new philosophy of Schoenmaekers' "plastic mathematics".

Mondrian met Schoenmaekers regularly, and their lengthy talks helped him to clarify his own ideas about the relations of art and life. Spurred on by these talks, he began to formulate his own thoughts. His writings on the theory of art later evolved from these notes. The explanation of the deep understanding reached by Mondrian and Schoenmaekers is no doubt to be found in the syncretistic "godly wisdom" known as theosophy on which Schoenmaekers' philosophic system was in part based. Mondrian had occupied himself before this with occultism and theosophy. In 1909 he had become a member of the Theosophical Society in Amsterdam, had written and published theosophical texts on several occasions. However, his critical attitude to the founders and leaders of the theosophical movement, Helena Blavatsky and Annie Besant, prevented him from becoming an orthodox theosophist.

Mondrian's contacts with Salomon Slijper were of similar intensity. Slijper, rooted in ancient Jewish tradition, was a representative of a simple, mystic philosophy. In his hitherto unpublished, extensive correspondence with Slijper Mondrian attempted to formulate his own opinions more exactly. They were instilled with the belief that humanity could be raised to a higher spiritual level through art. Mondrian's thoughts here come very close to those of Kandinsky as set forth in his "Concerning the Spiritual in Art".

The other acquaintances Mondrian made were of a quite different nature. In 1915 he displayed one of his "pier and ocean" compositions in a group exhibition in Amsterdam. Theo van Doesburg, then working chiefly as an art critic, gave the picture his careful attention in an article in the periodical "Eenheid". He probably visited Mondrian in Laren shortly afterwards, in early 1916. Although Van Doesburg describes Mondrian in a letter as being rather inaccessible and not very gifted for friendship, similar lines of thought seem to have brought the two different natures together. Bart van der Leck joined in their conversations a little later. According to Van Doesburg he established contact with them himself. Mondrian's recollection of the matter does not confirm this: "In this period I met artists with much the same intentions. First Van der Leck, who, although still figurative, painted in compact areas of pure color. My more or less Cubist technique ... came under the influence of his exact technique. Shortly afterwards I made the acquaintance of Van Doesburg. Full of vivacity and enthusiasm for the already international movement that was known as 'abstract', and a genuine admirer of my work, he came to request my collaboration in a magazine that he wanted to publish. He meant to call it 'de stijl'. I was happy to have the opportunity to publish my thoughts on art, which I was already busy writing down. I now saw the possibility of contacts with like minds."

Theo van Doesburg, whose real name was Christian Emil Marie Küpper, had first tried writing and had then, about 1900, turned to painting. He had been most deeply impressed by Van Gogh, the Symbolists and Japanese art. As a painter — and under the name of I. K. Bonset as an art critic — he had attentively followed modern developments. Expressionism and Fauvism had at first been his main interests. Then he had become acquainted with the works and writings of Kandinsky. This led him to a flat, rather highly stylized form of painting. A typical example is "The Cardplayers" of 1916, a picture in which the surfaces are bounded and divided by a linear pattern of horizontal and vertical lines and arcs. Evidently, Van Doesburg realized when he met Mondrian how much more advanced the latter's work was.

Much as in the case of Mondrian, but a few years later, a thrust into a new pictorial world expressed itself in Van Doesburg's work as a process of increasing abstraction. A series of studies of a grazing cow reveals to particularly good effect how the stylization is heightened from drawing to drawing. It soon leads to the dissection of the overall organic form into a system of rectangles and triangles that serves as a support for freely chosen colors. The process ends in 1916 in non-objective compositions built up from larger and smaller rectangles: uniform patches of primary and secondary colors on a white ground. The animal motif which was the starting point has been wholly eliminated; the picture does not pretend to be anything else but a geometric design animated by freely chosen rhythms. Van Doesburg's work has thus moved into the immediate proximity of Mondrian's (ill. pp. 75–77).

Bart van der Leck had worked in stained glass, and this fact had an important bearing on the contribution he was to make to Dutch art. A feature of stained glass is that the translucent areas are set in a pattern of leads which appear as black outlines when the glass composition is

Bart van der Leck: Composition No. 7, 1917

seen against the light. Van der Leck's professional work had involved practical collaboration with architects, in particular with Hendrik Petrus Berlage. His objective as a fine artist was also the integration of art in architecture. An active Socialist, he was skeptical about art for art's sake and regarded collaboration with architects as the only way to an art that would really be a part of society and life. A commission from the art-loving Helene Kröller-Müller to decorate the interior of her house St. Hubertus in Otterlo was to be an important milestone in his artistic career. It led, however, to violent arguments with Berlage, the architect of the house, and to the farsighted demand that the architect should really call in the artist at the project stage to decide on color schemes and not merely en-

trust him with cosmetic embellishment after the house was finished. Like Van Doesburg, Van der Leck was deeply moved by Mondrian's picture "Pier and Ocean" which was on view in Amsterdam in 1915. He too switched over in the course of 1916 from a highly stylized, flat figurative technique to purely geometric compositions consisting of colored rectangles (ill. pp. 72, 73).

The three painters Mondrian, Van Doesburg and Van der Leck were united not only by their analogous pictorial experiments but also in their determination to influence life by means of art and to create harmony in the world. It was not merely the wish to form a new group that prompted them to join forces. Their real and essentially ethical motive was an almost missionary zeal to change life through pure art based on harmonious relationships. In accordance with the ideas of Schoenmaekers, they wished to achieve a synthesis of mind and matter. This was the object of their association and of the publication of their magazine "de stijl".

The fourth and youngest artist in the Stijl group was Vilmos Huszar, a Hungarian by birth, who had come to Holland in 1905 and had soon become a popular portrait painter in The Hague. Around 1913 a Fauvist tendency appeared in his portraits, then a short phase of Cubist lithography and etching followed. In 1915 Huszar attracted great attention with "Hommage à Van Gogh", a very dynamic picture composed chiefly of spiral forms: the waving cypresses and rotating suns of the late Van Gogh have here been transformed into a pure Futurist rendering of motion. Probably this unusual work, which was executed wholly in shades of yellow and blue, attracted the attention of Van Doesburg. He felt that he must acquaint Mondrian and Van der Leck with the gifted Huszar (ill. p. 71).

It is typical of the intentions of this circle that even in the art field they did not wish to restrict themselves to painting. They soon accepted a new member in the person of the Belgian sculptor Georges Vantongerloo, who had come to the Netherlands after being wounded at the beginning of the war. In 1915 and 1916 he painted in the Pointillist style, and in sculptural work done at the same time he showed a growing interest in mathematical constructions. This proclivity for geometric problems no doubt strengthened his relations with the group centered upon the active Van Doesburg. Figurative sculptures were now replaced in Vantongerloo's œuvre by "space studies" in which the stylized figurative motif soon gave way to a moving and vibrating three-dimensional form. "Thus begins the destruction of the object," he wrote later, "and it is only the construction that counts." Immediately upon his entry into the Dutch group, Vantongerloo changed over from organic forms to cubic constructions of a pronounced architectonic conception.

Connections with architecture proper were also cultivated. Berlage's rationalism had set the younger generation of architects moving in a direction that was not far away from that taken by Van Doesburg and his colleagues. Jacobus Johannes Pieter Oud and Robert van't Hoff were the first to join the group. Oud, initially an admirer of Berlage, had familiarized himself in Germany with the latest trends toward Functionalism in architecture. Van't Hoff had been in the United States and had absorbed the work and theories of Frank Lloyd Wright. He had also collected, at least indirectly, some impressions of traditional Japanese architecture. Japanese models generally played an important part in the geometric Art Nouveau movement both in the United States and in Europe. It has been pointed out on several occasions that the geometric ornament in the early buildings of Frank Lloyd Wright, particularly the orthogonal leading of windows, shows astonishing parallels to the form-language of de Stijl.

The date of formation of the group and more particularly the date of birth of the journal "de stijl" are exactly known. The introduction written by Theo van Doesburg for the first modest issue was dated June 16, 1917. The founding members, apart from the untiring initiator, Van Doesburg, were: Piet Mondrian, Vilmos Huszar, the architect J. J. P. Oud and the writer Anthony Kok, who was to contribute to "de stijl" on the literary side. Further members and authors of articles appeared in the issues for the first year: the painter Bart van der Leck, the architects Jan Wils and R. van't Hoff, the sculptor and painter Georges Vantongerloo and, as a guest, the Italian Gino Severini. Later, many other personalities joined the circle, the first of them, in 1918, being the carpenter, interior designer and later architect Gerrit Thomas Rietveld (ill. p. 84).

It is quite understandable that a new group of artists should have adopted the programmatic name of "de stijl" (The Style), for it expressed a will to establish a new and soundly based style in a time of stylelessness and conflicting trends. As is evidenced by many statements made in 1917, the real aim of the Dutch group was not merely to introduce an art style, in the sense of just another "-ism", but to permeate life with art, and in the last definition to improve the quality of life itself. This explains the active interest in contemporary architecture, with which painting, sculpture and interior decoration were to enter into a synthesis, an aesthetic harmonization of the whole material environment.

It is consequently not surprising that the origin of the name of the group and its magazine "de stijl" has never been very carefully investigated. It must be remembered that the Belgian Henry van de Velde had already had a vision, about 1900, of a "new style" that should embrace all aspects of life. Van der Velde had also set a personal example: he had given up painting and become a designer of furniture, china, tableware and clothing, a lay preacher, art teacher and theorist as well as an architect and interior designer. His vision of a "new style" had been based on the idea of a "reasoned beauty" from which — as the typical social commitment of the time required — all men and not just certain individuals could benefit.

Hendrik Petrus Berlage, a contemporary of Van de Velde, held similar views. He was also largely in agreement with Frank Lloyd Wright, whose theories were then being attentively studied in the Netherlands. An important starting point of the Dutch discussions about a new style, a style more adapted to a technical and industrial age, was a book entitled (in translation) "Style in the technical and tectonic arts" in which the German architect and theorist Gottfried Semper had broached some basic problems in advance, to be exact in 1860/1863. The attention of the Dutch group had been drawn to this source by the writings of Jan Hessel de Groot. In his "Form-Harmonie" of 1912, which was being hotly discussed by artists at the time, De Groot devotes a good deal of space to Semper's book. He refers to the book with its complicated German title in the short Dutch form of "De Stijl". The term was therefore on people's tongues; everybody involved knew what assumptions and intentions were contained in it. When Van Doesburg formed his group of like-minded artists, it offered itself almost automatically as a programmatic password.

In the introduction to the first issue of "de stijl" Van Doesburg set forth its objectives:

"This little periodical seeks to contribute to the new sense of beauty. It seeks to make modern man receptive to what is new in the fine arts. It seeks to counteract archaistic confusion — 'modern Baroque' — with the logical

Theo van Doesburg: Study for a composition, 1922

principles of a maturing style that is based on the pure relationship of the spirit of our age and its media of expression. It seeks to unite the present-day lines of thought in the field of the New Plasticity, which, although similar in essence, have developed independently.

"The editors will endeavor to attain this goal by letting the truly modern artist, who can contribute something to the renewal of aesthetic understanding and to the self-realization of the fine arts, speak for himself. If the public has not yet grasped the new beauty of form, it will be the duty of the specialist to awaken a consciousness of beauty in the layman. The truly modern — i.e. conscious — artist has a double duty. Firstly: to produce the purely de-

signed work of art; secondly: to make the public susceptible to the beauty of pure creative art. A journal of an intimate nature has become necessary for this purpose, especially as public criticism has neglected to counteract the lack of appreciation for the beauty of abstract artistic expression. The editors will give specialists the opportunity to do this now . . ."

Van Doesburg closes with the statement: ". . . As soon as artists in their various domains of activity realize that their aims are basically alike, that they must speak a single common language, they will no longer cling anxiously to their individuality. They will serve a general principle beyond the confined personality. By serving this general

Theo van Doesburg: Study for a mural, L'Aubette, Strasbourg, 1926

principle, they will automatically create an organic style. It is not a social but a spiritual community that is necessary for the dissemination of beauty. A spiritual community, however, cannot come into being without ambitious individuality being sacrificed. Only if this principle is consistently applied can a new relationship of the artist to society lead to the new creative beauty manifesting itself in all things as style."

All the essential key words are contained in these statements: the aim is a style that shall embrace all creative domains and shall be "abstract" or non-representational. The artist is called upon to surrender all individual characteristics in the interest of this common style. He should not only make concrete contributions to it, he should also influence the public in the capacity of an educator and expositor, thus making the new aspects of art generally understandable. The "new beauty", though not exactly defined, is equated with the geometric, non-objective style affected by the artists concerned. Van Doesburg had originally intended to give the journal the more specifically programmatic name of "De rechte lijn" (The Straight Line). The more general but more ambitious title was due to the influence of Schoenmaekers. The "new style" was thus the art represented by the founders and in particular by Mondrian in 1917.

Mondrian was given the assignment of presenting "the

Theo van Doesburg: Counter-composition XIII, 1925/26

New Plasticity in painting" in a first programmatic essay. He allocates the leading role to painting: painting is best able to embody the pure shaping principle. His basic requirements for art are that its media of expression should be made more exact and more spiritual. Content in the descriptive sense must be replaced by the "representation of relationships". "We can perceive in nature that all relationships are governed by a primary relationship: it is that of the extreme One to the extreme Other." The right angle is recognized as the most balanced positional relationship, the mutual interaction of the horizontal and the vertical. For Mondrian abstract representation is universal representation. "The composition leaves the artist the

greatest possible freedom for subjectivization — if and as long as this is necessary. The rhythm of color and dimensional relationships (in exact proportion and in equilibrium) makes the absolute visible in the relativity of space and time. The New Plasticity thus becomes dualistic through the composition. As a result of the exact representation of the cosmic relationship it is a direct expression of the universal, as a result of its rhythm and the material reality of its execution it is an expression of the subjective and individual. In this way it unfolds before us a world of universal beauty without sacrificing the general human element."

Mondrian's further comments make it clear that he at any

rate did not see de Stijl only as an aesthetic, an artistic movement. A new life, a new reality was to be built up in accordance with universal principles. Results in the domain of aesthetic and creative research were equated with intellectual principles. Universalism, considered as an equilibrium of equivalent relationships, is the opposite of individualism, much as it is in a philosophical sense. Mondrian and his companions were not concerned merely with art and, inside of art, with a limited conception of style. Their aim must be understood as an "aesthetic vision of the universal". What is meant is a new culture, embodied in a new man. It is the artist's duty, as an individual with foresight, to lead the masses. The purification of art by the use of pure artistic means and the inclusion of all areas of creative art are only a first aesthetic goal. The ultimate moral goal is a new mankind. In this sense the objectives of the Stijl were Utopian as were, to a certain extent, those of Russian Constructivism.

While Mondrian's essay is in the last analysis a philosophical justification of the principles and aims of de Stijl, some of his paragraphs are devoted to concrete issues of creative art. Here he does not advance theories to which practical work must be adapted, but theories which have been derived from practice. The new approach is guided by reason. "The artist is no longer a blind tool of intuition. Natural feeling no longer dominates the work of art, it is the expression of an intellectual feeling—of reason and feeling in one. This intellectual feeling is by its nature accessible to reason."

Where Mondrian makes statements on the media of expression and composition, he speaks of a conscious or —as he repeatedly stresses—"exact" or mathematical handling of the medium. "Abstract-real painting can work in aesthetic-mathematical terms because it has an exact, mathematical medium of expression. This medium is color carried to a state of determinacy." To Mondrian this means a return from natural to primary color, a reduction of color to the surface and finally a confinement of the color within certain boundaries so that it appears "as a unity of rectangular surfaces".

Plastic effects, hitherto obtained in painting not only with natural colors but more often by illusionistic means, were also important to Mondrian. But he demanded a "new plasticity" which can be attained by "reducing the corporeality of things to an assembly of surfaces" which "create the illusion of lying in one plane". He continues: "These surfaces are capable, both through their dimensions (line) and through their tonal values (color), of creating space without expressing it in visual perspective." The dimensions of breadth and height can be read off direct from the composition, the depth dimension "appears as a result of the distance effect of the chromatic differentiation of the surfaces".

In this basic text, which appeared section by section in the first twelve numbers of "de stijl", supplemented by clarifying comments, and which Van Doesburg tells us was the binding result of joint deliberations, Mondrian outlined the fundamental tenets of the Stijl. It is quite understandable that in the work done by individual members at the time personal differences disappear almost entirely and the compositions are astonishingly alike. Even more than this stylistic concord, the readiness of each member to deal with special questions in texts pub-

lished in the magazine speaks for the unity of the group. Such contributions were devoted to the role of painting in architecture, the monumental cityscape, or the relations of art to the machine. The second annual volume opened with the "First Manifesto of 1918", which was signed by all members except Bart van der Leck and J. J. P. Oud. The manifesto calls for a new, universal consciousness that is ready "to be put into effect in all spheres, including outward life". The Great War is condemned, and the signatories express their fellow-feeling for all "who are struggling on the intellectual or material plane for the establishment of international unity in life, art and culture". Such people are expressly invited to cooperate in realizing the aims of de Stijl. It was to be the special assignment of Van Doesburg to put into practice the wish for expansion beyond the frontiers of the Netherlands.

The year 1918, however, already saw changes in the personal productions of the various artists. Mondrian returned from the use of color surfaces to the black line, a development which Van Doesburg soon followed, at least in part. Huszar filled his picture surface with grey rectangles. Van der Leck adhered most closely to the common form-language. Aware of the changes that were creeping in, however, he withdrew from the group in the same year and went his own way, which led to the resolution of figurative motifs into flat, elementary forms. The same year brought the first results in architecture and furniture design. Rietveld, for instance, produced his first chairs in the Stijl spirit. In the following year, 1919, came the first international contacts, and contributions to the magazine reveal a clear intention to furnish information on allied developments in other countries. The subsequent issues are marked by a stronger interest in questions of architecture and furnishing.

A phenomenon of some interest for the further development of painting were the attempts made by Mondrian and Van Doesburg to divide up the picture surface with a screen of horizontal-vertical or diagonal lines and to fit the color areas into this system. Mondrian, however, quickly returned to a freer form of the horizontal-vertical compositional arrangement, to the heavy black line and to pure primary colors. This may have been due to the fact that in 1918—perhaps under the influence of the former stained-glass artist Van der Leck—Huszar and Van Doesburg, and possibly Mondrian himself, turned their attention to stained glass. The colored panes of stained-glass windows are held together by the leads, which thus form a heavy black network around the translucent colors in the finished window. The geometric windowpane arrangements in some of the buildings of Frank Lloyd Wright have already been cited as a possible influence on the black, orthogonal line systems that appear in the paintings of the Stijl and of Mondrian in particular. In point of fact the artists of the Stijl did not need such models, for they had them before their eyes in the Netherlands—a point that has so far been overlooked: in countless anonymous buildings erected about the turn of the century in Amsterdam and other cities the entrances have fanlights with grilles, some of them in floral designs of wrought iron but more often with horizontal-vertical bars. These geometric grilles are not regularly spaced, but are mostly in free rhythms—striking in their resemblance to the black line patterns in Mondrian's pictures.

Piet Mondrian: Composition with Red, Yellow and Blue, 1930

How far these window grilles are due to Indonesian influences remains to be investigated. Reminders of the former colonial empire have survived in many aspects of life in the Netherlands.

The Stijl between 1916 and 1918 was the outcome of a unique convergence of ideas and trends. It was impossible that it should last for long. There were departures and new arrivals. As Van Doesburg became the propagandist of an extension and internationalization of the Stijl, Mondrian gradually fell back on his own resources. He remained true both to his earlier experiments, which he steadily pursued, and to his theoretical statements. In many respects his further work as a painter is an attempt to move step by step toward the Utopian vision announced in the magazine, toward a "Nirvana of radiant

purity and brightness", as the chronicler of de Stijl, Hans L. C. Jaffé, called it.

Unlike Van Doesburg, who—realistically and even pragmatically—expanded his thinking repeatedly beyond painting into other creative realms, the more spiritual Mondrian, while reducing his compositions to a simple system of black coordinates with sparingly integrated fields in the primary colors (ill. p. 79), brought his Neo-Plastic art into direct relation with the fundamental issues of human life. He once wrote with reference to his own goals: "In life the mind is often overemphasized to the detriment of the body. But sometimes too much attention is paid to the body, and the mind is neglected. In the same way content and form in art have been overemphasized or neglected in turn, because it was impossible to

Lajos d'Ebneth: Composition, 1926

Lajos d'Ebneth: Collage, 1926

attain their inseparable unity. If this unity in art is to be achieved, an equilibrium must be created. It is an accomplishment of our time to have produced such a balance. Imbalance implies conflicts and disorder. Conflicts are part of life and art, it is true, but they are not all life or the whole universal beauty. Real life is the interplay of two equal-ranking opposites — different appearance and nature. The visible expression of them is universal beauty."

While Mondrian, especially after his return to Paris in 1919, carried on his creative researches with sovereign discipline and consistency, Van Doesburg, seconded by the architects of the Stijl group and occasionally working as an amateur architect himself, devoted himself to the reshaping of the material environment in the spirit of the Stijl. The architecture of the Stijl went well beyond the "cubic" principles that are inherent in all architecture — flat floor, vertical walls and pillars, rectangular windows and doors and flat roofing — to work with smooth surfaces always placed at right angles to each other. The cubic form as an elementary space unit, however, is not used statically — in the sense of a mere assembly of compartments — but dynamically.

A building is looked upon as a zone of concentration in endless space; it appears as a complicated spatial configuration, as a raising of the two-dimensional relationships of surfaces — as embodied in the painting of the Stijl — into the third dimension. Inside walls are thus projected to the outside, walls interpenetrate each other; there are no front, lateral or rear façades in the traditional sense. Color plays a major part. As in Mondrian's pictures, only the primary colors red, yellow and blue are used in addition to white, grey and black. The buildings planned and in some cases carried out and suitably furnished by Oud, Van Doesburg, Rietveld and the younger Cornelis van Eesteren are very closely bound up with the Stijl painting. In their spatial character, however, they owe a good deal to the plastic experiments of Vantongerloo. It is only when we compare them with the functional architecture that developed in the twenties, particularly in Germany, that we realize to what an extent the Stijl architecture is aesthetic and not functional. In fact it is rather three-dimensional painting than architecture proper.

"We have studied the question together and discovered that architecture may be designated as the plastic sum of all the arts. This realization leads to a new style. We have investigated the laws of space and have found that all changes of space can be regarded as a unity brought into equilibrium." These are the words of the architects of the Stijl in a declaration intended for an exhibition of their common projects and individual work in 1923 in the gallery of Léonce Rosenberg in Paris.

The endeavors to transfer the principles of de Stijl into three-dimensional colored "architectural sculpture" seem to have brought to light fundamental differences in the views of Mondrian and Van Doesburg. Mondrian was a firm believer in the surface, although he could not overlook the fact that a system of black lines on a grey or white surface produces an illusion of space and that different depths are suggested in a picture by the use of the three primary colors and by the various shades of grey.

In 1925 Mondrian broke away from the Stijl altogether. As early as 1920, when he published "Le Néo-Plasti-

Piet Mondrian: Composition with Yellow, 1938

Georges Vantongerloo: Space Sculpture, 1935

the edge of the picture (ill. p. 79). Close scrutiny of the brushwork of some pictures of this period, especially those left unfinished (ill. p. 81), shows how Mondrian repeatedly tried to enhance the equilibrium of the pictures by subtle modifications of the dimensions of the black lines. The compositions in which these lines are parallel to the edges of the picture are easily in the majority, but from time to time Mondrian also fitted the right-angled composition into a square rotated through 45 degrees, with a corner pointing upward. Possibly these diamond-shaped pictures, with the resulting colored equilateral triangles in their corners, are an answer to Van Doesburg's counter-compositions. These diamond-shaped pictures continue to occur in Mondrian's work up to the very last.

By 1930 an extreme of asceticism seems to have been attained in the form and color structure of some of the compositions: restriction to one horizontal, two verticals, a single primary color, or even renunciation of all color in favor of the pure black-and-white line pattern. Then a counter-development sets in: the black lines are doubled or multiplied, occasionally producing dense grids that divide the picture area up into numerous small white or colored compartments. These dense grids have been related to the gathering gloom of the international political scene after the mid-thirties. There is no doubt that they appear heavier and more austere than the compositions dating from around 1930, which seem to float with almost acrobatic buoyancy because of their minimal use of form and color elements. These later paintings were done, however, at a time when changes were also taking place in Mondrian's daily life: in fall 1938, sensing that war was approaching, he moved to London. Two years later, on October 3, 1940, he arrived in New York.

His move to the New World left a visible mark on the works of his last years. The black lines vanished and were replaced by a dense network of colored strips which in the "Boogie-Woogie" compositions are transformed into a vibrating, serene and cheerful web of small rectangular color areas arranged in ribbon-like rows. Mondrian's titles were inspired by the dance rhythm popular at the time, which had developed out of a technique used by jazz pianists; what is more, the artist himself was stirred to the depths by this rhythm with its striking bass figures. From the early twenties on, in Paris, he had taken an intense interest in the relationships of timbre and rhythm in music and painting. A passionate dancer, he saw especially clear parallels between jazz and his own painting. His enthusiasm for the boogie-woogie is a culminating point in his search for an art-music synthesis. It must be seen against the background of a profound experience of the intoxicating atmosphere of New York. The years leading up to his death on February 1, 1944, thus bore all the signs of a transition to a new, dynamic style.

Mondrian's conception of de Stijl—"the work of art must point the way to a new revelation of our environment"—finally led to a moral claim: "Whatever is true in art must be true in life." Inspired by an almost religious belief in the power of these universal laws, Mondrian made well-nigh superhuman demands on art, which in his view was to serve the ends that in earlier times had been served by religion.

Van Doesburg took up a position which was more pragmatic, without betraying his own convictions. He believed

cisme" in Paris, he had tightened and clarified his theoretical arguments and had found a new name for his work. Another reason for his break with the Stijl was doubtless his rejection of a principle of composition which Van Doesburg began to apply consistently in 1924 and which he designated "counter-composition": the pattern of right-angled lines and surfaces is not placed parallel to the edges of the picture area but is turned through an angle of 45 degrees (ill. p.77). There are, no doubt, connections between these "dynamic" diagonal compositions of Van Doesburg and his isometric or parallel-perspective architectural representations done at about the same time. Van Doesburg called these new developments in his painting—which were soon to have many followers—"Elementarism", which we may perhaps take to be a counterblast to Mondrian's "Neo-Plasticism".

For Mondrian the following decade brought a subtle purification of the horizontal and vertical composition of strong black lines in which one to three primary colors are introduced into various peripheral areas, often cut by

Georges Vantongerloo: Composition II, 1921

in the message contained in the conception of de Stijl, and he worked with all his might for the acceptance of its basic implications in other countries. Shortly after the war he established important connections, in Germany with the Bauhaus at Weimar in particular, in Italy with the group "Valori plastici", in France with the architects Le Corbusier, Mallet-Stevens and others. New personalities entered the inner circle of the Stijl, for instance Cesar Domela Nieuwenhuis, Werner Graeff (ill. p. 94), Hans Richter, Frederick Kiesler and Friedel Vordemberge-Gilde-wart (ill. pp. 85, 86). Others were at least influenced by the thinking of the Stijl, among them Chris Beekman (ill. p. 68) and the Hungarian Lajos d'Ebneth (ill. p. 80), who was a friend of Huszar and had come to The Hague in 1923. The same applies to Willem van Leusden (ill. p. 70) and even Paul Joostens.

The manifestos that were published in almost regular succession in the magazine "de stijl" reveal how the interest of Van Doesburg and his companions was extended from painting to include the shaping of the whole human environment. In the years following World War I, collaborating closely with the architect and city planner Cornelis van Eesteren, he developed a socio-cultural concept for a new integral environment. In the third manifesto we read:

"Concentration and property, mental and material individualism were the foundations of the old Europe. It cannot detach itself from them. It is being tormented and ruined, and we stand and watch without turning a hair. Even if we could help, we would not wish to do so. We do not want to prolong the life of this old harlot. A new Europe is already alive within us." And the fifth manifesto adds: "We have found out in collective work that architecture is the plastic sum of all forms of art ... and we have reached the conclusion that the consequences will bring forth a new style ... The period of destruction has at last

Gerrit Rietveld: Berlin Chair, 1923

come to an end. A new constructive epoch is beginning."
These were not empty words. Behind them there were
remarkable examples of the building of a new material
environment: the structures of J.J.P. Oud, of Cornelis van
Eesteren and Gerrit Rietveld, who had begun as a joiner
and had become the designer of "Stijl" furniture (ill. p. 84)
and finally an architect. His Schröter House in Utrecht of
1924–1926 is, in its colorful exterior architecture and its
consistent interior decoration, an exemplar of a "Stijl"
architecture proper. El Lissitzky enthused about it after
his visit in 1926.
The new conception of de Stijl developed by Van Doesburg, for the most part in cooperation with Van Eesteren,
attaches more importance to the practical activity of the
artist than to his contemplative scope as seen by Mondrian. This reorientation involved a change in the role and
the responsibilities of the artist. On this point Van Doesburg says: "The things that are happening in architecture
and in the redesigning of our houses were prepared
some time ago by the plastic arts. Everything that for-
merly developed in the seclusion of the studio now
comes into existence in public, in the streets and in our
immediate surroundings ... Every work of art gives
expression to a statement which will be realized earlier or
later in life. In that resides the educational and creative
force of the work of art."
In 1927, on the tenth anniversary of the birth of de Stijl,
Van Doesburg was able to state in retrospect: "De Stijl as
a movement developed slowly out of de Stijl as an idea.
The movement spread more rapidly from year to year.
Initially only a small, timid, almost sect-like group which

partly dissolved again, it has today been strengthened by
many fresh forces and stands clear and challenging on the international stage." One of the most important connections that Van Doesburg was able to establish was that with Russian Constructivism, in the name
of which El Lissitzky took up contact with the Stijl while in
Germany. The crowning success of the efforts made to
internationalize the Stijl movement, however, was no
doubt the foundation of the "Abstraction-Création"
group in Paris in 1931.
Van Doesburg died on March 7, 1931, in Davos, shortly after his move to Meudon near Paris. His death signified
the end of the Stijl as a movement. The last issue of the
magazine, in January 1932, is dedicated to the memory of
its founder and initiator. In nearly fifteen years of existence the Stijl had not only produced significant works but
had generated new ideas directed toward changing the
relationship of art to life and placing it on a new plane.
For all its Utopian optimism—the creation of a new man
in a new world shaped by art—the Stijl had made the
public conscious that art can change, if not humanity as a
whole, at least certain human beings and above all the
visible world, and can change it for the better. This optimistic teaching has never been completely forgotten
since. The ideas of the Stijl, even though they have undergone modification, are still alive today.
In his introduction to the exhibition catalog "De Stijl,
1917–1931, Visions of Utopia" Hans L.C. Jaffé resumes
the concepts of de Stijl:
"What was de Stijl, and why has this losely organized,
mercurial group had a sustained influence on the visual
arts—not only painting, but architecture, typography and
furniture design—throughout this century? Never a cohe-
sive movement, in the beginning it included three painters, two architects, a sculptor and a poet, who came
together to exchange ideas in a public forum. The vehicle
for this exchange was a monthly magazine, "De Stijl".
Founded in mid-1917 in Leiden, Holland, it ceased publication in 1931 after the death of its founder, Theo van Doesburg, who was publisher and editor of the magazine and
the movement's primary spokesman. Without Van Doesburg, de Stijl as a movement fell apart.
"In visual terms, the group had a shared point of departure: the principle of absolute abstraction—that is to say,
the complete elimination of any reference to objects in
nature. Its means of visual expression were limited to the
straight line and the right angle, to the horizontal and the
vertical, to the three primary colors—red, yellow and
blue—with the addition of black, white and gray. But this
initial description reveals only the method of de Stijl, not
its scope or its philosophical outlook.
"In rejecting perceptible subject matter, the artists of this
movement did not abandon content or meaning in their
work. The essential content of de Stijl works is harmony,
a harmony that for these artists could only be rendered
by abstract means, through compositions unhampered
by associations with objects in the external world. This
search for harmony was the springboard and constant
goal of de Stijl. Yet de Stijl artists were not solely concerned with aesthetics. The movement was an effort to
renew the links between life and art. In creating a new
visual style it attempted to create a new style for living.
"Universal values, the absolute harmony, were the goals

Friedrich Vordemberge-Gildewart: Composition No. 23, 1926

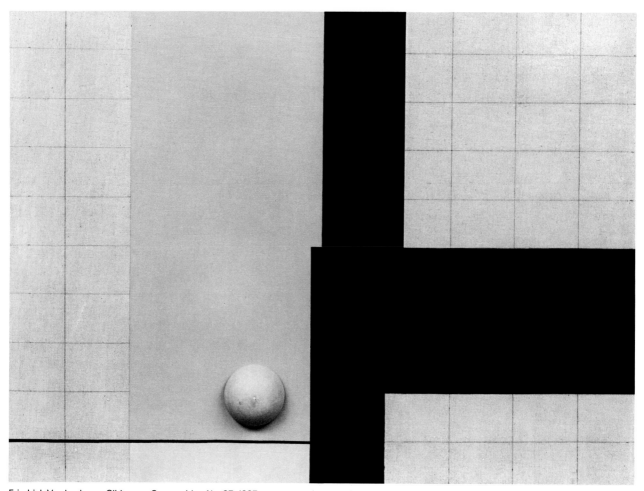

Friedrich Vordemberge-Gildewart: Composition No. 37, 1927

of de Stijl's work. To this end an absolute purification of the vocabulary and grammar of the arts seemed necessary. Abstraction and strict limitations on the elements of visual language were the consequences. Purification of the arts meant, in the first instance, the autonomy of the various arts, their independence from each other and their obedience to their particular laws. Independence had a double meaning: on one side it meant liberation from the arbitrary subjective temperament of the artist and the beholder, on the other, it involved the dissolution of every link with the perception of objects in nature. Abstraction granted freedom from external reality; the limitation of the means of expression excluded, by its elementary character, individualistic tendencies. It was a vital step towards a true vision of reality. This step was deemed necessary and logical to the history of art which was leading gradually from the representation of things to a rendering of the essential laws of creation. The arts

ceased to be the handmaiden of any other field of creative activity and became — like science, philosophy and religion — another way to approach universal truth in strict objectivity. Only an 'art of pure relationships' could fulfill this demand, could render a visual image of the laws of harmony, which dominate the entire creation and are related to every single appearance in reality as the theme in music is related to the variations based upon it. This conception of reality, parallel to ancient philosophical views of the world, brought with it far reaching implications.

"The artists and architects of de Stijl not only redefined the vocabulary and the grammar of the visual arts, they assigned a new task to painting, architecture and the other arts: to serve as a guide for humanity to prepare it for the harmony and balance of a 'new life'; to serve mankind by enlightening it."

On the Way to International Constructivism

Germany in the Bauhaus Period

At the beginning of this century the art scene in Germany was clearly dominated by Expressionism. The visits of the Norwegian Edvard Munch to Berlin and his exhibitions there shortly before the end of the century had brought about a first reaction against the then prevailing Academicism and German Impressionism. One of the results was the formation of the "Neue Sezession", the New Secession, in Berlin: a first and as yet moderate gathering of forces that sought liberation from the fetters of convention and rebelled against the emptiness of contemporary existence. Within the wide surge of the reform movement, groups of young artists began to form and were soon giving vent to explosive indignation against traditional formulas and demanding a new spiritualization, a new preoccupation with the inner man, or else a radical change in ways of living—though without, as yet, any political overtones. The eruptive and expressive urge which manifested itself no doubt sprang from a deep and unchanging substratum of the Germanic character.

In 1905 the architect Fritz Bleyl, the painters Erich Heckel, Ernst Ludwig Kirchner and Karl Schmidt-Rottluff joined to form the group known as the "Brücke" (Bridge). Life was to be renewed by art that was "direct and unadulterated", without ballast of any kind. "We aimed at pictorial vision, in contrast to the Impressionists, who had painted excerpts or motifs," Heckel said later about the aims of the "Brücke". Emil Nolde, Max Pechstein and Otto Mueller were also loosely associated with the movement. Aggressiveness, a wild insistence on intellectual freedom and uninhibited acceptance of their own feelings and instincts distinguished the work of the group, who must be credited with reestablishing the woodcut as a powerful medium of artistic utterance. The "Brücke" came into existence during the short flowering of French Fauvism, with which it has numerous parallels: an interest in primitive art, for instance, or the predilection for violent color contrasts. The German artists, however, were much wilder than the Fauves, who never quite abandoned a Latin moderation. The result of the breakthrough of these Dresden painters was a liberation of the forms and colors of German art, a service that was unaffected by the dissolution of the "Brücke" in 1913.

A second important event we must record here was the international exhibition staged in Cologne in 1912 by the "Sonderbund" (Separatist League) of West German artists. It confronted Germany for the first time with the new French painters: from Van Gogh, Gauguin and Cézanne to Matisse and the early Cubist works of Braque, Picasso and André Lhote. We know from the statements of many artists what a powerful impetus was imparted to the younger generation by this exhibition. When Herwarth Walden followed up in 1913 by presenting in Berlin —in the "First German Autumn Salon"—the modern works that had been rejected in Cologne, by artists such as Marc, Kandinsky, Klee, Carrà, Boccioni, Russolo, Severini and Arp, the inrush of modern influences could no longer be held up. As a patron of all new advances in art and poetry, Walden had already exhibited the Italian Futurists in his "Sturm" gallery in 1912 and had published Futurist manifestos in his magazine of the same title. The "Sturm" was to remain the most important interface for German and international art up to the end of the nineteen-twenties.

Meanwhile a third event was about to break in Munich. Around 1900, this city had already played a leading part among the art centers in Germany, when it had been the focal point of reform movements in the arts. The "Paris of Bavaria" had been the cradle of the "Jugendstil", the German branch of Art Nouveau, which had been so named for the Munich magazine "Jugend" (Youth). The most progressive artistic personality in Munich at that time was the Swiss Hermann Obrist, who as a sculptor found his way to non-objective, free or geometric compositions as early as 1900. As a teacher he encouraged his pupils to try their hands at dynamic abstractions which anticipated the Futurists. The painter August Endell had announced in an essay as early as 1898: "We are at the beginning of a wholly new art, the art of forms which mean nothing and represent nothing and recall nothing, but which stir up our souls as deeply and as strongly as only notes of music can." The North German leaning to Expressionism was evidently paralleled in the south, in Munich, by a leaning to abstraction. It was not by accident that Wilhelm Worringer's epoch-making study of art history, "Abstraktion und Einfühlung" (Abstraction and Empathy), was written in Munich.

The lively atmosphere that prevailed in Munich and the presence there of personalities such as the painter Franz von Stuck, one of the principal representatives of Symbolist painting in Germany, attracted artists from all over Europe. The young Paul Klee came from Bern, Wassily Kandinsky from Moscow. The Russians were particularly numerous among these guests and included—apart from Kandinsky—Marianne von Werefkin and Alexei Jawlensky. In 1901 Kandinsky founded his own art school and the Secessionist group known as the "Phalanx". While certain parallels might be drawn to the "Brücke" group in Dresden, the young artists who gathered around Kandinsky—Paul Klee, Franz Marc, August Macke, Louis Moilliet, Gabriele Münter, Werefkin and Jawlensky— differed in some basic respects from the isolated, introverted North German Expressionists. The Munich group

Willi Baumeister: Figurate with red ellipse, 1920

Lyonel Feininger: Cammin, 1934

Oskar Schlemmer: Relief H, Abstract figure, 1919/63

was from the first more open to outside influences. Kandinsky's relations with Russia occasionally brought avantgarde painters such as Vladimir Bekhteyev and Vladimir Burliuk to Munich. The contacts with Paris were also very close, and most of the artists from Munich passed longer or shorter periods there, in some cases making friends with the leading Parisian artists.

Robert Delaunay was one who imparted significant impulses to the circle around Kandinsky. Direct contact with him was established by Elisabeth Epstein, a friend of Jawlensky and Kandinsky, and Delaunay later took part regularly in the exhibitions of the Munich group. A visit paid to him by Macke, Marc, Klee and Jean Arp in Paris in 1912 shows how seriously his color research was taken. Theoretical texts by Delaunay were translated into German by Paul Klee, and some of them were published in "Sturm". An interesting sidelight on the acceptance of new styles by German artists is furnished by the fact that the analytic Cubism of Braque and Picasso evoked little response, but the transformation of Cubism embodied in Delaunay's Orphism was eagerly seized upon, especially by August Macke and Franz Marc.

After longish stays in Paris and Switzerland Kandinsky and his friends founded the "Neue Künstlervereinigung München" (New Munich Artists' Society) in 1909. This was soon very active organizing exhibitions and provoking discussions both among its own members and in public. Kandinsky was at that time working on the manuscript of his "Concerning the Spiritual in Art", and in 1910 he was to take the decisive step into the realm of non-objectivity. Before long he and Franz Marc had outgrown the framework of the New Artists' Society. They accepted the consequences and tried to gather together a new group of artists. These efforts were contemporaneous with their plan to present their own ideas in an almanach. They wanted at the same time to draw up a survey of the status of art in the various countries, setting forth the range of interests of the younger generation. A synthesis of art, a kind of total work of art—the "Gesamtkunstwerk"—was also being discussed. Their publication appeared in 1912 and bore the title of "Der Blaue Reiter" (The Blue Rider). It was to prove one of the most important programmatic statements in the art of the twentieth century: a compilation that reflects the excitement of those years, the variety of artistic interests and the international scale on which solutions were being sought and found.

"Der Blaue Reiter" was to have been followed by further issues, but the outbreak of World War I put an end to the project. Its second edition, issued in 1914, was nevertheless very widely read. The name, chosen jointly by Kandinsky and Marc, was from the first also applied to the group they headed, which attracted attention by a series of exhibitions between 1912 and 1914. But the war prevented any further activity. Kandinsky returned to Russia. Macke and Marc were both to fall in battle, the former in September 1914, the latter in March 1916.

It is clear from the paintings of Kandinsky, Klee, Macke and Marc at this time and from the substance of the editorial contents of "Der Blaue Reiter" that their real purpose was an advance into abstraction. Self-expression or spiritualization were no longer the motivation of their work, rather it was the idea of a new art. The placing of the ac-

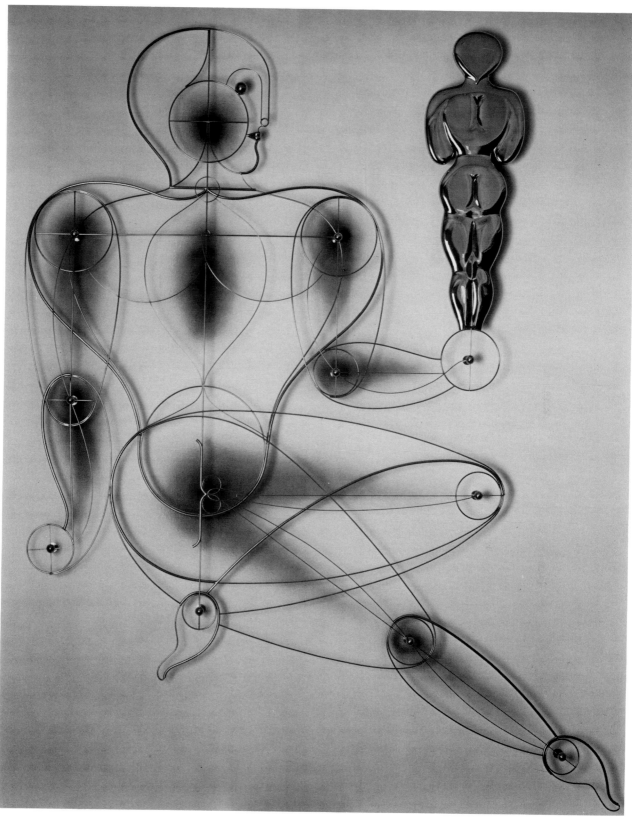

Oskar Schlemmer: Homo, wire figure, 1931/68

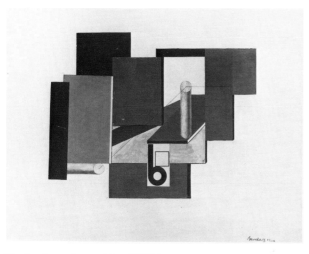

Max Burchartz: Composition, 1923/24

cent on pictorial means and on purely formal aspects shows that "Der Blaue Reiter" was aiming far beyond Expressionism. One of the important contributions dealt with the "elements of composition" in Delaunay's work. Kandinsky's main text was an investigation of "the question of form". The preponderance of music in the pages that were devoted to the other arts is significant. It seems to have been one of Kandinsky's principal aims at that time to establish the closest possible links between painting and music. There was certainly some contact with the composer Alexander Scriabin, who was working on a color and sound organ, and with Daniel Vladimir Baranov-Rossiné, who demonstrated his color piano in 1914. Kandinsky's stage composition "Der gelbe Klang" (The Yellow Sound), which closed the volume, must also be seen in this context, as a parallel to the other efforts that were being made at the time to introduce abstraction into the theater.

"Der Blaue Reiter" was not alone in furthering the cause of non-objective art in Germany. At the Academy in Stuttgart Adolf Hoelzel was teaching the systematic handling of pictorial means on the basis of a general theory of contrasts embracing both form and color. Hoelzel himself and a few of his students—including the Swiss Johannes Itten as well as Willi Baumeister and Oskar Schlemmer of Stuttgart—repeatedly tried their hand at non-objective color compositions around 1912/1914. Itten went furthest in this direction, arriving in 1914, by way of Cubist figurations, at geometric horizontal-vertical compositions. From 1916 onward he continued his experiments in Vienna, in his private art school, where he developed Hoelzel's theory into a comprehensive course of art. In his own paintings Itten used Futuro-Cubist elements along purely geometrical lines, producing crystalline compositions of a musical character. They show certain resemblances to the work of Delaunay and Kupka, although there was no direct connection. Itten's musical interests also led him to get in touch with the Viennese representatives of the New Music—Arnold Schönberg, Alban Berg, Anton von Webern and above all Josef Matthias Hauer. He and the dodecaphonic composer Hauer to-

gether investigated the relations between color and the notes of music. A generation later the painter and musician Robert Strübin of Basle was to explore similar lines of thought.

As Germany struggled on in the now hopeless war against the Allies, German artists found themselves ever more completely isolated from art developments abroad. Herwarth Walden admittedly managed to continue his informatory activity, with exhibitions in his "Sturm" gallery in Berlin, on a reduced scale, although he thus exposed himself to the charge of supporting the art of Germany's enemies. But this risky course enabled him, immediately after the end of the war, to present his international program in its full scope and to confront German artists with new trends in French, Italian and Russian art. In the newly proclaimed Republic, which had to face the hard facts of total defeat as well as grave political and economic problems, Walden and the art dealer Alfred Flechtheim succeeded surprisingly quickly in making Berlin an international forum for new ideas in art.

Kandinsky had returned to Russia by way of Sweden in 1914. For him too the October Revolution brought the chance of presenting his own ideas on the new art in courses for which he was officially responsible. In 1918 he accepted a professorship at the State Art Workshops in Moscow, set up new museums in Moscow and the provinces under the aegis of the People's Commissariat for Culture and in 1921 was made Professor of Aesthetics at Moscow University. About the same time the People's Commissariat for Culture published his autobiography in a richly illustrated volume, while he himself worked out a "Schematic plan of studies and work at the Institute for Artistic Culture". In this he took the view that all elementary art teaching must be both analytical and synthetic. The study consists of three parts: a theory of the individual arts, a theory of the relations between the individual arts, and finally a theory of monumental art or of art in general. The boldest part of this work is the unified review of the individual arts: painting, sculpture, architecture, music, dance and poetry. The text contains the seeds of all his later theoretical works on art. Although Kandinsky was at first deeply impressed by the opportunities the Soviets offered artists—an enthusiastic report of his was published in German newspapers under the title "Artistic Spring in Russia"—he left his homeland with official permission at the end of 1921. In a room of the "Non-Juried Exhibition" in Berlin in the winter of 1921/22 his work was represented again with four mural compositions.

A formal consolidation had already taken place in Kandinsky's painting about 1920, the inscriptional and expressive elements giving place to flat surface patterns, although the compositions were still very dynamic. Diagonals and circles now produced movement, rings and wavy shapes bisected and interpenetrated each other, creating spatial effects that were sometimes of cosmic dimensions. The titles were usually derived from one of the dominant motifs: "White Line", "Red Spot", "Blue Segment". Purely geometric forms now appeared in his pictures. At first sporadic, they were soon predominant: straight lines, zigzags, exact triangles, right angles, arcs. They increasingly supplanted the irrational, emotionally motivated forms and were no doubt the result of Kan-

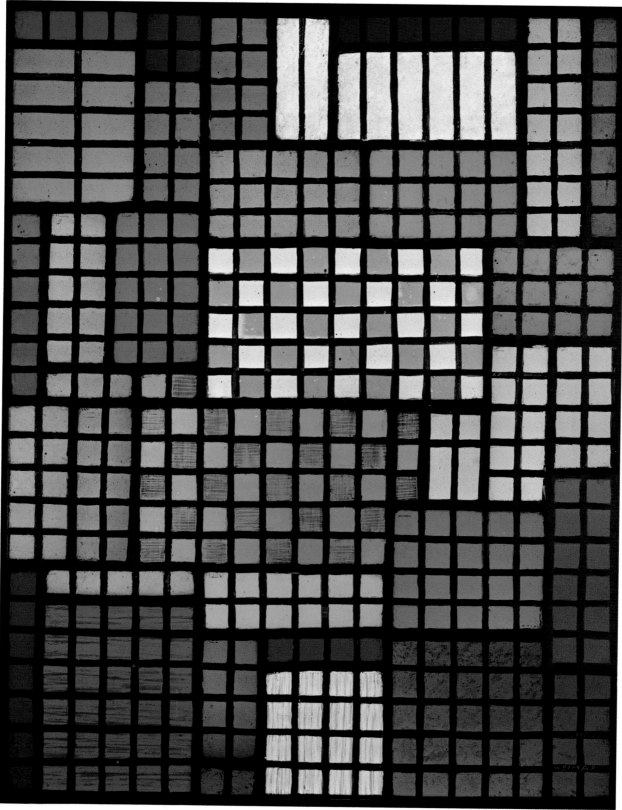

Josef Albers: Stained glass window, 1923/24

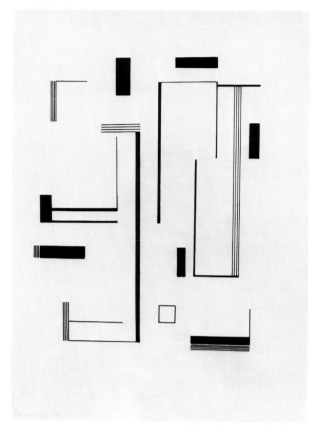

Werner Graeff: Construction, 1921

dinsky's preoccupation with Suprematism and Constructivism.

While Cubism had become the leading school in France during the war, Futurism had triumphed in Italy, de Stijl had offered its pure order as an alternative to the contemporary chaos in the Netherlands, and in Russia the avant-garde was trying to make, through Constructivism, an artistic contribution to the erection of a proletarian state, an avant-garde of a very different kind was forming on the small island of peace which was Switzerland. Exiled artists and writers of many different temperaments and origins had ended up in Zurich. The one thing they had in common was the conviction that the war, which they saw as the final fiasco of bourgeois society, was a pointless and senseless thing. They were in agreement that all the forms of traditional art had lost their validity and were to be condemned. An anti-art attitude comparable to that of the Futurists reigned among them. If destruction was the order of the day, then the museums and academies, the repositories of this obsolete art, had better be torn down too. It was in this anarchic and even nihilistic atmosphere that writers and artists joined forces to stage absurd performances in the "Cabaret Voltaire": a nonsense cult in which unsuspected depths were soon discovered, a game of chance whose secret rules suddenly turned out to be a reservoir of creativity, a mystification and provocation of the average townsman calculated either to shake him out of his lethargy or else to drive him to the lunatic asylum. The common denomina-

tor of the group that formed in February 1916 under the mysterious password "Dada" was certainly not a clear stylistic line but rather an affinity of mentality and attitude. "While butchery was going on all around us, we merrily devoted ourselves in Zurich to the fine arts," Jean Arp ironically stated later on. But the attack was really directed against this word "fine" prefixed to art. Instead, the refuse dumps of culture became a happy hunting-ground from which some surprising finds were brought to light.

These discoveries were made in the literary domain by Hugo Ball, Emmy Hennings, Richard Huelsenbeck and the main animator of the Zurich Dadaists, the Rumanian Tristan Tzara. The chief artists of Dada were Jean Arp of Alsace and the Swiss Sophie Taeuber, whom he later married, the German Otto van Rees and his Dutch wife Adja, the Rumanians Marcel Janco and Arthur Segal, and the Germans Hans Richter and Christian Schad, who, previously Expressionists or Futuro-Cubists, now turned to geometric or organic non-objectivity. Contacts between art and music were also set up in Zurich. The "Outline of a New Aesthetic of Music" by the Italian Ferruccio Busoni was carefully studied by the Dadaists. In the course of Busoni's stay in Zurich Hans Richter definitely took lessons in composition with him, and Jean Arp very probably did so too. In Richter's case this led to fugue-like geometric works, "roll pictures" in which each figure is logically developed from the one that precedes it. Richter undertook some of these studies in cooperation with the Swede Viking Eggeling. Dealing as they did with the problem of a sequence of movements and with the time factor, they must be regarded as forerunners of kinetic art. After 1919 the two translated their geometric sequences into films in Berlin and thus became the founders of the abstract film.

Berlin around 1920 was an ideal place for the meeting of progressive minds. The stimulating intellectual atmosphere of the city did a great deal to give a positive bias to the "transvaluation of all values" that had become necessary. Berlin was particularly well prepared to receive guests and travelers arriving from Russia. Konstantin Umansky's book "Neue russische Kunst, 1914–1919" (New Russian Art, 1914–1919) appeared in Potsdam in 1920. Threads that had been spun earlier were now strengthened. The German Dadaists Richard Huelsenbeck and Hans Richter had returned from Zurich. Joining forces with the satirical artist George Grosz, the writer and inventor of photomontage Raoul Hausmann, the master of political photomontage John Heartfield (Herzfelde), the inventor of the poetic collage Hannah Hoech and others, they founded the Berlin Dada movement, which was more radical and more politically oriented than that of Zurich. The fact that the Dadaists of Berlin identified themselves with the political aims of the left led them to take an active interest in the art of the Russian Revolution. At the first Dada Fair in Berlin in 1920 a notice was put up bearing the message: "Art is dead. Long live Tatlin's new machine art."

In Germany as elsewhere it was now necessary to redefine the position and function of the artist in a changed society. The "Art program of the People's Commissariat for Culture in Russia", which Paul Westheim had published in the magazine "Kunstblatt" in 1919, was attentively studied in Berlin. This program postulated an asso-

Erich Buchholz: Composition, 1920

Walter Dexel: Figuration A, 1926

Walter Dexel: loci, collage, 1926

ciation of all fine and applied artists as a circle of special-ists who were to carry out practical work for the people against the background of the handicrafts. The program was taken over almost word for word in the program of the "Arbeitsrat für Kunst" (Work Council for Art) issued in Berlin. The aim of this union of artists and architects was a more human and social architecture in which all branches of art were to be integrated. Its success de-pended on the reform of art education. Among the spokesmen of the "Work Council for Art" were the archi-tects Walter Gropius and Bruno Taut and the German-American painter Lyonel Feininger, who had been living in Berlin for a considerable time. In May 1919 Walter Gro-pius issued the first manifesto of the "State Bauhaus in Weimar" ("Bauhaus" meaning literally "Building house"). In substance the programmatic text was in keeping with the aims of the "Work Council for Art". The manifesto was adorned with an architectural woodcut by Feininger which later became known as the "Cathedral of Social-ism". The implication was that Gropius was reviving, in the Bauhaus idea, the building huts or workshops of the medieval cathedrals, in which architects, artists and arti-sans had pooled their resources. At the same time, he wished his art school to be considered as a leading edu-cational institution in a Socialist society.

In the early twenties, Berlin was an ideal place for interna-tional cultural exchanges. The part played by the Rus-sians was so great that people talked of a "Russian Ber-lin". "Berlin at that time, in 1919–1921," wrote Nikolai Nabokov in his memoirs, "was the principal center of the Russian emigrants ... the first and most important sta-tion of the Russian Diaspora; Paris assumed the role of the second station a few years later, but it never attained to the luster of Russian Berlin." Marc Chagall, who also passed a long period in Berlin on his way westward, de-scribed the city as a "Russian caravanserai". There were Russian theaters, stores, bookshops and pastry-shops, but first and foremost Russian galleries. In the Russian restaurants one might easily happen across El Lissitzky, the Punis, Antoine Pevsner, Naum Gabo, Alexander Ar-chipenko, Serge Charchoune or Yefim Golychev, the Da-daist writer, painter and musician. All of them and many others had come to live in Berlin. The zenith of this Rus-sian regnum was the "First Russian Art Exhibition" of 1922 in the Van Diemen Gallery, an enormous display which offered a wide if not complete panorama of recent Russian art, from the moderate successors of Cézanne to Constructivism. It also included work by students of the reorganized art schools of Moscow and Leningrad, as well as posters and stage settings. The catalog text was written by David Sterenberg, while the cover was de-signed by El Lissitzky, who was also responsible for the presentation of the exhibition.

The Russian art colony in Berlin was anything but homo-geneous. The emigrants had brought their basic differen-ces of opinion with them. The big Russian exhibition ac-cordingly sparked off violent discussions, for instance between Archipenko and Puni or between Vladimir May-akovsky and Serge Diaghilev. These controversies were recorded in the art magazines, both German and Russian. A few Russians who had come to Berlin convinced that they were bringing with them an entirely new art were now thrown into confusion, for they found that similar ob-

Carl Buchheister: Composition No. 27, 1927

jectives had been propagated by the western avant-garde before their arrival. The Russians had heard little or nothing of the aims of de Stijl, and thus found themselves advancing on paths that had already been opened up. On the other hand, for the bourgeoisie, which was hostile toward all forms of leftist or progressive art, the Russians in Berlin became a kind of scapegoat for everything that was looked upon as extravagant and crazy in art. It was really the resulting tensions that made Berlin's artistic atmosphere so attractive. This was reflected in heated discussions in the coffeehouses, in lectures such as those of the writer and poet Mayakovsky or the theater critic Alexander Tairov, and particularly in newspapers and magazines. The most interesting of the Russian magazines was "Vyeshch" (The Object), which El Lissitzky edited with the writer Ilya Ehrenburg in Berlin, where the Russian state publishing organization also had a branch. The German counterpart of this Russian art magazine was "G", a "magazine of elementary design" which Hans Richter had published since 1923 with Werner Graeff and El Lissitzky. Their subjects were architecture, film, art, typography and technology. This combination of all do-

mains of art and design was typical, as was also the information provided on work going on in a similar cause all over Europe. The activities of de Stijl in the Netherlands and of Russian Constructivism were here considered in combination for the first time. Berlin in this way proved to be the focal point at which exchanges between Russian Constructivism, personified primarily by El Lissitzky, and the Dutch de Stijl, represented by Theo van Doesburg, could come about.
It was not only the Russians who communicated in Berlin with the artists of Western Europe. Exponents of geometrical abstraction and Constructivism were also attracted from Prague, Warsaw and Budapest. Almost without exception, it was participation in exhibitions in the "Sturm" gallery that led to stays in Berlin. And since the Russian exhibition of 1922 enticed artists from all parts to come and see for themselves, it may justly be claimed that it was from Berlin that Constructivist ideas flooded outward over the rest of Europe.
The Polish artist who derived the most fertile stimulation from Berlin was no doubt Henryk Berlewi. He exhibited his work in the "Sturm" gallery, was a member of the pro-

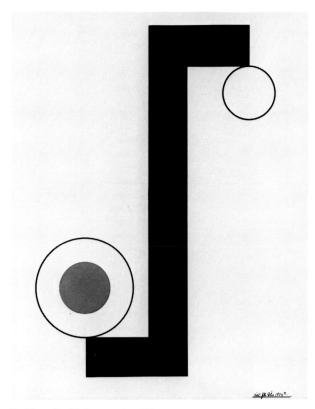

Karl-Peter Roehl: Construction, 1924

gressive "November group" in Berlin and was in close contact with El Lissitzky. His theory of "mechano-facture" sprang from this source: a study of materials and textures which, when superimposed in two-dimensional compositions, produced new spatial effect (ill. p. 99). In 1924 Berlewi and his countrymen Wladyslaw Strzeminski and Henryk Stazewski founded the Constructivist group "Blok" and the magazine of the same name in Warsaw. Another important contributor was Strzeminski's wife, the Russian sculptress Katarzyna Kobro (ill. p. 201).
The Hungarian avant-garde also played an active part. The group "MA" (Present) founded by Lajos Kassak together with a magazine of the same name established contact from Budapest with similar movements in Western Europe and Russia. It had a direct line to de Stijl through Vilmos Huszar, who had lived in the Netherlands since 1905 and had been one of the founders of the movement. The most prominent members of the Budapest group, after Kassak, were Laszlo Peri, Alexander Bortnyk (ill. p. 100) and Laszlo Moholy-Nagy (ill. pp. 103, 104). After the collapse of the republic in Hungary these artists had moved for a time to Vienna, where a "Book of New Artists" was published by Moholy and Kassak in 1922. The exhibitions in Walden's "Sturm" gallery attracted the Hungarians to Berlin from 1920 onward. A manifesto which was drawn up in October 1921 by Raoul Hausmann, Jean Arp, Ivan Puni and Laszlo Moholy-Nagy in Berlin and was published under the title "For an elementarist art" in the magazine "de stijl" in 1922 shows how international the exchanges were. The renunciation

of individual expression and of all links with the past was here postulated: instead of cultivating a multiplicity of styles artists should attempt to adopt a single style — the style, in fact. This art born of the present was called elementary because it was to be created solely from elements immanent in art, independently of all tradition and of all speculative and philosophical content.
A "Congress of International Progressive Artists" which was organized in Dusseldorf in May 1922 on the initiative of the "Junges Rheinland" (Young Rhineland) group was to have brought about the unification of all parallel or kindred endeavors to establish a new art. The spokesmen of progressive groups congregated from all countries to discuss the concept of progressivity and to study the possibility of a united front modeled on the Communist International. But no agreement was reached. The Dusseldorf Congress, in which the German organizers hoped to achieve a union of all progressive artists with the support of the majority of the participants, in reality only revealed an unbridgeable rift along the borderline between consistent Constructivist art and a half-hearted allegiance to geometric and abstractionist styles. Although the really progressive Constructivists were in the minority in Dusseldorf, they emerged as the victors: the tumultuous meeting led to a rapprochement between the groups represented by Theo van Doesburg, Hans Richter and El Lissitzky, which now joined forces in an "International Association of Constructivists". The major statements of the groups present at the Dusseldorf Congress, which included French and Belgian representatives, were published in the magazine "de stijl". From now on there was a multiplicity of personal contacts and a lively exchange of ideas taking place mainly in the magazines of the various groups.
A characteristic expression of the attempts to recognize the common factors of the new Constructivist trends without denying the differences of opinion was the trilingual publication "Die Kunst-Ismen, 1924–1914" (The Art-Isms, 1924–1914) by El Lissitzky and Jean Arp, which appeared in 1925. The two editors took a quotation from Malevich as the motto of their anthology: "The present is the time of analyses, the result of all systems that have ever existed. The centuries have brought the signs to our line of demarcation, we shall recognize in them the imperfections that led to division and opposition. Perhaps we shall only take the oppositional elements to build up the system of unity."
In the text the historical phases — from Cubism and Futurism to Constructivism and the abstract film — are dealt with in chronological order, sometimes with quotations from the protagonists, sometimes with exaggerated or ironic definitions supplied by the editors. The documentary pictorial section is arranged in the opposite sequence, beginning with 1925 and the question: "How does it go on?" At the end of the book we find the situation in 1914, or the starting point. As far as I know, it is one of the first examples of a retrospective historical treatment that moves step by step from the present into the past. The method reveals an attitude primarily concentrated on the present, from which an attempt is made to trace, by a backward movement, the path that led to the contemporary situation. The short definition of Constructivism given in the book reads: "These artists see

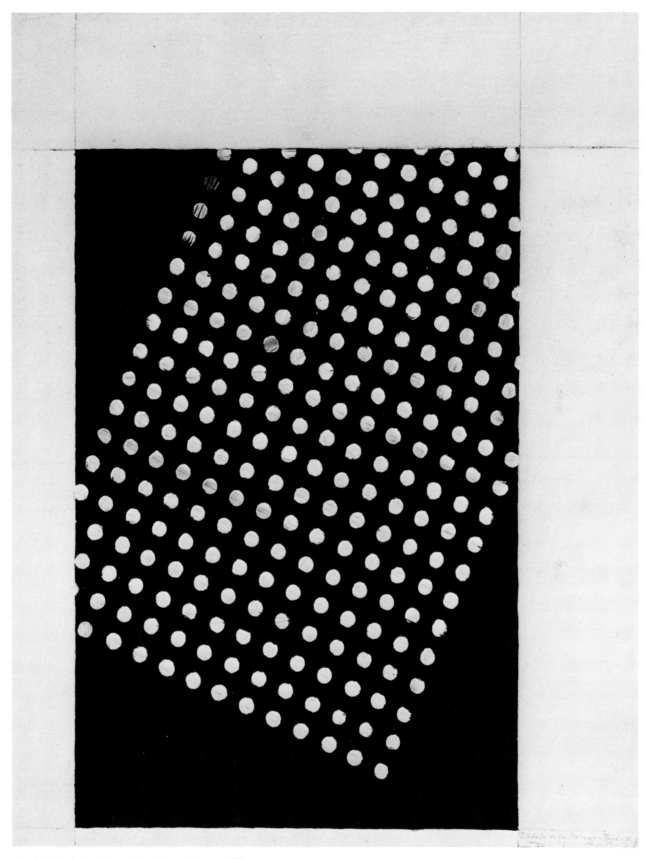

Henryk Berlewi: First Stage of the Mecano-Facture, 1923

Alexander Bortnyk: Geometric forms in space, 1923

the world through the prism of technology. They do not want to create illusions with paints and canvas but do their work directly in iron, wood and glass. Shortsighted observers see only the machine in this procedure. Constructivism proves that a boundary between mathematics and art, between a work of art and a technical invention, cannot be detected." This statement supplements Lissitzky's own definition of Proun: "Proun is the station where you change from painting to architecture."

This uncompromising attitude on the part of the Constructivists is in conformity with their statements made at the Dusseldorf Congress in 1922. As it had turned out there, most German artists, despite their sympathetic attitude to the developments they saw taking place, were unable to follow so consistent a line without certain reservations. In any case, the various outside influences did not lead in Germany to the formation of a unified school of geometric and non-objective art. In Berlin, it is true, the exhibitions in the "Sturm" gallery and the presence of the Russians produced a pocket of German Constructivists. One of them was Erich Buchholz, who made the acquaintance of Lissitzky as a result of his contacts with the Berlin Dadaists and absorbed Suprematist and Constructivist influences (ill. p. 95). Oskar Nerlinger worked in the

same direction, blending the influence of Paul Klee with that of the Russian Constructivists and producing "serial social art" with the aid of stencils. This was one of the contemporary attempts to enable broad sectors of the public to participate in progressive art and was at the same time an anticipation of the interest in the multiple, the serially produced work of art, that arose in the sixties. Another interesting figure of the time was Thomas Ring. He originally belonged to the circle of the "Sturm" writers, was connected with the experimental and political theater of Erwin Piscator and turned his attention for several years to drawn "machine art". Otto Nebel and Rudolf Bauer, who also hailed from the "Sturm" group, were only temporarily affected by Constructivism. Nebel, poet and painter, sought to combine the influences of his friends Paul Klee and Wassily Kandinsky in a free geometric art. Rudolf Bauer, with a proclivity for speculative theory, tried chiefly to emphasize the cosmic aspect of Kandinsky's painting, partly by geometric and partly by expressive means, and later founded a private museum for non-objective art. From 1936 onward he was closely connected with the Solomon R. Guggenheim Foundation in New York. The sculptor William Wauer was also only temporarily affected by Constructivism. As president of the "In-

El Lissitzky: Proun Room, 1923 (reconstruction)

ternational Association of Expressionists, Cubists, Futurists and Constructivists" he played an active part between 1924 and 1933 in promoting the so-called "Gruppe der Abstrakten" (Group of Abstract Artists).

Apart from Hans Richter, the main intermediaries between Russian Constructivism and the Dutch de Stijl were the Swede Viking Eggeling, who worked in Berlin on Constructivist films such as "Diagonal-Symphonie", and Werner Graeff of the Bauhaus, who was a member of the de Stijl group from 1922 onwards (ill. p. 94). There were also a number of Dadaists in Berlin who became deeply involved in Russian Constructivism. One of them was Raoul Hausmann, whose critical photomontages and photocollages are closely connected with the photomontages of Alexander Rodchenko and El Lissitzky. Much the same applies to Hannah Hoech, who repeatedly produced collages and color prints in a Constructivist vein, particularly in the early twenties.

Outside of Berlin, where the resident Russians took a direct part in cultural events, there were only a few individuals or small groups who took an interest in the ideas embodied in Constructivism. Ella Bergmann-Michel and Robert Michel, for instance, made their own use of Constructivist impulses in the seclusion of the Taunus. They

had begun with dynamic compositions of a Futurist character — so-called "explosions" — and continued to occupy themselves with problems of movement in the picture. Robert Michel sought interpretations of the mechanical and motoric while Ella Bergmann concentrated on kinetic effects.

A circle also formed in the Rhineland around Heinrich Hoerle of Cologne, who had founded the "Group of Progressive Artists" in 1919. The members of the group advanced from abstraction, in some cases via Dadaism, to geometric non-objectivity. The most powerful artistic force in the Cologne area, Max Ernst, was only marginally affected by Constructivist trends. His Surrealist work, beginning when he moved to Paris in 1922, is a direct development of his Dadaist compositions done in Cologne. Franz Wilhelm Seiwert was another member of the "Young Rhineland" group; like Hoerle, he was and remained interested in human and social problems and only gave up figural abstraction for geometric non-objectivity in isolated cases.

Max Burchartz of Essen, by contrast, became a serious exponent of Constructivism (ill. p. 92). As a member of de Stijl he engaged actively in the efforts to carry the formal principles and objectives of de Stijl beyond painting and into the spheres of architecture, commercial art and other domains. One of the most powerful figures of non-objective art in the thirties was certainly Otto Freundlich. A native of Pomerania, he had belonged to the inner circle of the Cubists in Paris before the First World War and in 1919 adopted a consistently non-objective style of painting. A friend of Seiwert, he had a decisive influence on the circle of Cologne artists before returning to Paris in 1924 to produce his mature painted and sculpted œuvre (ill. pp. 120, 121).

In Stuttgart, where young artists gathered around the pupils of Hoelzel, Willi Baumeister and Oskar Schlemmer, geometric non-objectivity was also to remain a phase, much as in Cologne. Schlemmer occupied himself with a figurative abstraction process, which led him to the "art figure" and abstract stage design (ill. pp. 90, 91). Baumeister was interested in mechanical compositions which at times turned into the purely geometric ordering of surface areas (ill. p. 88). His main interest centered on "surface forces" or "surface tensions". But Baumeister too returned to a form of figural abstraction which permitted him to broach themes connected with man and the machine and motifs from the world of sport.

Hanover was to become an art center of a very special kind. One person and one institution—Kurt Schwitters and the Kestner Society, privately founded already in 1916—turned what had once been a famous royal residence but was now merely a bourgeois and conservative provincial town into the scene of daring advances into new fields of art. This strange mixture of a bourgeois sense of order and a courageous and imaginative readiness to venture out into the unknown was uniquely personified in Schwitters himself. At the outset an Expressionist painter, fond of dark hues but otherwise with little to distinguish him, Schwitters first came into contact with the accurate fantasies of the machine world when he began to work as an engineering draftsman. In 1918/19 he went through a phase of Futuristic dynamism and then arrived, in a series of bold steps, at the pictorial style that really suited him. He launched out into his "Merzkunst" by incorporating foreign bric-à-brac in his paintings. This new personal form of art—described it with the word "Merz", which means nothing in particular—was in a way a development and deepening of Dadaism. Although Schwitters thus anticipated the "combine painting" and —with his material montages—the "assemblage" of the fifties and sixties, this is really less important than his attempt to find an art that would embrace all the creative domains, from plastic art to architecture, poetry, typography, theater, and music. Schwitters' "Merzkunst" is an isolated advance toward the "total work of art" and toward the transformation of life into art. In his search for new working methods Schwitters became convinced as early as the end of 1918 "that all values exist only by virtue of their relations to each other and that all limitation to one material is one-sided and small-minded". "It was out of this realization that I made Merz, at first as the sum of single categories of art . . . My ultimate goal is the combination of art and non-art in the Merz overall world-picture." Here, as an idea and a vision at least, the frontiers between life and art were dissolved.

In these objectives Schwitters was in tune with Futurism and Dadaism as well as with the Utopian visions of de Stijl and of Russian Constructivism. Lines of communication radiated from Hanover in all directions, many of them passing by way of the "Sturm" gallery in Berlin, where Schwitters had exhibited since 1920. He got to know Van Doesburg through the Berlin Dadaists, particularly Hans Richter. The two shared the Dadaist passion for new departures in poetry and writing. Part of the power of Van Doesburg's personality lay in his ability to submit to the discipline of rational composition and yet—under the pseudonym of I. K. Bonset—to devote himself to the imaginative and "absurd" word-games of the Dadaists. It was not by accident that after taking part in the big Dada congress in Weimar in 1922, Schwitters undertook a Dada campaign in the Netherlands with Van Doesburg and Vilmos Huszar. It was during such adventurous, scandal-provoking lecture tours, which had already taken him to Prague with Raoul Hausmann and Hannah Hoech, that Schwitters developed his sound-poems, a sort of non-objective poetry which lay outside of all linguistic logic and opened up with its word-montages, syllable and sound compositions new domains that were later to be explored more thoroughly by the exponents of "Concrete poetry".

The year 1925 brought an apogee in the contacts of Schwitters and El Lissitzky, which led to several joint publications. A stricter formal order had made its appearance in some of Schwitters' collages and montages from 1919 onward, in clear contrast to the free combinations and confrontations of heterogeneous scraps of foreign material. Under the influence of his friends of de Stijl and more particularly of Lissitzky and Russian Constructivism, Schwitters now adopted a tighter surface order for his collages and reliefs (ill. p. 105). The playful juxta- and superposition of fortuitous elements is interrupted from time to time by exact horizontal-vertical compositions. Questions of the equilibrium of colors or forms, surface contrasts or tensions, come to the fore, in isolated cases even dynamic diagonal and circular arrangements which can be directly related to Constructivist form concepts. Even hints of Suprematist space visions can be detected. This essentially Constructivist side of Schwitters' work is not limited to a clearly defined period, although it seems to be predominant between 1924 and 1926. Rational order was the opposite pole to poetic improvisation, and Schwitters' creative urge oscillated between the two extremes. The conception of a constructive shaping principle which he saw in the work of his friends was for him a part of the overall art he dreamed of. The fact that the "Merzbau" which in the course of the years mushroomed through the storeys of his house gradually turned from an eccentric Dadaist reliquary to a crystalline sculptural composition shows how deeply versed Schwitters was in Constructivist thinking in spite of his propensity for things irrational and incommensurable.

Hanover in the twenties stood, as we have seen, not only for Schwitters but for the Kestner Society too. Cooperation between Paul Erich Küppers, then president of the Kestner Society, his wife Sophie (later the companion of Lissitzky) and Schwitters brought modern works and representatives of the new movements to Hanover. Among the latter were the Van Doesburgs and the Moholy-Nagys as well as El Lissitzky, who took up residence in Hanover in 1923 as a guest of the Kestner Society. The cycle of lithographs entitled "Proun" appeared as the first of six

Laszlo Moholy-Nagy: Yellow Circle, 1921

Laszlo Moholy-Nagy: Suprematistic Q I, 1923

Kestner portfolios of graphic art, accompanying Lissitzky's exhibition in the Kestner Society, his first one-man show in the West (ill. p. 64). Encouraged by the success of this portfolio, the artist thereupon issued a series of figurines in Hanover under the title of "Die plastische Gestaltung der elektromechanischen Schau: Sieg über die Sonne" (The Plastic Representation of the Electromechanical Show: Victory over the Sun), before he was forced by the onset of tuberculosis to seek healing in southern Switzerland. The lithographs of the cycle "Victory over the Sun", inspired by the text of a singspiel by Alexei Krushchonykh, can be regarded as a pictorial comment on the way to a new society. The last composition bears the title "The New Man". It is a figurine which uses dynamic Constructivist form elements to characterize the new human being emerging from the Russian Revolution. Boris Pasternak later depicted this "New Man" in the person of Strelnikov in his "Doctor Zhivago": "He had two characteristic traits, two passions: an unusual power of clear and logical argument and at the same time great moral purity, a sense of justice: he was both passionate and honorable ..." This exactly describes the personality of Lissitzky. His portrait in the photomontage "Der Konstrukteur" (The Designer) had at that time impressed supporters of the new art: a cover illustration of a publication on experimental photography entitled "Foto-Auge" (Photo-Eye) and issued in 1929 by Franz Roh and Jan Tschichold. It showed the head and hand of Lissitzky, and the arc on the squared paper of the background seemed to imply clear thinking and manual precision.

El Lissitzky left other traces in Hanover, apart from his stay there as a guest in the studio of the Kestner Society. After his recovery he returned to Russia in 1925, but he repeatedly visited the West from 1926 onward as the representative of the "Wok", the Soviet government's organization for contacts with foreign countries. He was commissioned with the design of official Russian exhibitions in Western Europe, but he also accepted an assignment from Alexander Dorner, the new president of the Kestner Society, to fit out an exhibition room in the Provincial Museum. Lissitzky had done a "Proun Room" as a demonstration at the big art exhibition in Berlin in 1923 (ill. p. 101), and in 1926 he again designed a "Non-objective art room" for an international art exhibition in Dresden. The "Kabinett der Abstrakten" (Cabinet of Abstract Artists) — opened in Hanover in 1926/27, closed in the Hitler era, destroyed in the Second World War and since reconstructed — gives some idea of Lissitzky's interior design ideas. It is a unique, concentrated embodiment of Constructivist goals around the mid-twenties. The interior design, lighting, furnishings, and exhibits combine to form just that unity that was being demanded by progressive artists of East and West. In Lissitzky's words: "The room should not be decorated like a private salon. It should represent the standard for rooms in which new art is to be presented to the public."

Lissitzky's activity in Hanover contributed substantially to the influence exerted by this creative ambassador of Russian culture, who did so much to promote, especially in Germany, Switzerland and the countries of Eastern Europe, the dissemination of Constructivist thought and methods in painting, interior decoration, exhibition design, typography and other fields. In Hanover itself, Carl Buchheister among others upheld the Constructivist tradition with his elementary geometric compositions in the second half of the twenties (ill. p. 97).

The influence of Friedel Vordemberge-Gildewart, who came from Osnabrück, spread far beyond Hanover itself. The Lissitzky studio in the Kestner Society which he had taken over in 1924 became a relay point for new ideas and a meeting-place for those who shared his views and wished to use constructive principles as a means of establishing a new unity of art and life. Vordemberge's own work began in 1923 with non-objective geometric compositions, without any figurative or abstractive preamble, and remained consistently true to the concepts of Constructivist design up to the very last compositions of 1962. In 1924 Vordemberge had founded with Hans Nitschke the "gruppe k", a small group of Hanoverian Constructivists. In the same year he became a member of de Stijl and contributed to its international dissemination both as a publicist and through his own paintings. He succeeded in translating the trend to geometry and non-objectivity into a personal pictorial language which was to remain strict and objective but contained a striking measure of musical feeling, balance and optimism (ill. pp. 85, 86).

Weimar, too, had been a rather sleepy town and a former residence of German dukes; but if it now turned into a vital center of new ideas, the reasons were quite different from those applying to Hanover. Weimar had in fact long lived on the memory of Goethe's sojourn at the ducal court and regarded itself as a kind of national monument

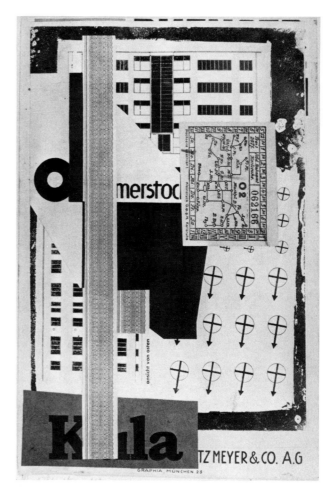

Kurt Schwitters: Karlsruhe, 1929

to the country's classical culture. All this was to change in 1902 when the Belgian Henry van de Velde arrived here. As an artist and architect, and most of all as an educator, Van de Velde was to make Weimar a center of art reform. In cooperation with Harry Count Kessler, a well-known diplomat and patron of the arts, he brought major works of the new schools into the classicist atmosphere of the city, where they were naturally found disturbing and shocking. He also founded a school which had a deep and lasting influence: his "Kunstgewerbliches Seminar" (Arts and Crafts Seminar) was a research institute of art and design where Van de Velde developed new teaching methods based on a systematic study of practical problems instead of the unthinking application of academic recipes. When the Belgian had to give up his teaching at the outbreak of war in 1914 — he was opposed by narrow-minded officials as being a foreigner and a "modernist" — he looked around for a suitable successor and found the young Berlin architect Walter Gropius. In 1911 Gropius had already made a first contribution to Functionalism in architecture with a factory he had designed for the Fagus Works in Alfeld.

During the war years Gropius prepared projects for the reorganization of the art schools in Weimar. In a report he submitted to the local government in 1916 he wrote: "It cannot be denied that there is a cleavage between the two groups of technical and artistic professions which must be bridged by better understanding on both sides." Gropius proposed a working community which should take as its model the medieval building workshops and should embrace architects, sculptors, painters and craftsmen of all descriptions. The joint mastering of contemporary problems, one of the most urgent of which was the training of the next generation, might well lead, as Gropius pointed out, to a new style, and even to a new lifestyle.

After he had been dismissed from military service into a civilian world full of unsolved problems, Gropius' ideas began to take on more precise form: "After that brutal interruption every thinking man felt the need for an intellectual change of front. Each one tried in his special field of activity to make some contribution to the bridging of the chasm between reality and idealism. It dawned on me then for the first time how enormous the mission was that an architect of my generation had to fulfill . . . I realized that a whole staff of collaborators and assistants was necessary, men who would not work like an orchestral ensemble, following the baton of the conductor, but independently, yet in close cooperation, in the common cause. I therefore tried to place the emphasis on integration and coordination, to include everything and exclude nothing."

In this line of thinking Gropius was at one with his architect and artist friends in Berlin who had joined to form the "November Group". Just as the revolution that had broken out on November 9, 1918, marked the end of the German Empire and the beginning of a new era, the union of artists in the "November Group" and the "Arbeitsrat für Kunst" (Work Council for Art) was to serve the ends of a reorganization of cultural life. The ethical objective of a reformation of society by a new unity of art and technology under the guidance of architecture brought these workers together and was for that matter very near to what Van de Velde had aimed at in Weimar. When in February 1919 Gropius reopened the united art schools of Weimar under his chosen name of "Staatliches Bauhaus in Weimar", he was putting into effect a program which reflected his own ideas as well as those of his friends. His first two collaborators and "masters"—used in the artisanal sense—were artists from Berlin: the German-American painter Lyonel Feininger, who had been closely connected with Weimar even before the war and was to remain an adherent of the Bauhaus in Weimar and in Dessau up to 1932 (ill. p. 89), and the sculptor Gerhard Marcks, with whom Gropius had collaborated at the 1914 Werkbund exhibition in Cologne.

The manifesto and program of the Bauhaus published in April 1919 opened with the statement: "The ultimate aim of all visual arts is the complete building." The union of all craftsmen and a return to the workshop system is demanded in exhortatory terms. The common purpose of all creative workers is to be "the new building of the future", which will be "everything in one: architecture and sculpture and painting". The training program is more concrete. It specifies handicraft training as the basis of the course of study, which is divided, in a concentric structure, into the essential components of design and technique. The student passes through the course in three stages: as an apprentice, a "journeyman" and a "junior master". The medieval training concept derived from the artisans' guilds is clearly emphasized. Most of the training takes place in the workshops, but is supplemented by general and theoretical subjects. A new feature of the program was that Gropius put "fine" artists in rotating charge of the workshops, though he gave them qualified craftsmen as workshop "masters". At the outset there was no instruction in architecture, although the "building" was regarded as the total work of art, as the receptacle of all creative production.

The school met with great interest from the first. Weimar had enjoyed a good reputation as a center of art education from the time of Van de Velde. Its name was also closely linked with the young German Republic. For since January 1919 the German national assembly had met in the theater of the Thuringian capital. It was here that the "Weimar Constitution" was proclaimed on August 11, thus leading to the designation "Weimar Republic" for the German state up to the seizure of power by the National Socialists, even though the parliament had actually moved to Berlin at the end of 1919. The chief attraction of the Bauhaus, however, was the array of personalities Gropius succeeded in enlisting and the lively way in which, with him, they put the novel program into practice.

The first two "masters", Feininger and Marcks, were joined in the fall of 1919 by Johannes Itten. Gropius had sought out this Swiss artist in Vienna because the elementary course he had developed at his private art school was qualified to fill a gap in the Bauhaus program. Students coming to the Bauhaus had had all sorts of previous training. Itten's task was therefore to provide a comprehensive grasp of fundamental art problems in an obligatory preliminary course, in which individual proclivities were to be recognized as a pointer to the allocation of the students to certain workshops and vocational directions. This preliminary or elementary course, which was modified by Itten's Bauhaus successors, ranks with the interdisciplinary workshop system as the most significant contribution of the Bauhaus to the evolution of art teaching. Art schools all over the world later borrowed this pedagogic system, which familiarizes the student with the objective laws of form and color composition while encouraging his or her individual talents.

Gropius had a gift for mobilizing strong personalities with widely differing characters, opinions and approaches in a common cause. In 1920 Paul Klee, Georg Muche and Oskar Schlemmer joined the council of masters; in 1921 Lothar Schreyer of the "Sturm" followed; in 1922 Wassily Kandinsky moved from his provisional domicile in Berlin to Weimar; in 1923 Laszlo Moholy-Nagy arrived from Berlin as Itten's successor. Each of these artists took over in turn one or more of the workshops, in addition to his own special subject. This rotation, together with the often heated discussions with colleagues and students, led to an intense give-and-take. The atmosphere of the Bauhaus was stimulating despite the strained economic situation, and it was rendered even more so by contacts with the outside world that were taken up from the very first —communications with persons and movements in Germany and abroad who were also interested in the relations of art and life. This applied particularly to the representatives of constructive art. It was these contacts that led the Bauhaus—not without some violent inner struggles—from an early phase that has often been typi-

Wassily Kandinsky: Soft Pressure, 1931

fied as Romantic or Expressionist into an ever more rational and progressive direction. Its changes of orientation can be connected in many cases with the stays of Theo van Doesburg in Weimar. Gropius had invited him to come and look around in 1921, perhaps even contemplating his active collaboration. But Van Doesburg was not at ease either with the arts and crafts workshops — he was a believer in the machine — or with the Spiritualist leanings of Itten or the marked individualism of some of the masters. Outside of the Bauhaus he represented a kind of private Anti-Bauhaus in Weimar, in his courses and lectures he consistently stood for the principles of de Stijl. In this way a Weimar Stijl group consist-

ing of students who had broken away from the Bauhaus and of young artists of similar persuasions was able to form around him. The members included Peter Roehl (ill. p. 98), Max Burchartz (ill. p. 92), Walter Dexel (ill. p. 96) and the group's spokesman, Werner Graeff (ill. p. 94). The international congress of Dadaists and Constructivists which Van Doesburg organized in Weimar in 1922, just after the ill-starred congress in Dusseldorf, may be regarded as a demonstration against the Bauhaus as it then was. This event, which was attended by most prominent artists, was a formal leave-taking from Dadaism and the beginning of a Constructivist International. As a result of manifestos, lectures and exhibitions there was a fusion of the forces of de Stijl, Suprematism, Russian and Eastern European Constructivism in an all-embracing Constructivism which included all the nuances of the various styles. A first consequence of this effort of integration was the Constructivist exhibition staged by Walter Dexel in Jena in 1923. At the same time the show offered an impressive survey of German Constructivism.

The activity of Van Doesburg and his friends was to have its consequences for the Bauhaus. Walter Gropius returned to his original Functionalism and disassociated himself more and more clearly from the Romantic and Expressionist trends in the Bauhaus, as well as from the buildings he had designed himself in the previous years. The choice of Laszlo Moholy-Nagy as Itten's successor reflects this change of heart. The idea of a combination of art and craftsmanship, as embodied in the artisanal workshops, was replaced in Bauhaus thinking by the more progressive slogan "Art and technology — a new unity". Adverse external developments also forced the Bauhaus into a more aggressive forward-looking policy. From about 1923 onward the institute was exposed to the unobjective criticism of increasingly reactionary authorities. The daily struggle against the petite bourgeoisie consolidated the ranks of the Bauhaus supporters and spurred them on to bolder and more mature achievements, which were then displayed in public exhibitions. But neither these achievements nor the experimental stage performances and bright festivals of the Bauhaus did much to improve the situation. The fate of the institute was finally sealed when the conservative majority of the Landtag, the state parliament, brought financial pressures to bear against it, and it was dissolved in December 1924 by a decision of the Council of Masters.

In the spring of 1925 the city of Dessau declared itself ready to take over the Bauhaus. A new era began, visibly announced by the fact that the educational and research institute was now to be housed in a new building designed for the purpose by Gropius and better suited to a university of art and design. From 1925 onward the Bauhaus also expressed itself more frequently on general questions of art and design in the books published by Gropius and Moholy-Nagy. The writings of Gropius, Paul Klee, Oskar Schlemmer, Piet Mondrian, Theo van Doesburg, Laszlo Moholy-Nagy, Wassily Kandinsky, J.J.P. Oud and Kasimir Malevich which were included in the series are among the most important books on art theory to appear in the twentieth century. They show that the Bauhaus had become, through its teachers and other artists attached to it, a center of the new constructive ideas. Much the same applies to the portfolios previously issued by the Bauhaus workshops: they comprised graphic productions not only of the institute's own masters, but of the whole European avant-garde.

In 1926 the new buildings in Dessau were opened. There was an architectural department and a theatrical workshop with an experimental stage, and in 1929 a photography department was added. The handicraft training that had originally been so marked in Weimar gave way to a kind of laboratory work for the development of standard types: the Bauhaus now occupied itself with the design of functionally and formally exemplary objects of use adapted to the requirements of industrial manufacture. Contacts were established with industry with a view to

ensuring their wide adoption and use. Gradually the political situation also began to exert an ever stronger pressure on the Bauhaus. Aesthetic considerations now took second place to functional and social ones. The drift toward a more radical political line led to the resignation of Gropius in 1928. His post was taken by Hannes Meyer, whose device "Building is a biological process, not an aesthetic process" clearly differentiated him from the art orientation of Gropius. After Hannes Meyer's departure Ludwig Mies van der Rohe took over in 1930. Soon after the accession of the National Socialists to power the Bauhaus was forced to disband by police action. This was in 1933. For most of its members — masters and students alike — a period of personal persecution now commenced, except where it was cut short by emigration. When the members of the Bauhaus were scattered all over the world, the era of its international influence began in earnest.

In no phase of its fourteen-year existence was the Bauhaus an art school in the usual sense. Its objectives were practical in scope: conscientious artist-designers or educators were to be trained here, men capable of making a constructive contribution to the qualitative improvement of standards of living. The products developed by the Bauhaus — tableware, metal implements, lamps, textiles, furniture and the like — served as models, as stimulating exemplars for consumer goods manufacture. Like typography, advertising graphics and exhibition design or the systematic architectural studies carried out by the Bauhaus, these models helped to shape the Functionalist style of the twenties, which is consequently often referred to — not quite accurately — as the "Bauhaus style".

In no phase of its existence the Bauhaus proclaimed stylistic uniformity.

It had been Gropius' wish, however, that the masters of the Bauhaus should not be specialists in their various domains but primarily fine artists. This felicitous but unusual feature of the teaching staff, combined with the open character of the instruction, made the Bauhaus an inexhaustible reservoir of unconventional and creative ideas. The same end would never have been attained with a staff of specialists for the various subjects. It was only through the collaboration of free artists that the basic goal of the unity of art and life, the permeation of life by artistic principles, was realized in some areas at least.

Neither their teaching nor the daily personal contacts led to a uniform style on the part of the Bauhaus masters. It was part of the free and stimulating atmosphere — in Weimar as well as in Dessau, where the masters formed a kind of artists' colony living in houses designed by Gropius — that every person had the right to remain true to his own convictions. Since each artist also had to formulate his own ideas on art and design accurately in his teaching, it was almost inevitable that the individual should develop his potentialities in a way that would hardly have been possible in the isolation of a private existence. The problems arising in the theory lessons or in the workshops, the talks with students, the discussion and assessment of their work — all these things threw up ideas that were of value to every Bauhaus master in his own exercise of his art. It is therefore no accident that these years were the most fruitful in the artistic activity and theoretical development of those concerned. If the Bauhaus

Wassily Kandinsky: White — Soft and Hard, 1932

was able to bring together so many personalities of the art world of the time and to keep them together for over ten years, the credit must go primarily to Walter Gropius; yet this unique constellation would never have come into being without a readiness on the part of each one to serve the Bauhaus idea.

The teaching, then, led to a clarification of the working aims of almost all the masters of the Bauhaus. This applies perhaps least of all to Feininger, who first headed the graphic workshop, but from 1925 lived at the Bauhaus without any specific teaching assignment (ill. p. 89). By contrast, the connection of teaching and work is particularly patent in the case of Paul Klee: there is a grand unity that can be followed even in detail between his artistic production and the ''Pedagogical Sketchbook'' as well as the writings on form and composition inspired by his Bauhaus teaching (''Creative Thought''). Much the same holds good of Laszlo Moholy-Nagy, who saw his preliminary course as a general introduction to the elements of art, including existing mathematical and geometric forms as well as freshly created forms and form-com-

plexes (ill. pp. 103, 104). He investigated dimensional relations, material values, light. The three-dimensional material and equilibrium studies in particular led to plastic structures which — themselves based on the cognitive experience of Constructivism — opened up new paths for constructive thinking. The so-called ''Light Display Machine'' which Moholy had been working on from 1922 onward for an electric stage, and which was finally carried out in 1930, belongs here: in reality a machine for producing non-objective light studies, it became a forerunner of kinetic art and of light sculptures.

There are also close relations between the teaching and the work of Kandinsky, who said of his lessons in analytical drawing: ''The teaching of drawing at the Bauhaus is a training in observation, exact seeing and exact representation not of the outward appearance of an object but of its constructive elements, the law-obeying forces (tensions) that can be discovered in some objects.'' In the color seminar the affinities of color and form were investigated. The theories Kandinsky summed up in his Bauhaus book ''Punkt und Linie zu Fläche'' (Point and Line to

Surface) are the outcome of his teaching activity as well as of experience acquired in his own work, which in these years gained considerably in clarity and purity (ill. pp. 107, 109).

Similar interrelations between teaching and painting can be observed in the case of Josef Albers. He came to the Bauhaus as a student with previous art training, later took over part of the preliminary course and the stained-glass workshop as a "young master" (ill. p. 93), and finally was responsible for the whole of the preliminary course. Central features of his "work course" were the study of materials and their deformability, or in other words of dimensions and energy; the study of motion, or statics and dynamics; and the investigation of expression as achieved by the use of line, surface, color, dimension and light. In his own work these studies have left their mark in his employment of the positive-negative principle, the optical effects of apparent spatiality, structure and texture (ill. p. 260). In the realm of color, the possibilities of which as a transparent medium Albers investigated in the stained-glass workshop, he developed a theory of his own based on subtle observation. It formed the basis of what he later called "the interaction of color".

It was the human being, and not elementary laws of form, that held foremost place in the art world of Oskar Schlemmer, who headed the stage workshop and taught figure drawing. In the mural workshop he based painterly and plastic wall compositions on a geometric "art figure" he had arrived at by a process of abstraction; in his own work he used it for wire "space graphics" (ill. p. 91) and in stage settings such as the famous "Triadic Ballet" as part of an abstract dance performance. Schlemmer was one of the first to realize what wonderful potentialities the theater holds for creative development in the educational field. Stage experiments at the Bauhaus, in which Moholy also took part, influenced the commercial theater of the time in many ways. Schlemmer retrospectively found a meaningful interpretation of the constructive conceptions and the basic humanist outlook of the Bauhaus in 1932 in his picture "Bauhaus Stairway" (New York, Museum of Modern Art).

The creative elements of form and color were investigated and tested in the Bauhaus courses more systematically than they had ever been before. The question of how much of this research could be usefully distilled out in the art productions of Bauhaus members and other contemporaries was a matter of creative resource and originality. The Bauhaus in any case provided an instrumentarium, especially for constructive work, which is still available today and by no means out-of-date as yet. In the Germany of the twenties and early thirties the Bauhaus did a great deal to make constructive art a widely understood language. It did this directly through the influence of its masters and students, and indirectly through its example, which was followed in many quarters. Together with de Stijl and the ideas of the Russian avant-garde, which were disseminated from Berlin up to and even after Malevich's memorable stay there in 1927, the Bauhaus contributed to the popularization of Constructivist thinking in painting and sculpture, in architecture and interior decoration, in typography, exhibition design, photography, film and theater. Its web of influence extended over the whole of Europe and to the United States. This latter development was due to a large extent to the interest of Katherine S. Dreier, who had first established contact with Berlin in 1920. She collected work for the "Société Anonyme" and repeatedly arranged for larger or smaller exhibitions in New York of the work of European artists, many of them members of the Bauhaus.

In Germany itself the seizure of power by Adolf Hitler in 1933 put an end to these developments. All the progressive trends in art became "un-German" and were supplanted by a sugary realism. Constructivist art was condemned as "internationalist" or "Bolshevist". Many of the most powerful personalities emigrated to other European countries, and either then or later to the United States. Those who remained in Germany were mostly forbidden to paint and withdrew into an "inward emigration". An impressive artistic movement was killed by the veto of power, much as in Russia, where with the strengthening of Stalinist dominion Constructivism was restricted to architecture, urbanism, propaganda, and exhibition design, while in art "Socialist Realism" was established as the officially approved idiom.

A comparison of the activities of the Bauhaus with the objectives of the Unovis group at the art academy in Vitebsk and later at the Inchuk in Moscow and Leningrad would certainly reveal some interesting parallels in the endeavors to combine constructive ideas with the Utopian vision of a "new man in a new world".

Abstraction – Création

France between Purism and geometric abstraction

Radically new ideas in art are mostly shaped into a valid idiom in an astonishingly short space of time by the group—usually small—of their initiators. It may take ten or more years, however, before a wider circle of artists, a whole "generation", has learned the language and can use it skillfully and with a personal touch. Yet it is only when a new artistic idiom has attained a certain general acceptance that the broad public is ready and able to recognize it as a contemporary style or at least as a distinctive stylistic trend. This was the course taken by Cubism in France. By the time the art world was prepared to accept and understand it, it had already passed through many hands, had lost some of its intensity and gained in variety. In 1918, just after the end of World War I, its initiators were following other lines of development.

If we take it that analytical Cubism breaks down reality —or rather corporeal and spatial phenomena—into comparatively simple geometric elements, while synthetic Cubism uses such simple elements to build up a new reality, an autonomous flat picture-reality, it may seem astonishing that in the formal sector the principle was never carried to its logical conclusion. This would have meant, for instance, reducing the elements found by Cubism, the geometric or stereometric character of which is evident, to pure basic forms of geometry, and building with this elementary form vocabulary, as with building blocks, a "non-objective world" obeying geometric principles. French art in the wake of Cubism did not take this step. The central sentence of the Cubist theory of Juan Gris is perhaps symptomatic: "Cézanne makes a cylinder out of a bottle, I make a bottle out of a cylinder." Cubism in its various phases sets out from the object and aims at the form, the stereometric body and the geometric surface. Precisely in Juan Gris, however, there are visible signs of a return to the object.

The outside observer would be inclined to regard the possible or even obvious step from Cubism into geometric non-objectivity as a specifically French alternative. A pronounced capacity for logical and rational thinking is after all commonly attributed to the French character. Cool Cartesian reasoning, the rationalism of the Enlightenment, the intellectualization of feeling—all this seems to justify the expectation that the Cubist advance in France would almost inevitably lead to a constructive geometric non-objectivity. This expectation was partly based on the example of Mondrian, in whose development between 1914 and 1918 the formalization of the Cubist dissection and geometrization of reality can be followed step by step up to the adoption of a non-objective horizontal-vertical ordering principle. But Mondrian was not a Frenchman.

A few contemporaries noted that the conclusions which seemed to follow from Cubist compositional principles were in fact never drawn. The attempts to avoid a relapse into Cubism by the adoption of a more or less abstract and at the same time aesthetic "peinture" were isolated efforts with little influence on the general run of events in France. There were two groups of artists who worked along these lines and tried to advance beyond Cubism, beyond the Orphism of Delaunay and the Futoro-Cubism represented, for instance, by Severini.

One of these groups belonged to the circle of the Dadaists: Marcel Duchamp, Francis Picabia, Jean Crotti are the most prominent names. They all have their roots in Cubism but broke away from it at an early date. Duchamp introduced the element of motion into Cubism as early as 1912 by the simultaneous depiction of the sequential phases of movement and came near to the conceptions of the Futurists with his "Nude Descending a Staircase" (ill. p. 240) and other pictures. His preoccupation with the phenomena of motion and his contemporaneous research into the relationship between objective reality and art (in the Ready-mades) led in 1913/15 to a study of the machine and thus of mechanical constructs. He said in 1914 of his "Chocolate grinder": "I felt finally liberated from the straitjacket of Cubism by the introduction of linear perspective and the highly geometric representation of a machine such as this chocolate grinder." The "Glider" of 1913/15, a "technical" construction of a sliding frame with built-in waterwheel, seen in perspective and mounted between semicircular glass plates, seems almost an anticipation of the later machine-like spatial constructs of the Russians. The apparatus, whose symbolic meaning we shall not investigate here, was later reutilized by Duchamp in his principal work, the "Large Glass". "Dry" works, as Duchamp called these anonymous pseudotechnical constructs, are exemplars of a sort of "machinism" which had its most passionate supporters among the Dadaists. This applies first and foremost to Francis Picabia, who painted pure machine pictures such as "Machine tournez vite" as early as 1916 and from 1917 onward executed a long series of "dessins mécaniques" which he reproduced in his own magazine "391" and in other Dadaist publications. They are compositions reminiscent of technical drawings for machines and equipment, linear designs that use very little color but are enriched with numbers, letters and enigmatic words. As befits the Dadaist mentality, they are ironically intended.

Both Picabia and Marcel Duchamp had belonged to the group of Cubists that gathered around Duchamp's brother Jacques Villon in Puteaux, taking a keen interest in mathematics and the ratiocinatory problems of chess and exhibiting their works as a group under the name of "Section d'Or". Duchamp's sister Suzanne and her later husband, the Swiss painter Jean Crotti, also belonged to the group. They took part in machine art with its emphasis on draftsmanship, as did also the Dadaist writer Georges Ribemont-Dessaignes. About 1920 Crotti in particular — he had turned his attention in 1915 to "Mechanical Forces" (the title of one of his principal pictures) — advanced in the direction of graceful spatial constructions. "L'Escalier sans fin" (ill. p. 117) is an example of these free geometric works in which problems of infinite space are also broached. Parallels to the Constructivism of Eastern Europe are unmistakable, but any direct contact is improbable. The geometric non-objectivity of Jean Crotti in particular is based on a musically interpreted Orphist Cubism and used the results of a formal confrontation with the technical and mechanical world to evoke serene, dreamlike and even mystic moods.

The members of this group were united by a biographical detail as well as by the bonds of family and friendship: they all repeatedly visited New York between 1912 and 1924, sometimes staying for long periods, and together with their friend Man Ray they were at the center of a movement that has been called "New York Dada". The only representative of the group who passed some time on all the scenes of the Dada movement in Europe in its period of florescence was Picabia. His connections extended via Zurich, where he worked with Jean Arp and Hans Richter, to the Dadaists of Berlin, who liked to be known as "Monteure" — "fitters" or "erectors". They took a lively interest in Picabia's machine style, finding that his absurd wheel systems had affinities with Russian Constructivism, which was also regarded as a "machine art". Picabia's influence can likewise be felt in the early works of Schwitters, in which three-dimensional "found objects" in the form of wheels and wire netting are incorporated. Indications of the importance of Picabia at that time can also be found in the magazine "MA" published in Vienna from 1920 onward by Lajos Kassak and Laszlo Moholy-Nagy. Finally, Theo van Doesburg issued the Dada magazine "Mécano" from 1922 onward under his pseudonym I. K. Bonset. It was inserted in the numbers of "de stijl" and betrays clearly in its title the taste for things mechanical. With the end of Dadaism in France in 1923, however, "machinism" gradually disappeared from geometric art in that country.

Marcel Duchamp was the only one who realized what potentialities the machine still had in the optical field. In 1920, when he was living in New York, he designed his "Revolving Glass Plates": five rectangular glass plates with black and white lines painted on them are mounted on the shaft of an electric motor and generate ever changing circles when the motor revolves at great speed. This apparatus is the beginning of a series of "optical precision instruments", Duchamp's investigations into "virtual forms", which found a temporary conclusion in the "Rotoreliefs" of 1926, made for the short experimental film "Anemic Cinema" turned in Puteaux (ill. p. 164). Duchamp had thereby done some vital preliminary work for all later kinetic art.

A second group of artists in France, from about 1918 on, was also moving by way of Cubism toward a rational geometric art. Their work began with a manifesto: in 1918 Amédée Ozenfant and Charles-Edouard Jeanneret published a pamphlet with the title "Après le Cubisme". It may be regarded as a reply to the theoretical essay of Gleizes and Metzinger on Cubism dating from 1912. The painter and art writer Ozenfant, who in close cooperation with Albert Gleizes and Roger de la Fresnaye had pleaded for a "return to order" within the framework of Cubist principles, had found in the young French-Swiss architect Charles-Edouard Jeanneret a stimulating partner for the further pursuance of his ideas. He persuaded Jeanneret, who had just settled down in Paris, to take up painting. "Après le Cubisme" appeared on the occasion of their first joint exhibition.

The publication is apparently directed only against the decorative dilution of late Cubism. Basically, however, it calls the very principles of Cubist composition in question. What its writers postulate is "Purism", which Ozenfant sees as not merely another school of painting but an expression of modern life as a whole. This explains the reference to the significance of the architect and particularly of the engineer, in whose works a "plastic beauty" comes into being. The essential gist of the argument is the unity of art and science. "There is nothing to justify the assumption that science and art are in any way incompatible. They have the common goal of reducing the universe to its basic equations. We shall prove that pure art and pure science are not wholly self-contained domains. They have a common spirit . . .; art and science are dependent on number." The Purist theory leads to a rationalist cosmogony: nature is not conceived as a great mystic secret but rather as a "calculable machine". The structural laws of nature are recognized behind its outward appearances. "Natural order emerges where the visible elements of nature reveal themselves to us in the terms of geometry." The fundamental concern is therefore with a synthesis of nature and geometry.

Unlike the Constructivists and Neo-Plasticists, Ozenfant and Jeanneret remained true to visual appearances in their painting. The "harmony of the cosmos" was mirrored for them in the form world of everyday objects (ill. p. 113). Purist painting uses essentially the requisites of Cubist still lifes: bottles, glasses, vases, plates, lanterns, turned handles. But the Cubist principle of dissection, of the breaking-down of an object into fragments, is rejected, the objects are perceived as coherent form organisms which are defined as stereometric structures by an emphasized plasticity. They appear in well-balanced compositions of a monumental character in markedly architectonic, imaginary picture spaces. Their suggestivity is heightened by strong shadows, exaggerated perspective and interpenetrations of transparent surfaces till they attain a theatrical, artificial reality which is sometimes reminiscent in its mood of the pictorial world of Italian "Pittura metafisica" — Giorgio de Chirico, Carlo Carrà or Giorgio Morandi.

A rational compositional order is consistently maintained in Purism. Nothing is left to chance. A will to harmonious relations of dimensions is manifested, clearly inspired by classical orders and going much further than Juan Gris did at the same time in his distillation of the Cubist heritage. The formal perfectionism of the Purist still life also has its dangers: aestheticism is occasionally carried to

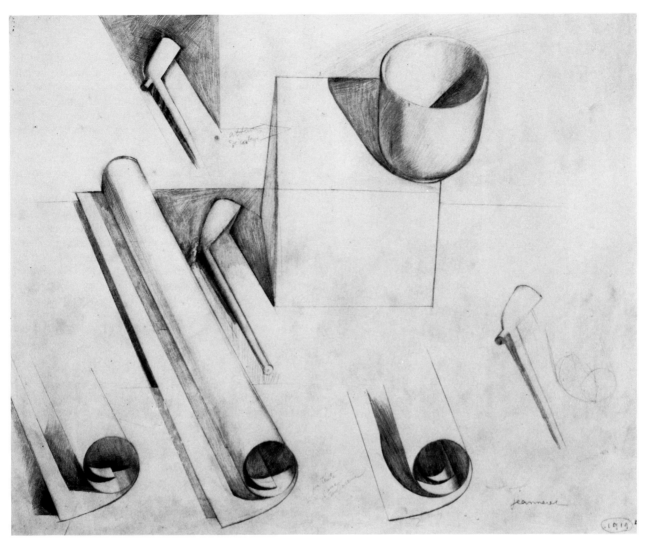

Le Corbusier: Cup, pipes and paper rolls, 1919

the point at which the delicately colored composition freezes into mere ornament. This formalizing element may be the expression of a longing for stability and security that is typical of the times. It can be found, though with a different emphasis, in many painters in France and elsewhere. In Germany Schlemmer and Baumeister aimed at a stylization and monumentalization of the human figure which is not far removed from the classicism of the Purist still life (ill. pp. 88, 90, 91).

The close collaboration between Ozenfant and Jeanneret in the years following 1918 involved far more than the joint development of the new pictorial language of Purism. Both were full of critical optimism, both saw themselves as called to help in building a better — and that meant a more reasonable and more beautiful — world. They were imbued with the spirit which Guillaume Apollinaire had referred to in a lecture in 1918, shortly before his death, as the "esprit nouveau".

In 1920 Ozenfant, Jeanneret and the writer Paul Dermée began to publish the international magazine "L'Esprit Nouveau", which was more than another art periodical. It dealt with all aspects of the "machine age", not only those of the visual culture. The title page of the first number of this magazine for "experimental aesthetics" included in its range of interests — over and above painting, sculpture and architecture — engineering aesthetics, literature, music, the theater, music hall and circus, sport, clothes, book art and furniture. In fact, the magazine laid claim to a universality similar to that displayed by Van Doesburg's "de stijl" or Hans Richter's "G". A "living aesthetic" embracing all the spheres of modern man's experience was the goal. Jeanneret signed his articles on architecture with a pseudonym: Le Corbusier. Before long he was using the same name as an architect, while he continued to sign his pictures with his surname Jeanneret till 1928. The choice of this pseudonym, with which he was to become known as one of the founders of modern architecture, was made just at the beginning of his independent career as an architect, town planner and architectural theorist. The texts published in "L'Esprit Nouveau" were collected in 1923 in the book "Vers une Architecture", which earned him an international reputation. The essays postulate a reform of our culture and civilization based on architecture. With the aid of the new

Victor Servranckx: Opus 16, 1924

mony with the universal order, deciding the multifarious movements of our mind and our heart: thus beauty becomes an experience for us." This train of thought runs parallel to the synthetic demands for a comprehensive, rational aesthetic as advocated above all by Theo van Doesburg in the magazine "de stijl". It was not by accident that the Stijl manifesto was reprinted in the second issue of "L'Esprit Nouveau", and that the magazine quite generally established farsighted contacts between persons and groups holding similar views.

The culminating and closing event of the "Esprit Nouveau" period was the inclusion in the "Exposition Internationale des Arts Décoratifs" in Paris in 1925 of a "Pavillon de L'Esprit Nouveau" which Le Corbusier built and furnished. The pavilion, which was boycotted by French officialdom, was a complete synthesis of architecture, interior decoration and integrated art. What Lissitzky had adumbrated on a small scale in Hanover with his "Kabinett der Abstrakten" was here realized in a spacious, harmonious and human "machine à habiter". In its blending of the functional and the formal the "Pavillon de L'Esprit Nouveau" demonstrated a consistently modern style of living which had its closest parallels in the architectural proposals of Rietveld and Van Doesburg.

Pictures by Fernand Léger hung in the pavilion alongside Purist works by Ozenfant and Jeanneret. Without becoming a Purist proper, Léger was the artist who made the most use of the movement's achievements between 1919 and 1928 or thereabouts. The development of his painting that set in immediately after the end of the war with the transition from the dynamic Cubist "Contraste de Formes" (ill. p. 25) to the "époque mécanique" would be unthinkable without the clarifying and ordering influence of Purism. He was also a close friend of Ozenfant and Le Corbusier and took an active part in the founding of "L'Esprit Nouveau". He opened a painting school with Ozenfant in 1924, and he did his first mural for Le Corbusier's "Pavillon de L'Esprit Nouveau" in 1925.

Ozenfant reviewed Léger's work from 1918 onward in "Art", a temperamental summing-up of the first quarter of the twentieth century published in 1928. "Léger was deeply moved by the fearful machinery of modern warfare, the precision of guns, grenades and cannon, and he understood the exact timing that is necessary to keep the thousand cogs of an army in smooth motion. His mind was ahead of his work, but in 1918/19 his pictures gradually freed themselves of the last traces of Impressionism. Léger was now ready to take up the ideas of Purism, and he was one of the first to realize that what was at issue was power, honesty and objectivity and not an imitation of the painting we were publicizing. From 1920 onward his paintings became ever more daring odes to the modern object, to living color. Léger has sung modern power with his mighty voice . . ."

It is precisely this element of physical and pictorial power that distinguishes Léger's Puristic period from the contemporaneous work of Amédée Ozenfant. Even when he subjected himself to a strict geometric order in his pictures, when he organized the dynamic elements from the world of mechanics in a system of rectangular surfaces, and even when he came closest to Purist classicism in still-life representations of objects, Léger's paintings retained the breathtaking rhythm of modern life. In the

means of expression now available to engineering and art, architecture was to initiate an evolution full of benefits for the future. Unlike the earlier appeals of likeminded reformers, Le Corbusier's arguments were free from all unrealistic romanticism. They embodied the logical thought of a creative rationalist who was able to support his theoretical proposals with convincing practical examples. These proposals never sprang from mere utilitarianism. They were put forward soberly but with feeling and are the expression of an all-embracing vision.

"Engineering aesthetics — architecture: both in their deepest nature identical and interchangeable, yet the one today in full vigor, the other painfully retrograde. The engineer, instructed by the requirements of economy and guided by calculation, puts us in unison with the laws of the universe. He attains harmony. By assembling forms the architect achieves an order which is the pure creation of his mind; through these forms he affects our senses deeply and powerfully, producing the excitement of creative design; through the relationships he achieves he awakens a deep response in us, furnishing us with the measurements of an order which we feel to be in har-

Fernand Léger: Le Pot rouge, 1926

monumental architectonics of his compositions vital life-bearing elements in figurative or vegetable motifs are repeatedly contrasted with rationally constructed forms. Léger believed in mechanical forces, but he also believed in life. In his later work he embodied it most impressively in the worker or the human being actively engaged in sport or in art. Like Le Corbusier, he saw the highest task of creative man as the building of a new — and, he believed, better — world. The very incarnation of the active human being for this "proletarian Utopian" was therefore the engineer-designer.

The Purist phase was extremely important to Léger. He himself says that he used geometric forms for only three years from 1918 on, but the effect of Purism can be felt well beyond his mechanistic period proper up to about 1930, when the free objective and figurative work of his maturity begins. He is referring to the clearly ordered still lifes of the twenties, which include "Le Pot rouge" of 1926 (ill. p. 115), when he makes this typically Purist statement: "I have distributed my objects in space and brought them into relationship by letting them act outward from the plane of the canvas. The whole is a free play of chords and rhythms produced by the ground and surface colors, by leading lines, distances and contrasts." The object is a maximum of formal force: "I can attain

this powerful effect only by the uncompromising use of absolute contrasts: flat parts in pure tones, modeled parts in gray, plus realistic objects."

In this period Léger would have been a great mural painter. But the opportunity was lacking, except for Le Corbusier's assignment for his pavilion "L'Esprit Nouveau". One line of development, however, was open to him: the provision of curtains, settings and costumes for modern ballet performances. Shortly after making the experimental film "La Roue" with Blaise Cendrars (1921), he was able to design the setting for Arthur Honegger's "Skating Rink" (1922) for Rolf de Maré's Ballets Suédois: a purely geometric, predominantly black and green design. In the following year came the Negro ballet "La Création du Monde" by Darius Milhaud, with a setting built up of staggered backdrops in black, white and ocher and imbued with primitive power. In both ballets Léger tried to make the dancers' costumes geometric. He was thus following a trend toward the "abstract theater" which was represented at the same time in Germany by Oskar Schlemmer with his "Triadic Ballet". In the film "Le Ballet méchanique" (1924), a rhythmic sequence of moving objects and fragments of sentences based on arithmetic principles, Léger came even nearer to abstract kinetics. Like Man Ray and René Clair, who were working along similar

Gustave Buchet: Construction, c. 1920

Florence Henri: Black-White-Silver, 1921

tion of an abstraction divorced from the object. French art critics, though they felt its austerity to be pedantic, have admitted that it stimulated "peinture pure", painting free from all representational reminiscences, whose subject is only the relationship of forms and colors.

This "pure painting" comprised both the free geometric disk compositions of Robert Delaunay, with their concentration on simultaneous contrast, and Kupka's harmonic horizontal-vertical works (ill. p. 29). In this context we should also mention Alberto Magnelli, who from 1915 on advanced through Cubism and Futurism to dynamic nonobjective compositions which, with their clear surface patterns, often look like painted collages. Much the same applies to Gustave Buchet, who had moved from Geneva to Paris in 1916 and there gravitated from Cubo-Futurist abstraction toward Purist severity and calm (ill. p. 116). The influence of his countryman Le Corbusier, who actively encouraged him, can be clearly felt. A friend of the sculptors Ossip Zadkine and Alexander Archipenko, Buchet was also a member of the "Section d'Or" and a student of harmonious numerical relations. The balanced compositions suggesting still lifes which he executed between 1925 and 1930 — one of them is entitled "L'Esprit Nouveau" — radiate very strongly that delight in harmonic proportions which Le Corbusier was soon to propagate in the universal standard of his "Modulor". This preoccupation with proportions, harking back as it did to the classical Greek conception of man as the measure of all things, led in almost all the artists concerned — Le Corbusier, Léger, Picabia, Magnelli, Buchet, and others — to a return, in some cases only temporary, to figurative art.

Auguste Herbin, who was later to be called the "primitive master of Constructivism", was also affected by Purism. From 1917 on he developed compositions in the synthetic Cubist style from which he derived, about 1920, a severe, purely geometric approach with an impact that suggests the poster. The principal feature of this work is a consistent symmetry about a central axis which makes the very colorful pictures somehow reminiscent of idol shapes. This phase with its striking geometric signs ended in 1922. It has been spoken of as "magical-barbaric decorative art" and it included colored reliefs of wood and concrete as well as Purist frescoes. Then Herbin returned to a figurative and objective style of painting, which was to be succeeded by a further abstract phase toward the end of the twenties, after which came an organic-dynamic and finally a geometric non-objectivity (ill. pp. 123–125).

The work of Florence Henri shows how typical this line of development was in France at that time. This cosmopolitan artist, a trained pianist who had switched over to painting in Munich, came under the influence of Ozenfant and Léger in Paris, which led her to balanced geometric abstraction of a Purist character (ill. p. 116). Although her pictures show a kinship with works of Buchet, Magnelli and Herbin done about the same time, Florence Henri did not return to a painterly figurative style. After a course of study at the Bauhaus in Dessau, she took up Constructivist photography in Paris in 1929 and soon ranked among the leading photographers of the day. Through her photographic mirror compositions and portraits she remained closely connected with the small circle of Constructivist artists in Paris in the thirties.

lines, he therefore made an early and important contribution to "cinéma pur". The essay entitled "The Aesthetics of the Machine", which he published in 1924 in the "Bulletin de l'Effort Moderne", shows how deeply fascinated he was in those years by the machine and by mechanical motion: "Modern man lives more and more in a predominantly geometric order. Every human creation, whether mechanical or industrial, depends on geometric factors." Even though Purism did not establish a general stylistic trend, it had a purifying effect in France in the first half of the twenties. It strengthened the position of those who were attempting to pursue synthetic Cubism in the direc-

Jean Crotti: L'Escalier sans fin, 1920

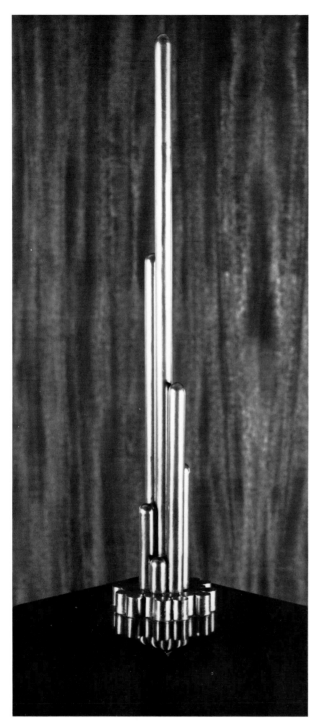

Etienne Béothy: Project for a monument, 1919

In the early twenties the history of stage settings and costumes for ballet performances is closely linked with developments in the art world. The beginnings must no doubt be sought in Russia, where the potentialities of non-figurative art were first exploited both for ballet and for drama. The names of Natalia Goncharova and Mikhail Larionov in particular are intimately linked with stage decoration. Their accomplishments in this field would admittedly have been hardly possible without the influence of the great animator, Serge de Diaghilev. At the outbreak of war in 1914, Diaghilev remained in Western Europe to make cultural propaganda for his country with his "Ballets Russes". His stay in Paris later became a permanent exile which the couple Larionov-Goncharova shared with him from 1915 on. Both worked in Paris for the tournées of the Ballets Russes in Western Europe until the death of Diaghilev in 1929, and they remained true to stage art even beyond that date. Diaghilev's Russian artist collaborators, however, hardly progressed beyond a Cubo-Futurist style in their ballet settings. It was only through its connections with French composers and artists that Diaghilev's ballet became a "painter's theater". This avant-garde development was initiated by Picasso's stage design for "Parade" by Eric Satie, performed by the Ballets Russes in Rome in 1917, and followed — again in Rome in 1917 — by Giacomo Balla's designs for Stravinsky's "Feu d'artifice". Subsequently Braque, Gris, Matisse, Derain, Miró and others worked for Diaghilev, but none of their designs attained the daring and logical consistency of Léger's work for the Ballets Suédois. It was only at the very end of his career that Diaghilev made another advance into the field of Constructivist design: Naum Gabo and Antoine Pevsner, both at that time living in Paris, designed a three-dimensional setting of partly transparent sheets and circles for the Constructivist ballet "La Chatte", which was performed in Monte Carlo in 1926. In the following year Yuri Yakulov (Georges Jacoulov) transformed the stage for "Le Pas d'acier" into a mechanical construction of cogwheels, bridges and platforms. These Constructivist stage settings in France were an echo of post-Revolutionary Russian theater decoration. They were based on the "Theater October" proclaimed by Vsevolod Meyerhold in 1920, which was theoretically anchored in "Biomechanics", as he called his Constructivist theatrical art. Meyerhold's rival, Alexander Tairov, was just as important in the area of stage design in Russia. Alexander Wesnin and Varvara Stepanova, Yuri Yakulov, Liobov Popova and Alexandra Exter played some part in Constructivist stage design in Russia along with Tatlin. Popova died in 1924, and in the same year Alexandra Exter emigrated to Paris and exerted an influence there as a teacher of stage design at Fernand Léger's school.

The Constructivist stage design of the Russians — familiar in Western Europe from the early twenties onward from guest performances, theatrical exhibitions and publications such as Tairov's "The Theater Unchained" — initiated analogous developments in Germany: Oskar Schlemmer at the Bauhaus in Dessau, the political theater of Erwin Piscator in Berlin, and the stage settings of Moholy-Nagy at the Kroll Opera. In France this influence was felt only in isolated cases, although the Constructivist theater was featured in the Russian pavilion at the International Exhibition of the Decorative Arts in 1925. French taste transformed every Constructivist tendency into modernist decoration, which was soon to celebrate triumphs in the "Art Déco" style. The failure of the attempt to create a theater of abstraction is exemplified in the anti-theater play "L'Ephémère est éternel" which was written by Michel Seuphor in Rome under the influence of Marinetti and Balla in 1926 and for which Mondrian sup-

Antoine Pevsner: Le dernier élan, 1962

119

Otto Freundlich: Abstract composition, 1930

only outcome was that the leading French magazine "Architecture vivante" devoted a special issue to the Dutch movement.

When Theo van Doesburg settled in Paris, both of the central figures of de Stijl were present in the French capital. They had, however, long given up active collaboration, and in 1925 came the final separation. In voluntary solitude, supported only by a small circle of friends, Mondrian went on with his work, behind which loomed the vision of an aesthetic Utopia: human society was to be changed and man guided toward greater harmony by way of painting, architecture and the shaping of the material world around him. Van Doesburg's temperament, directed more toward practical achievements, was quite opposed to this Utopian and prophetic attitude. In his activities as a writer he had repeatedly pointed out that the artist's task was the active endeavor to improve imperfect living conditions. While Mondrian was thinking about the people of the future, Doesburg was demanding that the artist should occupy himself with the people of the present. This approach is also expressed in the manifesto of "Elementarism" published in 1926, which is in a sense an answer to Mondrian's Neo-Plasticism. Van Doesburg saw architecture as the best means of directly influencing his contemporaries. He had written as early as 1922: "I am firmly convinced that the moral consciousness of man will unfold in a cleanly designed environment."

A splendid opportunity to put this theory of practical activity by the artist to the test presented itself in 1926 with an assignment to renovate the whole interior of the "Aubette" restaurant in Strasbourg. The work was entrusted to Jean Arp and Sophie Taeuber-Arp, who had just settled in Meudon near Paris. They spontaneously enlisted the aid of their friend and neighbor Van Doesburg. A list published in "de stijl" shows how the commission —interior decoration of restaurant, brasserie, tea saloon, several bars, dance floor and cabaret in the cellar, billiard room, large and small gala halls, lobbies and other rooms— was divided among the group. Early in 1928 the new restaurant—in a historic building that had long been a favorite meeting place of the citizens of Strasbourg—was reopened. The undertaking only materialized because the owners, who were collectors of avant-garde art, placed full confidence in the artists. We know the "Aubette" today only from photographs, a few original models, plans and contemporary descriptions. Ignorance, modifications to suit the tastes of the public and finally deliberate obliteration as "degenerate art" during the German occupation of 1940/44 led to the complete destruction of this "modern fairy-tale".

Working on similar principles but without in any way denying their individual differences, the three artists created in the "Aubette" a total work of art which conformed exactly to Van Doesburg's idea of the integration of the arts. The organic interconnection, the uses of the various rooms, the furniture and lighting, the design and coloring of walls, ceilings, floors and staircases and the interior architecture combined, thanks to the extensive use of elementary forms and color schemes, to form a unity of unique impact. Arp's murals incorporating playful organic shapes were fantastic in their festal atmosphere. Sophie Taeuber restricted herself in wall and ceiling treatments, floor mosaics and windows to horizontal-vertical rhythms

plied the designs for three settings. These had already been made and the rehearsals were under way in Lyons when the enterprise was abandoned. It was only in 1968 that Seuphor's play was finally staged for the first time in Milan with reconstructions of Mondrian's stage designs.

At that time geometric constructive art proper met with little understanding in France, although the preliminary conditions for its acceptance were fulfilled: Mondrian lived in Paris from 1919 to 1938 and developed the principles of his Neo-Plasticism there. Léonce Rosenberg, who published "Le Néoplasticisme" in 1920, was one of the few champions of the new trend. In his gallery "L'Effort Moderne" he displayed examples of constructive art, as a logical development from Cubism up to Mondrian, under the title "Du cubisme à une renaissance plastique" in 1922. In the following year he devoted an exhibition to de Stijl. This gave Theo van Doesburg an opportunity to propagate in Paris the design ideas of de Stijl, which extended into all spheres of life and had many points of contact with Le Corbusier's theories. It was this event that persuaded him to make Paris the center of his international endeavors from that time on. The impact of the exhibition was considerable on an international scale, but in Paris the response was weak. The fate of a Stijl exhibition in Nancy in 1925 was no better. The lack of interest of the leading Parisian circles in the Stijl is exemplified by the fact that in 1925 the Dutch group was excluded from the International Exhibition of the Decorative Arts. This admittedly evoked a violent international protest, but the

Otto Freundlich: Composition, 1930

Sonia Delaunay: Rythme coloré, 1953

delicate in color and corresponding to human dimensions in their proportions (ill. p. 127). Theo van Doesburg also made use of rectangluar forms, but placed diagonally like the compositions which at that time characterized his painting. These "counter-compositions", as he called them, gave his rooms — in contrast to the more severe, filigree designs of Sophie Taeuber-Arp — a disquieting dynamic force (ill. p. 75). The integrated decoration of the ten rooms of the "Aubette", which was celebrated in a special issue of "de stijl" in 1928, was one of the greatest painterly and plastic achievements of the constructive spirit. Jean Arp, himself from Strasbourg, said later that it "would have been a highlight of the town with hardly any parallel in modern architecture".

The overall concept for the interior decoration of the "Aubette" was doubtless due to Van Doesburg: the creative use of color in space. A "synoptic effect" of painting and architecture was the aim. "To attain this end the painted surfaces had to be in relation with each other both architecturally and as paintings. The whole had to be designed as a solid body: construction and composition, space and time, statics and dynamics held in a single grasp." The "Aubette" embodied a — perhaps immemorial — painter's dream which Van Doesburg shared with his companions: that of placing the observer not in front of the art work

but in the midst of it. Art has returned periodically to this dream ever since.

Sophie Taeuber was the one who had most to do with the actual execution of the "Aubette" renovation. She supervised all the work down to details such as the placing of the electric switches. Born in Davos, Sophie Taeuber had undergone most of her art training in Germany and was very well equipped for this integration of even secondary elements in an artistic whole. From 1916 to 1929 she taught textile design at the School of Applied Art in Zurich. Starting from the principle of the interpenetration of warp and weft as used in weaving, she had begun to paint purely geometric horizontal-vertical compositions on her own initiative in 1916. These formed the foundation of her later constructive work. Having been introduced to the circle of the Zurich Dadaists by her friend and later husband Jean Arp, she also appeared as a dancer in the performances of the "Cabaret Voltaire" and in 1918 composed the abstract puppet play "König Hirsch" (King Stag), with robot-like figures of cylindrical character. In her paintings and reliefs, which she developed systematically from the middle of the twenties on, purely geometric compositions of strictly ordered lines, bars, rectangles, triangles and circles predominate, although biomorphic forms also occur sporadically. Her constructive

122

Auguste Herbin: Le Nid, 1955

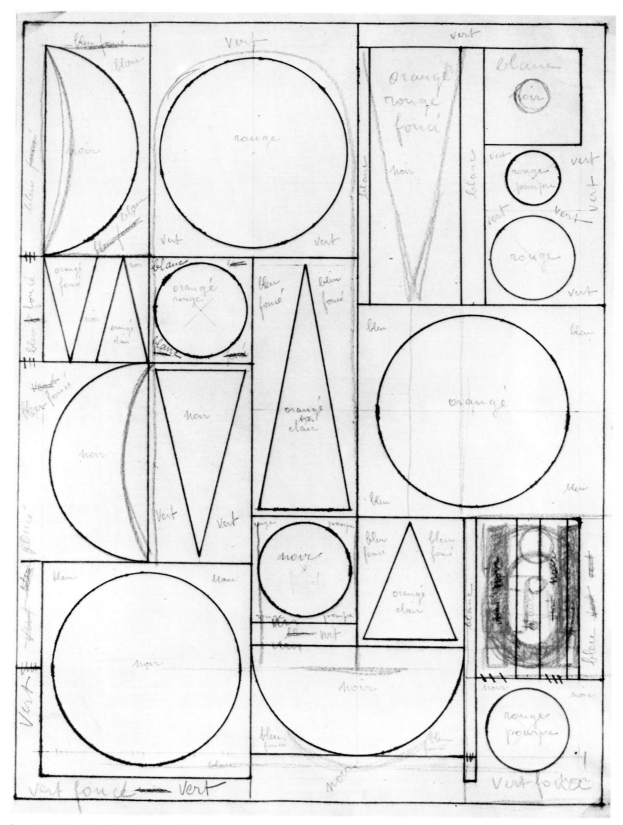

Auguste Herbin: Project for a painting, c. 1955

124

Auguste Herbin: Main, 1960

Jean Arp: Tête-Heaume I, 1959

tive tendencies. It belongs instead to the "Concrete Art" which Arp himself helped to establish, an art which is not arrived at by abstraction but must be understood as the "concretization" of mental, not objectively inspired form-ideas (ill. p. 126).

Michel Seuphor, chronicler of the art developments of those years in Paris, describes the situation around 1930 in his retrospective account "Le Style et le cri": "It was a sad time for painters, and especially for those who had devoted themselves to geometry. The hopeful euphoria of the years following the war had sunk into the past. In 1929 the galleries of Paris sold nothing, not even the works of the Surrealists, although these were splendidly supported by the advertising ballyhoo that this movement had made use of for years. Kupka, disappointed and embittered, lived wholly withdrawn from artistic life. Herbin was not yet Herbin . . . Vantongerloo, who had settled in Paris in 1927, could hardly make ends meet on the pension he received as a former Belgian combatant. The Delaunays applied art to fashion: Sonia had temporarily given up painting as a survival measure. Mondrian sold a picture from time to time to a rare art lover from Central Europe and was able to manage by austere housekeeping . . . Many others were on the closest of terms with sheer poverty."

The list of painters and sculptors working in the constructive idiom in the Paris of the twenties—often in an almost conspiratorial atmosphere—is astonishingly long. Few of the artists, however, were French; most of them were foreigners who had come to stay in Paris for a time or had settled there permanently, either of their own free will or because they had been forced to emigrate from their own countries. Among the French—apart from Auguste Herbin—were Marcelle Cahn (ill. p. 162), André Heurtaux (ill. p. 132), Jean Gorin (ill. p. 130, 131), and Jean Hélion (ill. p. 133). They were all born between 1895 and 1905 and worked along geometric and constructive lines but with marked individual differences. They were influenced mainly by de Stijl and in some cases directly by Theo van Doesburg. Around the year 1930 all of these artists were beginning their mature work.

While some of the foreigners were isolated individuals, others lived in "artists' colonies". The largest of these consisted of Russian emigrants, but there were only very few among them who participated actively in the further development of constructive art. Natalia Goncharova and Mikhail Larionov, for instance, returned to figurative art in their theatrical work. Ivan Puni took the same step even more decisively, returning by a rather curious route from Suprematism via a new Cubo-Futurism to traditional realist paintings which he signed with the name Jean Pougny. Alexandra Exter, Pavel Mansurov and to some extent Mikhail Andreenko, Yuri Annenkov, Yuri Yakulov and Serge Charchoune continued to work in the Constructivist style. One of the strong personalities in this group was Sonia Delaunay-Terk, who from 1910 on was engaged in a constant give-and-take with Robert Delaunay. She developed in the twenties a free and forceful geometric style in which squares or triangles and particularly concentric circles and arcs predominate. The color rhythm, based on the principle of simultaneous contrast, echoes the rhythm of the forms (ill. p. 122). Sonia Delaunay's work for the theater as well as her fashion design

work, often black and white or in two colors, but occasionally in a rich range of differentiated hues, reveals her from the first as an artist independent both of de Stijl and of Eastern European Constructivism. Sophie Taeuber's pictorial concepts—basic patterns employing similar elements but offering wide scope for variation—led her to a strictly rational but sensitively controlled constructive art of her own which was to set a trend in the thirties (ill. pp. 127–130). It has—except for some joint compositions—only marginal points of contact with the free shapes occurring in the reliefs of Jean Arp. The latter's sculptural work, beginning in 1931, is organic, sensual, irrational and biomorphic in character and has little to do with construc-

Sophie Taeuber-Arp: Composition Aubette, 1927/28

familiarized the general public with the "style simultané", and in this way she helped to prepare the path for "Art Déco".

Of the Russian sculptors living in Paris, Ossip Zadkine and Jacques Lipchitz continued to follow the Cubist tradition. Antoine Pevsner, who had left Russia in 1923, produced his Constructivist sculptural work in Paris in accordance with the principles set down in the "Realist Manifesto" he had published with his brother Naum Gabo in Moscow in 1920. If art is to correspond to the realities of modern life with its overload of science and technology, it must be based on two main elements: space and time. In the sculptural domain volume is not the only means of spatial expression. Kinetic and dynamic elements offer a possibility of expressing real time, which static rhythms can never do. In Pevsner's work the complete breakaway from the figurative motif takes place between 1924 and 1928. He dismantles volume into a complicated system of surfaces of metal or transparent plastic which are assembled at acute or obtuse angles to form intricate constructions and thus to permit the surrounding space to flow into the skeleton of the sculptural shape. The straight or curved edges of his plates enter into dynamic relationships with each other. This gives the relief-like or free-standing "Constructions in space" the suggestion of high tension, of concentrated force. They are sinewy sculptures with a "dynamic rhythm", to use Pevsner's own term. They are also a logical development of Tatlin's and Naum Gabo's three-dimensional ideas, and they led Pevsner almost inevitably to resolve the surfaces that constituted his spatial compositions into clustered lines of force. He took this step in the early thirties. From this time on Pevsner saw the individual surface as the product of a line displaced about given axes in time by an operative force. Technically, this led him to the formation of surfaces by means of soldered brass wires (ill. p. 119).

Compared to this logical and personal development of the Constructivist heritage, the Hungarian sculptor Etienne Béothy remained merely within the confines of a partly geometric, partly free and often elegant non-objectivity (ill. p. 118). Much the same applies to his countryman Alfred Reth, whose pictures and reliefs did not diverge from the Cubo-Futurist tradition.

Among the German artists who found a second home in Paris, Hans Reichel deserves mention. He incorporated constructive impulses received from his friends Klee and

Sophie Taeuber-Arp: Composition à cercles à bras angulaires superposés, 1930

Kandinsky in a non-objective pictorial world which reveals in its forms and colors the musician and poet as much as the painter. Otto Freundlich, painter and sculptor, was unquestionably possessed of a more powerful talent. He had lived in Paris, with some interruptions, since 1909. He proceeded from abstraction to a type of free geometric composition that belonged to no particular school. The picture surface always consists of free geometric shapes which are mostly divided into rectangular patches of color. The tones grow lighter or darker, with a wide range of gradations, from one rectangle to the other. Freundlich used a technique of thick color application involving an accentuated craftsmanship. The subtle interplay of the bright, luminous zones, mostly in the center, and the darkly glowing or twilight zones nearer the edges depends on a rich palette of hues (ill. pp. 120, 121). The result is an impression of rich splendor reminiscent of Byzantine mosaics. Living entirely for his art and often struggling to survive, Freundlich regarded himself as an exponent of an intellectual renaissance guided by reason and his work as systematic, constructive art. "The work of the artist is a sum of constructive actions," he

said, and believed in an artistic revolution which was to lead finally to a new, active and creative life.

The strongest, most compact and influential group consisted of the members of de Stijl who had moved to Paris, even though their personal relations were sometimes strained, as were those between Mondrian and Van Doesburg. The Dutch artist Cesar Domela, who had joined the Stijl in 1924, had gone beyond Mondrian's Neo-Plasticism and had developed, parallel to Heurtaux (ill. p. 132) and Gorin (ill. pp. 130, 131), the principle of the diagonally arranged rectangular counter-composition postulated by Van Doesburg. Later he attempted—much as Gorin did, and in full conformity with the precepts of de Stijl—to expand the painting from its surface existence into the three dimensions of the colored relief. This led him in the thirties to the "tableau-relief" in which the materials—metal sheets and acrylic plastic—also play an important part. These dynamic creations in space are lacking in the constructive discipline evinced, for instance, by the "plastic structures" of Gorin.

The Belgian Georges Vantongerloo, who had lived in Menton since 1920, came to Paris in 1928. As can be

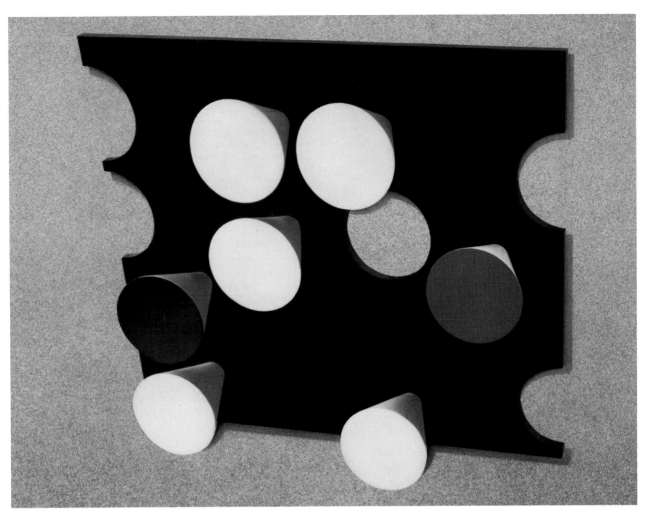

Sophie Taeuber-Arp: Relief à cercles découpés et cônes surgissants, 1936

gathered from his "Reflections" on space and time published in "de stijl" in 1918, he was interested primarily in problems of space. He found solutions to them in sculptural compositions that were concerned with the relationships between volumes. In his painting Vantongerloo occupied himself at that time with delicate horizontal-vertical designs which must be understood as pictorial representations of mathematical functions (ill. p 83). They consisted of patches of color set sparingly between finely drawn coordinates on a white ground. In the thirties fine colored curves on a white ground, expressing energies, replaced the straight lines running at right angles to each other (ill. p. 135). In Vantongerloo's late work, characterized by a preoccupation with the "incommensurable" and thus with cosmic space, sculptures of colored acrylic plastic predominate.

The weak response to these various constructive trends in the art world of Paris cannot be attributed only to a traditionalist spirit. The reproach repeatedly leveled against Constructivism by the critics of the day — that it was lacking in "lyricism" — is also only half the truth. Nor does the charge raised by Ozenfant in 1928 in his publication "Art"

get to the heart of the matter: "Arrested by the mechanical spectacle of modern machine life and impressed — under the influence of Dadaism and Purism — by Léger and by earlier memories of Archipenko, the Constructivists produced constructed paintings that smack of the machine. A few talented artists were occasionally successful and interesting. The school for a time had a big reputation in Central Europe and Russia; today it influences stage decoration and with Gabo and Pevsner has found its way into Diaghilev's Russian ballet, as for that matter have all modern schools with the exception of Purism, which is not decorative enough for the purpose."

The true explanation of the lack of understanding for constructive art at that time is to be found in Surrealism. André Breton's "Surrealist Manifesto" of 1924 had initiated a literary and later an artistic movement that attributed primary importance to the emotional and irrational sources of creative inspiration and expressly rejected the rational, the controlling understanding. The leading figure of this movement was not the engineer but the psychoanalyst. Attention was turned to the unconscious and the dream, and association was held to be more interesting

Sophie Taeuber-Arp: Echelonnement désaxé, 1934

Jean Gorin: Composition No. 18, 1961

than construction. This implied a shift of emphasis from the form to the content of art, to the symbolic cipher and even to the figurative and objective motif. The principle of "écriture automatique", automatic writing, postulated by Breton, was a radical break with the conscious handling of pictorial elements. Surrealism remained the leading school in France till the end of the thirties, and by virtue of its penetration into all domains of life it was the art form with which people were best able to identify themselves—a Romanticism that touched upon the mysterious and nameless reaches of human existence with all its secret wishes and fears, and a form of self-defense against the rationalization and mechanization of life. André Breton had written as early as 1924 in his Surrealist Manifesto: "We still live under the dominion of logic. Yet, today logical processes are applied only to the solution of second-rank problems. The still fashionable absolute rationalism allows us only to consider facts that are closely dependent on our experience. I do not need to point out that experience has also had to accept limits. It is going round in circles in a cage."

To constructive artists with their rational working method, their optimism, their idealistic belief that they were helping to build a more beautiful and better world, Surrealism inevitably appeared as a relapse into a prelogical world of magic and hocus-pocus. It was also their great adversary in the everyday world of art in Paris, down to the window display. Some constructive artists gave up and retired, like Mondrian, into the peace of their studios. Others saw Surrealism as the enemy against which they must take arms. Something had to be done. Their leader and spokesman was the Belgian writer Michel Seuphor. He had published the magazine "Het Overzicht" (The Overview) with the painter Josef Peeters in Antwerp in 1921–1925. Through this publication he had been in contact with the leading representatives of non-objective art in all Europe and had helped to disseminate the new ideas in Belgium. The painters Félix de Boeck and more particularly Victor Servranckx had thereby become important supporters of de Stijl (ill. p. 114). Seuphor himself, like Van Doesburg, had established personal relationships with the main representatives of constructive art in the course of extensive travels throughout Europe. He collected like-minded artists around him after settling in Paris in 1925 and presented their work to the public in a number of exhibitions. The regular meetings of Mondrian, Vantongerloo, the Futurist painter and musician Luigi Russolo, the couples Arp, Pevsner and Van Rees in Seuphor's apartment led, on the initiative of the Uruguayan painter Joaquin Torrès-Garcia, to the founding in 1929 of the group "Cercle et Carré". It was under this programmatic name that the group presented in April/May 1930 an international Constructivist exhibition uniting 130 works by 46 painters and sculptors from all parts of Europe. All the leading names were represented with the exception of Theo van Doesburg, who chose to keep his distance, and Moholy-Nagy. The exhibition and the magazine of the same name published by Seuphor at the same time were meant as a challenge to Surrealism. And in fact "Cercle et Carré" for the first time opened up a breach in Paris for geometric non-objective art. Even so, there was, as Seuphor reported, not a single positive review in the French press. The rest of Europe, however, responded

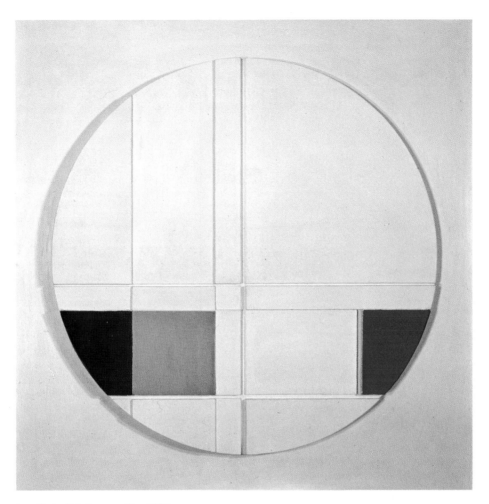

Jean Gorin: Relief composition, 1937

Jean Gorin: Contrepoint No. 31, 1948

André Heurtaux: Untitled, 1939

with enthusiastic approval. Seuphor, falling seriously ill, had to leave Paris and cease all work; he was therefore unable to follow up his first success. The small magazine "Cercle et Carré", though it was important because of the texts of Seuphor, Mondrian and Le Corbusier and its international scope, did not survive more than three numbers, and the group itself disintegrated in the absence of its leader.

Van Doesburg, who had obstinately kept away from the group, perhaps because of Seuphor's friendship with Mondrian, managed to start a fight with Vantongerloo at the preview of "Cercle et Carré". He issued a small magazine of his own under the title "Art concret" in May 1930, while the exhibition was still running. The magazine was to be the mouthpiece of an opposing group of the same name, which included Van Doesburg, the Swede Otto-Gustaf Carlsund, Jean Hélion, the Russian Leon Tutundjian and a little-known artist by the name of Marcel Wantz. The group—if it really existed—remained insignificant, and the magazine ran only to one issue. But Van Doesburg had created an opportunity to present his new concept of a non-objective art going beyond de Stijl, Neo-Plasticism, Elementarism and Eastern European Constructivism.

Van Doesburg's "Manifesto of Concrete Art" is dated January 1930 and opposes abstraction: "Concrete and not abstract painting. For we have left behind us the time of searching and of speculative experiment. In seeking for purity the artist was forced to abstract from the natural forms that concealed the plastic elements. In order to express himself and to create art-forms he was compelled to destroy the natural form. Today the idea of the art-form is as obsolete as the idea of the natural form. We look forward to the era of pure painting. For nothing is more concrete, more real than a line, a color surface. Are, say, a woman, a tree, a cow concrete elements on a canvas? No—a woman, a tree, a cow are concrete in the natural state, but in the painted state they are far more abstract, illusory, indefinite, speculative than a line.—Concrete and not abstract painting. For the mind has reached the state of maturity: it needs clear, intellectual media to manifest itself in a concrete way." Van Doesburg then

turns against individualism, against all emotionalism. "Only the mind is creative . . . It is the thought that is really important in all spheres of human activity. The evolution of painting is nothing else but the search of the intellect for the truth, as a culture of the visual. Everything is measurable, even the mind . . ." In another passage he writes: "In painting only color is true. Color is a constant energy, determined by its contrast with another color. Color is the basic substance of painting; it signifies itself only. Painting is a means of realizing a thought in optical terms: every picture is a color-thought . . . The work exists as a whole in the consciousness before it is translated into materials. It is also necessary for the execution to be of a technical perfection that is equal to that of the mental project." Van Doesburg expressly rejects all handicraft, everything that is merely incidental in the artist's handwriting. "We work with the magnitudes of mathematics (Euclidean or non-Euclidean) and of science, that is, with the medium of thought."

The conception of "Concrete Art" in the sense of the concretization of a pictorial thought without any dependence on visible reality is not Van Doesburg's invention. The German Constructivist Max Burchartz had used it earlier, no doubt prompted by a new edition, in 1922, of the "Aesthetics" of the German philosopher Georg Wilhelm Friedrich Hegel. In accordance with his dialectical method, Hegel explains the process of art as a concretization of abstract thought and thus considers "concrete" as being the opposite of "abstract".

Max Bill, who repeatedly returned to Van Doesburg's definition from 1936 on to clarify its exact implications, said: "The purpose of concretion is to make abstract thoughts accessible to the senses in reality." An essay by Mondrian in the second issue of "Cercle et Carré" also shows that this interpretation of "concrete" was in the air in 1930: in a critical comparison of "Realistic and Superrealistic art" (by which latter term he means not Surrealism but geometric non-objectivity) he investigates the nature of "morphoplastic" and "neo-plastic" art. Only the second, he concludes, is able to reveal by plastic means the laws of a truly human life. This life—the result of the exploration and shaping of a "concrete equilibrium" (équilibre concret)—is the essential thing for the Neo-Plastic artist. Since the term "concrete" was first used by the circle of the geometric and constructive artists, it was soon being equated with "geometric". Such a narrow interpretation of their "universal language" was not the intention of Van Doesburg and the artists who identified themselves with this terminology: Jean Arp, Wassily Kandinsky and Max Bill. Paul Klee says aptly in his essay on "Exact Experiments in the Realm of Art" (1928): "We construct and construct, but intuition is still a good thing."

In Van Doesburg's own work the simultaneous counter-compositions (ill. p. 77) are joined in 1930 by purely arithmetical works which give an accurate idea of his conception of Concrete Art. How would his painting have developed from this point onward? Events such as the "International Exhibition of Concrete Art" in Stockholm occupied his time, as did the building of his house in Meudon, his talks and lectures. In increasing distress as a result of his asthmatic complaints, he died on March 7, 1931, in Davos. He had lived to see a new union of progressive artists being formed, not without some contribution from

Jean Hélion: Composition orthogonale, 1932

his side. After the demise of "Cercle et Carré" Vantongerloo had attempted, with Herbin and Béothy, to rally the scattered members and other non-figurative artists. In May 1931 the international group "Abstraction-Création, Art non-figuratif" was officially founded. With the aid of a magazine of the same name the movement very quickly evoked a wide international response. For a time it united as suscribers over 400 artists living in Europe and in North and South America. The magazine, with Arp, Gleizes, Hélion, Herbin, Kupka, Tutundjian, Valmier and Vantongerloo as editorial collaborators — Pevsner acted as reader — appeared between 1932 and 1936 in five annual issues. Almost all the significant non-objective artists of the time contributed. "Abstraction-Création" published programmatic statements and manifestos as well as a good deal of illustrative material.

In retrospect "Abstraction-Création" appears as a faithful and many-faceted mirror of constructive trends in the first half of the thirties. The intention of Mondrian, Van Doesburg and Seuphor to confront triumphant Surrealism, with its prevalence of unreal and emotional elements, with a pure art of rational sensibility seemed to have been realized with "Abstraction-Création". The group had become a repository for the various tendencies within the field of non-figurative art, and it was free from any stiff dogmatism. Artists of the same bent were united in numerous exhibitions in Paris and the rest of Europe. Important impulses from the center of the movement reached groups of constructive artists in the various countries. The most impressive example of this is the group of Polish Constructivists. Michel Seuphor had collaborated with Jan Brzekowski, who published a Franco-Polish magazine in Paris, as early as 1929. He was one of those who now initiated the union of the revolutionary artists Karol Hiller, Katarzyna Kobro, Henryk Stazewski, Wladyslaw Strzeminski and others in the group "a.r.". The cooperation of these Poles in "Abstraction-Création" was one of the factors that led to the founding of the "International Collection of Modern Art" in the Museum of Lodz. By 1932 the collection already comprised 72 works, most of them donated or exchanged by members of the "Abstraction-Création" group.

In spite of the social and economic problems due to the worldwide slump, the exponents of geometric constructive art were optimistic in their theoretical utterances. The development of technology, science and industry, and the phenomenon of the big city with its ever denser traffic were seen from a positive angle in the sense that the responsibility of the artist in the shaping of this modern world was underlined, and it was repeatedly suggested that art in its conventional forms must disappear, making way for the participation of the artist in the integral design of modern ways of living.

In a text written in 1939 but published only after his death on "The new plastic reality", Jean Gorin is not content with the historical derivation and justification of geometric abstract art but extrapolates its role into the future:

"It was Cubism that took the most consequential step known to art history when it attacked the real problems and made it possible for art to free itself completely from dependence on the subject, from a descriptive literary role and from imitation by the systematic geometric analysis of objects. Working with forms became a truly creative act. True, Cubism did not advance to absolute non-objective painting. For a time collective, almost anonymous work was pushed forward in hieratic constructions of pronounced severity, and the pictures appeared almost crystalline. Shortly afterwards, however, individuality got the upper hand again and the last goal was not attained.

"At the same time, in the countries with an advanced civilization, a big international movement was born whose aim was the realization of a non-objective art, the study of a pure plastic art that was freed of every figurative element, or in other words was purely abstract and constructive.

"The decisive reasons for this plastic renaissance are easy to understand; it is enough to contemplate the times we live in. Art was always linked to life, but the plastic requirements of the man of the steel and machine age and of the scientific revolution can never be the same as those of the caveman. Man has reached such a stage of evolution that his intellectual, poetic and plastic needs are very marked and highly sensitized. The machine has completely changed our environment, industrialization and standardization have brought a new, clear and precise optical perception. The spirit of science and of truth guides the cultured human being, and the artist must today satisfy all his requirements.

"Constructive, non-objective art is in keeping with this new spirit and reveals the true plastics of art. Pure plastics, says Mondrian, is the aesthetic expression of comprehensive reality (the cosmos) and of things (the microcosmos), which man can create solely with a picture of lines and pure colors or of planes in space, without any figurative element. This is what the new plastic reality consists of: it points to the future, seeking the constructive basis of a synthetic, free, static, dynamic, and even kinetic art. It is the shortest connection between man and the universe, enables structures and the timeless values of art to shine in their full brilliance and expresses universality, unity and the cosmos."

The optimism that initially inspired the spokesmen of "Abstraction-Création" and led to international successes was, however, not destined to endure. The "battle" against Surrealism had been fought with some success, and constructive art as a legitimate form of artistic expression had been publicized all over the globe. But new difficulties, this time of a political nature, loomed ahead. The victory of National Socialism in Germany in 1933 began to cast growing shadows on the international political scene. Gloomy presentiments, gathering after the middle of the thirties, gave way to open fear of an imminent war and began to paralyse artistic developments. Constructivist artists in Germany became the victims of the Nazi art policy and were condemned to choose between emigration and silence. Some of them chose Paris as their new home; they hoped to find a fertile artistic and human atmosphere in the center of "Abstraction-Création". Foremost among the new arrivals was Wassily Kandinsky, who in 1933, after the closing of the Bauhaus, moved from Berlin to Neuilly and remained there till his death in December 1944, free from all teaching duties and able to devote himself to his late work.

The outbreak of the Spanish Civil War in 1936 was a fore-

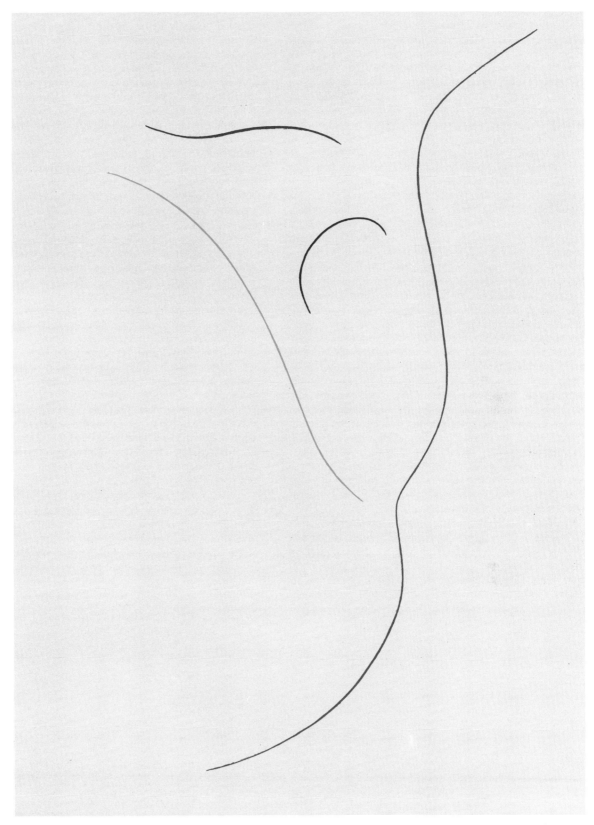

Georges Vantongerloo: Relations de lignes et couleurs, 1939

taste of things to come. But it was not only the political scene that presaged ill; the economic situation was likewise tense, especially in France at the time of the Popular Front. Artists suffered from this more than others. Constructive art hardly had any buyers. The magazine "Abstraction-Création" succumbed as much as anything to the economic strain. In 1937 Sophie Taeuber-Arp attempted to provide a modest substitute when she issued, on her own initative, the trilingual magazine "Plastique". The first number was devoted to the memory of Kasimir Malevich, the last appeared in 1939 just before the outbreak of war. Some lines by the Zurich art historian Sigfried Giedion contained in it characterize the situation then prevailing: "On the one hand a public art of enormous bulk, on the other the work of half a dozen painters upon whose shoulders all research and discovery rested. They knew that as far as success and confirmation were concerned their position was hopeless. The right to recognition which every ordinary individual can claim for his work was ... almost without exception denied them. The fact that such people do not die out, that they create their values at the expense of their own lives is an example of a heroic attitude that takes a different form in every epoch. Outwardly, they lived in the greatest isolation. At the time their work was moving further and further away from the taste of the public, of critics and collectors. In return a type of artist came into being whose work approached ever nearer to that of the inventor, the investigator and explorer. The less an artist tries to please a public, the greater is the chance of his striking those subterranean springs from which every era draws its sustenance."

The optimistic and "heroic attitude" of the small group of artists Sigfried Giedion refers to can be detected in a text published in 1937 by Mondrian in "Circle", an international survey of constructive art:

"We live in a difficult but interesting epoch. After a secular culture, a turning point has arrived; this shows itself in all the branches of human activity. Limiting ourselves here to science and art, we notice that, just as in medicine some have discovered the natural laws relating to physical life, in art some have discovered the artistic laws relating to plastics. In spite of all opposition, these facts have become movements. But confusion still reigns in them. Through science we are becoming more and more conscious of the fact that our physical state depends in great measure on what we eat, on the manner in which our food is arranged, and on the physical exercise which we take. Through art we are becoming more and more conscious of the fact that the work depends in large measure on the constructive elements which we use and on the constructions which we create. We will gradually realize that we have not hithero paid sufficient attention to constructive physical elements in their relation to the human body, nor to the constructive plastic elements in their relation to art. That which we eat has deteriorated through a refinement of natural produce. To say this appears to invoke a return to a primitive natural state and to be in opposition to the exigencies of pure plastic art, which degenerates precisely through figurative trappings. But a return to pure natural nourishment does not mean a return to the state of primitive man; it means on the contrary that cultured man obeys the laws of nature discovered and applied by science.

"Similarly in non-figurative art, to recognize and apply natural laws is not evidence of a retrograde step; the pure abstract expression of these laws proves that the exponent of non-figurative art associates himself with the most advanced progress and the most cultured minds, that he is an exponent of denaturalized nature, of civilization.

"In life, sometimes the spirit has been overemphasized at the expense of the body, sometimes one has been preoccupied with the body and neglected the spirit; similarly in art content and form have alternately been overemphasized or neglected because their inseparable unity has not been clearly realized.

"To create this unity in art, a balance of the one and the other must be created. It is an achievement of our time to have approached such a balance in a field in which disequilibrium still reigns. Disequilibrium means conflict, disorder. Conflict is also a part of life and of art, but it is not the whole of life or universal beauty. Real life is the mutual interaction of two opposites of the same value but of a different aspect and nature. Its plastic expression is universal beauty."

Incubation and Radiation

Concrete Art in Switzerland

The political climate of Europe in the nineteen-thirties was unfavorable to Constructivist trends, and for that matter to art in general. In every European country the growing fear of war, even more than the economic depression, paralysed the progress of art — not so much the actual artistic activities as the readiness of wide sectors of the population to recognize modern art as an integral part of social life. The instinctive desire to preserve the traditional and accepted culture made every bold artistic experiment look like an attempt to undermine established values. The Utopian conceptions behind constructive art forms were inevitably felt to be revolutionary and subversive. From a present-day viewpoint the reactionary art policy of National Socialist Germany from 1933 on can be seen as merely an extreme expression of what was in fact a widespread attitude. It added a new note to this resistance to everything new only in so far as the breakaway of European art from objective realism — then already a historical fact — was openly declared to be internationalist and consequently un-German. To the Nazi rulers all developments since Expressionism were blasphemous and destructive attacks on human dignity and were opposed by the proclamation of another ideal — that of a bogus naturalism that was claimed to be the art of the people. Critical movements such as Dadaism and advances into non-objectivity or into geometric constructive idioms were branded as intellectualist, Bolshevist or Jewish aberrations and heresies. Hitler's tirades against "degenerate art" make it clear with what utter lack of differentiation everything progressive was damned as being noxious to the people. Even in countries that watched the rise of the Third Reich with trepidation this condemnation of contemporary art fell on willing ears, although the specifically German ideology was rejected and the resistance to modernism was justified as an expression of the national (and thus often anti-German) character and conscience.

Switzerland, a small democratic country at that time imprisoned between Italian Fascism and German Nazism, was not immune to this reactionary attitude to art. But developments here revealed what a great deal a few committed believers can achieve when they are determined to defend a cause against a broad but passive opposition. These few individuals succeeded in making Switzerland a center of constructive art from which the movement could once more radiate into the outside world after 1945. The role that Switzerland was to play in the history of constructive art also depended on a few other considerations. After 1900 Ferdinand Hodler had gravitated from Art Nouveau to a Symbolist and later to a purely painterly Expressionism. His successors Cuno Amiet and Giovanni Giacometti, though never forfeiting their own individuality, had joined the school of Pont-Aven and had passed on to Fauvism, while Augusto Giacometti had been practising since 1905 a form of non-objective painting with dots of color that anticipated Tachisme by half a century. Between 1910 and 1912 a group of Swiss painters also adopted Cubism, adding Orphist and Futurist elements to produce a locally colored Futuro-Cubism. Alice Bailly, Gustave Buchet, Jean Crotti, Johannes Itten, Oskar Lüthy, Louis Moilliet and Otto Morach all took part in this development. The really new impulse, however, was to come from Weggis, where in 1911 a number of young artists, led by Oskar Lüthy and Jean Arp, joined forces to form the "Moderner Bund" and obtained the support of Matisse, Picasso, Othon Friesz, Auguste Herbin, and other Parisian artists for exhibitions in Lucerne. Connections were also established through Paul Klee and Louis Moilliet to the "Blaue Reiter" (Blue Rider) in Munich, which led to exhibitions of the internationally constituted "Moderner Bund" in Munich and later in the "Sturm" gallery in Berlin. In 1912 an exhibition in the Kunsthaus in Zurich embraced all the Cubists working in Paris as well as Kandinsky, Klee and Marc of the "Blue Rider" movement in Munich. It was the beginning of a series of exhibitions of international contemporary art which went on till 1914, the most important of them being a Picasso exhibition in the Kunsthalle at Basel. As far as can be ascertained, this was Picasso's first exhibition outside of France and his first in a public art institution anywhere.

Two private galleries — Tanner and Neupert — which represented Cubism, Orphism and Futurism gave Zurich a leading place among Swiss art centers from about 1912 on. After the outbreak of war in 1914 the city also became an international turntable for economic and cultural exchanges in the no-man's-land between the two belligerent groups. Switzerland benefited in particular from the artists and intellectuals who, as refugees or Pacifists, found their way to Zurich. Jean Arp, whose situation in France was jeopardized by his Alsatian origin, settled in Zurich in 1915, gathered a few friends from the "Moderner Bund" around him and presented his collages, Cubist in inspiration but already non-objective, in an exhibition. His partners in the show were Otto and Adja van Rees. "These works," wrote Arp in the catalog, "are constructions of lines, surfaces, shapes, colors." At the exhibition he met Sophie Taeuber, who was busy on even more radical compositions with geometric surface elements. The two were soon producing joint works — "duo-dessins", as Arp called them later — that explored the possibilities of strict horizontal-vertical orders. Together with the surface compositions which Johannes Itten was painting independently at the same time in Stuttgart, they represent the inception of Swiss constructive art.

Arp and Sophie Taeuber continued this geometric work parallel to their activity in the Zurich Dada movement, which was founded by Arp in conjunction with the writers Hugo Ball, Richard Huelsenbeck, Tristan Tzara and the painter Marcel Janco in February 1916. While Arp developed an "organic" style — in part non-objective, in part abstract and with an ironic touch — that was chiefly embodied in wood reliefs, Sophie Taeuber concentrated her efforts, both in her own work and in her teaching at the School of Applied Art, on purely geometric orders. She built up motifs evolved from rectangles, triangles and circles as "elementary shapes" into complex compositions. Starting with the settings for an "abstract" puppet play based on Pocci's "King Stag", completed in 1918, she took up geometric painting in oils (ill. p. 139), producing an occasional wood relief no doubt due to the influence of Jean Arp.

This geometric and constructive movement was strengthened for a time in Zurich by Hans Richter from Berlin and by the Swede Viking Eggeling, who were both interested in the study of gradually modified geometric compositions, or in other words in fugal movements. Both investigated, in their "plastic counterpoint", relationships with musical composition. The Swiss painters in the Dadaist group were more interested in the suggestions for the treatment of color furnished by Delaunay's Orphism. There was hardly any contact at that time with contemporary Russian art, apart from friendly relations with Kandinsky, whose work from his "Blue Rider" period had been shown in Zurich through the good offices of Jean Arp. The situation of Russian art before the war, however, was represented by the work of Alexei Jawlensky, who was a regular guest at the Dada soirées in Zurich with his friend Marianne von Werefkin. Nothing is known at all about contacts with de Stijl, which had been founded in the Netherlands in 1917. It seems in fact that the overtures to constructive art made in Zurich between 1915 and 1918 were autonomous. The key figure of the movement, and possibly its real initiator, was Sophie Taeuber.

Some influence was also exerted by Francis Picabia, who joined the Dadaists in Zurich in 1918 and was greeted as the founder of machine art. He took part in their publications and for a time issued his own magazine "391" from Zurich. In the meantime the group known as "Das Neue Leben" (The New Life) had been founded in Basel, uniting Cubists and abstract artists. An exhibition in the Kunsthaus in Zurich led in 1919 to the fusion of Swiss and foreign artists in the group "Artistes radicaux". The Swiss Futuro-Cubists were among its spokesmen, as were also Arp, Eggeling and Richter. Their politically motivated manifesto reflects the conviction that progressive artists should take an active part in the creation of a new, socially just and internationally conciliatory society after the war: "As representatives of an intrinsic domain of culture, we artists wish to participate in the development of the ideas of the State: we want to exist within the State, as part of its life, and we want to share in all its responsibilities ... The spirit of abstract art represents an enormous development of the human being's sense of freedom ... Our highest endeavor is toward the creation of an intellectual basis for the mutual understanding of all

people ..." The Swiss "radical artists" were soon to find agreement on these Utopian social objectives in the avant-gardes of Germany, the Netherlands, Eastern Europe and Russia. The opportunity for contacts was provided by the international congress of progressive artists held in Dusseldorf in 1922 and the congress of the Constructivists in Weimar in 1923, which was also regarded by its participants as a farewell party for the Dadaist movement. The pioneer period of abstract, non-objective art in Switzerland had thus come to an end.

The social tensions that began to come to a head after World War I announced themselves in Switzerland with a general strike in 1918. The artistic avant-garde was leftist and supported the cause of the workers. The advance toward the establishment of a Socialist state in Russia that began with the October Revolution encouraged a belief in the dawn of a juster age. Only a few artists and intellectuals, however, saw parallels or connections between social and cultural progress. The great majority of the workers were culturally conservative, their views being modeled on those of the "petite bourgeoisie". The middle classes, who rejected all really progressive art as "Bolshevist", were prepared to accept only a moderate form of modern art that busied itself with the great strides made since the time of Cézanne. The Swiss art scene was dominated by a type of painting based on Cuno Amiet and Giovanni Giacometti and characterized by a certain reserve toward international developments. The influences of Cubism, Fauvism and Expressionism were blended in an artistic idiom that differed from region to region and showed marked individual traits. A formally controlled, expressive style of painting, sometimes cheerful and optimistic in its coloring, sometimes dark and melancholic, was prevalent in the exhibitions. Sorties from this circumspect world of art were rare, leading into constructive areas chiefly in strictly composed murals. More often, attempts to break away only heightened the expressive component.

A few young architects from Basel and Zurich were important exponents of artistic progress and of a constructive approach. They were believers in the "neues bauen", the "new building" envisioned by Walter Gropius in his first Bauhaus book "International Architecture" in 1925, by Adolf Behne in "Der moderne Zweckbau" (The Modern Purpose-Built Structure), and by Le Corbusier in his programmatic essay "Vers une Architecture" (Towards a New Architecture). The ideas of this new architecture, which was no longer to consist of erected structures but of spaces designed on constructive principles, were closely bound up both in the East and the West with the advances of constructive art. There was therefore a direct confrontation, this time in the architectural field, with Russian Constructivism and de Stijl in the Netherlands.

The onset of tuberculosis had forced El Lissitzky to leave Hanover for treatment in Southern Switzerland in the late fall of 1923. At Brione above Locarno, where he stayed, he soon gathered a circle of friends around him and began to develop his theories and to publish his writings. He was instrumental in the launching of the progressive magazine "ABC, Beiträge zum Bauen", which was edited from 1924 to 1928 by the two Swiss architects Hans Schmidt and Emil Roth and the Dutchman Mart Stam. In addition to essays by Moholy-Nagy, Mondrian, Vanton-

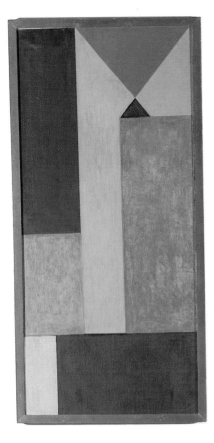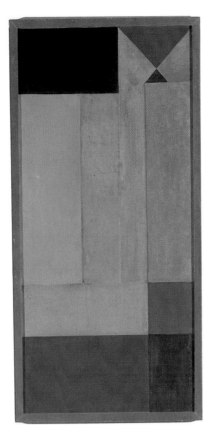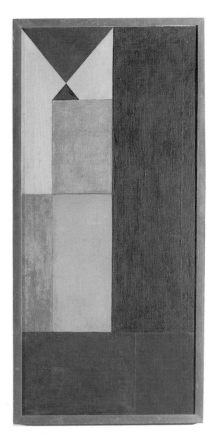

Sophie Taeuber-Arp: Triptych, 1918

gerloo and others it contained an important text by El Lissitzky entitled "Element und Erfindung" (Element and Invention). It was also during his stay in the Ticino that Lissitzky prepared the illustrated work "Die Kunst-Ismen" (The Art-Isms) which he published with Jean Arp in Zurich in 1925. More important still, he worked out with the architects Mart Stam and Emil Roth the details of the Utopian "Wolkenbügel" or "cloud-hanger" project, a high-rise office building standing on three gigantic columns and intended for Moscow. This urban project was reproduced on the cover of Adolf Behne's book "Der moderne Zweckbau". When he was forced to leave Switzerland, Lissitzky returned to Russia in the summer of 1925, but the intellectual excitement and fresh ideas he had imparted to his Swiss friends continued to be effective.

Contacts with Russia through Lissitzky and others remained so close that several Swiss architects later went to work in the Soviet Union, among them Hans Schmidt of Basel and Hannes Meyer, who — after acting as director of the Bauhaus in Dessau from 1928 to 1930 — was Professor of Architecture in Moscow and as chief architect of several urbanist institutes prepared various projects in Russia from 1930 to 1936. Shortly before this Le Corbusier had won the contest for the "Centrosoyus" building, seat of the Union of Cooperatives in Moscow, with a project of 1929–1931 which was not carried out.

The contacts with the Bauhaus were close. Johannes Itten and the friend of his youth, Paul Klee, had belonged to its teaching staff while it was still located at Weimar. The work and program of instruction of the Bauhaus were presented in an exhibition in the Museum of Applied Art in Zurich as early as 1923, and in the Dessau years further exhibitions followed in Basel and Zurich. The Bauhaus also had its attraction for young Swiss artists: the painter Hans R. Schiess of Basel, Max Bill and Hans Fischli of Zurich were decisively influenced by Albers, Moholy-Nagy, Kandinsky, Klee and Schlemmer in Dessau between 1927 and 1929. Fruitful inspiration also came from the exemplary Weissenhof development in Stuttgart, which was completed in 1927 and comprised numbers of buildings by leading international architects including the Swiss Le Corbusier and Pierre Jeanneret, the Stijl members J. J. P. Oud and Mart Stam of Holland, the Germans Walter Gropius, Mies van der Rohe, Ludwig Hilbereimer and Hans Scharoun. The erection and appointments of the two houses by Le Corbusier were in the hands of the Zurich architect Alfred Roth, who worked in Le Corbusier's studio in Paris. The Swiss Camille Graeser, at that time an interior designer in Stuttgart, took part in the furnishing of the buildings by Mies van der Rohe.

The international cooperation of leading architects on the Weissenhof scheme in Stuttgart was one of the factors contributing to the foundation of the CIAM (Congrès Internationaux d'Architecture Moderne) at the castle of La Sarraz in French Switzerland in June 1928. The collector Hélène de Mandrot had made the medieval castle a meeting place of artists through a foundation known as "La Maison des Artistes". When she made the acquaintance of Le Corbusier, it also became the meeting place of leading architects. The International Congresses of Modern

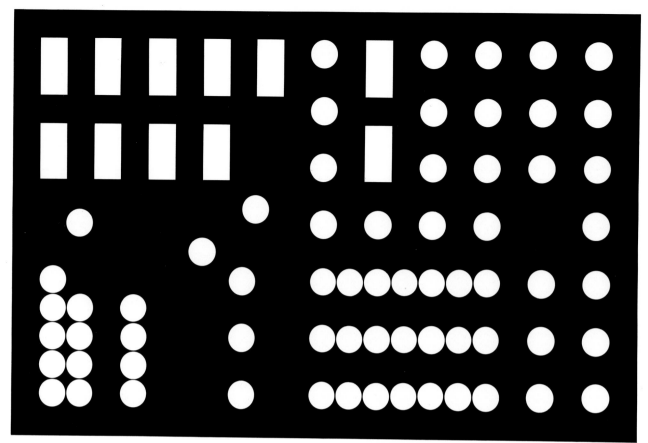

Sophie Taeuber-Arp: Composition schématique, 1933

Architecture continued to play an important part in architecture and town planning as instruments of social research up to their discontinuation in 1956. This was due in no small part to the activity of the critic of architecture and art Sigfried Giedion of Zurich, who was secretary-general and motive force of the CIAM. There were close connections between the member architects and the exponents of constructive art. Both parties were convinced that they were working toward the liberation of man from the fetters of convention. That is made clear, for instance, by the fact that Lissitzky was invited to the first congress at La Sarraz, though visa difficulties prevented him from being present.

Three art museums — the Kunsthalle in Basel and in Bern and the Kunsthaus in Zurich — acted as intermediaries in this development. Hotly discussed exhibitions afforded a good overview of contemporary art in France, Italy, Belgium, Holland and Germany. An especially influential exhibition was, in 1929, that of the Bauhaus masters Albers, Feininger, Kandinsky, Klee and Schlemmer in the Kunsthalle at Basel, accompanied by performances of the "Triadic Ballet" of Oskar Schlemmer and other Bauhaus stage experiments. Hardly less important was an international exhibition in Zurich's Kunsthaus in 1929, when works by forty of the leading practitioners of applied art in Basel and Zurich also provided information of a more practical nature on the current trends. The new design principles put forward by de Stijl, the Bauhaus, the Russian Constructivists, and Le Corbusier were de-

monstrated in the form of new architecture and town planning, interior and industrial design, photography, typography and graphics. These practice-oriented exhibitions underlined the fact that both constructive art and functional architecture were really aiming beyond mere aesthetics at a complete renewal of man's environment.

A powerful impression was left by the "Russian exhibition" staged in the Zurich Museum of Applied Art in 1929. El Lissitzky helped to organize the exhibition and designed an effective photomontage poster. This exhibition likewise demonstrated the relationship between art and architecture, between the fine arts and industrial design, typography, photography, theater and film. The problems of the abstract theater — as represented by Oskar Schlemmer, Laszlo Moholy-Nagy and the Russian Constructivists — were also reviewed in 1931 in an international exhibition of theater art in Zurich.

The spokesmen of the new trends, and particularly of constructive art, were the art critics Sigfried and Carola Giedion-Welcker in Zurich and Georg Schmidt, art critic and director of the Museum of Applied Art, later of the Kunstmuseum, in Basel. They encouraged young artists on their way to a constructive style, they drew attention to the importance of the Bauhaus in Dessau and of the "total work of art" represented by the "Aubette" in Strasbourg. They established personal contacts between foreign and local artists. Their motivating influence on collectors in Basel, Bern and Zurich was also significant: the nuclei of some important Swiss collections of con-

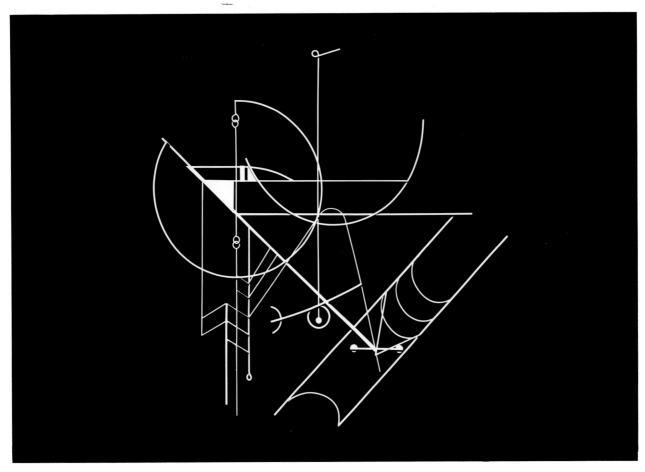

Walter Bodmer: Wire mural, 1937/39

structive art were built up in the late twenties, in many cases in direct contact with the artists concerned. The works were mostly acquired in the year of execution, and this applies equally to Mondrian, Van Doesburg, Kandinsky, Klee, Arp and Sophie Taeuber. Some of these collections are today in the possession of Swiss museums.

Young non-figurative Swiss artists were strengthened in their aspirations by the founding of the international movement "Abstraction-Création" in Paris in 1931. Many of them took part in the group's public manifestations. At the beginning of the thirties artists of the same persuasion had to close their ranks, for the world crisis was destroying the basis for the continued existence of experimental and socially nonconformist artistic activities. The news from Russia was as disheartening as the economic situation. The progress of constructive art in Russia had been cut short when the Stalinist era began and Socialist Realism was proclaimed. An alarming piece of news had also reached Western artists and architects in 1931 when the Russian authorities had demonstratively announced that the governmental palace in Moscow for which Le Corbusier had worked out bold plans on an official commission in 1929–1931 was not to be carried out.

Not all Western artists and architects who were active in the Soviet Union came away with such positive impressions of the "Russian adventure" as the architect Hannes Meyer of Basel, who held official positions there in 1930–1936: "When I strike a balance of my work in the Soviet Union, I am grateful for the unexpected enrich-

ment of my life. Gone was the uncertain situation of the Western intellectual, dictated by economic worries, threatened in both mental and material respects; a new cultural circle, a firm ideological basis and thus a new relationship to architecture. I feel younger, stronger, more creative than before." Hannes Meyer and his colleague Hans Schmidt, also of Basel, were no doubt the exceptions in their praise of the conditions in Russia. Other deeply disappointed observers, among them André Gide, were well aware of the growing intolerance of the Stalinist regime.

This rejection of progressive art by the rulers of a state in which Western artists had placed great hopes was not to be the only blow. In 1933 the Nazis seized power in Germany, and the political suppression of all experimental work in the cultural field was now near at hand. Progressive artists retired underground or emigrated from Germany. Prague, Paris, London and Switzerland became places of exile for many exponents of modern movements. The ever more critical plight of the fine arts in Germany called forth a spirit of resistance among Swiss artists, critics, museum directors and collectors. While in the political domain Switzerland had to come to some sort of terms with her German neighbors, the progressive forces in art, literature and the theater showed great moral courage in organizing active opposition. "Group 33", founded in Basel in 1933, included Expressionists, Surrealists and Constructivists. The attitude of these artists was more important than their particular school. The absence of

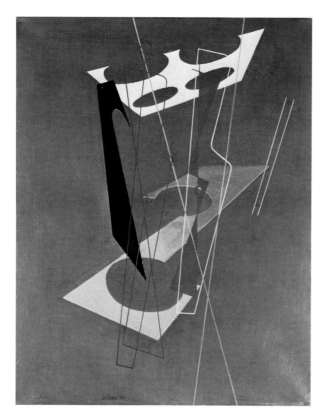

Leo Leuppi: Forms in space IV, 1937

any division into -isms was characteristic of the situation of art in Switzerland at that time and mirrored the tolerance shown toward others. Representatives of Constructivism and Surrealism joined forces to defend the cause of modern art, no doubt realizing that both elements, the

Leo Leuppi: Filetage sur blanc III, 1963

rational and the irrational, the conscious and the unconscious, belong to the complete human being.

This view found exemplary expression in an exhibition mounted in the Kunstmuseum in Lucerne in 1935 ("Thesis, Antithesis, Synthesis"). The foremost exponents of Purism, Abstractionism and Constructivism were hung beside Pittura metafisica, Dadaism and Surrealism with the somewhat Platonic aim of "obtaining by synthesis the elements of a new art". To underline the didactic purpose of the exhibition, the catalog contained an anthology of texts on modern art (by Jean Hélion, Anatole Jakovski, Wassily Kandinsky, Fernand Léger and James Johnson Sweeney, for instance) as well as an excellent bibliography, one of the very first of its kind.

In the following year the Kunsthaus in Zurich presented the work of forty artists of the Constructivist and Surrealist schools under the title of "Problems of the Times in Swiss Painting and Sculpture". This exhibition provided the impetus for the founding in 1937 of "Allianz", an association of modern artists in Switzerland. It was within this association that the group later to be known as Swiss Concrete artists was formed. Zurich has remained its chief center to the present day.

The vigor of these constructive artists may have been one of the reasons why Georg Schmidt decided to present an exhibition titled "Constructivists" in the Kunsthalle in Basel in 1937 which in retrospect must be ranked as an event of major importance. The artists represented, many of them with excellent groups of works, were Lissitzky, Malevich, Tatlin, Kliun, Rodchenko, Gabo, Pevsner, Moholy-Nagy, Stazewski and Strzeminski from Eastern Europe; Van Doesburg, Mondrian, Van der Leck, Vantongerloo and Vordemberge of de Stijl; the Frenchmen Hélion and Gorin; the Germans Richter, Dexel, Baumeister, Schwitters and Freundlich; the Swede Eggeling; Marlow Moss from Britain and Alexander Calder from America. Sophie Taeuber, the only Swiss, contributed a rich selection of work. The influence imparted by this exhibition to constructive artists in Switzerland and to a number of collectors was a powerful one. Georg Schmidt deepened the impression it made by giving it the full support of his stimulating personality. The closing words of his inaugural address are still quoted: "Although Constructivist artists no longer recognize the natural phenomenon as the subject matter of art, their art is all the more deeply founded on obedience to and love for natural laws. Released from its attachment to natural phenomena and bound to natural laws, this art gives the feeling and shaping mind, the creative imagination, the greatest possible freedom. — This art demands three things from the observer: constant refinement of the senses, serenity of spirit, and alertness of the mind. And to those who are willing to learn its language it returns these three things, the most precious that we can possess, with interest: refinement if the senses, serenity of spirit, and alertness of the mind."

The "Allianz" brought together artists with a similar attitude rather than members of a single school, just as "Gruppe 33" had done in Basel. From the first, non-figurative art held a prominent place in its productions, both in the free, organic form typical of the amicably disposed Jean Arp (ill. p. 126) and in its geometric, constructive style modeled rather on Sophie Taeuber-Arp (ill. pp. 127–129,

Max Bill: Construction, 1937

140) and, in a wider context, on international Constructivism. There was also a strong contingent of Surrealists to represent the Swiss proclivity for the fantastic and grotesque. It was unmistakable from the first joint appearance of this loosely assembled group that the main emphasis was on geometric and constructive art. A sidelight on this is provided by an "Almanac of new art in Switzerland" that was published in 1940. It already contains the names of the artists, most of them domiciled in Zurich, who are still regarded today as the leading representatives of constructive art in Switzerland.

The founder, president and guiding spirit of the "Allianz" was Leo Leuppi. Rational and emotional elements complement each other in his painting, which developed from Cubist and Purist beginnings to integral abstraction about the middle of the thirties, then moved to non-objectivity. Even in his purely geometric compositions the linear construction is determined by a musical and often choreographic or acrobatic sensibility. The concept of "équilibre", of subtle balance, gives Leuppi's painting a poise and poetry that moved Arp to lyrical praise. Particularly in the colored line constructions placed against wide blue backgrounds, dating from 1935–1945 (ill. p. 142), there are space-time elements that recall the atmosphere of older constructive works by, say, Lissitzky or Moholy-Nagy. Leuppi on several occasions turned his attention to monochromy and the transformation of the picture into a relief. The white "filetages" or networks made up of cords are the culmination of these experiments in Leuppi's work (ill. p. 142). Some wire sculptures which were intended as models for monumental works, but which mostly remained in the project stage, show affinities to

the wire sculptures of the painter and sculptor Walter Bodmer of Basel (ill. p. 141).

The motive force behind the "Allianz" was from the first Max Bill. He had been trained as a silversmith at the School of Applied Art in Zurich and had attended the Bauhaus in Dessau between 1927 and 1929. The lessons of Albers, Kandinsky, Klee and Moholy-Nagy there were less important to him than the experience of new forms of creative work in which the artist was not restricted to the "fine" arts but was able to engage in the visual shaping of his whole environment. From 1929 onward Bill worked in Zurich as an architect, painter and sculptor. In addition, in the framework of this universal concept of the artist's activities, he designed exhibitions and posters, was a typographer, a designer of industrial products and jewelry, a publicist and an art theorist. It was due to the determined initiative repeatedly taken by this champion of progressive art—comparable in his versatility to the "uomo universale" of the Italian Renaissance—that from 1932 onward lively contacts were maintained with the "Abstraction-Création" movement. Thus Bill returned to Van Doesburg's definition of "Concrete Art", formulated in 1930, and in 1936 drew up a programmatic statement of its principles in the catalog of the exhibition "Problems of the Times in Swiss Painting and Sculpture". This near-manifesto was given its final wording in the catalog of an exhibition of "Concrete Art from Zurich" which toured Germany in 1949. Bill's clear if repeatedly modified definition of Concrete Art was an endorsement and an incentive: "Concrete Art is, by virtue of its special character, an independent entity. It has an equally valuable existence of its own alongside that of the natural

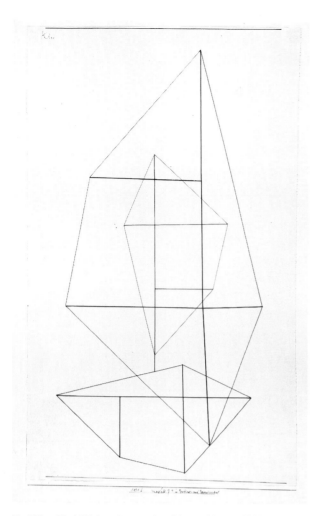

Paul Klee: Model 7a in a change of position and format, 1931

Paul Klee: Floating (Before the Ascent), 1930

phenomenon. It is the expression of the human spirit, intended for the human spirit, and it should be of that incisiveness and unequivocality, of that perfection that can be expected of works of the human spirit." This was the light in which Bill presented the works of his Swiss colleagues against the background of international constructive art in the exhibition he organized in the Kunsthalle, Basel, in 1944. If the "Allianz" not only survived as the hard core of constructive art but commanded growing respect from 1945 onward, this was due to the publications of the "Allianz Verlag" directed by Max Bill and to the magazine "abstrakt-konkret" which he published for the gallery "Des Eaux-Vives" in Zurich in 1944/45.

Bill's activities have extended into the areas of art education and even of local and national politics, but the work of art has always held a central position in them. From the first, painting and sculpture ran parallel in his œuvre and were closely interconnected even though he broaches specific problems in each of the two domains. A feature common to both is that every work is a seemingly quite simple and elementary, but all the more convincing solution to a problem that the artist has set himself. The obviousness of the solution conceals the reasoning that has led to it. Reduction of a problem to its elementary terms — the finding of a sort of lowest common denominator — combined with great perfection in its material embodiment is what characterizes every work of Bill's.

This "elegance of thought and realization", as Margit Staber puts it in her monograph on Bill, can be compared with a logical reasoning process in the exact sciences, as for instance a mathematical proof. Such a reference to the exact sciences is legitimate: Bill gives a great deal of thought to scientific problems, they are indirectly contained in his definition of Concrete Art, which he says is an expression of the human mind that aims at the unambiguous statement and searches for a law. Since painting and sculpture are first of all problems of planes, of bodies and of space (and color, in addition, a problem of optics and physiology), it is natural for Bill, following up the reasoning of other constructive artists, to occupy himself with geometry, stereometry and trigonometry, permutations and equations, or in a word mathematics. In his conviction that mathematics and art have a great deal in common Bill is in line with his many forerunners. Yet, he is far from equating the two domains; what he sees is analogies between mathematical and artistic reasoning.

Those who expect art to have an emotional or thematic content regard constructive art, as practiced by Bill, as being merely the visualization of mathematical facts with artistic means. This assumption cannot be substantiated. Bill has repeatedly pointed out that art and mathematics are two independent areas with laws of their own, though there are close parallels between the problems and working methods of mathematics and those of Concrete Art, and more particularly constructive art. In an essay on "Mathematical thinking in the art of our time" published in 1948 Bill set forth his views on these questions: this type of art is no longer a copy but a new system, the "translation of elementary forces into sensuously perceptible forms". Bill continues: "One might perhaps say that art has thereby become a branch of philosophy, part of the description of existence ... And I therefore assume that art can present thought in a way that will make

Paul Klee: Superchess, 1937

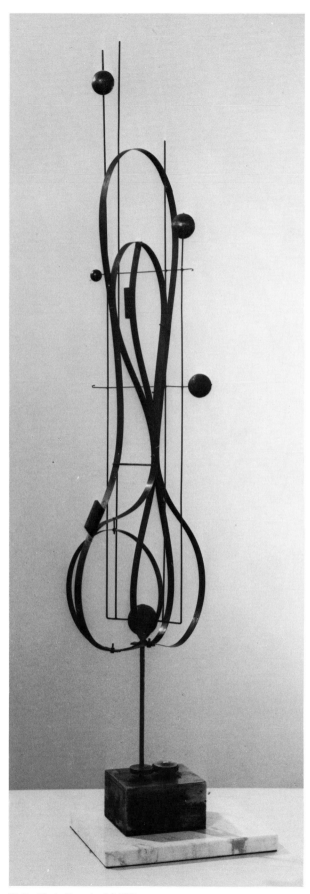

Walter Linck: Fleur du ciel, 1961

it directly perceptible ... And the more exact the process of reasoning, the more homogeneous the basic idea, the more the thought will be in harmony with mathematical thinking, the closer we approach to the primary structure, and the more universal art becomes. Universal in the sense that it expresses itself directly and without ambages, and can be understood directly and without ambages." The text closes with the remark: "Art has entered fields that were previously closed to it. One of these fields uses a mathematical form of reasoning which despite its rational elements contains many philosophical components which extend outward beyond the frontiers of the explicable world."

In his painting Bill began in the middle thirties to work on "constructions" which show divisions of a surface by the consistent application of a principle or, conversely, the building-up of a whole from related elements. His "Construction" of 1937 (ill. p. 143) is an example of this. It is related to a sequence of lithographs entitled "Fifteen variations on a single theme", done in 1935–1938. The accompanying text, which explains the principle of these line-and-surface, monochrome and polychrome variations on a single idea, also underlines the value of the exercise as a paradigm. Bill shows what a variety of possible solutions, often of diametrically opposed character, may be contained in a single valid problem. This work has consequently become a kind of key to the understanding of Bill's work and of Concrete Art in general.

His later painting also comprises variations on a definite basic idea which Bill calls a "theme". Apart from the objective laws applying in each case, a subjective decision has to be made as to which of the possible variants is to be carried out. The difference between two solutions to a given problem may often consist in the color combinations chosen. One of them may use a dramatic confrontation of primary and secondary colors, another may opt for a poetic blend of paler and more delicate hues. The logic of the color system may derive from the mixing of two colors or from the expansion or contraction of the color areas. In most cases the title of the work contains some indication of the basic design principle (ill. p. 153).

A similar approach is embodied in Bill's sculpture. Here again he exploits the possibilities of the systematic division or segmentation of an exactly defined form, such as a sphere, which was his starting point for the discovery of a large range of plastically expressive hemispherical configurations. Or the three-dimensional complex may result from the agglomeration of identical parts such as half rings. Constructions made of round, triangular or square bars, usually combined with a solid core, produce some surprising spatial structures. The crystalline "Construction from prisms" (ill. p. 151), a hanging mobile, is an example. The monumental spatial sculptures consisting of beams of uniform dimensions should also be mentioned in this connection, as for instance the "Pavilion Sculpture" in Zurich (ill. p. 283). The extreme is reached, for example, in the "Construction of 30 equal elements", 1938/39, in which an imaginary prismatic body, defined by round bars, becomes a constructional element for a self-supporting spatial structure.

The "single-surface" sculptures, mostly of gold-plated brass sheet, are one of Bill's important contributions to contemporary sculpture. Setting out from the so-called

Johannes Itten: Space composition I, 1944

Mary Vieira: Polyvolume, interruption semi-développable, 1953/66

Möbius strip, a three-dimensional surface figure made famous by the mathematician August Ferdinand Möbius, Bill has developed a large number of "surfaces in space". Their distinctive feature is the limitation of the surface by a single "endless" line, so that they are in effect endless loops. The "Endless Spiral Surface" (ill. p. 150), developed from a circular disk, is a hanging mobile of chromium steel conceived as a counterpart to the "Construction from Prisms". It is a monumental contribution to the series of ribbon forms in space. Rational as the principle of these works is, their effect is quite irrational—a splendid illustration of Bill's argument that rational developments based on mathematical reasoning may lead to results that border on the mysterious and inexplicable.

The affinity of attitude among Zurich's Concrete artists did not initially lead to similar works, nor has it done so in the course of their development. They frequently broach similar problems, and like expedients may be used for visualization; but the results are so different, so colored by individual leanings, that there is hardly any risk of their productions being confounded. It might even be true to say that the proximity of these artists, both geographically and in their design approach, over a period of almost

forty years has been a stimulus for each to differentiate himself from his colleagues.

A characteristic œuvre is that of Verena Loewensberg, who, after meeting Auguste Herbin and Georges Vantongerloo, began to take part in group exhibitions in the late thirties. Initially she used black or colored sign-like elements to build the patterns of her compositions (ill. p. 152). Before long, she utilized color and shape in such a way that they could no longer be separated, especially when the principle of chromatic penetration or superimposition binds the surface elements inextricably together. The picture arrangements follow from the rational grouping or graduation of the colored forms—triangles, squares, bars or circles, of similar or progressively increasing dimensions. In spite of the essential surface quality of the compositions, the color relations soon began to produce pronounced spatial effects. The real canvas thus becomes a "zero plane" before or behind which the pictorial happenings take place, often about a clearly defined center. One of the special features of Verena Loewensberg's work are the apparently "irrational" shapes. They are produced when simple and geometrically exact surface shapes are combined to form composite shapes defying definition, for instance when segments of increasing radius become roundish angular conglomerates whose exact construction can hardly be discerned. Closely related to these phenomena is also the dynamic expansion or deformation of shapes in space, anticipating the principles adopted by Op Art in the late fifties. A comparison with the works of Max Bill, whose starting point is perhaps nearest to that of Verena Loewensberg, shows how individual these strongly color-oriented compositions really are.

Comparable differences from the work of his colleagues are evident in the paintings of Camille Graeser. A Genevese by birth, he moved in his youth to Stuttgart and worked there in the twenties as an interior architect and product designer, being responsible, for instance, for the interior decoration of an apartment house by Mies van der Rohe erected as part of the Weissenhof estate around the year 1927. A pupil of Adolf Hoelzel, Graeser also painted, moving from Expressionist and Futuro-Cubist compositions toward integral abstraction. In 1933 he returned to Switzerland, where from 1938 on he produced an increasingly individual œuvre. After experiments with free two-dimensional compositions including curved forms, he soon began to concentrate on straight lines. He saw the picture plane as a place of both static repose and dynamic movement. The subjects investigated are clearly reflected in his titles: the dynamic elements in concepts such as rhythm, concentration, rotation, progression, contact, thrust, energy, dislocation; the static elements even more frequently in concepts such as concretion, location, coordination, equivalence, relation, polarity. However great his interest in the formal subject matter, the effect of his clear compositions in their generous simplicity depends primarily on their coloring. The choice of colors is by no means emotional—on the contrary, Graeser usually restricts himself to primary and secondary colors; the principle of the contrast of complementaries contributes largely to the rightness and effectiveness of his color combinations. The relations of forms are always color relations as well. The equilibrium of color

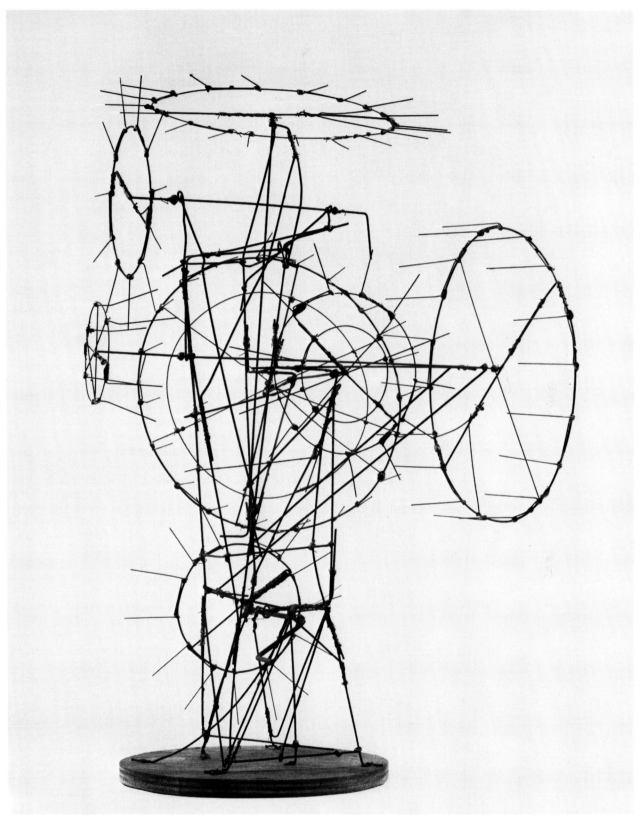

Jean Tinguely: Méta-Mécanique, 1954

Max Bill: Endless Spiral Surface, 1973/74

quantities plays a decisive role. The ordering principle of the composition, always logical and comprehensible though often not visible at first glance, is based on a horizontal or horizontal-vertical division of the whole surface. Relationships are sought not only in the areas of the component surfaces but in the colors defining them. This comes out most clearly in the works that display certain area and color relations exclusively in the rhythm of horizontal bands (ill. p. 157). These band or strip pictures, which the artist repeatedly returned to after 1960, anticipate paintings of American Minimal Art without there being any actual contacts.

The wealth of forms which Graeser extracts from this extremely disciplined and sparing use of the artist's means is particularly evident when he "dislocates" one square from an integrated group of squares and through this minor mechanism demonstrates the fundamental principle of all movement (ill. p. 156). The rational tips over into the irrational in the color domain when several surfaces of equal size but different colors are answered by an area equal to the sum of the surfaces in a color which is the quantitative sum of their colors, exactly mixed, for instance the active complementary couple of red and green as against a blunt and sluggish dark brown. Here an apparently elementary and completely rational method of painting may well stimulate meditation on the unlikenesses inherent in the like. Graeser himself was content to express his ideas in his pictures, leaving it to the viewer to use them as food for thought over and above the perceptual pleasure of looking at them.

The exclusive study of compositional problems is always in danger of ending up as an aesthetic game played in an ivory tower. Yet investigation of the laws of shape and color can also lead to an understanding of methods of organizing parts in a whole which goes beyond art. Art is then only a field of experiment in which the work is favored by the exactly controlled conditions. The œuvre of Richard Paul Lohse must be seen as research and experimentation in this sense. An essential feature of it is the displacement of the creative process from the phase of execution to that of planning, from material to concept. Lohse began in the thirties with floating, carefully weighed curves placed against a background. These geometric figurations were at first flying things, imbued with expressive diagonal dynamism. About 1940 the vertical began to assume increasing importance as an ordering element. The dualism of background and geometric figure disappeared. At the same time the individual pictorial motif was replaced by an "anonymous" vertical structure covering the whole surface. The "vertical rhythms" that materialized around 1942 set the stage for the experiments Lohse pursued from then on.

He begins with standardized elements. These are combined to form groups, which the artist takes as his theme. This theme now becomes a standard unit in its turn and can be repeated or arranged in rows. "I try to conceive a picture with the simplest possible basic elements: square, line, ribbon elements that are in structural relationship with the bounding lines of the composition. Since 1943 I have used rectangular forms only." This statement was made by Lohse in an interview. Using a simple instrumentation of anonymous pictorial elements, "microcells" as it were, he develops systems whose special character lies in their variability. In handling systematically ordered groups he comes up against the problem of the color row: color turns into shape, and the form structure into a color structure. Color and form no longer are opposites but act as a unit. This may be the starting point for a principle Lohse has often applied: quantitative equality of the colors used in a picture.

There are two different ordering principles that chiefly govern Lohse's work: modular and serial. The module is a standard dimensional unity, often square, with which a predetermined order is created by certain manipulations: by rotation about a center or axis, by arrangement in rows, by interlocking or interpenetration, by progression or degression, by movement in a horizontal, vertical or diagonal direction. The module changes from work to work, as does the operation which it takes part in.

In the works embodying a serial order, which can be recognized as structures of vertical bands (ill. p. 154), there is an identity of picture area, form structure and color structure. The basis is a model that follows automatically from the predetermined number of color-forms. Continuous color processes — rows, bands or chains of color — are arranged in groups according to the structural principle chosen. This is most impressively exemplified in works with 15 or 30 vertical systematic series of colors, whose 225 or 900 color compartments are sometimes of the same dimensions — mostly squares — or else undergo horizontal or vertical "concentration" (ill. p. 155). When such concentration takes place at the borders of the composition or on the central axis by a progressive or degressive change in the size of the color compartments, the pattern seems to produce motion or even apparent three-dimensionality. With regular quadrature of the picture area, the arrangement of the color series, by means of the systematic shift of analogous color compartments, produces a color movement or pulsation. This kinetic effect can be heightened by coupling colors of equal brightness or contrasting light and dark. Irrational and inexplicable effects are thus obtained by rational and explicable expedients.

The methodical consistency of Lohse's procedure in handling open, flexible systems is the determinant feature of his work. Scrutiny reveals that the structural models are exactly fitted to the picture area but can be extended beyond it by the application of the underlying principle of combination. This possibility points up the relativity of picture dimensions and the unlimited nature of the structural laws. There are no primary and secondary shapes in Lohse's painting, and thus there is no hierarchical principle. He calls his structures "democratic": the elements enjoy equality in their system, they are dependent on each other for the formation of the whole. This lends Lohse's art the character of a model extending beyond its merely pictorial significance. "Serial and modular design methods are by virtue of their dialectical character parallels to expression and activity in a new society." Lohse of course knew that non-hierarchical social structures are Utopian. He nevertheless did not tire in the interest he took, above and beyond his own work, in questions of the environment, the humanization of our living space and the implementation of social justice.

Numerous painters and sculptors turned to constructive art after 1945 without actually belonging to the group of

Max Bill: Construction from Prisms, 1973/74

Verena Loewensberg: Painting No. 111, 1950

Concrete artists. An outstanding figure among them was Johannes Itten. He had returned to Switzerland for political reasons in 1938 after having been active in the field of art education in Germany. In Zurich he had been appointed head of the Kunstgewerbeschule, the School of Applied Art. He was thus still able to make use of his preliminary course, a comprehensive introduction to the practice of art and design, which he had developed at the Bauhaus in Weimar in 1919–1923. This foundation course met with extraordinary success and is, in fact, still being utilized in all parts of the world today. He was also able to communicate to young designers and artists the color theory he had formulated on principles first expounded by Adolf Hoelzel. Itten had been painting alongside his teaching work since his own student days. In his late years in Zurich he returned to non-objective art, which he had been one of the first to attempt when he was studying under Hoelzel in Stuttgart in 1914. He turned his attention once more to horizontal-vertical patterns, some of them strictly orthogonal, others freely geometric. This playful form of composition was employed also by the friend of his youth, Paul Klee, in his constructive phases. Itten differed from the circle around Max Bill in his conviction that the coolly rational and constructive always needed to be completed by an emotional and expressive component. His belief in the totality of human potentialities explains the painterly, mood-dictated coloring of his geometric works and the irrational elements, spontaneously added, that intrude upon the logical compositional principles. Itten's painting is in fact characterized by a poetic geometry in which the pulse of life can always be felt (ill. p. 147).

Walter Bodmer and Theo Eble of Basel, who belonged to the "Allianz" from the first, were closer to the spirit of constructive art. Their subjects were weightless, hovering constructions placed on a surface or in space. Bodmer has produced, apart from his linear paintings, a large body of plastic works of individual character executed in wire. Free geometric line structures suggesting fantastic rigging (ill. p. 141) are placed before white or black grounds. Sometimes metal surfaces, which may be colored, are fitted in the angles of the wire patterns and give the constructions optical and spatial cohesion. The rational poetry of these wire reliefs often recalls drawings by Paul Klee that formed part of his teaching work in the early thirties (ill. p. 144). Though Bodmer's wire reliefs are little known outside of Switzerland, they had a marked influence on the early work of Jean Tinguely, who was a pupil of Bodmer's at the School of Applied Art in Basel and began with fragile wire construction (ill. p. 149). Hans Hinterreiter, who later emigrated to Spain, also belongs to their group. From about 1940 on he designed highly dynamic geometric compositions, applying Ostwald's color theory and the principles of rotation and mirror reflection. Their tightening or expanding space rhythms are painted in colors whose gradations Hinterreiter determined by the laws of harmonics. Robert Strübin, although not connected to the "Allianz", moved in a similar intermediate zone between practical and theoretical art. His experiments in the translation of musical scores into geometric compositions (under the influence of synaesthetic theories) and the architectural fantasies with astonishing optical effects which he produced around 1935 were known only to a small circle of friends in Basel during his lifetime.

One of the founders of the "Allianz" was the Zurich-born Fritz Glarner. His constructive work began with abstractions of external and internal spaces, with which he was represented at the exhibition "Problems of the Times in Swiss Painting and Sculpture" in 1936. Architectural

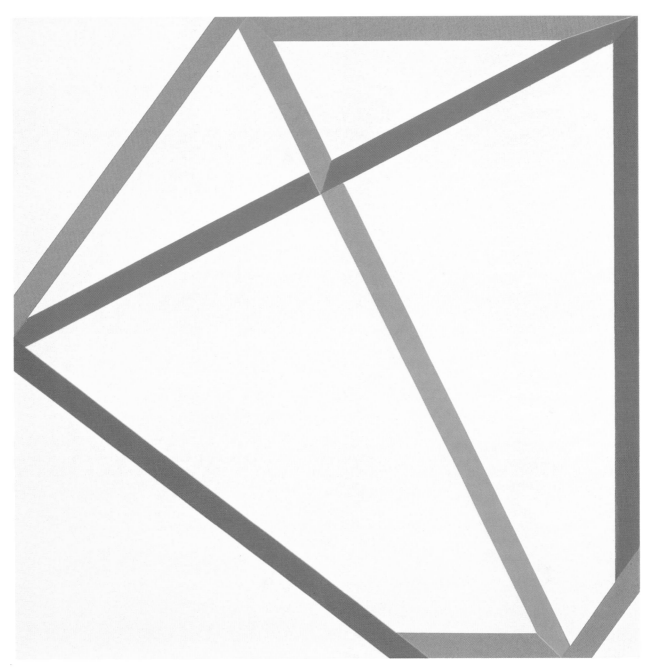

Max Bill: Interchanges, 1983

complexes are broken down into geometric surfaces which — mostly in delicate outline — are pushed behind, above and into each other in almost monochrome structures. These architectural constructions are the immediate forerunners of the "Relational Paintings". They materialized under the impact of city architecture and in an amicable dispute with Piet Mondrian in New York, where Glarner settled in 1936 (ill. pp. 246, 247).

The circle of Concrete artists also included a few sculptors from the outset. Unlike Bill, whose sculptures had been based, from the "Endless ribbon" or the "Construction with a suspended cube" of 1935, on rational constructive principles, these sculptors were almost without exception exponents of the "organic concretion" which

Jean Arp, also one of the founders of the "Allianz", had popularized from about 1930 on, when he changed over from reliefs to fully three-dimensional work. After this first generation of Concrete sculptors — their number included Adolf Weisskopf and Willi Hege — constructive trends only reappeared among Zurich stone carvers about 1960, in the works of Hans Aeschbacher, Oedön Koch, Hans Fischli and others.

In metal sculpture constructive ideas appeared about 1950. A widely noted example is to be found in the work of Jean Tinguely, who began to make a name about that time with experiments in various materials. His aim was to replace the traditional static sculpture by works that were in motion. Motion has since dominated his whole

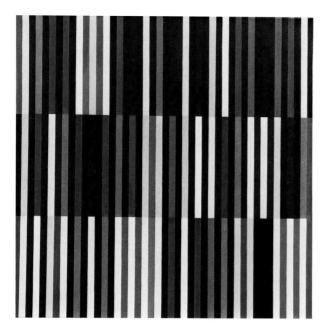

Richard Paul Lohse: Serial elements concentrated in rhythmic groups,
1949/56/63

development. It was created initially by wind or water power, later by a crank operated by human muscle and finally by the electric motor. A result of this obsession with movement is the approximation of the sulpture to the machine. The emphasis placed on the mechanism is a return to an idea first taken up by Dadaism and by Russian Constructivism with its early "machine art". One of Tinguely's sources of inspiration are Picabia's machine pictures, another is the ironic interpretation of the machine reflected in Marcel Duchamp's "Ready-mades" and the "Large Glass". Tatlin's tower might also be counted among the ancestors of this machine art.

In Tinguely's early work two types of mobile sculptures can be distinguished: reliefs and three-dimensional constructions. In the reliefs white or colored segments turn at different speeds on eccentric axes before a black background. The continuously changing compositions are reminiscent both of the organic reliefs of Jean Arp and of the arrangements of lines, rods and bars in Constructivist pictures. This kind of motorized box may be regarded as a relief in motion, as an extrapolation of painting. The moving three-dimensional constructions — skeleton-like wire lattices — belong instead to the domain of sculpture (ill. p. 149). They are austerely conceived spatial drawings whose component parts — girders, wheels, shafts, spokes, gears, cranks — have or at least suggest functional purposes. About 1955 the concept of "meta-mechanics" occurs in connection with Tinguely's work, meaning, as a parallel to the dematerialization of the plastic body, the transformation of practical mechanisms into a different state of "purposeless" function. That is, the contrivances operate in a world divorced from everyday practice. The artist's further development led to the use of scrap, of spare parts taken from real machines and apparatuses. In the form of montages or assemblages of these "found objects", the motorized sculptures once more assumed corporeality. Painted black and erected in accordance with mechanical laws and technical principles, the contrivances constitute a counter-creation to the world of useful machines, one in which homage and irony are equally contained. This phase in the artist's work began around the time of the foundation of "Nouveau Réalisme" by Pierre Restany in 1960. Tinguely belonged to this group from the beginning.

The Bernese sculptor Walter Linck arrived at the mobile from a different quarter. As a representative of Surrealist sculpture he had occupied himself with mythological and musical subjects, with the circus, acrobats, and conjurors, before he turned to the mobile in 1951. He now succeeded in expressing himself in technically perfect contrivances, in most cases meticulously composed, without making use of a figurative motif, but embodying weightlessness, subtle equilibrium, gentle swinging of the pendulum or dying motion (ill. p. 146). Linck exploits all the properties of his materials as an engineer would: elasticity of steel wire, flexibility of rods, spring force of metal strip. His mobiles are set in motion by a light touch or by the wind. Motorized mobiles are exceptions, but the weight of falling water has been used in fountains to power ingenious dynamic processes. In his artistic attitude he shows an affinity with Leo Leuppi: rational and constructive media set the stage for the expression of poetic and musical moods.

Bernhard Luginbühl began his career as a sculptor in wrought iron with ponderous space-hooks or meshing C-shapes that had something of the earthiness of his farming ancestry. The development of "Strahler" (literally "radiators"), structures reminiscent of radar equipment or solar power plants, next led to machine-like sculptures made of prefabricated iron components. Here he has affinities with his friend Tinguely. But while the latter is primarily interested in the operation of his ghost machines, Luginbühl's attention is concentrated on the constructive and sculptural content of his metal montages. They usually suggest attributes of living creatures — aggression, concentrated effort, upward struggle — and remind the observer of the bold engineering achievements of nineteenth century workers in iron. In Luginbühl's drawings and prints this admiration for technical structures comes out in a "constructive Expressionism", not without a fantastic component that recalls the "Carceri" of Piranesi.

The work of sculptors such as Linck, Tinguely and Luginbühl is no doubt an extension if not a transformation of constructive thinking. By comparison, the plastic work of Angel Duarte and Mary Vieira is a continuation of earlier constructive experiments along the lines of mathematical thought. The Spaniard Angel Duarte, who has lived in Switzerland since 1961, is interested in problems of space. Along with his reflex structures with mirrors, which may be considered as contributions to kinetic art, he has turned his attention to hyperbolic paraboloids. He has made these figures a structural element of his designs and has developed a module from several of them. His three-dimensional structures composed of identical modules may be considered as models for architects; they can be manufactured industrially and permit endless variations. Duarte's most important advance, however, has been made with lattice-like space sculptures employing curved planes, visualizations of problems of three-dimensional analytical geometry which are a further devel-

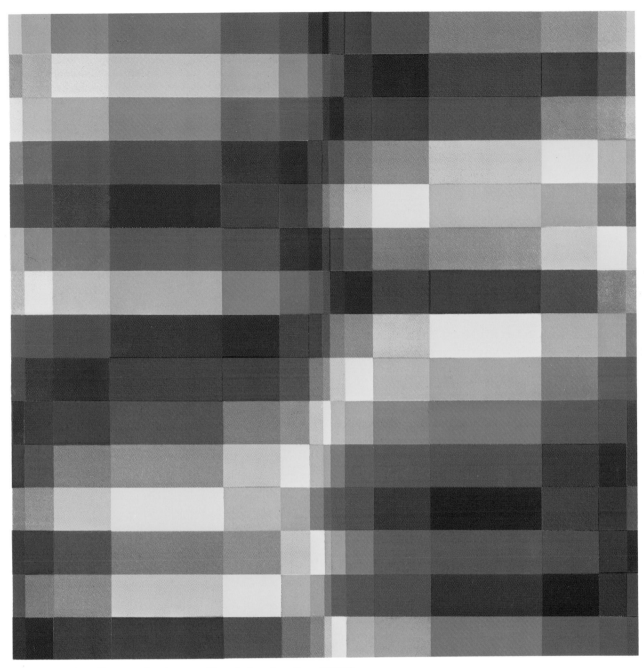

Richard Paul Lohse: 15 systematic color rows with vertical condensations, 1950/68

opment of the sculptural and spatial research of Pevsner and Gabo.

The works of Mary Vieira, born in Brazil and now resident in Basel, are based on mathematical principles such as division and multiplication. The steps she takes to develop a three-dimensional body are absolutely logical and easily followed by the observer. The system on which she evolves her "Monovolumes" automatically includes progressive movement in space, and consequently the element of time. With her invention of "Polyvolumes", bodies built up wholly or in part of elements amenable to manipulation, the idea of participation is also included in her sculptural work. The object can be changed by "inter-

actions" within the strict limits set by the artist. In these "Polyvolumes", mostly conceived by Mary Vieira as integrated parts of architectural interiors or open-air spaces, the modifiable parts are in direct dimensional relationship to the whole. In spite of the rational nature of the sculptural idea, the changes — for instance in laminated parts that can rotate about an axis — lead to seemingly irrational forms: static stratifications can be turned into a dynamic helix in space (ill. p. 148).

Angel Duarte and Mary Vieira are members of a generation that has been encouraged by the champions of constructive art to continue the investigation of the principles of Concrete Art. A characteristic feature is the choice

Camille Graeser: Translocation, 1969

of a definite problem complex and its systematic exploration. While Jean Baier, Willi Müller-Brittnau and Jakob Bill are primarily interested in problems of color and form on a surface, Hansjörg Glattfelder and Andreas Christen concentrate rather on the relief. Christen develops complementary structures in white reliefs, the positive projections being cancelled out by corresponding negative depressions. The incident light is allowed for in the design and turns the various facets into differing shades of grey, so that monochromatics give place to an apparent color effect. Glattfelder operates with structures of pyramids whose four sides carry colors, so that graduated color movements result, either in the order of the spectrum or in the interpenetration of two color systems. These pyramid reliefs are kinetic in the sense that the observer can bring about a transition from one color sequence to another by a change of position.

While Andreas Christen has always remained true to his monochrome white reliefs, Glattfelder has since reduced colored relief structures to the surface. In doing so he has disturbed the regularity of the structure by systematic expansion or compression of the forms and a corresponding lightening or darkening of the colors, which creates a surprising color-form dynamism. Setting out from these experiments, Glattfelder has investigated problems of non-Euclidean geometry and arrived at compositions that use surfaces to conjure up self-contradicting spatial visions. Glattfelder calls these works "non-Euclidean metaphors". By this he means a breakaway from the Euclidean parallel axiom, which states that through any point lying outside a straight line only one parallel can be drawn to the given straight line.

Karl Gerstner works in a similar area and has also been active as a publicist, a theorist and a champion of constructive art—this particularly in his essay on the situation of painting today entitled "Kalte Kunst?" (Cold Art?),

in which he presents exact chromatic and formal analyses of works by constructive artists. Gerstner exhibited his first modifiable works in 1952, his first programmed compositions in 1953. Through the logical development of serial principles he arrived at his "Chromorphoses" and later his "Color sounds". For Gerstner the exploration of forms is a science, their geometry being amenable to construction and proof; but the exploration of color is a form of speculation. He does not want to leave color to the incertitude of sensation, however, but believes that here too accuracy can be achieved. Gerstner's model is Josef Albers, whom he sees as the explorer and "designer" of color. His "Color sounds" are reliefs with graduated projections and depressions composed on a fixed geometric system: intraversions and extraversions. They comprise in each case twelve hues which change by small steps, but which bridge a very large interval between the first and the last, which may even be complementary colors. Exact as the color mixtures are on the electronic balance, the hues nevertheless flow into each other and pulsate in a most uneven way. Obviously, the metric regularity of the changes of tone is quite out of step with the irrational scale of perception. The fluctuating psychic effect of the various hues is simply not measurable.

Another of the many possible lines of advance in geometric and constructive composition is exemplified in the paintings and three-dimensional work of Gottfried Honegger. Initially a graphic designer, he had progressed from expressive abstraction to non-objectivity in his painting by 1950. An interest in structures and in scientific methods led him, about the middle of the fifties, to reduce his vocabulary to the square and the circle and to convert the picture area into a low relief. What Honegger calls a "tableau-relief" is for technical purposes a collage with cardboard elements which completely cover the canvas. This strictly geometric relief, which nevertheless reveals a measure of craftsmanship, is then covered with glazes of paint or graphite in a series of delicate working processes (ill. p. 159). In compositions made up of squares, the pattern results from the addition of identical elements, multiplication or division of the squares, or diagonal division of the whole square. In compositions made up of circles, differing radii, arc lengths and segments play a part. Square and circular elements are often combined. The dimensional relations of the various elements, which follow from the method used to divide up the whole area, are based on simple arithmetical progressions.

The activation of the picture area by this form of delicate relief leads to a closer study of layering phenomena and of the role of light in rendering the structure legible. The use of several layers makes it possible to provide window-like cut-outs in the top layers and thus to free glimpses of the deeper layers. In this way two different structures can be dialectically related. The views of deeper layers also reveal that what is not visible can be imagined and that the visible can in its turn become invisible and secret. Occasionally part of the relief is covered by a metal sheet, as in a Russian icon, and thus obscured from view. Where marginal zones that can easily be imagined, and are therefore irrelevant, occur in a composition, for instance where progressions lead outward from

Camille Graeser: Three color groups against black and white, 1969

a core, they are cut away. This can leave Honegger with a "shaped canvas". He frequently makes use of this to allow the work a virtual extension on the wall beyond its actual boundaries. From 1955 or thereabouts Honegger's reliefs became monochrome, with the mostly sonorous colors modulated in a painterly vein. This results in a dialogue between a rational, mathematical form of composition and a painterly, emotional execution, which may lead in some cases to a solemn and even religious mood that raises the work to the plane of the meditation diagram.

Honegger's interest in the language of signs induced him to reduce geometric shapes to fragments which still define the nature of the complete figure: the circle to a quadrant, the square to the right-angled isosceles triangle obtained by dividing it diagonally. This opened up the possibility of using a computer for working through a program. The resulting plotter-produced computer drawings record all possible combinations of all variables. Honegger used random numbers for the choice of the variant to be carried out. Very soon he dispensed with the aid of the computer but retained the basic system, in which calculation and chance form a unity. The "Structures" show this clearly; they are chromium steel sculptures combining exactly definable shapes in accidental combinations. "My relief pictures and sculptures are built up of simple geometric structures. The drawings are programmed, the composition is fortuitous" (ill. p. 158). In later work the

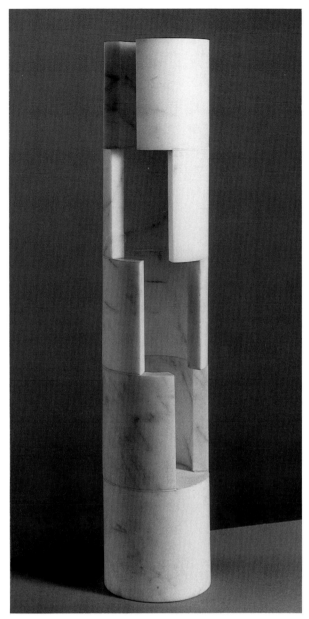

Gottfried Honegger: Monoform 1a, 1981

have radiated from Switzerland into the surrounding countries. In Switzerland itself the founding generation of the Zurich Concrete artists — Bill, Glarner, Graeser, Loewensberg, Lohse — was followed by another which included Carlo Vivarelli. Both of them safely survived the turbulence caused by the informal art of the fifties and early sixties as well as the effects of American Pop Art. They remained an important faction, respected even by their opponents, in the heterogeneous field of Swiss art. Today a younger generation is at work with artists such as Marguerite Hersberger, Nelly Rudin and Shizuko Yoshikawa, and they too withstood the expressive outbreak of the "neue Wilden" in the early eighties without falling foul of the recent neogeometric trends.

Since the fifties Switzerland's geometric constructive art, as intended by pioneers such as the members of de Stijl, has affected other fields of visual design far beyond painting and sculpture. This is only partly explained by the fact that Bill, Lohse, Vivarelli, Honegger and others have repeatedly worked as visual designers. Influences are also evident in architecture, industrial design and perhaps most of all in graphics. In poster art and other branches of advertising design, as well as in typography, the logic and clarity of the constructive approach have found wide expression.

Precisely in Switzerland, constructive thinking has not been limited to problems of form and aesthetics but has become typical of a way of seeing, feeling and acting. Max Bill perhaps brought this out most clearly in a talk with Margit Staber in 1972: "Art is just as pluralist as our society. If you move among present-day problems you naturally have to grapple with them all, and this generates the picture of the world from which you derive your creative impulses. In the course of time you take an independent attitude, you regard past and present critically in the light of your studies and your own experience. I can only produce my pictures and sculptures by constantly following political and economic developments, scientific researches and discoveries. And all this is combined with my experience in practice, for example in architecture . . .

"It is proven that works of art influence people. I try to make pictures that trigger positive influences in the viewer by their coloring, mood and compositional idea, for instance causing activation, tranquilization, concentration, harmony. A sculpture should awaken new impressions of space and volume, new knowledge and emotions . . .

"It is my opinion that art has a unique chance to form a counterpole to an over-technicalized, polluted and commercialized consumer world. And it can do that with comparatively modest material resources, but with the application of all the more intellectual discipline."

In his "Lines of Development" Richard Paul Lohse notes in 1984: "Geometric art forms have a range extending from the esoteric to democratic orders. Constructive art is an encyclopaedic art, an art of reason, a moralizing, ideological, political art, at once analysis and order. The integration into society of new systems and methods of designing will not become feasible until society acquires the ability to see in it an analogy to its own behavior . . . It is necessary to create an awareness of the resulting problems, that is, the conversion of the unidimensional principle into an individualized multidimensional one."

rational program takes second place to textures produced by strokes executed in the spirit of action painting and revealing the artist's hand. Traces of his activity cover the constructive framework. Their anonymity make Honegger's drawings and graphite pictures hermetic tokens of a silent art (ill. p. 159).

Switzerland's constructive art, in 1940 a cause passionately championed by a small circle only, has since developed into a broad and richly ramified movement and has remained an essential aspect of the Swiss art scene. Since Switzerland has been, internationally considered, a haven of constructive thinking since the late thirties, it is natural that when political and intellectual frontiers were opened again after the war constructive concepts should

Gottfried Honegger: Tableau-Relief NY 665, 1972

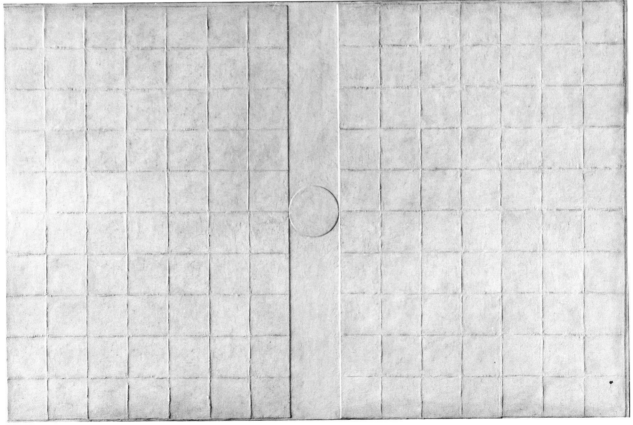

Gottfried Honegger: Tableau-Relief PZ 19, 1962/63

Max Bill, Half Sphere around two Axes, 1966

Max Bill: Pyramid in Form of one-eighth of a Sphere, 1965

New Realities

From Geometric Abstraction to Kinetic Art in France

"Geometric abstraction", the term still used in France for constructive art, was faced by many difficulties in Paris even after 1945. Initiated in the thirties by representatives of the "Abstraction-Création" group, from the first the movement registered only a partial success. The reason for this is a specifically French conception of art. Surrealism had a wide appeal because its poetic and literary content was open to intellectual appreciation, while a free, painterly abstraction visibly suited the French sense of form and color. But geometric abstraction was rejected, the opposition to it increasing as it became mathematically stricter and more constructive. Geometric art was regarded as hard and cold, and was occasionally described as "Germanic". The small magazine "Plastique" published by Sophie Taeuber-Arp with friends of the same persuasion in 1937/38 has distinct traits of an underground publication braving a hostile world.

There was no readiness on the part of the Parisian art world to raise any interest in an art that was felt to be foreign and imported. This is revealed by the lives that many representatives of constructive art led in Paris. Although Kandinsky, for instance, resided in Paris from 1933, he achieved only superficial success during his lifetime. Antoine Pevsner, who settled in Paris in 1923 and in 1930 became a French citizen, remained a marginal figure till after World War II. The case of Mondrian is still crasser: he worked in Paris from 1918 till 1938, but he remained practically an unrecognized and unknown outsider. Much the same happened to Georges Vantongerloo, who was Vice President of "Abstraction-Création" between 1931 and 1937 and was thus a spokesman of geometric and constructive art, but whose functional studies of curved lines on a surface (ill. p. 135) and in space met with less and less understanding. The list could be continued, for instance by way of Jean Hélion (ill. p. 133). What Theo van Doesburg had postulated in Paris in 1930 under the designation of "Concrete Art" was obviously unacceptable to the French.

When social and cultural life returned to normal in Paris after the armistice, the protagonists of constructive art again appeared on the scene. In 1946 the first "Salon des Réalités Nouvelles" was organized, resuming the prewar activities of abstract art. It attracted constructive artists from other countries as well as French exponents from both the older and younger generations, and thus brought a welcome internationalism into art life in the French capital. But an article by Léon Degand on this first attempt at an international overview (a "Defense of abstract art") reveals that the movement had to be vigorously defended against a hostile public. Some 400 works by 90 artists of many nationalities were exhibited: "the best

documentation of abstract art one could imagine". Degand's arguments today leave us with the impression that he was writing an introduction and apologia for something until then quite unheard of in Paris. After defining the principles of the various groups, Degand comes to the conclusion that all the trends could be grouped under the concept of "Art abstrait", that "decried, unknown and misunderstood art". He explains its attributes by quoting analogies from music. The second part of his essay is particularly instructive. All the objections to non-objective art—repeatedly heard even today—are listed and disproved in a fictitious dialogue. But his efforts were all in vain, or at least it must seem so to anyone who reads the review in which the art historian Bernard Dorival poured scorn on the second "Salon des Réalités Nouvelles" in 1947.

In 1950, after another exhibition under the same title, the poet, painter and publicist Michel Seuphor published his book "L'Art abstrait, ses origines, ses premiers maîtres". It served two purposes. At a time when the term "abstract art" was being bandied about it set out to show that such an art had existed since 1910/12, that it had its history, its great masters and its clear trends and affiliations. The book also left no doubt that abstract art had from the beginning taken two quite different lines: expressive abstraction (Kandinsky, 1910), based on Fauvism and Expressionism; and rational abstraction (Delaunay, Kupka, Mondrian), which had grown out of Cubism and had also been influenced by Seurat. Seuphor saw the two extremes connected by many intermediate trends and certainly not fundamentally opposed to each other. For him abstract art was "any art that is free of relations to visible reality and thus contains no suggestion of observation, whether as a starting point for the artist or not". Seuphor considers the work of Kandinsky and of Mondrian as the two extremes between which abstract art was developing and would continue to develop.

The third "Salon des Réalités Nouvelles" of 1948 had presented 700 pictures and sculptures by artists from 17 countries. Despite this, it had not been a complete review of the state of the art. According to Seuphor it had "furnished proof that abstract art offers innumerable possibilities for renewal, whereas subjects drawn from the visible world are much less numerous, much more limited, and above all much more worn-out than those found in the world of the mind".

Seuphor's book, the first attempt at a description of constructive art as a whole, did a great deal to persuade numerous younger artists to join the pioneers working in France—Sonia Delaunay, Auguste Herbin, Jean Gorin, Antoine Pevsner, Georges Vantongerloo, etc. And this in

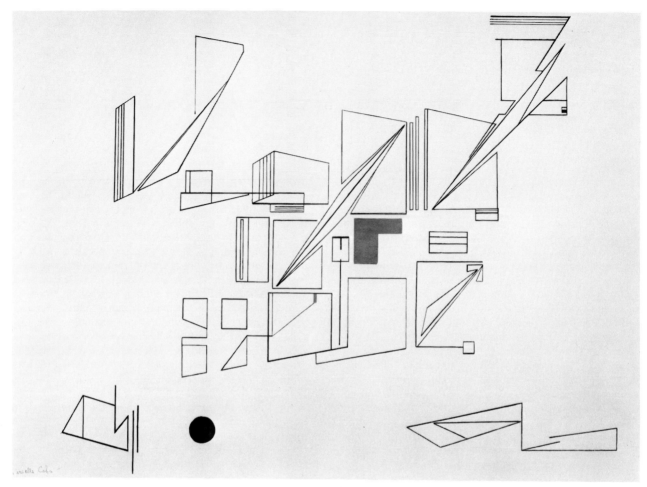

Marcelle Cahn: Reversible II, 1952

spite of the dominant position of the painters of the "French tradition" active in Paris around 1950, who have since become known as the "School of Paris": Bazaine, Bissière, Estève, Lapicque, Manessier, Singier and de Stael; and in spite of the free, expressive "abstraction lyrique" which conquered Europe from Paris in the fifties and challenged the more objective and disciplined constructive art with its extremely subjective non-figurative gestures. Next to this Tachisme of Wols, Mathieu, Fautrier, Soulages, Hartung and others, born of an understandable need for the uninhibited self-expression of the individual after the war, the constructive artists with their cult of clarity and order were at a disadvantage. Their situation was rendered even more difficult by the fact that few galleries in Paris had the courage to swim against the tide.

The most courageous of those who did so was Denise René. She began work in 1945 with the aim of creating a center for the representatives of geometric abstraction. The "Denise René Group" was quickly formed and was not restricted to Paris or even to France but soon attracted artists of similar leanings from abroad. The exhibition "Tendances de l'art abstrait" of 1948 embodied a clear and by no means narrow program. The institution, in 1946, of a "Prix Kandinsky" with the moral support of Nina Kandinsky, the artist's widow, and of Charles

Estienne and Léon Degand had already demonstrated that the object was an artistic one and not merely a commercial success. "The future thus seemed full of promise, but the game had not by any means been won for abstract art," Denise René declared later.

The Denise René Group, which changed its composition continually, had a common denominator in what she herself called "the constructive line of abstract art". As an alternative to the vague term "art abstrait" she proposed "art abstrait constructif international". The basis of the movement was provided by the pioneers of constructive art, some of them by this time already dead, including the exponents of Eastern European Constructivism as well as members of de Stijl, artists from the Bauhaus, with the emphasis on Josef Albers, and the seniors of "Abstraction-Création". Denise René did not wish merely to bring the past up to date, however; she also wanted to encourage present endeavors, and from the first she took a predominant interest in young contemporary artists.

Along with Auguste Herbin, who had launched into his masterly late work with its radiantly colorful surface designs of triangular, rectangular and circular shapes (ill. p. 125), Jean Gorin, who advanced from Neo-Plasticism to three-dimensional constructions, his so-called "compositions plastiques spatio-temporelles" (ill. p. 131), the reserved Marcelle Cahn with her line constructions on a white ground, partly static and partly dynamic (ill. p. 162), new personalities soon made their appearance in Denise René's circle. There was the group of the Swiss Concrete artists, Bill, Glarner, Graeser, Lohse, and later the young Karl Gerstner. The trio Richard Mortensen, Olle Baertling and Victor Vasarely were also closely associated with the gallery for many years. The two Scandinavians — Mortensen was a Dane and Baertling a Swede — brought new impulses into the constructive movement by replacing rational severity by a freer, more intuitive approach to geometric forms. The dynamic or expressive element of the diagonal — not a measured 45 degrees between horizontal and vertical, but at any acute or obtuse angle — repeatedly broke up the surface, or the expansive movements of the shapes seemed to dissolve the confines of the picture area. While in Mortensen's work the adjoining and superimposed surfaces, pushed in front of one another like set pieces on a stage, evoke an idea of dislocated spaces (ill. p. 163), the movement of Olle Baertling's shapes is limited to the plane. Oblique black lines radiating from the edge of the picture or from a point outside it produce a fan-like line pattern into which the flat fields of color are inserted (ill. p. 165). Both artists apply their color flatly to the surfaces, avoiding all signs of personal brushwork. This color is not restricted to the primaries but includes blended hues, in Mortensen softer, more muted and passive, in Baertling more violent and contrasty and therefore more active and vital. In his theoretical writings Baertling has pointed out that by moving the points of intersection of the lines outside of the picture area the shapes can be made to open up to the surrounding space. Many of his compositions give the impression of a show of colored floodlights whose rays widen toward infinity. In his "Prologue to a manifesto of open shape" Baertling summed up the thoughts behind this endeavor to open up the picture: a sort of phenomenology of the open shape.

In connection with this open shape there is much talk of "forces" and "energies", and thus necessarily of motion. In the work of Baertling, who repeatedly pointed out his debt to Léger and particularly to Herbin, this element of motion and even of speed no longer depends on circular shapes as in, say, Geneviève Claisse, but consciously avoids these. Lines and families of lines shooting out into space become the only carriers of this motion. Kinetic energy is expressed at its purest in the sculptural works, where the lines, detached from the rest of the composition and invested with independence, shoot out into space like flashes of lightning. The sense of motion is enhanced by the use of black lines that diverge from a straight course and seem to oscillate.

Baertling was not by any means alone in evincing this interest in motion at the beginning of the fifties. "Kinetics" was a magic word that fascinated many of the exponents of geometric abstraction. This brings us to one of the fundamental problems of art: the reproduction of movement in static terms. In the spring of 1955 Denise René mounted the exhibition "Le Mouvement". It comprised work by Agam, Bury, Calder, Duchamp, Soto, Tinguely and Vasarely and was accompanied by a manifesto with the same title that has come down to posterity as the "Yellow Manifesto" because of the color of the paper on which it was printed. The texts are by K. G. Pontus Hultén, Roger

Richard Mortensen: Laura, 1962

Bordier and Victor Vasarely. Hultén, the real initiator of the undertaking, contributed two basic articles. In the one — "Movement — time, or the fourth dimension of the kinetic sculpture" — he took the view that the inclusion of the time factor was one of the great innovations of contemporary art. "Movement is a spark of life that makes art human and truly realistic." The element of movement was a chance for the artist to free himself and to employ all his faculties. As a result of elements of motion, "that symbol of the artist's freedom", "the pictures leave their static positions, joining themselves to us and initiating a fruitful dialogue". The supplementation or even the replacement of static art by a "dynamic art" was regarded as an act of liberation and at the same time as a possible and necessary way of bridging the gap between the work of art and the viewer. The latter is released from his passive role and drawn into active exchanges with the work.

In a second article in the "Yellow Manifesto" Hultén explains that this "kinetic art" — the word "kinetic" now appears more and more frequently — has its forerunners. He gives a chronology of modern art's preoccupation with time and space, which began with the Cubists and Futurists. He finds an ancestor of the movement in Marcel Duchamp, who had produced the first "kinetic ready-made" with his movably mounted bicycle wheel in 1913. Hultén also calls to mind Tatlin's mobile architectural projects and the "Realist Manifesto" of Gabo and Pevsner, in which kinetic art is first mentioned theoretically as a future possibility. In the same year, 1920, Gabo's "Virtual kinetic volume" had seen the light, a steel strip set in mo-

163

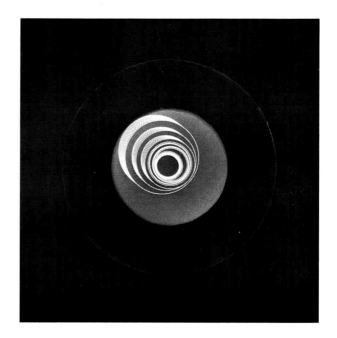

Marcel Duchamp: Rotoreliefs, 1935/53

tion by an electric motor and producing a virtual volume by its oscillation. It was also in 1920 that Duchamp's experiments with rotating glass disks began, in which a pattern painted on the disk, basically spiral in form, creates by rotation an immaterial body or space. The "Rotoreliefs" that Duchamp placed on the market in 1935 — the first real "multiples" — were the last products of his study of rotary kinetic illusions (ill. p. 164). Hultén's chronology also recalls the fact that it was Duchamp who gave the name of "mobiles" to the first of Alexander Calder's space sculptures to be moved by hand or by a motor. These pioneering achievements were followed after the end of World War II by an increasing number and variety of experiments directed toward the integration of motion in art.

The facts contained briefly in Hultén's chronology were made the subject, in 1961, of a comprehensive exhibition that was staged in the Stedelijk Museum, Amsterdam, under the title of "Bewogen Beweging" (Moved Motion). The concept for this first fundamental exhibition of kinetic art again came from Hultén. He produced both a who's who of the artists who had devoted themselves to kinetic art up to that time and a researched documentation of kinetic art in the twentieth century. He was to turn to the subject for the third time in the exhibition "The Machine as seen at the end of the mechanical age" in the Museum of Modern Art, New York, in 1968. Here he was less concerned with kinetic phenomena in art than with the relation of the artist to the machine, culminating in the study of technologies and their use for the purposes of art. This extension, variation and deepening of the theme of kinetic art mirrors the enormous development of interest in aspects of motion in art from the fifties on. It has also furnished the theoretical and historical foundation for trends that really reach far beyond art: the critical and self-critical, disturbing and sometimes ironic questioning

of the machine world at the end of an era. (In his major work, "Mechanization Takes Command", Sigfried Giedion had described in 1948 the beginnings of this mechanical age in the nineteenth century, with all its boundless belief in progress.)

The artists who supported the manifesto "Le Mouvement" in 1955 were hardly thinking of such consequences. Motion was a magic word that could be applied to many things. That is clear from the main contribution to the "Yellow Manifesto" by Victor Vasarely. He first outlines the developments leading up to the events that chiefly interest him and his companions: the triumph of pure painting over the anecdote in Manet; the first interpretation of the visible world through geometry in Cézanne; the conquest of pure color by Matisse; the breakdown of figuration in Picasso; the switch from an outer to an inner vision in Kandinsky; the translation of painting into architecture, an architecture articulated by color, as in Mondrian's Neo-Plasticism; the advance to the great plastic syntheses in Le Corbusier; new three-dimensional alphabets by Arp, Sophie Taeuber, Magnelli and Herbin; the renunciation of volume in favor of space by Calder. "Space", "pure composition" and "unity" are the passwords for Vasarely, whose new line of advance involves the complete discarding of all former routine and leads to the acceptance of new functions for art and to the "conquest of dimensions beyond the surface".

In a second section Vasarely turns to the artist's media. He recognizes "pure composition" — by which he means an autonomous order, free of allusions to visible reality and primarily geometric — as a significant achievement of modern art. But he criticizes the fact that the handling of form has been restricted to the articulation of surfaces. He points out that a sensation of space is inherent in the relations of positive and negative shapes, which can produce an illusion of motion and duration. He regards it as

Olle Baertling: Ogri, 1959

significant that in the new painting he proposes color and shape have become an indivisible unity. From this fact he derives one of the fundamental tenets of his artistic theory: two color-shapes, which necessarily contrast with each other, form a "plastic unit". These "plastic units" are the cells which Vasarely uses to build his later compositions.

Vasarely goes on to discuss what happens in the "frame", inside the horizontal and vertical boundaries of the picture. To frame is to limit a surface or to cut a piece out of space. A screen for the projection of slides or films leads beyond such two-dimensionalism. It is, like the picture, two-dimensional. But since corporeal or spatial entities—and in the film motion too—can be projected on it, it becomes three- and four-dimensional, it becomes space. From this reasoning Vasarely deduces for painting, which he understands as "création plastique", the requirements for an animation of the plastic world. Firstly, movement in the direction of an architectural synthesis, the monumental three-dimensional work being so conceived that its constant metamorphoses are produced by the movements of the viewer. Secondly, automatic plastic objects which, in addition to their own intrinsic value, are highly suitable as a means of animation for recording on film. Thirdly, the methodical inclusion of cinematography in the domain of abstract art. Vasarely announces a new era: "The age of plastic projections on flat and recessed surfaces, by day and in darkness, has begun." Moholy-Nagy had already had visions of this kind.

The conviction that an "expansion" is taking place in art is closely bound up with this vision. It relates not only to designing processes, to new goals and new techniques, but also to new functions of art in society. "The art of tomorrow will be the common possession of all or will be nothing at all . . . Our living conditions have changed, and now our ethics and our aesthetics must change. Whereas the idea of the work of art has hitherto been based on execution by hand and on the myth of the unique artifact, it is today confronted by the idea of repetition, of multiplication." By analogy with the duplication of literary or musical works, Vasarely postulates the "multiplied work of art", the "multiple".

Vasarely's "Notes on a Manifesto" of 1955 sparked off a series of theoretical statements by other artists. These formed the background of an artistic practice in which all the possibilities of kinetic art were experimentally rehearsed. The favorite word of the day was "recherche" —research, experiment, exploration. A good deal of both theory and practice was at cross purposes; the concept of "kinetics" and its derivatives did more to confuse than clarify the issue. It appears to be established that Naum Gabo was the first to use the term "kinetics"—a branch of dynamics concerned with the motion of bodies—in relation to art as far back as 1920. "Kinetic energy" is the mechanical energy stored in a moving body which can be released when its motion is modified, for example when a vehicle is braked. In art this type of kinetic energy is rarely involved. And kinetic art certainly has nothing at all to do with the kinetic theory of gases founded in 1738 by Daniel Bernoulli, which is concerned with the movements of molecules.

If we apply the word "kinetic" to everything in art that has to do with motion, we soon realize that there are several different types of motion. We have to differentiate, for instance, between virtual and real movement. In the course of its history art has found many ways of representing movement which we need not review here. This representation of movement differs from the suggestion of movement achieved by compositional means, by coloring or contrast. Here again many approaches have been tried out by artists. A major change came only with the advent of photography: the instantaneous shot enables the phases of a real movement to be frozen in such a way that the illusion of movement remains. This fact has brought about a fundamental modification of the artist's way of seeing since Impressionism. But it was not until the motion photography of Etienne-Jules Marey and Eadweard Muybridge that movement could be broken down into its phases and thus made accessible to observation. The cinematography of Edison and Lumière finally enabled motion to be reproduced by the use of film at the speed at which it had originally taken place.

The photography of motion, above all chronophotography as first demonstrated by the American Thomas Eakins in 1885 with multiple exposures on the same plate, and finally culminating in stroboscopic photography, inspired the Futurists to suggest dynamic movement in their pictures. Their attempts to paint several phases of a movement simultaneously remained a mere episode, for in this area photography and film were superior. The artists who turned their attention to the phenomena of motion after 1950 could of course point to Marcel Duchamp's "Nude Descending a Staircase" of 1912 (ill. p. 240) as a forerunner worthy of veneration. But in geometric constructive art the representation of moving figures or objects was not of interest. Attention was turned rather to motion in itself; the idea, the illusion of motion was to be created.

The illusion of motion can be created in different ways. Processes of perception long known to the physiologist can be exploited so that the static viewer is deceived by optical effects and seems to see movement in the picture. Such illusions of motion may be such that the two-dimensional impression is not destroyed, or else the surface can be set in apparently three-dimensional pulsation. The psycho-physical processes involved in this "surface kinetics", as Vasarely has termed these optical effects, can be initiated either by black-and-white or by colored shapes and structures.

Both types of surface kinetics have no doubt interested artists at all times. Optical effects are not by any means an invention of our own era; the generation and observation of them go back to antiquity. But it was only with the scientific investigation of optical and physiological laws and phenomena in the nineteenth century that artists were provided with a firm basis on which they could probe into optical effects on the surface with the tools of drawing and painting. This work was begun by the Impressionists and continued by Georges Seurat and Paul Signac in particular. It was later to be a springboard for Op Art, which takes purposeful and effective advantage of the mechanisms of human perception.

In black-and-white patterns—parallel bands, concentric circles or squares, chessboard patterns and the like— pulsating effects are the commonest. A disturbing element, for instance a diagonal or curved line crossing a pattern of stripes, may be added to produce the "moiré

Victor Vasarely: Minato, No. 301, 1951

effect". The modification of a shape by distortion, compression or expansion gives it a plastic appearance; compression suggests depth, expansion causes surfaces to "bulge".

In the use of colors to create the illusion of movement the relation of the colors plays a part. If a color depends on its neighboring or surrounding color, a "simultaneous effect" is produced through the principle of simultaneous contrast. Our eye demands, as a companion to a given color, its complementary color, purple to yellow, orange to blue, green to red, to mention only primary and secondary colors which are opposite each other in the color circle. The simultaneous effect consists of a modification of the affected color toward the complementary of the surrounding color. In blue surroundings, for instance, red is modified toward orange, whereas in yellow surroundings it moves toward purple. The complementary effect occurs when a color produces its complementary color when perceived by the eye. The phenomenon has not yet been fully explained scientifically but belongs to the after-image effects which — ostensibly as a result of fatigue in the receptors of the retina — are also observed in dark and light contrasts, and thus in black and white figures.

Disturbing effects are also produced by irradiation, the spread of a color beyond its actual surface area. If two interacting color areas are confined, the result is not equal irradiation, the simultaneous effect, but the so-called "Bezold effect": one color is displaced toward its neighboring color by the irradiation of the stronger color. The "Mach strip" or edge contrast on either side of a line dividing two adjacent color areas is also very important. Flutter or vibration may occur along the line depending upon the relationship of the two colors. Strong vibration effects are observed when color contrasts occur in small-scale patterns. These color effects, resulting from the processes of vision, have long been known and described alongside the laws of color, both in scientific color theory and in art color theories developed since Chevreul and

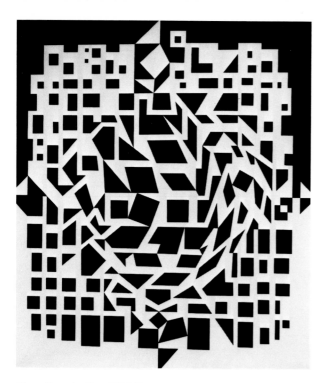

Victor Vasarely: Citra, 1955/59

Goethe. All aspects of these color effects have been explored in kinetic art to create the illusion of movement.

A different kind of kinetics is involved when the movement is not an illusion on a two-dimensional surface, and thus a merely perceptual phenomenon, but is instead produced optically by the movement of the viewer, as for instance in a relief that reveals a continuously or successively changing structure or color composition as we walk past it. The "kinetic effect" may also be produced by two structures that are superimposed but separate — two different line systems or a line system and a color surface — whose relationships are modified by the movement of the viewer. If a pattern on a transparent medium, such as glass or acrylic, is placed above but at a certain distance from another basic pattern, moiré effects and distortions may result. Such vibrations suggest movement to the observer. They are faster and more violent than his own movement.

A fundamentally different form of kinetic art operates with real motion. This is not illusionary or due to movement of the observer, but is produced by air movements — breath, updrafts, wind, or air flows generated by fans — or by direct mechanical actuation by hand, water power or spring force, by the use of electromagnetic fields, by electric motors or electronic drives. In the case of mobile hanging objects — hung in relief before a wall or as three-dimensional elements in space — no drive as such is needed. Where mechanical force, and more particularly motors, are used for creating motion, the work of art moves in the direction of the machine.

A special category of kinetic art comprises works in which light effects are used, either alone or in addition to other movement, for instance by means of the projection, reflection or refraction of light. Combinations of light and

mechanical kinetics are possible when the light sources are mechanically or electronically controlled or the object itself is moved under a static light source. Changing reflections are then produced, or the moving object may even be used for casting a changing shadow.

The applications of kinetics have expanded into an ever larger and more differentiated domain of geometric constructive art. The different types of kinetic art can hardly be terminologically distinguished, for the conceptual divisions are blurred by the subjective preferences of the artists concerned and a measure of overlapping makes it difficult to draw clear lines. The sector Vasarely has called "surface kinetics", which has to do with phenomena of perception, has come to be known as "perceptual art" (Albers). Since the problems involved are of an optical nature, the name proposed in "Time" magazine in 1964, "Op Art" (optical art — by analogy with Pop Art), was at once universally accepted. Within the whole range of the arts of motion, kinetic art proper might be limited to those applications in which the apparent movements are due to the movement of the viewer or the object is set in real motion. Where light effects are combined with motion, we are dealing with light kinetics.

Action painting and experiments with cameras and video equipment make it clear that since the fifties many artists outside of geometric constructive art have developed an interest in the problems of motion. All the efforts to produce or to suggest motion have one thing in common, a desire on the part of the artist to activate the observer and in the extreme case to induce him to participate. The deeper purpose is to break out of the "isolation" of art and to re-integrate it in society. Vasarely referred to these new functions of art in his contribution to the "Yellow Manifesto" of 1955.

Though Vasarely's written commentaries were stimulating enough at the time, it was really his work that sparked off new investigations into visual phenomena. His geometric abstractions in the period beginning about 1945 do not yet show any great interest in kinetics, being sensitive, painterly surface arrangements in muted tones, inspired by natural impressions (shells, gravel, waves), and often clearly revealing the hand of the artist (ill. p. 167). "It was only in 1947 that the abstract was really and truly manifested to me when I realized that the pure color-shape was capable of signifying the world." After 1930, when he had settled in Paris, Vasarely had worked as a graphic designer and had familiarized himself with the working principles of Surrealism, including optical illusions based on graphic patterns. Attention has already been drawn to this work as helping to explain his later development. Vasarely himself has repeatedly pointed out, however, that during his training under Alexander Bortnyk in Budapest in 1929 he became acquainted both with Constructivist thinking and with the working methods of the Bauhaus in Dessau, though he never studied there himself.

About 1948 his painting became markedly geometric. The irrational, organic curved shapes gave way to crystalline patterns. At the same time his palette was sharply reduced. Vasarely concerned himself once more with the axonometric cube with which Bortnyk had familiarized him. Paintings using axonometric projections of three-dimensional bodies (in parallel perspective) take on a

Victor Vasarely: Tridim W, Gestalt, 1969

striking appearance of corporeality, an illusion of depth. Vasarely was to return to this later.

He now dropped color temporarily, however, in order to investigate in black and white the behavior of regular line systems whose parallelism is in some way disturbed. The surface is set in motion, spatial illusions are created. In his "Photographisms" in 1951 Vasarely tried out the large-scale projection of such dislocated structures and the kinetic effects resulting from the superimposition of two systems. His observation of the increased surface movement tempted him to transfer these projected figures to painting. "After my excursions into the fluid domain of the overdimensioned I found myself back on the surface. I noted that two dimensions are not by any means exhausted as yet. Was optics an illusion, was it not involved in kinetics? Was an attack on the retina not best achieved by setting it in effective vibration? The greatest contrast was no doubt black and white . . ." In the next few years Vasarely investigated dislocated line systems, grids, small chessboard patterns and bar structures with almost scientific exactitude. He observed attentively the different effect made by the same composition when executed

Nicolas Schöffer: Lux 9B, 1959/68

From about 1960 on, using the principles of permutation and an ever richer color spectrum, Vasarely developed in numerous series the outline of what he calls his "planetary folklore". Systematization of the elements and hues, plus the use of permutational principles, permit unlimited variation and bring the designing processes very near to cybernetic procedures.

While in his serial work the principle of the addition of similar elements takes first place, Vasarely has not dealt exclusively with it. His interest in problems of apparent depth and corporeality led him to return to compositional principles he had broached at the beginning of his study of surface kinetics. The effects obtained in the dark-light contrasts of his black-and-white compositions were now enriched by the use of color. Thus he returned to his "concentric" rectangular bands or frames in the "Vonal" series of 1968, in which the increasing or diminishing thickness of the bands is optically intensified by an analogous graded color modulation. The result is a disturbing spatial effect that confuses the observer, who cannot decide whether a pyramidal stepped relief is approaching him or a corridor is pulling him into its depths. The effect is even more dramatic in the series that predominated after the late sixites, which might be termed the "expanding chessboard": the pattern of rows of identical units arranged regularly over the whole field is distorted, and an apparent hemispherical convex deformation of the surface is produced toward the center because of the increased size of the units, or else a concave deformation due to their reduced size. The effect is heightened by a brightening or darkening of the colors. Going beyond the principles of color and shape explored in such works — concave-convex, light-dark, hollow-full, circle-in-square, square-in-circle — Vasarely has also proposed pairs of astrophysical concepts such as perigee-apogee and nadir-zenith.

The "Tridim" series based on a hexagon composed of three rhomboids, or the projection of a cube standing on one corner (ill. p. 169), takes matters a step further than these "breathing" surfaces. The rhomboids, in different colors, form cube-like projecting and retreating bodies. This can be recognized only because the surfaces in the same position show the same color brightness. The differing degrees of brightness enable the observer to "read" the stereometric structure in either of two contrary senses: convex or concave. Since the two "readings" are incompatible and the inversive figure is therefore illogical, a final choice between them is impossible. This phenomenon of perceptually ambivalent figures, which has turned up repeatedly since antiquity, and the accompanying perplexity or aporia, the impossibility of making a visual decision about them, have long occupied perception theorists. Maurice Merleau-Ponty dealt with them in some detail in his work on the phenomenology of perception published in Paris in 1946. Similar "visual paradoxes" have also turned up in cybernetic aesthetics, a field in which the computer is used for the production of permutational graphics.

The series of the "Tridim" compositions, which Vasarely has termed "homage to the hexagon" (by analogy with Josef Albers' "Homage to the Square"), do not stop at the presentation of such paradoxes. They are visual riddles that set out to awaken a "multidimensional" impres-

as a positive — in black on white — and as a negative — in white on black. Vasarely worked his way through these black-and-white kinetic compositions, sometimes proceeding quite systematically, sometimes taking certain liberties and trying out non-logical modifications. Intriguing patterns were obtained when a basic composition was fitted together in its negative and positive forms to make a single whole. In his "Citra" of 1955 the mirror image of positive and negative, top and bottom, left and right, is so manipulated by the introduction of disturbing factors that the impression of a dynamic surface dislocation is created which cannot be rationally explained (ill. p. 168). The principle of the combination of identical positive and negative compositions — known as "inversion" — was later used by other geometric constructive artists, for example by Aurélie de Nemours (ill. p. 176), who belonged to the "abstraction géometrique" movement in Paris after 1950.

Setting out from grid-like black-and-white patterns that are brought into apparent movement by expansion, compression and other types of deformation, Vasarely studied, from the mid-fifties on, the changes in binary structures. Simple geometric units — squares or circles, circles in squares, squares in squares, rhomboids in squares — now gained in importance. The "plastic unit" consists, as Vasarely says, "of two constants: the core shape and its surrounding complement, the square background. Apart from this two-shape aspect, the unit necessarily has a two-color aspect, which is harmonic or oppositional and at the same time positive-negative. As a pure contradiction, this unquestionable unity is a synthesis of pure dialectic." The square character of the unit and its "mobile scale" offered maximum scope for rational manipulation.

sion over and above the spatial illusion. And in the final analysis they are meant to invite thought on the "surface that is more than a surface".

Other artists also turned to kinetic art in Paris after 1950, some of them in complete isolation. In many cases they became aware of the work in progress in this field only when it appeared in exhibitions, for instance in the annual "Salon des Réalités Nouvelles" from 1952 onward. Meetings took place chiefly through Denise René, and the convergence of the individual lines of advance then became evident. One of these isolated artists was the Israeli Yaacov Agam, who had lived in Paris since 1951. He had taken Johannes Itten's course in Zurich, had become familiar with Concrete Art through Max Bill and had learned something about space-time relationships from Sigfried Giedion. The works he produced after 1952 and exhibited for the first time in the Galerie Craven in 1953 were a markedly individual achievement.

"I set out to create a picture that can be looked at by the observer in an unlimited number of situations — each situation exactly calculated in advance and determined by the totality of single elements constituting the work. The observer should be able to choose the situation that suits him best. The freedom thus granted him raises the question of whether I am not thereby relinquishing my rights as creator of the work, whether the observer does not in fact change it. To this I can only say that the observer himself creates nothing; he only chooses one of the many positions, situations, propositions, which are virtually contained in my work. The observer can find no shape that I have not provided and approved." The freedom of the observer, in other words, consists only in the subjective choice of one of the given possibilities that particularly appeals to him; his freedom is a limited freedom. If Agam nevertheless attaches a good deal of importance to this act of choice, it is because he believes that participation permits a more spontaneous, personal and intense contact with the work than would be possible if the observer were only a passive consumer.

All of Agam's two- and three-dimensional works offer this possibility of transformation either by manual adjustment or by a change of the viewer's location. In his earliest compositions, mostly black-and-white reliefs, the position of the mobile elements could be changed on a baseplate with a regular or irregular pattern of perforations. The scope for structural change contained in such a system is designated by Agam as the "expressive potential" of the work. The modifiable reliefs mostly consist of white lines, bars and circles on a black background. In a second group of works, non-mobile relief structures formed of parallel vertical triangular bars, color becomes important. These works challenge the observer to change his viewing angle. Using a principle already applied in the laminated sectional pictures in European popular religious art of the eighteenth and nineteenth centuries, Agam utilizes the two visible faces of the triangular bars for his geometric color compositions: each yields, regarded from left or right, a complete picture. Looked at from the front, the two subjects blend into a third composition. The ribbed structure also seems to move as the viewer changes his angle of observation to the left or the right. The work can therefore be understood as presenting a continuous change from one subject to the other. Agam

gave these relief structures such a richness of color and shape that ever more changing themes were captured in them, in a spirit comparable to that of polyphonic musical composition.

Agam's purpose of freeing the picture from the wall led to the free-standing display of two-sided relief structures. Such "metamorphoses" become three-dimensional color bodies. As the work can only be observed in the process of walking around or past it, it also involves the time dimension. Experiments with color bodies of this kind have repeatedly been made since the early fifties by Bill, Vasarely and others. The transformation of the colored relief structure, the kinetic picture proper, however, has remained a specialty of Agam. He is also interested in plastic problems, as is shown by the early vibrating reliefs that appeal to the sense of touch, and by the spatial structures of the late sixties. Here round metal bars arranged parallel to each other in three imaginary surfaces are at

Pol Bury: Sphère sur un cylindre, 1969

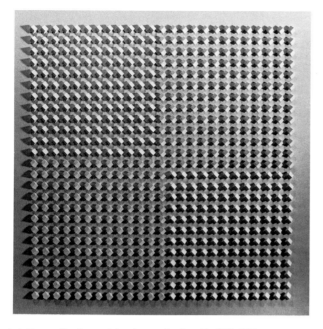

Luis Tomasello: Atmosphère chromoplastique No. 300, 1973

Julio Le Parc: Continuel Mobile, blanc sur blanc, 1968/69

right angles to each other and therefore point in the three directions of space. Agam calls these structures "In all directions". The intersections of the bundles of bars are continuously displaced by the changes of position of the observer. The works are in fact a transference of the optical impression of intersecting line structures to three dimensions (ill. p. 173).

The realization, repeatedly activated since 1950, that optical effects can also be obtained by the superimposition of two or more pattern systems is also the basis of the kinetic work of Jesus Rafael Soto. This Venezuelan, who settled in Paris in 1950, was the first Latin American to play a major role in constructive art and more particularly in its optical-kinetic branch centered on Paris. With an interest in Mondrian, Malevich and the Bauhaus, Soto first attempted in 1951 to develop geometric surface patterns from a single, systematically repeated form. These "repetitions" resulted in pure surface textures in which the picture area was only part of a pattern extending to infinity in all directions; Soto talks of their "universal character". The repetitive principle can be understood as a serial ordering system if it leads to dense, coherent rows in which the single — identical — elements lose their individuality. The impression of a relief structure, of apparent corporeality, is produced when Soto chooses his basic shapes so that the horizontal-vertical arrangement with rectangles or bars is joined by a diagonal component with triangles, trapezoids, rhomboids. If color is added to black and white, a "spatial" light-and-shade structure results. Serially developed patterns of this kind yield fruitful results particularly when the principle of repetition is combined with progression, penetration or rotation.

Soto made use of acrylic for the first time in 1953. He mounted two plates, each covered with a dot pattern, at a certain distance from each other. When the viewer moves in front of this two-layer transparent picture, the dot pat-

terns begin to interact. This was the starting point of Soto's investigations into kinetics. He formulated its principles with Agam and Tinguely in 1954. By 1955, the year of the exhibition "Le Mouvement", he had his own kinetic productions under control. They consist essentially of two or more linear figures or patterns that are superimposed with a certain interval between them so that they are relatively displaced when the viewer moves. Because of the constantly changing configurations that result they produce a marked optical movement, for instance the moiré effect. Most of the "kinetic structures of geometric elements" that Soto developed after 1955 show these in-depth kinetic effects.

An extension of the possibilities came around 1960 with the study of optical vibrations, and vibrations characterize the two groups of works with which Soto chiefly concerned himself after this date. The prerequisite is a basic pattern consisting of a dense horizontal or vertical, regular or hand-drawn hatching, either dark on light or light on dark. In one group of works Soto uses a suspension device to hang a horizontal bar or one or more vertical balanced wires or bars from a nylon thread in front of this hatching. The movement of the almost weightless mobile as a result of drafts or intentional contacts produces a secondary optical movement due to its slight displacement in front of the pattern of lines (ill. p. 175). Real and apparent motions are thus combined. In the second group of works Soto fixes square monochrome plates — mostly blue or black — in a strict order in front of the hatched ground, suspending them invisibly (ill. p. 174). Even the slightest change in the angle of observation sets these "static" tableaux in vibration.

It has been mentioned above that these kinetic works, for all their relief character, really express the intentions of a painter: articulation of the surface by means of shape and color. Commissions for monumental objects and

172

large works developed especially for exhibitions showed in the next few years, however, that Soto was also intensely interested in space. In his "Extensions" —spaces filled with serried rows of standing bars—and his "Penetrations"—spaces filled with a dense "rain" of hanging nylon threads—he turned his shaping principles to the creation of environments. In the first instance the viewer walks around the closely packed, colored forest of rods and perceives the changes in the persons and objects behind them. In the second he is himself the actor who experiences, as he advances into the nylon curtain, the disappearance, the dematerialization of his surroundings, and as he emerges again their gradual materialization and restoration. In other words, an increasing and diminishing identification of the observer with Soto's articulated space takes place. Space, time and material become one, according to Soto, who considers himself as a research worker and his art—or art altogether—as a science proving what cannot be proven by other means: "Art is the sensuous experience of the immaterial."

This statement might also have been made by a second Venezuelan, Carlos Cruz-Diez, who settled in Paris in 1960 and for whom color is the most powerful of stimulants. He uses strips or lamellar structures in horizontal or vertical arrangements as a scaffolding of low intrinsic significance for his experiments in color kinetics. The interpenetrating parallel color strips generate effects of color vibration which can be considered as "chromatic happenings" (ill. p. 174).

The pioneering kinetic works inspired active participation and pursuance of the new ideas among young artists, a phenomenon that had hardly characterized other advances in constructive art. Opportunism and the ease of making such art evidently played some part here, and this led to optical and kinetic art being relegated to the sphere of the fashionable and ephemeral. A more important aspect was that the impulses imparted by the pioneers also turned a latent interest in the fundamentals of perception into a readiness to carry out concrete experiments. Groups of artists now formed in Paris and elsewhere and exchanged their results like scientists in the laboratory, some of them even tackling kinetic problems in concert.

One of the first of these groups was the "Groupe de Recherche d'Art Visuel" founded in Paris in 1960 and disbanded in 1968. Among its founders, in addition to Vasarely, Agam and Soto, the Argentinian Hugo Demarco and the Frenchman Yvaral (ill. p. 173), was the Argentinian Julio Le Parc, who had lived in Paris since 1958. The whole spectrum of the kinetic research undertaken in this circle is found in his work. It reflects the objectives which the group formulated in 1966: "This research sets out from the independent work with its final and self-contained character and is directed toward the open, non-final work that is subject to conditions such as arise from direct contact with the observer. This observer, usually a passive spectator, can be won over to active and decisive participation. Parallel to this, the—overestimated—role of the creative artist is called in question. It is easy to imagine that the inspired artist will now be replaced by searchers, contrivers of elements and inventors of situations, in short by animators who by their productions and activities will reveal the contradictions of present-day art and will create the conditions for an opening-up of art in direct collaboration with the observer. An opening-up which may lead to the surmounting of the antinomy of art and public."

Le Parc turned his hand to all branches of kinetic art: optical phenomena on the surface, penetration of various structures, virtual and real movement. His work extends from kinetic pictures to mobile relief structures moved by hand or by electric motors, from "continuous mobiles" to kinetic light reliefs and light sculptures. Foreseeable movement, unforeseeable "surprise movement" and experimental objects such as his "glasses for a different vision" are among his studies. The "continuous reliefs" belong to Le Parc's more important productions. They are mobile structures hanging on threads in front of a monochrome ground, consisting of identical elements of reflecting metal or transparent acrylic, and they are kept in constant but unpredictable motion by air movements, continuously changing their relative positions and, as the light falls on them, projecting their real movement onto the wall (ill. p. 172).

Yvaral: Instabilité, 1960

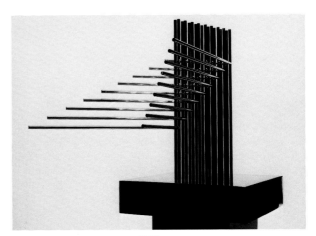

Yaacov Agam: In all Directions, 1969

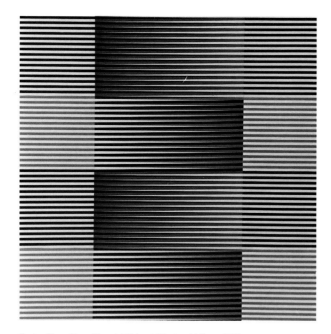

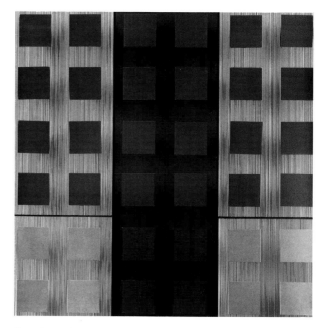

Carlos Cruz-Diez: Blue + White + Black = Yellow, 1970

Jesus Rafael Soto: Vibrating Squares, 1968

The Argentinian Luis Tomasello, who came to Paris in 1957, investigated relief structures and phenomena of color reflection. As a member of "Nouvelle Tendance" he took part in the major kinetic exhibitions. His leitmotiv is the "chromoplastic atmosphere", and all his wood reliefs bear this designation. As a rule small cubes standing on end are fixed in horizontal-vertical or diagonal rows on a square base. The three visible faces of the cubes are painted white, like the base. A differentiation as between white, light gray and dark gray relief zones, between illuminated, half-shaded or fully shaded surfaces, is created according to the position of the groups of surfaces and the incidence of light. The three faces of the cubes turned away from the viewer are systematically painted in the primary colors, all faces of the same orientation being in the same color. These color surfaces are not visible in the front view, but their reflections appear on the base. As the viewer or the light source moves, the pattern of delicately colored shadows on the white ground and on neighboring surfaces also changes. The subtle chromatic beauties of Tomasello's relief structures depend on the immaterial nature of color. It is not the hues themselves, but only their effects, that are visible (ill. p. 172).

Another of the founders of the "Groupe de Recherche d'Art Visuel" was the Frenchman François Morellet. He began in 1952 to produce pictures whose arrangements were not subject to his own aesthetic decisions. He developed rigorous systems by which identical elements were combined in larger patterns. The rules of the game, as Morellet calls them, are such that the serial procedure permits a plurality of patterns of equal value. Line grids appearing on the surface or as wire nets in front of the surface became a specialty of Morellet's. As a result of perceptual phenomena the observer has the impression of movement, of instability in line patterns which are in

fact quite static. The grids turned in 1958 to "trames", line screens whose superimposition produces kinetic and vibration effects. In his "spherical screens" — orthogonal metal grids in a sphere suspended as a mobile (ill. p. 177) — Morellet combined virtual and real kinetics in 1962 with light kinetics produced by reflection and projection in the form of moving shadows on ceiling, walls or floor. These spherical screens extend the problem of circle-in-square or square-in-circle raised by Vasarely to the three-dimensional domain of cube and sphere. Morellet is himself more concerned with demonstrating the perspective changes in regular spatial grids as a result of the mobility of the object or of the observer. After studying fortuitous patterns around 1962 — for instance in the form of small black squares on a large white square surface — the engineer Morellet later transferred these aleatory principles to light kinetics with rhythmical interferences of colored neon tubes.

Nicolas Schöffer, who came to Paris from Hungary in 1938, also worked with spatial structures, motion and light. His early horizontal-vertical structures of prefabricated metal elements were based on Mondrian's Neo-Plastic principles. To this framework he later added rectangular metal plates, which sometimes had reflecting surfaces. In 1948 a development began to which Schöffer gave the name of "spatio-dynamism": the constructions are enriched with new elements, the bounding and dividing plates have openings or are perforated to form screens. Light is utilized, producing reflections on the metal surfaces and casting the shadow of the real three-dimensional structure as a distorted projection on the wall. An intermittent or mobile light may replace the static light source. Another expedient is to use a motor to rotate the rigid object (ill. p. 170). All this follows up suggestions made by Moholy-Nagy between 1922 and 1930, when he devel-

Jesus Rafael Soto: Gray and white vibration, 1966

Aurélie de Nemours: Proposition inverse 16, 1968

oped his "Light Display Machine for an electric stage". Schöffer, who sees himself as an artist, architect, engineer and futurologist and who believes in teamwork in the workshop and in the industrial manufacture of the "products" he thinks up, says that the object of his spatio-dynamics is "the constructive and dynamic integration of space in the sculptural work". His "lumino-dynamics" serve the purpose of "provoking, defining and dynamizing a spatial entity" by means of spatio-dynamics: "The colored or colorless light penetrates the spatio-dynamic sculpture and by illuminating the structures and the transparent or opaque surfaces causes plastic developments that liberate a huge potential of aesthetic values together with considerable energies." Through the light and movement, the "chrono-dynamism", the work forfeits its plastic independence and becomes the generator of an optical and kinetic spectacle which — particularly in the cybernetically controlled monumental productions — develops all the pathos of a public performance. From here it is only a step to visions of a "cybernetic city", with which Schöffer's ambitious ideas merge into the world of science fiction.

The work of the Belgian Pol Bury also belongs to the category of kinetic sculpture; he was already represented in the exhibition "Le Mouvement" in 1955. Neo-Dadaism is combined with Constructivist ideas in his mobile reliefs and objects, of which some are of wood, others of metal. Absurd, droll phenomena of motion alternate with the mechanically rational. The incomprehensible and illogical, the instability of the seemingly solid and the menacing might of gravity are all contained in these "kinetizations". Gravity, magnetism and motors are used. Spheres and cyl-

inders frequently play an important part among form elements (ill. p. 171). While Bury's works illustrate the action of either law or chance, the movement that can be observed and experienced is a negation of speed. It is characterized by a striking inertia, by slow motion. Later works by this "slowest of the kinetic artists" often take the form of wooden sounding-boxes, and steel strings serve to give the movements a long-drawn acoustic accompaniment, as in the Aeolian harp.

Very many artists took an active part in the "Groupe de Recherche d'Art Visuel" and the numerous other groups, such as "Equipo 57" in Paris, "Gruppo N" in Padua, "Gruppo T" in Milan, "Mac" (Movimento Arte Concreta) also in Milan, "Gruppo Uno" in Rome, "Novi Tendencije" in Zagreb, "Nul" in the Netherlands, "Zero" in Düsseldorf and "Arte Madi" in Buenos Aires, and most of the members also joined the international "Nouvelle Tendance" founded in 1963. They explored the field of optical-kinetic art with more or less originality and with more or less innovation. If the number of international exhibitions is any valid criterion, 1965 marked the zenith of kinetic art. Denise René provided an international survey in "Mouvement 2", which presented the work of 48 artists. Sixty artists were represented in the excellently documented exhibition "Licht und Bewegung" (Light and Movement) in the Kunsthalle, Berne. In New York the Museum of Modern Art offered a general review of the artist's concern with optical and kinetic phenomena in "The Responsive Eye".

William C. Seitz, who was responsible for this show, characterized the works exhibited as follows: "This is an art of appearance, not factuality. Like the apparatus of a

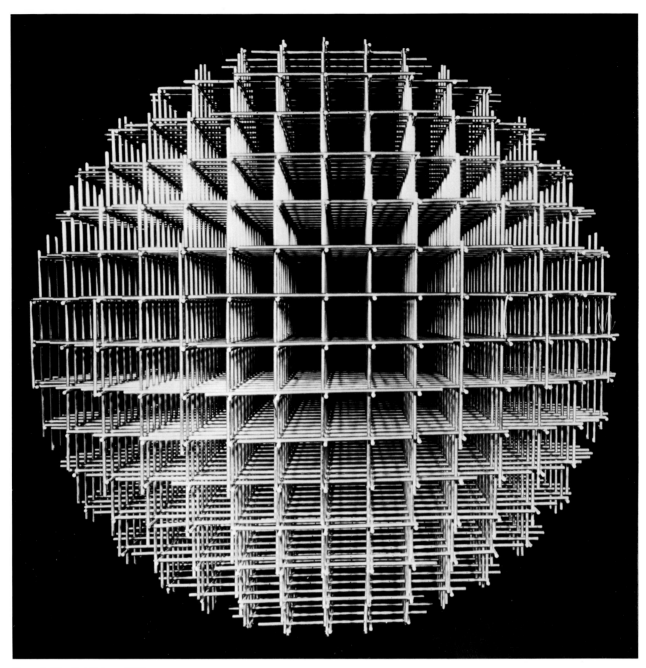

François Morellet: Sphere, 1962

stage magician these objects do not exist for their true physical form but for their impact on perception." He concludes his introduction to the catalog: "It is impossible to generalize about individual artists. For many, perceptual abstraction is only a means, one to which they may have given hardly a passing thought. But it can be said without falsification that, seen together, these works inaugurated a new phase in the grammar of art that has already spread among free-brush abstract as well as figurative painters and has had its effect on sculpture too. Every new development merges at its periphery with other tendencies; purity is not necessarily a virtue in art. It is clear also how close to the border of science and technol-

ogy some of the 'hardcore' optical works are, and they remind us at the same time how close to art some of the images of science are. — The question of the connection of ends to means remains the most fascinating. Can such works, that refer to nothing outside themselves, replace with psychic effectiveness the content that has been abandoned? What are the potentialities of a visual art capable of affecting perception so physically and directly? Can an advanced understanding and application of functional images open a new path from retinal excitation to emotions and ideas?"

The visualization of perceptual processes and kinetic art proper met with a lively response from exhibition-goers and later from the general public. The visually attractive optical and kinetic effects and the dynamism of moving three-dimensional objects had the fascination of novelty and even a touch of the sensational. Art could once more be experienced as a spectacle and approached either with the naive curiosity of the child or with the superior amusement of the culturally pampered. Something was happening, the individual was even invited to participate. This art seemed vital, positive and optimistic. It thus accorded well with the optimism of the time, which was inspired by the hope of a better and happier future. It seemed as though with the advent of optical and kinetic art an age had dawned in which art was not to be quite as grave as heretofore, and not so difficult to understand. This superficial affirmation served to suppress the uneasiness and perhaps even existential anxiety which might well be inspired by the insoluble riddles inherent in our perceptual processes and in the phenomena of motion.

Discussing optical phenomena in his historical survey of "Constructivism" (1967), the sculptor George Rickey said: "Artists have long ignored the peculiarities of human vision. The eye has been merely a window onto a world where every object had local qualities. Yet the eye has qualities of its own; there is a world inside the window also. In recent times, the responses to outside stimuli which take place in the eye and brain have begun to interest artists. For example, the eye responds in a direct and selective way to certain color situations, line arrangements, and patterns of alternating black and white patches or stripes, as immediately as a finger does to heat and cold. These sensations are in the mechanism of the optical system itself and are not an interpretation or evaluation of the source of the stimulus. In fact, the eye may be so shocked that attempts to interpret the stimulus may be futile. In another type of situation, the eye may read the evidence and interpret it clearly but wrongly. This is optical illusion. Again, the eye may be baffled, confused, and frustrated by ambiguous visual situations. Such responses, generated in the observer, become — under a skillful manipulator — a means of direct access to the observer as an organism. Artists now see this access as an opportunity for a new kind of intimate artist-spectator interchange. They are beginning to explore the range of the eye's responses, sometimes borrowing from science, sometimes unsystematically duplicating, on their own, what science has long been aware of, sometimes pursuing variations of a discovery science has noted and left behind. These phenomena are as old as the human eye and have occasionally in the past been examined as curiosities. It is only in this century, however, that they have been added to the artist's repertory of means . . . There is, of course, no guarantee that the use of such phenomena and physical sensations makes art. As always, it is the artist who makes it."

An Insular Aesthetic

Constructive Trends in Britain

British art has always followed developments on the Continent hesitantly and at a certain distance. This may be due to a strong insular awareness of the country's own values and criteria which leaves little room for impulses from the outside. A proud independence, in the last analysis the expression of a special historical position that has been defended for centuries, can still be clearly felt in the domains of literature and art. In art in particular the specifically British literary or emotional interest in the object represented has always been so strong that the step into an abstraction wholly divorced from the real motif or into pure non-objectivity has been taken in no more than a handful of instances. It would in any case be unjustified to speak of an independent development of constructive art in England. The inclination of the Briton to exaggerate the aesthetic element, as postulated for example by Roger Fry in his theoretical and philosophic writings on art, has led only by way of exception to any purely formal art. The interest in the phenomena of human relationships and behavior, in hidden and sometimes mysterious stirrings of the psyche, has been much more powerful. In the twentieth century, taken as a whole, Expressionism and more particularly Surrealism have evoked a much more positive response than Constructivism. This is witnessed, for instance, by the cordial reception given in London to the literary Expressionism of Max Beckmann or to the cosmopolitan Expressionism of Oskar Kokoschka.

This reserve toward geometric art was already manifested in the way Britain received Cubism and Futurism: late and for a limited period of time, and thus without any lasting consequences. It was almost with regret that Roger Fry said in 1923 of the painter Duncan Grant, who had been one of those involved in Cubism: "It was perhaps inevitable that, coming at a time when the movement of creative artists was in favor of insisting almost exclusively upon the formal elements in design, he should have tended to suppress his natural inclination to fantastic and poetic invention." The fantastic and poetic come more naturally to the Englishman than the rational.

Cubism and Futurism of course had some effect even on British painting. The appearances of F. T. Marinetti in London in 1910, 1912 and 1913 triggered an avant-garde movement of which the uncompromising painter, writer and philosopher Wyndham Lewis soon became the spokesman. This movement, which adopted the name of Vorticism (the vortex is an obvious analogy to the "Sturm" in Berlin), absorbed and applied the influences of the French Cubists and Italian Futurists. But the British who were caught up in the vortex were less concerned with the stylistic exploration of new possibilities of expression than with an intellectual atmosphere of rebellion and an escape from traditional social and behavioral patterns. The movement left its mark with only two numbers of the provocative magazine "Blast", published in 1914. Rebellion was expressed in the title and in the individual contributions. The magazine was influenced by the young Ezra Pound, to whom the Vorticists also owed their name. Vorticism — which hardly became known outside of Britain — can best be understood as a blend of Futurist and proto-Dadaist elements. It turned out that the Cubism of Picasso and Braque, in essence an intimate dialogue between the artist and his canvas, was — as in Russia at the same period — unable to satisfy the younger generation. Futurism, which in the last definition was more concerned with life than with art, and Dadaism, which set out with its nonsense productions to carry social and artistic conventions ad absurdum, were more to the taste of youth before and during World War I because of their basically anarchic attitude. Within the Vorticist movement, whose members exhibited regularly in the "Rebel Art Center", the principal figures — apart from Wyndham Lewis — were Frederick Etchells, David Bomberg, Helen Saunders, Vanessa Bell and the Frenchman Henri Gaudier-Brzeska. They all favored a geometric-dynamic style which was seen to best effect in graphic art. The most forceful works, which stirred up some scandal in London, were contributed by the New-York-born sculptor Jacob Epstein: his bust "Rock Drill", developed from a montage of technical equipment, is an unmistakable formulation of the mechanistic and dynamic trends of the Vorticist movement. The artistic élan of the movement, however, was quickly broken by the outbreak of war. The attempts of the Vorticists to create furnishings and articles of daily use embodying a style of their own also failed to lend their efforts duration. Compelled to accept the harsher truths of life when they served as war artists at the front, most of the members of the group later returned to a sober, representational style.

The war experience, and perhaps even more the "English mistrust of dogma, English interest in the ebb and flow of surrounding life", as Sir John Rothenstein once remarked, strengthened the opposition to the blandishments of an aesthetic purism. Roger Fry would easily have been able to provide the background theory for a specifically English variety of Purist art in the twenties. But neither Wyndham Lewis nor Paul Nash nor Stanley Spencer took that direction. On the contrary: when Surrealism conquered the world from France, they found in it support for a fantastic figurative art in which John Piper and Edward Burra particularly excelled. It was the same source as was later to feed the expressive painting of Graham Sutherland and, somewhat later, Francis Bacon.

In all justice it must be added that Kandinsky's painting and message had met with an early response in England, more so than the work of Mondrian, whose puritanical severity was at odds with what both Roger Fry and Clive Bell referred to in their writings as "aesthetic emotion". Possibly it was this aesthetic emotion that in the late twenties lent a poetic magic to the highly stylized, delicately colored still lifes and landscapes of Ben Nicholson. Nicholson was soon trying to transfer their musical quality to the purely geometric, yet more intuitive than constructed, paintings and reliefs which made him known beyond British shores in the mid-thirties: a synthesis of Cézanne, Picasso and Braque on the one hand, of Giotto, Uccello and Piero della Francesca on the other. These non-objective works answered an awakening need for "some adventure in art", as Paul Nash put it in the first manifesto of the group "Unit One" in 1933, a group in which Nicholson — together with other non-objective artists of the "7 and 5 Society", such as Cecil Stephenson (ill. p. 182) — was an active participant. The art of this group, to which Henry Moore and Barbara Hepworth also belonged — an art tending toward a free geometric style of a Purist character — was soon to be confirmed by the founding of "Abstraction-Création" in Paris. At the invitation of Jean Hélion, Nicholson and Hepworth spontaneously joined the "Abstraction-Création" group in 1933.

Nicholson's first "white relief" was done in 1935. In the same year he paid his first visit to Mondrian in his studio in Paris. The talks between the two artists revealed parallels and contrasts in their artistic thinking. The orthogonal colored compositions that Nicholson did alongside his white reliefs show how successfully he maintained his independence (ill. p. 180). He formulated his own thoughts on non-objectivity in 1941 in his "Notes on abstract art". In the meantime he had joined the editorial staff of "Circle", which in 1937 undertook an "international survey of constructive art". Its main initiators were Hepworth, Nicholson and Naum Gabo, who had settled in England and, like Mondrian at a later date, lived in close companionship with the Nicholsons. With its important contributions by Gabo, Mondrian, Le Corbusier, Herbert Read and others, "Circle" gave an account of international constructive tendencies on the eve of World War II, as they had also been made manifest in major exhibitions in Basel and London.

Nicholson's white reliefs, in which circular motifs are let into patterns of layered rectangles, were an important contribution to the constructive art of the late thirties. From our present-day vantage point we can state that they anticipated later ideas incorporated in the "tableau-relief", for example by the Swiss Gottfried Honegger. Barbara Hepworth, at that time married to Nicholson, worked

Ben Nicholson: Abstract composition, 1936

Ben Nicholson: Locmariaquer 5, 1964

with him, passing from the free organic forms of her earlier sculptures to austere combinations and interpenetrations of stereometric bodies, but in the forties returning to irrational, rounded form-complexes. Chords stretched across the empty spaces in her sculptures make fields of force visible, much as in the works of Gabo and Henry Moore. In this sculptress's later work purely rational forms continually alternate with irrational and even markedly emotional compositions. Barbara Hepworth made her clearest contribution to constructive art between 1937 and 1947 with constructive geometric drawings which obtain their pictorial effect from color tones sparingly applied in gouache.

In Ben Nicholson's postwar work strict geometry also made way for a lyrical, sometimes representational play of lines in front of a delicately colored, freely composed but geometric relief background (ill. p. 181). A gentle serenity exhaling a suggestion of classical Antiquity distinguishes these works, which Nicholson himself has referred to as "musical and architectural", comparable perhaps to the poetic use of organic forms by Jean Arp or the cheerful, hovering dance of the mobiles of Alexander Calder, both artists to whom Nicholson was bound by personal friendship.

It is interesting to record that it was a woman who made Britain's most compact contribution to constructive art: Marlow Moss. She was a strong personality who went her own way from an early age. For the sake of her art

she broke so radically with the society she originated from that she was even ready to change her name. After studying sculpture, philosophy and mathematics, she took up painting in 1926, saw works by Mondrian in Paris and shortly afterwards met the artist himself. She now gave up lessons under Léger and Ozenfant to practice Neo-Plasticism. The black bar systems of her cool pictures on white grounds, with which she took part, at Mondrian's suggestion, in the first exhibition of "Abstraction-Création", at first recall the contemporaneous work of Mondrian. The two were involved in frequent and lively discussions, and there was a brisk give-and-take of ideas. In 1930 Marlow Moss replaced the simple black bar in her compositions with the more dynamic and plastic double line, which did not appear in Mondrian's work until after 1933. From the double line Marlow Moss advanced to the colored line, and before long to a sculptural line in the form of a cord relief (ill. p. 182). This move toward relief and occasionally to three-dimensional constructive work carried her farther and farther away from the Neo-Plastic concepts of Mondrian. In her paintings, however, she remained true to a horizontal-vertical surface composition with sparingly applied areas of primary colors (ill. p. 182).

After World War II a younger generation of artists in Britain had to find a new approach to constructive art. Victor Pasmore was the first to break with representational painting. In the late forties his highly stylized landscapes,

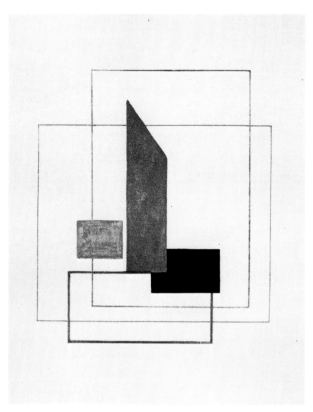

Cecil Stephenson: Composition I, 1939

reminiscent almost of Chinese calligraphy in their strong sign character, tightened into structural compositions with a suggestion of spiral movement. The definite breakthrough came with a mural for the Festival of Britain in 1951. Like Marlow Moss, and in some respects in a parallel development to Jean Gorin or Cesar Domela, Pasmore was henceforth interested in three-dimensional painting,

the colored relief. First of all colored bar elements grew out of the picture like ribs of varying dimensions, strictly orthogonal to begin with but soon displaying an ever greater freedom. In the fifties this "relief painting" was replaced by the use of a transparent base plane of Perspex. It enabled Pasmore to employ sculptural elements, mostly of painted wood, that projected from both sides of the transparent base plane. Straight-sided cubic forms were soon joined by curves, and the penetration was thus rendered more dynamic. These transparent spatial constructions, which Pasmore called "projective painting", constituted an individual achievement in the field of Concrete Art. Pasmore's works are never the product of mere calculation; they always display a personal sensibility that is of almost Far Eastern subtlety.

After 1950 the constructive sculptress Mary Martin, like Pasmore, explored the sculptural relief. Her interest, however, was concentrated less on color than on the spatial effect of the stereometric elements projecting from the base plane. In the white reliefs shadows replace color articulation (ill. p. 190). It is the shadows which, despite the severity of these compositions, give such an impact to the contrast and the interpenetration of the real and the apparent. With her keen interest in the positive-negative effect of the raised plastic elements and the ground, Mary Martin made a real contribution to a relief art which, executed in monochrome white, relies entirely on light effects. Although her work is in some ways akin to that of the American and Canadian representatives of Structurism, such as Charles Biederman, she took a definite step forward in the "transition from painting to relief", as Jean Gorin formulated this development.

The younger Anthony Hill worked in the same area, having graduated about 1955 from abstract painting to three-dimensional constructive work. Initially he would use several similar black elements — squares or equilateral triangles — silhouetted in flat relief and carefully disposed on a white ground (ill. p. 183). In his later work the relief has

Marlow Moss: Black and White, 1949

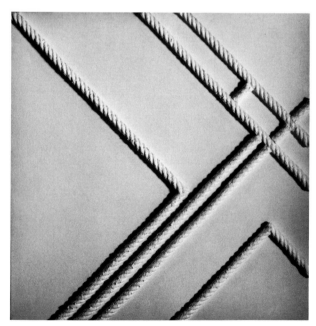

Marlow Moss: White with Rope, 1940

been further developed into a multiplane spatial structure. Hill makes use of the different qualities and colors of Perspex, white vinyl and brass or aluminium. The precision of the work, combined with its structural and architectural quality, gives these relief constructions an anonymous technical character.

While the work of Mary Martin and Anthony Hill—like that of Jean Gorin in France, Joost Baljeu in Holland or Charles Biederman in the United States—involves the sensitive border region between colored constructions on a plane and in space, the Chinese-born Richard Lin, who lives in England, remains true to the surface. In his light and airy pictures parallel groups of bar elements are meticulously placed to create rhythmic patterns, most of them in the same delicate shades as the ground, so that the

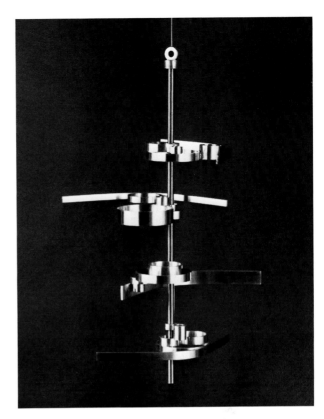

Kenneth Martin: Rotary Rings, 1967

equilibrated tones produce gentle vibrations. The whole is done with great formal economy and chromatic discipline. Lin avoids strong optical effects and remains within the bounds of a poetic constructive style in compositions that have something of the richness of faded Oriental silks.

A very different relationship to the potentialities of color and form combinations for the creation of optical effects is evident in the work of Bridget Riley. The basic principles of such perceptual phenomena have long been known to opticians and physiologists, but art has only turned them to account in our own century. They were systematically investigated at the Bauhaus by Johannes Itten in his preliminary course, and even more thoroughly by Josef Albers. Bridget Riley approached them from a different quarter: from her study, as a painter, of the systematic brush techniques of the Neo-Impressionists and Pointillists. Encouraged no doubt by the investigation of "virtual movements" on a surface, or in other words of "kinetic structures", by Soto, Vasarely and others, Bridget Riley began at the end of the fifties to sound out the artistic possibilities of this kind of surface design—initially in black and white—with a system and perseverance that have been unparalleled in spite of the widespread interest in optical effects. Her starting point was a distortion of a regular checkerboard pattern, first in one and then in two directions. It was at once apparent that regular modification of a surface structure can lead to spatial and dynamic illusions. A wider scope was offered by zigzag lines, the staggering of which, on the basis of a wave system, produced the effect of a ribbed relief and even of

Anthony Hill: Constructional relief 2, 1955

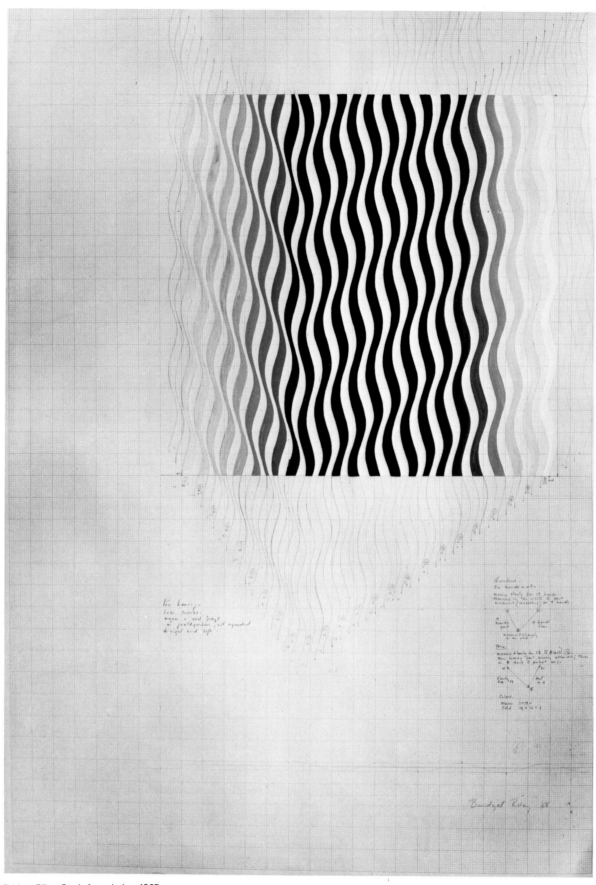

Bridget Riley: Study for painting, 1965

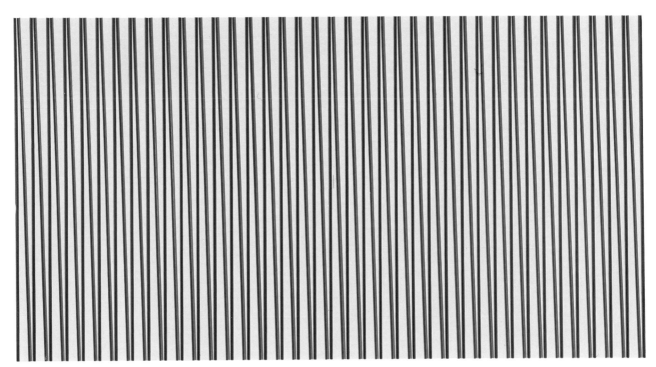

Bridget Riley: Red and blue elongated triangles, 1968

visual torque (ill. p. 185). Patterns of flow, blockage, expansion, and ballooning could be created, while similar techniques applied to a circle resulted in pulsating and rotating effects.

From these kinetic black-and-white compositions Bridget Riley proceeded in the early sixties to the use of color. She first applied the knowledge which she had so far acquired to color gradations. As the number of tones is increased, the tempo of the optical effect is changed: the more numerous the gradations, the slower and gentler the apparent motion (ill. p. 184). Finally pure color contrasts were added to the contrasts in tonal values. Bridget Riley at first restricted herself in each painting to two colors — for example red and blue — and to simple structures of straight or undulating lines (ill. p. 185). In her subsequent work she usually used three colors, sometimes supplemented by intermediate shades, plus black and white, in pictures suggesting wave forms. As the composition is in most cases not centered, it appears as an excerpt from a form-color movement that can be thought of as extending to infinity. It is only in these later works, which dispense with all loud Op Art effects, that simple, very real and easily reproducible means yield an effect that links the rational and the irrational. Fundamental principles of all life — change and constancy, rest and motion, growth and decay — are made tangible in these compositions, which can be fully grasped only through long and attentive contemplation: a realization which has led Bridget Riley herself to seek analogies in Eastern thought. Whether one is prepared to follow her on a path that also led to Chinese picture titles or not, the fact remains that fascinating effects are here obtained with elementary pictorial means and with a working method that is closely allied in its systematic procedure to the sober and almost mechanical precision of science and technology. These effects cancel out the opposition of the rational and the irrational and turn a simple creative principle into an unsolvable riddle before our eyes.

While Bridget Riley produces apparent spatiality or corporeality with linear means, other constructive artists in Britain have investigated actual three-dimensional structures, or in other words, sculpture. Kenneth Martin, for instance, who began as an abstract painter, turned from

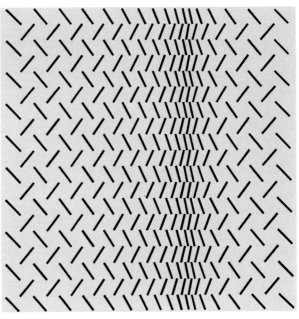

Bridget Riley: Fracture, 1964

Phillip King: Crest, 1970

the early fifties to constructions of wire or metal strips which give the impression of rotary motion or which are mobiles that actually move in space, especially hanging sculptures that produce helical effects when turning (ill. p. 183). While the wire mobiles developed by Lynn Chadwick about 1950 were only an episode in his work, Kenneth Martin has continued his kinetic studies systematically. His designs take up ideas that were first formulated by the Russian Constructivists, Tatlin and more particularly Rodchenko. Martin deploys them systematically in constructions that are accurately calculated and perfectly executed.

In Britain as elsewhere, the art world was caught up about 1960 in a trend which may be understood as a new realism. First touched off by a collage of Richard Hamilton's, it soon conquered the world as Pop Art. Even more than the informal art which had preceded it, Pop Art, inspired by the trivial culture of a consumer society, left little room for the comparatively reserved constructive art, which was considered by many as asocial and formalistic. While artists such as Merlyn Evans, John Hoyland and Paul Huxley affected a free and painterly geometric style, Peter Sedgley was one of the few to explore kinetic effects. Unlike Bridget Riley, who worked with perceptual anomalies, Sedgley was interested in radiation patterns. These are particularly strong in centered pictures which

use a simple circular motif in which the color spectrum is manipulated in a sequence of concentric zones. The resulting unbounded flow of color produces a light effect that can attain an almost cosmic character.

Excursions into the no-man's-land between painting and sculpture were repeatedly undertaken in the sixties. Seen from the painter's angle, this meant an advance from the two-dimensional plane into corporeal and sculptural surfaces. Richard Smith was active in this area, his first venture being to stretch his canvas over a spatial skeleton instead of the usual flat stretcher and to paint on it in a free geometric style with a marked painterly touch (ill. p. 187). A further step led to the transference of the "shaped-canvas" principle into three dimensions. The painting itself was now less important than the possibility of making manifest a progressive change of form in a series of three-dimensional elements. This end was best achieved when the work was kept monochrome.

Approximations to the monochrome are also found in the work of the painter Alan Green. Setting out from the "square-in-square" compositional principle already used by Malevich and—to a different end—by Albers, Green first adopted color combinations that were often rather dull—dark green, olive and brown shades, or black—to create works that had little to offer in the way of form but a good deal in their coloring: a kind of meditative han-

Richard Smith: Surfacing, 1963

dling of color. In subsequent work the formal component is reduced to the function of a mere frame, and the pictorial effect depends almost exclusively on the dense, crafted, painterly, polyvalent surface (ill. p. 189). This approach to painting puts this English artist in the proximity of American Silent Art deriving from Mark Rothko and Ad Reinhardt.

The boundary zone between painting and sculpture presents the sculptor with a different set of problems. Here the question is not "What effect does painting have on volumes?" but "How do colors influence sculptural forms?" Metal plates, rods and tubes that could be painted and colored plastics were the technical prerequisites for colored sculpture. The formal impetus was derived from constructive combinations of simple form elements in "primary structures" which may be regarded as a rejection, in the sculptural domain, of both abstract Expressionism and Pop Art, and for that matter of every form of anthropomorphism. It was precisely in Britain, where contemporary sculpture had entered a period of florescence with Moore and Hepworth, with Reg Butler, Lynn Chadwick and Kenneth Armitage, that a younger generation of sculptors turned to these elementary but constructed and mounted rather than carved or molded forms. This was tantamount to a reaction, in the early sixties, against what

Anthony Caro had apostrophized as an "excessively totemistic kind of abstract sculpture". What Caro wanted to see was a maximum of freedom. This must consist not only in the free choice of materials but above all in the demystification of sculpture. Brought down from its pedestal, the sculptural work was to take its place in everyday life. Along with Caro himself, Robert Adams, Eduardo Paolozzi, William Turnbull, William Tucker and Phillip King adopted this new approach.

In the works of these artists, which can hardly be said to show any stylistic unity, two basic characteristics of British art are nevertheless apparent: moderation on the one hand, wildness on the other. By contrast with the American representatives of Minimal Art, with whose primary structures the productions of these young British sculptors can be compared, there is, rather than an enigmatic banality, an uninhibited eccentricity. This is reflected in the colored, space-probing linkages of Anthony Caro and William Tucker, as it is in the space structures of the younger Nigel Hall.

Caro is no doubt the central figure of this generation of British sculptors, and he has influenced sculptural thinking far beyond British shores. His spatial linkages, often using semi-finished products of the steel industry, combine in their technoid character ideas from the industrial

187

Anthony Caro: Early One Morning, 1962

world with irrational or emotional form configurations that recall nothing familiar to us and therefore often have an enigmatic aura. An aspect that is important in Caro's spatial constructions of rods, plates, beams, and expanded metal surfaces is the intense coloring of individual elements. Whether placed in urban or rural surroundings, they do not appear to be integrated, but are foreign and different, and therefore in a sense "artificial" (ill. p. 188). This alien quality is also found in the "Table Pieces", structures that either rise above the surface of the table or grow down from its edge.

In her work "Passages in Modern Sculpture", a thorough review of the subject, the American art writer Rosalind Krauss attributes a key position to Caro's spatial structure "Early One Morning" (ill. p. 188). She regards it as an exemplar of a fundamental self-contradiction in modern sculpture: that between its outward-reaching spatial structure as a physical object and the pictorial organization of the work as an image resulting from linear expression and particularly from color. This "linear gesture" follows logically from the sense of a work which insists on the incompatibility of the two conditions of a constructed and colored object/image and which can be seen as three-dimensional and spatial or as two-dimensional and pictorial, according to the position of the observer.

Much the same applies to the complex and richly colored metal and plastic deformations of Phillip King (ill. p. 186). As King has repeatedly pointed out, the surface quality is important, but what it covers or enshrouds is equally important. In his attempts to formulate his artistic concern, along with nature, which he takes very seriously and uses as a measure of his work, King develops a concept of "characterization". He understands his work as a "listening in" for "character". It is no accident that he has

Alan Green: Red-Pink, 1985

made a very close study of Tatlin. It fascinates him to see how in Tatlin's corner constructions "gravity has not been taken for granted, it has been retransformed". And on the subject of color in sculpture King says: "Color for me is the life-line into this invisible world where feeling takes over from thinking."

The ideas of a younger generation of constructive artists in Britain are reflected in King's statement: "The mistake that many Constructivists made was to think that there could be relatively neutral forms, and that the rectangle was the most neutral and therefore something unrelated to the external world and having a more universal meaning. But I don't think any really neutral form exists, all forms are psychologically loaded. It is only in their relations that forms can lose some of their associational contents and take on more neutral ones."

Mary Martin: White Relief, 1952

Geometric Art: from Intuition to Programming

Italy's Contribution to Constructive Art

Futurism could not have originated in any country other than Italy. The Futurists' belief in modern life, in the dynamism of the city, in the noise and speed of racing cars, in electric light that turns night into artificial day—this Futurist creed of progress and "modernità" is specifically Italian in character. It reflects the Italian's feeling for and instinctive understanding of the productions of engineering and industry. The radio research scientist Guglielmo Marconi, who in 1901 flashed the first telegraphic messages across the Atlantic and in the twenties made important contributions to the development of radio technology; Umberto Nobile, the daring aeronaut and polar explorer; the Savoia flying-boat designers; pioneers of motor racing such as Ettore Bugatti, Roberto Biscaretti di Ruffia and Cesare Goria Gatti; the engineers of Alfa Romeo and Maserati; the Turin industrialists Giovanni Agnelli and Vincenzo Lancia; Camillo Olivetti, designer of typewriters —all of them were typical Italians in their enthusiastic acceptance of a new technical era. Even though the Futurist architecture of Antonio Sant'Elia appeared Utopian at the time, the brilliant engineer and architect Pier Luigi Nervi was later to furnish proof of the feasibility of equally bold and aesthetically perfect constructions in concrete. This fervor of the Italians for the impetuous advance of the mechanical and industrial age is in a sense paradoxical because no other country in Europe is quite as steeped in history as Italy. The marks of a great cultural past are evident everywhere in the everyday life of the country, all Italy is in a sense a huge museum. Marinetti's challenging remark that a racing car is more beautiful than the Winged Victory of Samothrace only shows that this cultural heritage may also be felt as a burden. The Futurists' exhortation to set fire to the museums came well before any other demonstration against museum art.

Even Benito Mussolini's Fascism, of which F. T. Marinetti was no doubt one of the intellectual forerunners, revealed—over and above its nationalist aspirations, its ambition to restore the Roman Empire—a very positive attitude toward technical progress and modernism. It differed in this respect from German National Socialism, which sought to disguise its radical exploitation of technology behind a false mask of old Nordic allegiance to the land. Under the Fascist regime the art Biennale in Venice and the Triennale of design and architecture in Milan presented worldwide surveys of the latest modernist trends. Even in the twenties Italy had already been well disposed toward avant-garde movements in architecture and design. The buildings and the theories of Le Corbusier, the functional architecture of Walter Gropius and Mies van der Rohe sparked off analogous developments in Italy. The architect and publicist Alberto Sarto-

ris, who was on friendly terms with most protagonists of the international avant-garde, was here the chief intermediary. Almost without exception the centers of artistic advance were in the highly industrialized north, where the work of the Bauhaus in Dessau was followed very closely. The elimination of the old boundaries between fine art, applied art, product design and architecture was very much in keeping with the Northern Italian conception of a "stile nuovo", a rational style of the times.

Giacomo Balla had shown with his "compenetrazioni iridescenti" (iridescent interpenetrations) in the early years of Futurism, around 1912, that problems of color and form can be presented in art without any objective and figurative accompaniment. These pictures, which are astonishing if only for their early date, use simple geometric structures to produce kinetic effects which anticipate Bridget Riley's compositions half a century before her time. It is interesting to note that Balla's experiments had no direct sequels either in his own work or in that of his Futurist colleagues. Balla did actually make some designs for dynamic three-dimensional works, particularly in wire, around 1915, and these may be regarded as harbingers, for example, of the spatial constructions of Naum Gabo. In the early twenties Balla went on—no doubt aware this time of the developments in the rest of Europe—to produce surface compositions with circular and spiral motifs which are a sort of dynamic rejoinder of the former Futurist to the severe geometry of de Stijl and of Eastern European Constructivism (ill. p. 35). These mature works of Balla's are one of the starting points of constructive trends in North Italy.

From 1920 onward the works of Dutch artists were being discussed, for example in the magazine "Bleu" published in Mantua. Mondrian's theory of Neo-Plasticism was especially closely studied. Later the Galleria del Milione in Milan, which was run from 1933 on by the painter Gino Ghiringhelli, became a discussion center. It established contacts with artists in the rest of Europe. Kandinsky, Albers and Vordemberge-Gildewart were among those whose works were exhibited there. The main burden of this exchange of ideas was borne by Edoardo Persico, who was also the motivating force for the formation of a group of constructive artists. In a letter to the art historian Will Grohmann, Kandinsky reported on the expansion of constructive art in 1936. On the strength of his own observations he expressed the opinion: "The most radical representatives are to be found in Italy, where there are perhaps twenty of them. They sprout like mushrooms there after a downpour."

The most important figure in the Milanese circle was Luigi Veronesi. A friend of Vantongerloo's from 1932 on, he

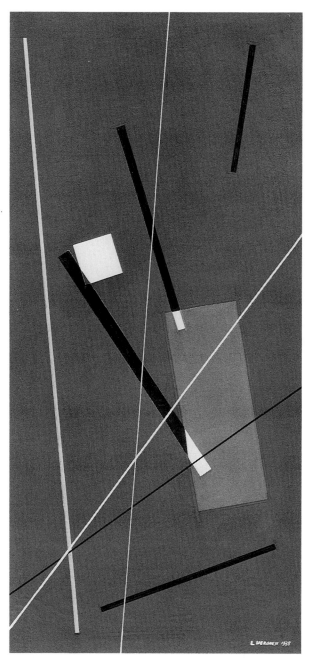

Luigi Veronesi: Composizione, 1938

later turned his attention to de Stijl and Eastern European Constructivism. In 1934 he exhibited non-figurative etchings for the first time in the Galleria del Milione, in conjunction with a show by Albers. This was the beginning of an artistic œuvre of considerable amplitude and significance. Line tensions, color areas and surface interpenetrations combined even in the first compositions to produce a pictorial dynamism that occasionally recalls Moholy-Nagy. There was also a personal friendship between these two artists which produced an extensive correspondence. It was perhaps instrumental in leading Veronesi to study the photogram and the relations between painting and photography. From about the same time

he also took part in the exhibitions of "Abstraction-Création" in Paris (ill. p. 192).

Despite the common artistic attitudes of the Milanese Constructivists — the "artisti astratti", as they called themselves — there were pronounced differences in their ideologies. Some of them, basing their arguments on the publication "Kn" by Carlo Belli — this daring book was the subject of passionate discussion in 1935 — regarded constructive art as a form of artistic expression well suited to the strict Fascist order. For others, some of whom were active anti-Fascists, geometric art was the expression of a liberal democratic attitude and thus a weapon in the underground struggle against Fascism. Connections with artists in Paris, London and New York encouraged a cosmopolitan outlook that was diametrically opposed to the strongly nationalistic leanings of Fascism. Veronesi was the spokesman of the internationalist group and thus, like the pro-Communist Osvaldo Licini, Mauro Reggiani or Attanasio Soldati, a declared opponent of the Fascist regime. This opposition became even more bitter when the government tried to suppress contacts with the avant-garde abroad. In the war years many of the Milanese Constructivists became active members of the resistance.

Como, the center of the North Italian textile industry, also played an important part in the development of constructive art after 1930. A group of painters and sculptors of about the same age, all of whom had found their way individually from abstraction to "geometria-sentimento", an intuitive geometry, here set the standard and were supported by architects of a similar persuasion. The group comprising Mario Radice, Manlio Rho, Carla Badiali, Aldo Galli and Carla Prina and the architects Giuseppe Terragni, Pietro Lingeri, Cesare Cattaneo and Alberto Sartoris represented the concept of "geometria spaziale di volumi semplici": a spatial geometry of simple volumes. The key work of the movement was the "Casa del Fascio" built by Terragni in 1933/36. Seat of the municipal authorities of Como, it was converted into a "Casa del Popolo" after the overthrow of the Fascist regime. The building still ranks as one of the earliest and purest examples of functional concrete architecture in Italy.

Mario Radice, a specialist in interpenetrating surfaces and doubtless the strongest personality in the Como Group, carried out some constructive murals for the main halls of the Casa del Fascio. They embody the aim of the group, inspired by the Bauhaus, de Stijl and Le Corbusier: the integration of architecture, painting and sculpture. The architect Cattaneo, with whom Radice designed many churches and fountains, spoke of the "translation of the one intellectual message into various languages". The artists belonging to the Como Group at first considered the direction of their endeavors to be entirely in keeping with the progressive spirit of Fascism. It was only the polemic confrontation with the "classical Roman" school of Fascist architecture and the big-muscled idealistic-realistic style of its painted and sculpted decorations that made it clear to Terragni and his "Movimento Italiano per l'Architettura Razionale" that art and politics were here at cross purposes. Edoardo Persico had the courage to point out repeatedly in the magazine "Casabella" from 1929 on that the rational, constructive trend in architecture and art was by its very nature

Lucio Fontana: Concetto Spaziale, Attese, 1959

anti-nationalistic and therefore anti-Fascist. He paid for this belief in an International of constructive art with his death in the concentration camp of Mauthausen in 1943. The Milanese architect Gio Ponti was a better tactician. As director of the Triennale he gave rationalist architects and constructive artists many opportunities to display their work from 1933 on and presented their latest productions in his magazine "domus".

The work of the Italian avant-garde evoked little response abroad. It is difficult to say whether this was a result of its isolation in the years immediately preceding World War II. No doubt, there was some skepticism on the part of leading international Constructivists toward the "not entirely reliable" Italians because their style lacked the unconditional purism of a Mondrian, the passionate consistency of a Van Doesburg, a Moholy-Nagy or an Albers. Even when the Italians were professing rationalism, they could never eliminate from their work the last trace of Mediterranean irrationalism, or perhaps it would be fair to call it simply poetic feeling. They remained representatives of a people molded by the sensualism of the Roman Catholic church. In the last analysis they were not really at home with the enlightened atheism of many Constructivists nor with Mondrian's puritanical Calvinism. This comes out very clearly in Veronesi. In a manifesto which he signed and which was issued in 1935 on the occasion of the first collective exhibition of "abstract Italian art" in Turin, the participants designate themselves "as champions of order, as unyielding enemies of chance, which may admittedly lead to subjectively valid results in convul-

sions of the world of experience, but without these representing any binding form of expression". Many members of the Italian avant-garde in fact remained true to the subjectively valid results.

Apart from his painting and his photographic experiments (especially in his later political posters, inspired by Russian models), Veronesi occupied himself extensively with stage design. In work that is comparable only to that of Enrico Prampolini, who had previously been a Futurist, he made a major contribution to "abstract" ballet and theater decoration after 1940, and thus to the popularization of constructive art in general. Possibly even greater importance should be attributed to his theoretical studies of the relations of music and art, or to put it more exactly the relations of notes and colors. After 1959 he experimented with the chromatic visualization of sounds, equating the twelve notes of the scale with the twelve principal colors of the spectrum. This "sonorizzazione visiva", which was also used to translate musical scores into systems of colored fields, is a return to a subject that had interested others before him. He had had predecessors, for instance, in the Russian avant-garde musicians, in Kandinsky, who had conducted sound studies in 1912, and in the Viennese dodecaphonic composers. Other non-objective painters have since turned their attention to these parallels between sound and color.

The oscillating position of Italian constructive art became apparent in the postwar period. In the headlong development that began about 1945 the varied and sometimes contradictory tendencies within non-objective Italian art

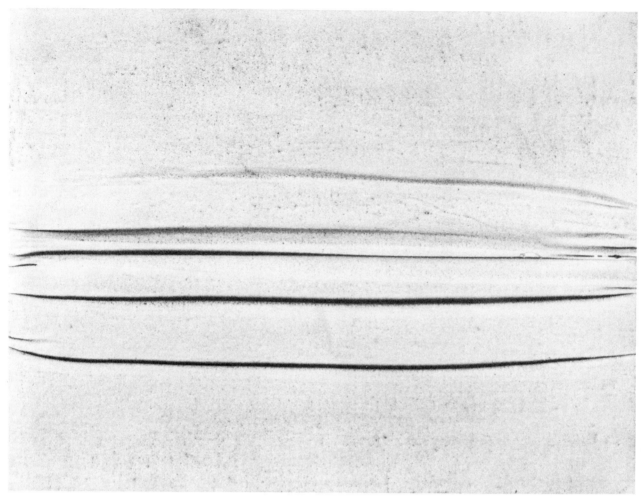

Piero Manzoni: Achrome, c. 1960

came to the surface. Even if we disregard the free abstraction which had been derived from Cubism and Futurism — as represented, say, by Alberto Magnelli and as tri-
umphantly disseminated by the Ecole de Paris — the diversity of viewpoints in Italy's non-figurative art was still
striking. The extreme positions were held by the representatives of a partly organic, partly geometric but markedly irrational non-objectivity — a kind of "lyrical geometry" — on the one hand and on the other hand by the
mostly young supporters of "arte concreta", who were
chiefly influenced by the Swiss Max Bill and Richard Paul
Lohse but had also had recourse to a new and thorough
exploration of de Stijl, Constructivism and the Bauhaus.
The poetic-geometric style of the former group is embodied in the paintings, gouaches and drawings of Arturo
Bonfanti from 1950 on even more clearly than in the late
work of Veronesi and Prampolini. A feeling for refined
form and subtle color announces itself here that is related more to early Italian painting than to prewar constructive art. The lyricism of fourteenth-century Siennese art is
just as much in evidence as the graceful linearity of the
early Florentine Renaissance. A comparison with Nicholson or Pasmore shows how eminently Italian the forms
and colors of Bonfanti are. Although the colored draw-

ings of these three artists have much in common, Bonfanti's poetic compositions are nearer to the quiet, representational mysticism of Giorgio Morandi than to the
aestheticism of the British artists.
A contrary trend was established under the influence of
the "art informel" of the early fifties. Geometric art, which
looked with disfavor on all signs of the artist's hand, preferring complete anonymity of execution, was confronted
by an openly individual pictorial idiom characterized by
the spontaneous and subjective expressive gesture. Italy
delegated a few important representatives to this movement, which originated in Paris with Wols and Georges
Mathieu: Basaldella Afro, Alberto Burri, Roberto Grippa,
Emilio Vedova and others. The most significant contribution, however, came from the Argentine-born Milanese
Lucio Fontana. He too had belonged in the thirties to the
abstractionists in Milan and to "Abstraction-Création".
Returning to Argentina during the war, he there issued
with a few artist friends a "Manifiesto Blanco". This
"white manifesto" lent a new impetus to the Milanese art
scene when Fontana returned to Italy in 1947. Among its
conclusions we find the following statements: "The position of rationalist artists is wrong. In their endeavor to
overvalue reason and to deny the function of the sub-

194

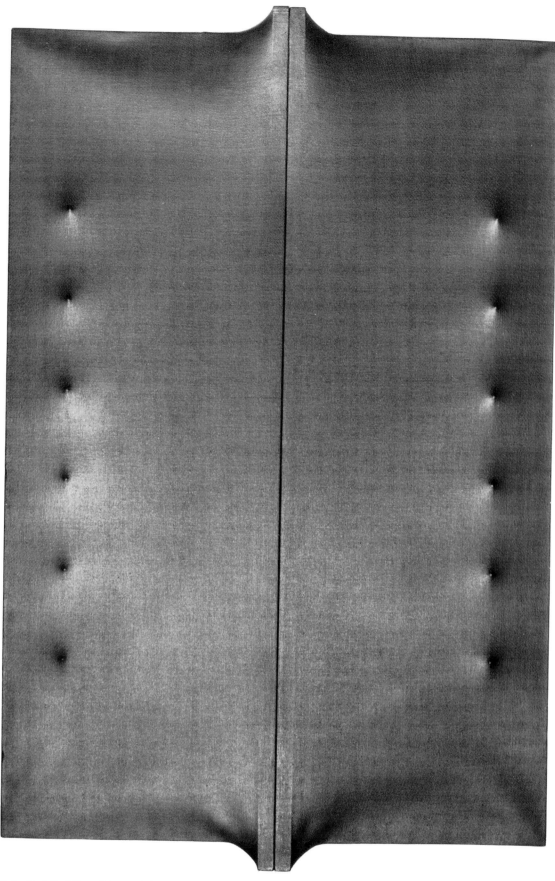

Enrico Castellani: Superficie nera 4, 1964

conscious, they only succeed in making its presence less visible... Reason does not create. In the creation of forms its function is subordinate to that of the subconscious. In all his doings man acts as a function of the totality of his faculties. The free unfolding of these faculties is a fundamental condition for the genesis and the interpretation of the new art. Analysis and synthesis, meditation and spontaneity, constructing and feeling are values that cooperate in a functional unity in the integration of the new art. And their development by experiment is the only path that leads to a perfect revelation of human life." Fontana closed his manifesto with the remark: "The new art demands the interaction of all man's energies for its creation and interpretation; existence manifests itself as a whole in the fullness of its life force."

This passionate statement of his position was the starting point for Fontana's concentration on problems of pictorial and real space. The results are to be found in the manifestos of 1948 on the subject of "Spazialismo". Fontana tried his hand at light sculpture, which was then in vogue, in the form of fluorescent tubes projected in dynamic sweeps of several hundred yards (Triennale of Milan, 1951) and in the illumination of spaces with ultraviolet light. Parallel to this went experiments in which he perforated and disfigured his canvas, boring holes in it in vehe-

ment attacks with an awl or inflicting spontaneous gashes with a razor blade. These assaults on the "sacred surface" were gestures entirely in conformity with the action painting at that time practiced by numerous artists, the crucial point, however, lies less in the gesture than in the forcible destruction of the two-dimensional nature of the painted surface. Fontana leaves no doubt, with his "Spatialism", that there is something in front of this surface and something behind it: space, mysterious space extending to infinity—or into nothingness. It was not by chance that Fontana chose the term "concetto spaziale" for his canvas "piquages" of the fifties, to which designation he often added "attese"—expectations. He was more interested in spacial transformations than in painting as such. This almost inevitably led him to monochromy. What had previously been a picture was now a single-color relief, a canvas which was pushed or bellied outwards, pierced or rolled (ill. p. 193).

With this conversion of the surface into a monochrome relief Fontana touched off experiments that were carried out in a few studios far removed from the noisy progress of action painting and "art informel": in those of Yves Klein in Paris and Piero Manzoni in Milan. Both tried, through the creative gesture, to turn the picture into a relief, and both used monochromy. Yves Klein preferred the blue of infinity, Manzoni in his folded or sewn reliefs the white of nothingness (ill. p. 194). Like Fontana, the two young artists—Klein died at 34, Manzoni at 30—were more interested in the concept than in the work itself. Their self-observation as they worked and their contemplation of the result of their work produced an artistic approach that was later to be designated as "conceptual".

Fontana posed problems that were to become important for various schools of art. The repercussions of Spatialism can be felt in many groups of artists that were formed after 1948 and often lasted only for a short time before their members broke up and joined new groups. One of the earliest groups was called "Mac" ("movimento per l'arte concreta") and was founded in 1948 by the critic and philosopher Gillo Dorfles with Bruno Munari and Mario Soldati. The painter and sculptor Munari and the painter Soldati had long been active in the constructive field. After the end of the war they again got into touch with artists of similar leanings in other countries. The Biennale in Venice and the Triennale in Milan became centers of international exchanges in the early postwar years. The idea that connected the various seekers was a new unity of art, architecture and product design along the lines adumbrated by the Bauhaus. The development of Concrete Art in Switzerland was followed with close attention. The programmatic work of Richard Paul Lohse, the painting, sculptures and universal activities of Max Bill and his theoretically formulated renewal of Van Doesburg's ideas on Concrete Art met with a good deal of interest in Milan. A more systematic organization of constructive trends was the result. In addition to Munari, Enzo Mari and Marcello Morandini, both untiring experimenters, championed a systematic constructive art. The experiments first consisted of trying all the possible variations of simple surface elements. Then three-dimensional units were combined to form relief structures, often in long series of variations. Morandini in particular also assembled spatial structures from identical elements. The

Gianni Colombo: Cromostruttura, 1961/70

Mario Nigro: Project for chessboard painting, 1950

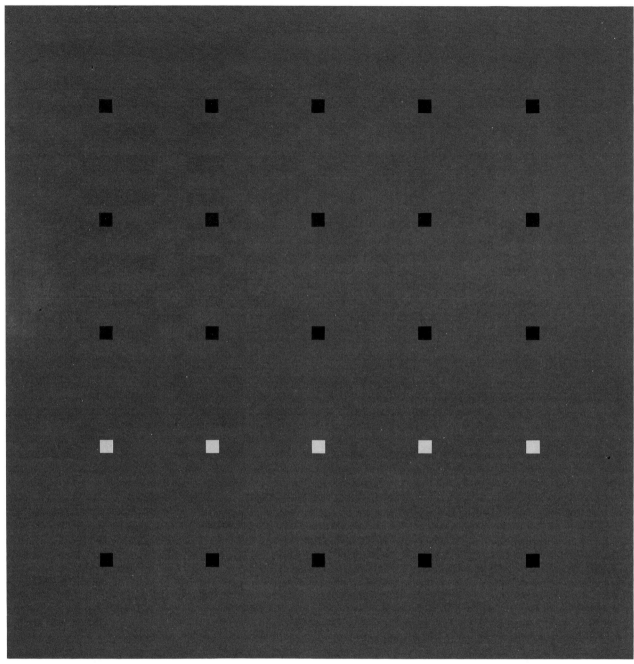

Antonio Calderara: Costellazione 24, 1969/70

representatives of this truly rationalist art broached many different sectors of art over a wide range of experimentation. Some of them analysed perceptual phenomena and finished up with kinetic structures, mostly in black and white, belonging to the domain of Op Art. Among these artists were Getulio Alviani, Marina Apollonio, Marcello Morandini, Alberto Biasi, Angelo Bertolio, Franco Grignani and Mario Nigro.

In the case of Mario Nigro, also a member of the Milanese Concrete group "Mac", the development began with horizontal-vertical compositions built up of small elements, which he called "projects for chessboard paintings (ill. p. 197). They led to close-meshed linear structures of a kinetic character. Nigro referred to them as "spazio totale" and gave the same title to a manifesto issued in 1954. After 1968 he produced loose structures consisting of short diagonals on a white background. They brought him up against the problem of "total time", to which he devoted another manifesto. The role of the observer is of some importance in his art, and the concept of perception is central to it. The single picture loses its autonomy, becoming part of "strutture fisse con licenza cromatica" ("fixed structures with chromatic license"). In the seventies these groups of works took on the char-

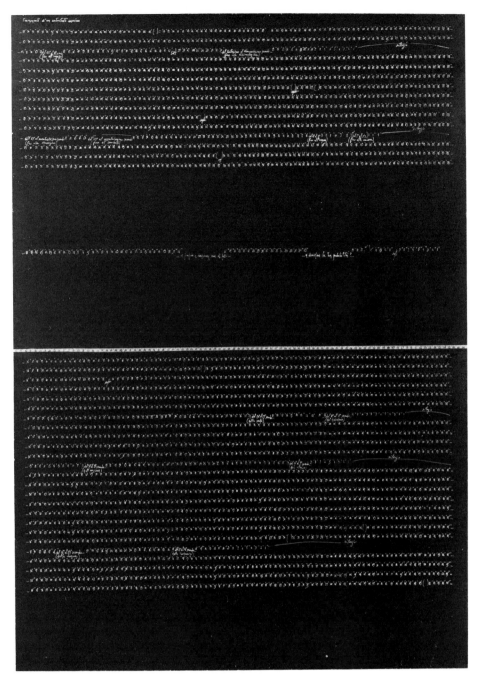

Carlo Alfano: Fragments of an anonymous self-portrait 16, 1972

acter of multicomponent cycles. The interest of Nigro and of a few other artists in systematic work has led, under the influence of the computer, to the production of works of art by way of computer programs, known in Italian as "arte programmata". The single works produced are the possible solutions to the problem posed; those that are aesthetically unsatisfactory can be simply passed over.

This art is easily accessible to intellectual interpretation, but that is not the only reason why it has provoked theoretical discussion as well as being based on theoretical considerations. Contacts have been established — partly as a result of impulses coming from Max Bill — with the philosopher Max Bense of Stuttgart, whose "information aesthetic" has had just as stimulating an effect as the later investigations of Abraham A. Moles in information theory. One statement made by Moles is obviously very apposite in the case of the Italian exponents of computer art: "The artist is no longer the creator of works, but the creator of ideas for works."

The Italian art scene proves that systematic work, for which the modular and serial systems of Richard Paul Lohse served as a model, need not lead to uniformity. Even though starting points are the same and the theoretical knowledge — information aesthetics, semantics and semiotics, Structuralism and the models furnished by communication theory and sociocultural thought—is accessible to all, it is still personal dispositions and propensities that decide the approach of the individual artist. This comes out in the work of Getulio Alviani, who may be regarded as a representative of a "programmed Constructivism", as the art critic Gillo Dorfles called it. His vocabulary is determined by a structural principle by which horizontally or vertically striped squares are composed in checkered variations. The shading is heavier or lighter toward the edges, and this creates the impression of concavity or convexity. The effect is thus primarily kinetic. By using new materials—with a reflecting surface, for instance—Alviani has obtained "vibration structures", and has proceeded by way of fluted elements into the range of three dimensions. This has made it possible to design vibrating environments. The Milanese artist Gianni Colombo, another representative of programmed Constructivism, is concerned with mechanized pulsating structures, with kinetic and luminous objects (ill. p. 196).

Spatial problems are even more predominant in two other followers of Fontana, Agostino Bonalumi and Enrico Castellani. Both want to turn the picture into something palpable, both regard the canvas—or the fabric that replaces it—as a skin that can be stretched over a frame so that it projects or retreats and thus takes on the character of an object. The sculptural deformation follows constructive principles; motifs are repeated in systematic sequence, axes are used, statics and dynamics are brought into compositional and spatial equilibrium. This is most impressively exemplified in Castellani's monochrome reliefs, a white or black surface ("superficie bianca" or "superficie nera") whose spatial modulation is only brought out fully by light (ill. p. 195). Calculated reflections add striking highlights to the protruding forms. In both Bonalumi and Castellani the technique of stretching an elastic skin over a framework produces sculptural forms which we feel to be irrational. They show some resemblance to the "minimal surfaces" known to mathematicians as surfaces of minimum area in differential calculus. They are visualizations of extreme properties of surfaces in space.

Color plays only a minor part in the programmed art of the Italians. Black-and-white and monochrome works are predominant. In this respect Antonio Calderara, who gave up engineering for painting in the twenties but only began to paint Concrete pictures in 1959, is an exception. On the grounds that no right-angled system occurs in nature, Calderara uses a strictly orthogonal order. A monochrome ground, often divided horizontally in upright paintings, forms the basis for a systematic arrangement of fine bars or rows of squares (ill p. 198). The usually delicate coloring is restricted to a low-contrast confrontation of colors that are often very close to each other. The reduction of the pictorial arrangement to an elementary and easily surveyed scheme makes the color contrasts effective in spite of their delicacy. Added to this is the power of color to influence neighboring zones of gray or other neutral hues, the simultaneous effect. This irradiation of color beyond its actual confines is a major theme of Calderara's painting. It presupposes a high degree of sensibility to color stimuli in the viewer. While the forceful contrasts of the primary and secondary colors predominate in many painters of the Concrete school, Calderara operates with subtle nuances within a limited scale of tones. This awakens the impression that the picture is flooded with radiant light: a dynamic, vibrating brightness which—Calderara believes—suggests infinity.

From this specifically painterly and at the same time lyrical position within Italy's Concrete Art one direct line of communication runs to the quiet painting of color vibrations as practiced by Francesco Lo Savio, who died in 1963, and later by Claudio Olivieri, Claudio Verna and Gianfranco Zappettini. In this kind of painting the subjective emotional coloring is more important than the geometric order of the picture surface. Structures lose their objective anonymous character and are replaced by a personal touch. Carlo Alfano operates in this area. In his paintings white horizontal line-and-dot systems on a black ground act as scriptural, almost seismographic notations. He calls them "Fragments of an anonymous self-portrait" (ill. p. 199). Alfano's method of making highly personal feelings the enigmatic content of the painting has affinities—in substance, but not in form—to the poetic "visualizations of thinking processes" of the Italian representatives of Concept Art, the adherents of "Arte povera".

The Heirs of Constructivism

Tendencies of Eastern European Art

In Western Europe Constructivist art has been able to develop more or less continuously from its beginnings, with the sole exception of the caesura of 1933–1945 in National Socialist Germany. It admittedly has not attained the same volume and the same intensity in all countries; national idiosyncrasies have repeatedly colored and modified the movement. But it is precisely these regional differences that have brought out the wealth of possibilities contained in constructive art and in the last analysis have helped this movement to remain very much alive up to the present. The formal aspects of this art permit manipulations of form and meaning that have allowed it to remain open to new tendencies. Its various facets are not difficult to survey, for innumerable exhibitions have drawn attention to them by presenting single phases of what is now a seventy-year history or by comparing the work of the pioneers with that of their successors. Selected examples in the museums of all cities enable anyone who so wishes to study and evaluate the movement. In the Eastern European countries conditions are quite different, and it would be misleading to speak of the situation there with any degree of generalization.

The constructive art of Russia, which must claim first place in any review, was prevented from developing organically and from making any further progress by the repressive art policy of the Stalinist era. The splendid flowering of the early twenties was followed either by an abrupt break or by slow extinction. The artists who did not emigrate or conform to the program of Socialist Realism took refuge in some form of applied art in which

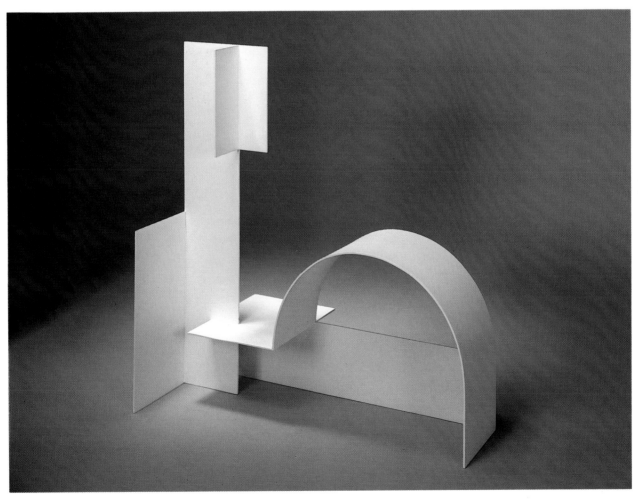

Katarzyna Kobro: Construction in space (3), 1926

Alexander Grigoriev: Radiation, 1967

there were acceptable functional arguments for constructive design concepts: town planning, structural engineering, photomontages for political propaganda, exhibition design and the like. Since the works of Suprematist and Constructivist artists were banned from the museums after the establishment of the Stalinist regime and were not accessible even in the repositories, there was no way for the younger generations to study the achievements of the pioneers. The fragmentary information that they could obtain by roundabout routes was and still is insufficient to fill the gap.

It was only possible to break down little by little the almost complete isolation of young Russian artists after cultural de-Stalinization began to take place in 1961. Fol-

Galina Bitt: Presentation of a tension, 1965

lowing the same underground channels as the jeans cult, rock music or beat poetry, a knowledge of recent developments in Western art seeped through to Moscow and Leningrad and was eagerly seized on by a generation thirsting for contacts and exchanges. The absorption of Western influences officially condemned as "soft" or "Imperialist" and therefore prohibited or unwillingly tolerated, and in any case regarded with suspicion, involved certain dangers of its own. This is evident, for instance, in recent Russian poetry. Young Soviet poets knew something about Mayakovsky's absurd Dada verses, but they were hardly prepared for the American beat poets whom they got to know in the post-Stalin era. There was simply no comparable historical basis, and the Russian beat poetry of Yevtushenko or Vossnessensky is for the most part a misunderstood imitation of foreign models. Parallels can also be found in Russian "underground art", where for instance, in the absence of the sociocultural context of the Western consumer society, the influences of American Pop Art produced some imitative efforts. The situation of constructive art is somewhat more favorable. Even though artists have only had very limited access to the source material and there has not been any uninterrupted tradition, they at least have some idea of the nature of the pioneering work. They have nevertheless moved on rather uncertain ground, since for all practical purposes they have had no knowledge of the changes and developments that have taken place in constructive art in the West since the twenties. It is consequently inevitable that in art the new rapprochement should display some haphazard and one-sided aspects.

The group known as "Dvizhenie" (Motion), led by Lev Nussberg, attempted in the early sixties to take up the thread of Suprematism and Constructivism where it ended in 1930, while enriching its legacy with Western influences. This underground group made the principles of kinetic art and the dynamic effects of Op Art the main foundation of its constructive activities. Its chief protagonists were its initiator Lev Nussberg, Galina Bitt (ill. p. 202), Tatiana Bystrova, Vladimir Grabenko, Alexander Grigoriev (ill. p. 202), Francisco Infante and Claudia Nedelko. It made its first public appearance in an exhibition in Moscow in 1963. It was hardly by chance that the members of this collective were designated as "Ornamentalists", for in many of their works variations on a given form principle are used to produce ornamental surface designs. The basic form is often a square which is converted into a lattice pattern by repeated halving and incorporation of the diagonals. The result suggests a crystalline structure, especially if the compartments thus created are filled with color. The layman who experiments in the progressive geometrical division of a surface will arrive at comparable results.

A feature of all these straight-lined surface patterns, as of the compositions constructed from arcs drawn with a pair of compasses, is axial symmetry. Lev Nussberg has explained this principle, which heightens the ornamental character of the work, as being symbolic of the harmony of man's relations to infinity. It is difficult to say whether this is based on any real conviction or is only a useful explanation after the fact. In any case the Western observer who is familiar with asymmetrical orthogonal harmonizations of form and color values, for instance in Mondrian,

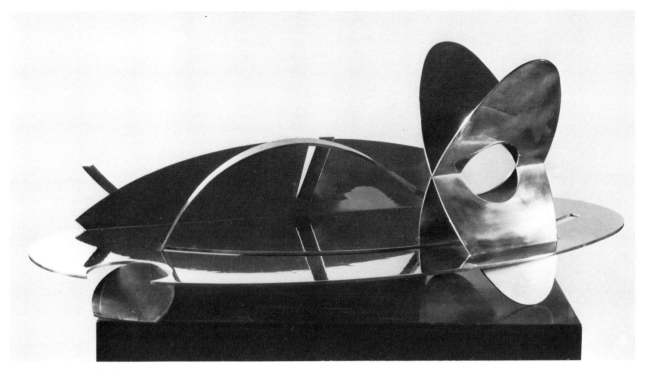

Karel Malich: Project II, 1970

or with the balance of diagonal and circular elements in Moholy-Nagy and others, will miss an endeavor on the part of these young Russians to produce a more daring form and color equilibrium or to create tensions by subtle imbalances. The compositions are completely devoid of any disturbing factor in either colors or forms.

It would be unfair to the group, however, to judge them purely in the light of painting and graphics which have become known in the West. For these works of theirs are only a product, perhaps even a by-product, of much wider activities. In 1967, for instance, the group contributed monumental works, some of them mobile and others kinetic, to the street decorations in Leningrad on the occasion of the fiftieth anniversary of the Revolution. Their efforts are in fact chiefly concentrated on urbanist projects, for instance a children's town in which kinetic designs are used to create a fairy-tale atmosphere. It may be that the collective's preference for gigantic architectural and urbanist projects reflects a deliberate intention to follow up the "Architectona", "Planites" and other Utopian schemes of the Constructivist era. Or it may be that this preference only serves to provide a pretext — as it did among the Constructivists themselves — for work which really runs contrary to official directives. That may also apply to artists such as Edward Steinberg and Victor Stepanov. An urban project realized by Nussberg's group in 1970 was the "artificial kinetic space" in Moscow.

In the eighties conditions in the Soviet Union have begun to change radically. In 1977 a big exhibition in London was still presenting unofficial art from that country, with a large number of unknown artists who worked there but rejected Socialist Realism. Only a very small fraction of these artists, for the most part those already mentioned,

contributed works showing a constructive approach. The liberalization process has meanwhile opened the way for art not in conformity with the system. It has brought greater tolerance, though this does not by any means imply official recognition. The thaw has triggered a keen but sometimes uncritical interest in the West in recent Russian art. One-man and group exhibitions are becoming more and more frequent. As far as can so far be judged, the work of the principal artists — to whom Eric Bulatov, Ilyi Kabakov and Ivan Chuikov belong — consists in a combination of realist settings and styles with constructive additions, often in the form of written elements and symbols that recall the graphics of the Russian Revolution. This blending of realism with constructive components may also appear as an echo of Pop Art and in this sense is an understandable effort to catch up with Western developments, though the artists do not relinquish their own, frequently political images.

Conditions in other Eastern European countries are considerably more favorable. Constructive art still has to stay more or less underground, according as the reins of cultural policy are tightened or slackened at any particular time. If we forget for a moment the official doctrine of Social Realism, however, we must concede that exchanges with each country's own artistic past and with developments in non-Communist countries have always been possible. While there are discrepancies due to the national character and to differences in historical background, developments in Czechoslovakia and Poland, for instance, have been analogous in many ways. As the flourishing poster art of these two countries — in the absence of private enterprise it is devoted primarily to the cinema and the theater — and their fine graphic arts show, the interests of art-

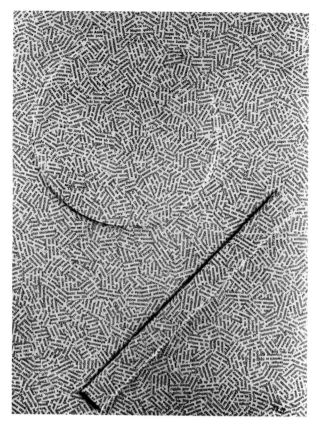

Jiri Kolar: Circle and bar, collage, 1970/71

ists are directed more toward the fantastic, the Surrealistic and a macabre, Kafkaesque brand of humour than toward any purely formal art. Constructive art has remained the concern of a few. It is noteworthy, however, that the works of Frantisek Kupka and of the Cubist school in Czechoslovakia have never disappeared for long in the repositories of the museums, that the modern museum of Lodz in Poland, where Constructivism is cultivated, has never been suppressed but has remained an active national institution and has maintained contacts with artists and art institutions in the West. The fact that artists of a constructive persuasion have repeatedly come last — for instance in official exhibitions staged in the West — or have got into difficulties because of their nonconformist views is quite another matter. There was, after all, a Czech branch of "Abstraction-Création".

In Czechoslovakia constructive art has no real tradition. The later developments of the Cubist movement, as personified by Bohumil Kubista, Emil Filla and Josef Capek in the twenties and thirties, were too much a part of the trends in Germany and France to permit the establishment of an independent Czech school. Jiri Kolar, who tends more to Surrealism than to constructive work and came to art by way of literature, stands alone in the field in which he displays such consummate skill: in his use of the collage for constructive purposes. He demonstrates this in his so-called "chiasmages", simple geometric relief compositions over which text and picture collages have been stuck to produce ever new patterns (ill. p. 204); or in the works which usually consist of two identical

color reproductions which he cuts up into strips and then reassembles. These latter, christened "rollages" by the artist, display surprising form and color structures that are geometric in character, even though Kolar's work is primarily an intellectual game in which the familiar and banal is transformed into the strange and fantastic. It has affinities, on the surface at least, with the photocycles of the Dutch artist Jan Dibbets, conceived with quite different objectives.

A specifically constructive group of Czech artists was formed in the mid-sixties. It includes personalities sharing similar outlooks but using different working methods. Karel Malich is chiefly concerned in his reliefs and plastic work with the transformation of surfaces into bodies. Usually starting from a circle or ellipse, he destroys the surface of a metal sheet by carefully calculated cuts. He then bends or creases the cut-out forms in various directions, thereby creating spatial structures of a dynamic character (ill. p. 203). The rational procedure of the pattern cutting takes on an irrational aspect when raised to the third dimension, especially when spirals of sheet metal are twisted into free spatial configurations. Malich does not regard these works as autonomous sculptures but as projects for a "Utopian architecture" which is accompanied by an edifice of Romantically colored philosophic thought.

A constructive concept comes out more clearly in the mirror reliefs of Hugo Demartini. A rectangular baseplate or a cube usually serves to carry polished or mirrorized hemispherical elements, sometimes concave, which are arranged in strictly organized series. The rational principle of arrangement in rows is in strong contrast to the illusory effect produced by round surfaces whose curvature turns them into distorting mirrors. Each of the works derives its impact primarily from the repetitive mirroring of extraneous surroundings. Rhythmic reflections are produced, identical or oppositional according to the sequence of convex or concave mirrors employed.

Jan Kubicek is also concerned with the relief, or to be more exact with the relation between surface and line. The line is either a passive boundary between two differently colored or unequally high relief surfaces or else an active dividing bar or rib with sculptural qualities, which catches the light or casts shadows (ill. p. 205). The orthogonal or diagonal patterns of squares which Kubicek calls "counter-positions" can be considered as systematic Structurist investigations, following up the compositional ideas of de Stijl. — Zdenek Sykora also works with systematic structures, namely circles and semicircles inside squares, and exploits the positive and negative effects of light and shade. The raw material of his structural compositions, which may be placed at any angle in the rectangular picture area, are numerical series supplied by the computer. Sykora first sets up a rule which takes account of the problem of the "neighborhoods" of the elements employed. He has explored his structure systems in black and white and in a limited range of colors (ill. p. 206). Similar working processes lead to the black-and-white variations which Milos Urbasek obtains with the use of segments of circles in a square field. By including color in his repertoire of forms, Urbasek has brought his series of segment arrangements into the realm of "objective color research".

Jan Kubicek: Principle Z in the square, 1972

Hungary played a major role in the early phases of Constructivism. Several Hungarian pioneers had a powerful impact in the new homes to which they moved for political or personal reasons: Vilmos Huszar and Lajos d'Ebneth in the Netherlands, Moholy-Nagy first in Germany and later in the United States, Béothy and later Vasarely in France. A very different position is held by Attila Kovacs, who came to West Germany in 1964 and only gave up objective painting after his arrival. He then turned to systematic structural experiment. A feature of his work is the mathematically programmed process. The aim is not to arrive at a static shape on a surface or in space, but only to follow up a structural development, the gradual and logical transformation of one form into another, for instance the transition from a square surface via a linear system of coordinates to a line relief and finally to a hollow cube (ill. p. 207). In these two- and three-dimensional structural developments, which he terms "Substrates", and in the "Coordinations" and "Transmutations", which he constructs on a surface, he is interested exclusively in the "dynamics of the process", in mathematical kinetics (ill. p. 207).

Recent constructive art in Poland has quite different antecedents. The concept of constructive design has never lost its legitimacy in Poland's artistic life. This is partly due to the fact that the fruitful activity of various

Zdenek Sykora: Polychrome structure, 1965

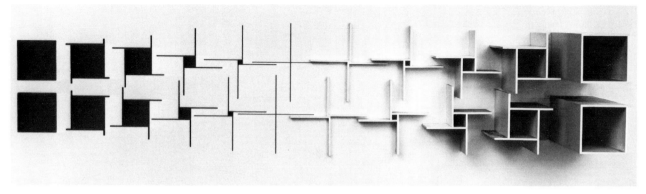

Attila Kovacs: Substrate K/H/7, 1967/71

constructive groups between 1923 and 1936 left its mark on the public consciousness. The work of Berlewi (ill. p. 99), Karol Hiller, Katarzyna Kobro (ill. p. 201), Stazewski and Strzeminski and their affinities with developments in Russia and in Western Europe are still remembered. The elementary white or colored space structures of the Russian-born Kobro, for instance, are among the leading achievements of early constructive sculpture (ill. p. 201). They anticipate the spatial surface deformations of a younger generation by half a century. Both the theoretical writings of Strzeminski and the incomparable international collection of the Sztuki Museum in Lodz form a bridge from the past to the present. This continuity of constructive art in Poland is nowhere more impressively demonstrated than in the work of Henryk Stazewski. He resumed in 1945 the artistic activities he had broken off in 1939, but did not return to his own past, preferring to make his contribution to the solution of new problems of design. His work has been done mainly in the domain of the "tableau-relief", the outward growth of elements of form and color from the surface into the third dimension (ill. p. 209). At first restricting himself to white reliefs, he went on in 1965 to metal reliefs of an elementary square structure, then in 1967 to colored reliefs consisting almost exclusively of orthogonally arranged squares. "I have been concerned with the problem of color. In my recent reliefs I submitted myself to extremely severe limitations, making them resemble tables used in optics and colorimetrics. Colors are distributed along the prismatic spectrum. All contrasts have been eliminated and only gradual transitions are allowed. Most often a relief contains 16 squares arranged into 4 ranges. Colors on the squares are distributed along horizontal and vertical gradients, and their juxtapositions are determined by a numerical principle ... Mathematical precision of choice is warranted by intuition. There is a measure in our eye that makes intuition infallible. It is intuition that prevents artistic creation from being a mere illustration of laws already discovered."

Ryszard Winiarski, more than forty years younger than Stazewski, goes far beyond the Structurist relief arrangements of the Nestor of constructive artists in Poland. To the pioneer Stazewski the unity of form is still the great experience. In Winiarski's work the form is split up, reduced to the anonymous building block of a small square, perhaps comparable to what Vasarely has called, in another context, the "unité plastique". Winiarski uses this anonymous element to build up a complex picture area that can be summarily described as an irregular multiplex chessboard. The elements from which his "surfaces" are constructed are regarded by Winiarski as "statistical material". Every composition is based on a program, a collection of rules which begin with a certain dimension of the basic element and determine the dimensions of the "surface". An important feature of the programming is the introduction of variables based on the random result

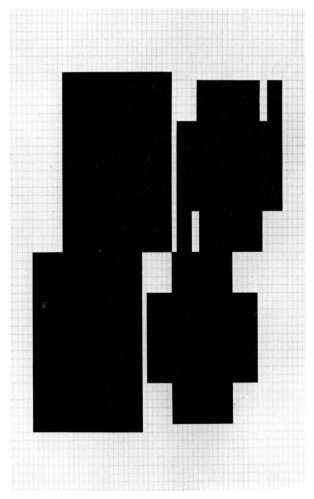

Attila Kovacs: Coordination 3/4 E, 1970/73

207

Ryszard Winiarski: Surface 94, 1971

obtained at a throw of the dice. While some of Winiarski's black-and-white or colored "surfaces" remain in the plane and are strictly orthogonal in arrangement, others have an apparently spatial dimension as a result of the use of diagonals and vanishing points (ill. p. 208). This illusionist element makes the permutational structures of Winiarski — as they might be christened after Abraham A. Moles — even less accessible to rational analysis.

In 1974 Winiarski made the following statement: "The theme of my recent work is the penetration of what may in the simplest way be called the space of the image. Occasionally, this space is taken to the letter — by the formation of thicknesses of spatial depth — or else, illusorily. In the latter case, the layout of statistical elements, appear-

ing in imaginary depths, is seen on the surface of the space, thanks to the different forms of perspective. The formation of an illusory space is often tied to the participation of the chance factor. The statistical notes of chance, the visual code and the statistical analysis create a whole world where Technology and Art meet."

The same unexpected flip from the real to the irrational, from the logical into the "impossible", is found in the works of Roman Opalka, which are also systematic but can be allocated to the sphere of constructive art only with certain reservations. After 1965 the artist did nothing but enter numbers from one to infinity in dense rows in white paint on a gray ground. Every picture begins with the number following the last one in the previous picture

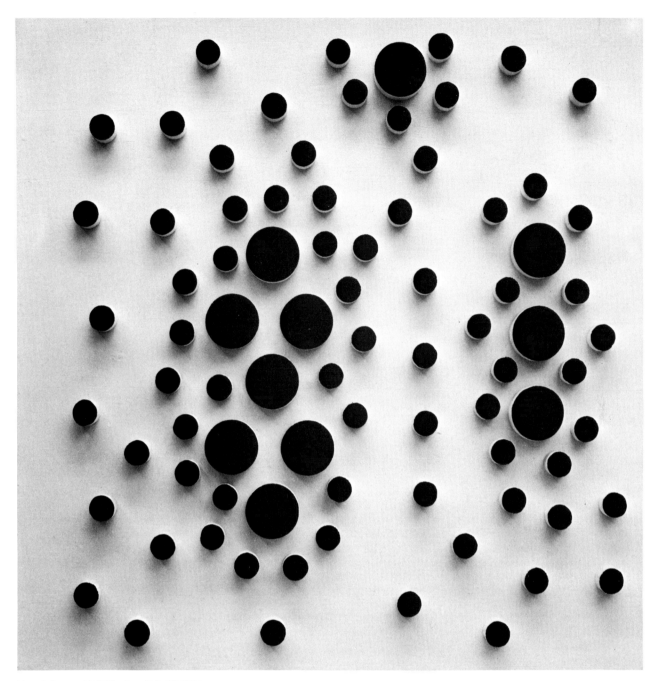

Henryk Stazewski: White-Gray Relief 6, 1964

(ill. p. 210). This method is a kind of scriptural painting, gestural and calligraphic in the added sense that the color in the brush becomes weaker as the artist writes and the intensity of the white therefore decreases, paling almost to illegibility before the brush is dipped in the paint again. The composition thereby takes on a painterly tonal character, and the dense rows of figures turn the canvas into a vibrating and pulsating surface. The magic in the monotony becomes even more powerful if the viewer also listens to a tape of Opalka counting aloud as he writes down the numbers. The endless series of numbers moving one by one in an unchanging rhythm strangely loses all its banality. The spell is stronger for those who share with the artist an awareness of the unattainable goal, the approach to infinity. Behind the "painterly" surface of this art is a rational concept related to systematic structural art, but its fulfillment is displaced to an infinite remove. Or, if one prefers, this concept leads to final nothingness, for the gray ground of each picture is slightly paler than that of the preceding one. As the march to infinity proceeds, the figures thus gradually move toward the oblivion of white on white and will finally become altogether invisible—long before Opalka approaches infinity.

Roman Opalka: Detail 843.802–868.148, 1965

The Serial Principle

Constructive Art in Germany since 1945

Art developments in Germany after 1945 cannot be rightly assessed without keeping one or two historical facts in mind. As a result of the reactionary art policy of the National Socialist regime from 1933 on, the free development of German art had been suppressed, as had also the exchange of ideas with other countries and every form of serious art criticism. When Germany came to reestablish its civilian life, there was a powerful urge toward intellectual and artistic reorientation. But almost all the prerequisites were lacking, and not only those of a material nature.

The artistic elite had emigrated or died, had given up in despair or been killed in the war. European art since Impressionism had been removed from the museums in the thirties, and some of it had been sold to collectors abroad. The German art trade had been forced to manage without this "degenerate art"; anything that remained in private ownership had had to be hidden away. A large number of twentieth-century works in public or private collections were destroyed in air raids during the war — the exact figures are not known even today. The younger generation after 1945 was thus without the material evidence of the development of European art in this century. The study of progressive movements in art, literature and music had been systematically stifled in schools and universities after 1933. Art schools had replaced experimentation with materials and methods, as initiated by the Bauhaus, with academic instruction. Germany's young artists thus faced the future with immense gaps in their knowledge. Although the era of National Socialism had only lasted twelve years, it had produced a profound caesura in Germany's cultural life which was not going to be easy to bridge.

The occupation forces set out to satisfy this hunger for intellectual nourishment by making their own art productions known in Germany through liberally conceived cultural programs. This enabled artists, art lovers and teachers to become familiar with the new work that was being done elsewhere — even if the information was often rather haphazard or nationally colored — and to catch up on the advances that had been made in the meantime. The efforts of the French, British and American cultural services, backed by the other countries of Europe, to meet the needs of the three zones of West Germany soon brought results. The other half of Germany, which was occupied by the Russians, was admittedly excluded from this reintegration in the international cultural scene. The dichotomy between West and East, which was to become a lasting reality with the creation of the Federal Republic of Germany and the German Democratic Republic, was thus already making itself felt in the cultural sphere.

One of the main negative factors affecting this new beginning was the loss of the old capital. Up to 1933 Berlin had been one of the great centers of art as well as one of the major cities of Europe. After 1945, divided into four sectors and isolated from the rest of Germany, it could no longer play this part. The lack of a capital was felt in West German art, and regional fragmentation was the result. But in the meantime the art scene has found new points of concentration in Cologne, Dusseldorf, Munich, and Frankfurt. The insular situation of Berlin has produced an artistic climate there that differs markedly from that of the West German cities. Constructive art, for instance, meets with less interest in Berlin — once the European focal point of Constructivism — than the new expressionist or realist trends. The sociocritical commitment of art is greater in Berlin than in West German art centers such as Cologne or Dusseldorf.

The modern classics that had been out of sight since 1933 were absorbed in a surprisingly short space of time. The great experience of the first awakening, however, was the free, painterly abstraction of the Ecole de Paris. It permitted the longed-for return to privacy after years of total war and was at the same time an escape from the misery of the times into a problem-free world of beauty and of sensuous enjoyment of the painter's craft. A no less powerful influence was exercised by Surrealism, which now went through a late flowering in Germany, with Max Ernst the principal source of inspiration alongside Dalí and Miró. This Neo-Surrealist trend is as understandable as the escapism of abstract painting: expressive and realistic art forms could be used to invoke, reprocess and thereby neutralize the burden of fears and nightmares left by the harrowing years of war.

After a first survey of international art, and particularly of the various forms of abstraction, a rediscovery of the schools and artists that had long been condemned in Germany set in. The German Expressionists were rehabilitated, and so were Kandinsky, Klee, Schlemmer, Baumeister and Schwitters. This led to a reconsideration of the move toward non-objectivity made in Germany a generation before, to an examination of the Expressionist gesture, of Constructivism, of the construction of the human form, of the Dadaist integration of chance in art and the revalorization of the worthless found object.

An Expressionist school of painting soon made its appearance, with the younger painters quickly jettisoning all allegiance to objective and figurative reality. The starting point must be sought in the free improvisations of the early Kandinsky. The expressive gesture was a form of self-liberation that the artist thirsted for after years of uniformity, of the suppression of all individualistic impulses.

Adolf Fleischmann: Untitled, gray, yellow, black, c. 1958

It permitted him the relief of subjectivity and spontaneity. And German painters soon discovered that they were not alone with this expressive gestural art. About 1950, they found backing in similar developments in France, where two artists of German origin — Wols (Otto Wolfgang Schulze) and Hans Hartung — had helped to launch the school of Tachisme or "art informel". Similar developments were also under way in the Netherlands and Scandinavia, dominated by the wildly expressive, formless painting of the "Cobra" group, founded in 1948. Reassurance next came from the United States, where Abstract Expressionism and Action Painting proper — developing partly out of Surrealism — were very influential between 1945 and 1955. German postwar art had thus come into line with art developments elsewhere.

Below this surface adoption of modern tendencies, however, the pursuance of German prewar departures went on. One of the information gaps that had to be filled was that relating to Paul Klee, who had returned to Switzerland in 1933 and had died there in 1940. While his work was still being discovered, his writings on aesthetic theory appeared in 1956 under the title of "Das bildnerische Denken" (translated as "Creative Thought", literally "pictorial thinking"). The book was soon important reading matter in any study of the artist's means. The same applies to "Das Unbekannte in der Kunst" (The Unknown in Art) by Willi Baumeister, doyen of German postwar artists, who made himself, through his protean œuvre and the weight of his impulsive personality, the spokesman of a many-faceted German art.

In the early sixties, Abstract Expressionism or informal art, to which Germany had made a substantial contribution both in artistic practice and in theory, was at its zenith. The flamboyance of Action Painting, which startled the general public, pushed other aspects of the reassessment of past movements into second place. The study of Kandinsky, Klee, Schlemmer, and Baumeister, however, had led to the rediscovery of the achievements of the Bauhaus. This interest was strengthened by the huge problems with which reconstruction confronted architects and town planners and the need for well-designed, practical and economical objects of everyday use. From 1955 on publications on the Bauhaus began to supply accurate information on the cultural accomplishments of the Weimar Republic. This information was to be of use in solving contemporary problems. Former members of the Bauhaus now came forward, they presented their old and new artistic productions, most of them Constructivist in spirit, they accepted major assignments as architects and product designers. Their influence was particulary fruitful in art education. The preliminary course of the Bauhaus was now adopted in the instruction programs of Germany's newly organized art schools. Johannes Itten acted as a kind of missionary with his essays and lectures on questions of art education, and later with publications on the "Art of Color" and the preliminary course at the Bauhaus. From the United States came the counsel of Walter Gropius, founder of the Bauhaus, and of other personalities who had further developed Bauhaus ideas in the meantime, such as Josef Albers and Herbert Bayer.

The postwar situation in Germany with all its social, economic, architectural, urbanistic, artistic, educational and

Günter Fruhtrunk: Two Red to One Red, 1970

design problems clearly invited a revival of the Bauhaus movement. And this was in fact achieved by a synthesis of the progressive forces in Germany with the American support for cultural reconstruction in the country. A former member of the Bauhaus, the Swiss Max Bill, had already been thinking of the creation of a design university which would be based on Bauhaus practice and would turn out a new type of designer. The Geschwister-Scholl-Stiftung, a foundation in memory of a resistance group that had perished in the struggle against the Hitler regime, entrusted Max Bill with the preparation of a project for the erection of such a school in Ulm. Thanks to the active support of the American High Commissioner, John J. McCloy, the project was soon on the way to realization with financial aid from the reeducation program. In 1950 the "Hochschule für Gestaltung" in Ulm was opened with Max Bill as founder and rector. The school was intended as a "place of research and training for the design problems of our time", and as a pioneering establishment it exerted a powerful attraction on the younger generation. In 1955 faculty and students moved into the new buildings designed by Bill, which were to provide the setting for the teaching of industrial design, architecture, town planning, visual communication and information theory.

The Ulm experiment was even less an art school in the traditional sense than the Bauhaus had been. It was instead an attempt, as Max Bill said later, "to make a real contribution to the emergence of a culture that is in tune with the facts and requirements of our time". In spite of the emphasis it placed on fundamental and practical aspects of the shaping of the environment, the Ulm school had close ties with contemporary fine art. It had particularly close ties with Constructive art, partly because of the artists among its guest lecturers, partly as a result of the constitution of the faculty itself, which included — in addition to Max Bill — Friedel Vordemberge-Gildewart, who

Günter Fruhtrunk: Separating White, 1973

Herbert Oehm: Additive layers of color, 1967

became head of its visual communication department in 1954. The Ulm school in fact made important direct and indirect contributions to the growing interest in a rational art as a counterweight to the dominant, markedly emotional approach of Tachisme and Action Painting. It also provided support for the efforts made by others to revive constructive ideas, particularly through the theories developed by Max Bense as the foundation of a rational aesthetic during his collaboration with Max Bill. Bill had also planned some fine art studios in Ulm as part of the training, but only for students who had already graduated in some field of study. Since he left Ulm in 1957, however, only very few students had taken up fine art, among them Almir Mavignier, who now combines painting with his visual communication assignments.

The currency reform of 1948 furnished the material foundations for the evolution of a vital postwar art in Germany. This radical change in the monetary system marked the beginning of a faster reconstruction phase and soon brought immense economic growth. The improvement in economic conditions, coupled with an uninhibited belief in progress, favored the reception of contemporary art. A great deal was soon being done to popularize and disseminate it: museums and exhibition halls had their buildings renovated or rebuilt and intensified their activities. The growing prosperity encouraged private art collecting. The confusing multiplicity of the German art scene — mirrored in magazines and art books, galleries and exhibitions, public support of art, private collecting and patronage — was also reflected in a more condensed and selective form in the manifestations of the "Documenta" in Kassel. This quadriennale of art was a discerning attempt to add to the biennales (Venice, São Paulo, Tokyo and later Paris) an equally international survey of contemporary art which was, however, based on a uniform criterion of selection.

The first Documenta in 1955 marked the reentry of West Germany into the mainstream of contemporary art. It presented a retrospective of the work done between 1933 and 1945, in the years of German isolation. The second Documenta in 1959 concentrated on art from 1945 to 1955 and thus provided more information on postwar trends. The third Documenta of 1964 was devoted to the five preceding years and thus caught up with art developments. In the fourth exhibition in 1968 the historical approach was given up in order to single out the more important aspects of a now many-faceted contemporary art. Even though Kassel's "Museum of the 100 Days" had always made the force of an artistic personality the criterion of its choice, there was a confrontation, in 1968, between Pop Art and what Barbara Rose, speaking of the American situation, had called "post-painterly abstraction", in other words American constructive art. This could now be compared with constructive art in Europe, and both parallel and contrasting traits became visible. Constructive art had actually been represented in Kassel before this, and with some of its leading exponents.

In the fifth Documenta of 1972 a development began which was to be continued up to the eighth Documenta of 1987: prevailing trends, basic themes, and special sectors of contemporary art were dealt with, the presentations differing only in the personal outlooks of successive commissaries. Among these various aspects of art in progress, constructive art played only a marginal role.

Every Documenta provoked passionate discussion and sparked off a wide variety of activities among art institutes and galleries in Germany. The competition was at times hectic. Among the aspects of art that received support, constructive art was very much to the fore. The exposure it was now given was all the more important for its survival and development because many of its representatives lived in local isolation, a result of the decentralized character of German art life. The critic Eduard Trier had already stated in 1959, in connection with the flood of Action Painting: "It is unimaginable that a painter of twenty-five should give himself up to this inebriating self-abandonment and persist in it to a ripe old age." A response to this justified criticism came around 1960 with the evolution of the "Neue Figuration" (New Figuration) from Action Painting. Constructive art also had an answer ready in its own stock-in-trade, as yet far from exhausted and quite capable of renewal.

The sources of such renewal were to be found first of all in the historical incunabula, which soon began to turn up in exhibitions and galleries and were also being bought by museums. Then there were a few surviving exponents of the German Constructivism of the twenties. Among these — they now emerged from obscurity once more — were Ella Bergmann-Michel and Robert Michel, Carl Buchheister, Ernst Buchholz, Max Burchartz, Walter Dexel, Werner Graeff, Oskar Nerlinger, Thomas Ring and Karl-Peter Roehl. Many former students of the Bauhaus also came forward to take posts in art teaching, architecture and industrial design.

Among the few German Constructivists who had emigrated and now returned to Germany — we have already mentioned Friedel Vordemberge — was Adolf Fleischmann of Stuttgart. Impressed by Delaunay and Gleizes, Fleischmann had worked in France from 1938, had become a member of "Réalités Nouvelles" in 1946 and had moved to New York in 1952. His extensive late work — produced between 1950 and 1965 — is a highly individual synthesis of various constructive tendencies. His preference for an oval picture area recalls Cubist compositions (ill. p. 212), and the division of the surface into meshing L-shaped elements may also be regarded as a systematization of surface arrangements as used by synthetic Cubism. These surface forms are produced by horizontal or vertical hatching on a dark, neutral ground. The parallel strokes, applied freehand, which lend order and rhythm to the whole picture area and also carry the color, can be ascribed to Neo-Impressionist methods of color application. The resulting structure sets the color in vibrating motion. The contrast of the dark ground with the color nuances and textures laid upon it also creates a spatial movement which is sometimes heightened by vertical bars of color. Without having recourse to the surface kinetics then in vogue, Fleischmann investigated the problems of virtual motion in the picture by painterly methods, with free, unconstrained brushwork. When he began to use stiffened corrugated board in a sort of collage technique about 1956, problems of relief presented themselves. The color texture was now joined by a relief structure reacting to the incidence of light. Fleischmann's painterly geometric art, with the harmonious proportions of his surfaces and a delicate coloring reminiscent of Georges Braque, has repeatedly invited a comparison with chamber music.

The mention of textures and structures brings us to a subject in which young constructive artists in Germany have long taken a special interest. The first impulse came — in part at least — from the Swiss Concrete artists. Group exhibitions from Switzerland and one-man exhibitions of the work of Max Bill and Richard Paul Lohse drew the attention of the young Germans to a further develop-

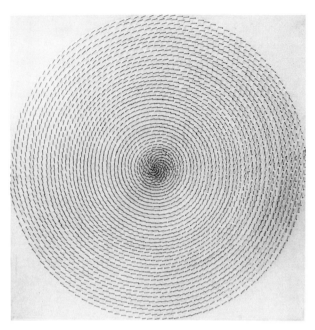

Günther Uecker: Spiral 4, 1968

ment of constructive art that was based on mathematical thinking and rational, systematic procedure. The informational aesthetic propagated by the new school of design in Ulm was able to use this type of Concrete Art in the investigation of certain phenomena of perception.

The philosopher Max Bense of Stuttgart had revealed the close connection between art and mathematics in his basic work "Konturen einer Geistesgeschichte der Mathematik" (Outline of a History of Mathematical Thought, 1946/49). Bense's investigations might be considered as an attempt at a synthesis of the philosophies of mathematics and of art. The upshot of his historical research is the theory of "the original unity of aesthetic and mathematical categories". He finds that "like the product of nature, the product of art, provided it is real, is distinguished by mathematical properties". In his other writ-

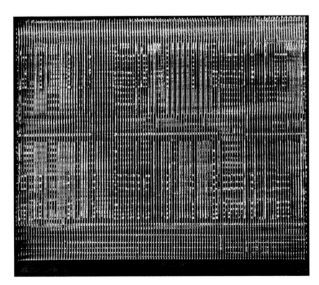

Heinz Mack: Untitled, frottage, 1960

215

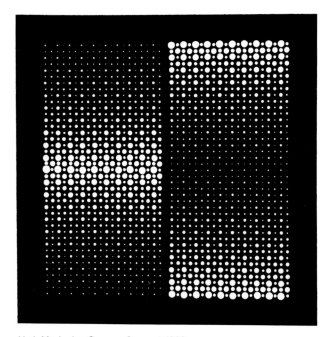

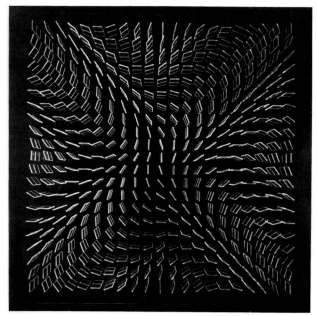

Almir Mavignier: Concave-Convex I, 1962

Hartmut Böhm: Square Relief 27, 1966/68

ings (collected in "Aesthetica", 1966) Bense studies the "programming of beauty" and its influence on communication, society and criticism. Bense's publications, lectures and exhibitions, from the early fifties on, greatly stimulated thought about all fundamental aspects of art. He may be regarded as the founder of information aesthetics in Germany. The conclusion that "art is communication", or in other words that art is a message transmitted by one individual to another, connects up to the principles of cybernetics which were brought to the attention of art theorists by Norbert Wiener's presentation of this science ("Cybernetics", 1948). Contributions to the new thinking on aesthetics were also made by the philosopher and sociologist Theodor W. Adorno of Frankfurt and the psychosociologist Abraham A. Moles of Strasbourg. Moles's book "Informationstheorie und ästhetische Wahrnehmung" (Information Theory and Aesthetic Perception, 1958/1971) became an important instrument for the study of perceptual phenomena such as those on which the systematic development of constructive design principles is based. Most of the work of the younger generation of German artists would be unthinkable without this background of information aesthetics, however different the work of the various artists may be.

The painters and sculptors who have renewed constructive art in postwar Germany mostly belong to a generation that was born in the twenties. They received their training, after the delay of the war years, in the second half of the forties, and they have been producing independent work since about 1950. Some of them entered the field of geometric constructive art directly, others gravitated into it by way of free abstract art or as the result of a deliberate rejection of Abstract Expressionism about 1960. This last course was taken by Georg Karl Pfahler, who gave up a very painterly, expressive and gestural subjectivism for systematic arrays of simple, anonymous color-shapes. "For me at that time it was a matter of getting away from the uncommittedness of Tachisme

and painting pictures that would lead to a new formal discipline and terseness." Together with the color-objects of the sculptors Utz Kampmann and Thomas Lenk, Pfahler's forceful painting represented German art in the exhibition "Formen der Farbe" ("New Shapes of Color") that was staged in Amsterdam, Stuttgart and Berne in 1966/67 and brought together European Constructivists and exponents of American Postpainterly Abstraction (ill. p. 219). The sign-like shapes that characterized this art, together with the optical shock of its colors, led to its being designated as "Signal Art" when it appeared in exhibitions, as it did first in Basel and Berlin in 1965. But the designation was not to last, any more than the term "Musische Geometrie" (Lyrical Geometry) that was coined for an exhibition in Hanover in 1966. While the former name alludes to the power of suggestion of the sign-like shapes and to the aggressive colors, the second is a reference to the intuitive rather than constructed nature of the shapes and above all to the psychic effect of the colors.

The significance of color and of its laws and effects was brought home to young German artists both by Johannes Itten and by Josef Albers, who in 1955 was a guest lecturer at Ulm. His theory of color interaction was one that could be studied in exhibitions of his paintings (ill. p. 259). Eugen Gomringer, exponent and theorist of Concrete poetry and for many years a collaborator of Max Bill's, had repeatedly pointed to the importance of Albers from the mid-fifties onward. Albers' study of color has given the idea of the "color space" first put forward by the Abstract Expressionists a new meaning in constructive art.

One of the first Germans to find his place in international constructive art was Günter Fruhtrunk. After studying under Fernand Léger he settled in Paris in 1954 and began by developing a dynamic geometric style with rectangular and circular elements which can best be compared with the painting of Herbin or with some of the work of the young Vasarely. Around 1960 the configurations of cir-

216

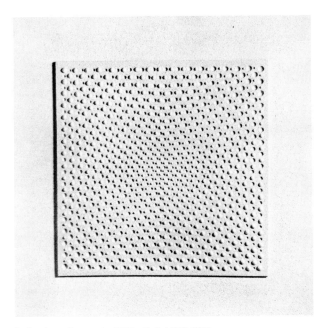

Gerhard von Graevenitz: White Relief 12/3, 1961

Gerhard von Graevenitz: Kinetic Object, 1970

cles and rectangular planes begin to change into structures of parallel rods or bars (ill. p. 213). Initially a dynamic mosaic of interpenetrating "particles", his vertical, horizontal or diagonal bar patterns gradually take on an expression of repose, of collected strength and grandeur. The determinant feature of the black-and-white compositions is the rhythm created by the changing thicknesses and intervals of the bars. Where color — sometimes made more aggressive by luminescent pigments — stands beside black, the surface kinetic effect is enhanced by fine dividing lines of a different color that produce optical vibrations. "Pure color," says Fruhtrunk, "is made to display a maximum of its inherent light intensity. Interpenetrating color structures and particles that lose their natural color as a result of quantity ratios and mutual influences cancel each other out by their dividing and uniting simultaneity as a possible space." Fruhtrunk — unlike the English artist Bridget Riley — does not go so far that the viewer's optical adaptation limit is overstepped and the eye is dazzled. He stops on this side of optical provocation and thereby permits a close, in-depth scrutiny. The arrangement and the rhythm of the pattern evokes the idea of a wide field, only a detail of which is captured in the picture.

Starting from abstract shapes, Heijo Hangen arrived after 1950 at constructive work of "a Suprematist order", to use his own words. From 1956, stimulated by the methods of the Swiss Concrete artists, he translated numbers and dimensions into pictures, at first using systematic square divisions. The "Chromatic regression with 7 squares" of 1957 (ill. p. 218) is an example of this phase. The principle of superimposed surfaces, introduced in 1960, then led to the "schematic-methodical art" Hangen has been practicing since. The basic element is a module with which he operates on a square picture area divided into 16 smaller squares. This module, developed from a grid system and based on two form elements, can be used as a linear shape, as a structural module, or else as a surface shape or surface module. A vast range of

solutions is possible within the system by methodical manipulation techniques such as reversal, rotation, regular or progressive displacement and combination. While the shape module is fixed, the artist is free in the choice of his colors. "Primary colors objectify the form-rhythm. Color extends the combination range of form."

Almir Mavignier also belongs to this generation. When he came to Europe in 1951 and settled in Ulm in 1953, however, he admittedly brought a different background with him, partly as a Brazilian, partly as a result of his antecendents, his art training and his practice as art therapist in Rio de Janeiro. He studied at the Hochschule für Gestaltung from 1954 to 1958, in the visual communication department. His preceptors were chiefly Max Bill, Josef Albers and Max Bense. In 1954 he completed his first picture using a punctual structure. He set out from an idea that Paul Klee had developed when teaching at the Bauhaus: the intersection of two lines creates a point, a point of energy that embodies the action of the one line against the other. The structural principle developed by Mavignier is based on the marking of the imaginary points of intersection of a dense network of rectangular lines by "active" points. These grow in accordance with certain rules, rather like the dots of screen tints used in reproduction techniques, so that the intervals between them seem to become smaller (ill. p. 216). Systematic enlargement of the light points of color on a dark ground leads to a brightening of the whole texture. An apparent convexity or concavity of parts of the surface — a kinetic illusion of spatiality — can thereby be produced, according to the pattern of the composition. The points of color themselves — made of impasto pigment that grows out of the surface in small mounds — turn the microstructure of the picture into a relief with a crafted quality. A serial principle is thus given an unmistakable personal stamp. The interplay of waxing and waning brightness also brings Mavignier's painting very near the domain of lumino-kinetic work.

Structures and lumino-kinetic problems were also the

217

Raimund Girke: Horizontal-Vertical, 1967

subject matter of a group of Dusseldorf artists of about the same age: Otto Piene and Heinz Mack, who published the magazine "Zero" from 1958 and who formed the Zero Group in 1962 with Günther Uecker. Inspiration for this group came less from early Constructivist art than from the "Mouvement" school in Paris. The theoretical concepts and practice of the Zero Group embrace many of the problems that were being discussed in the late fifties. "Zero" here means the reduction of all the elements of art — the vocabulary of shapes and the sensuous wealth of colors — to an absolute minimum. Mack, for in-

Heijo Hangen: Chromatic regression with 7 squares, 1957

stance, renounced color altogether in 1958 and restricted himself to the light-and-dark effects of black and white. In return, vibration and light phenomena took on greater importance. "The constant return of black and white, of light and shade, the constant return, that is my strength, that is my weakness, that is your strength, that is your weakness" runs a passage from Mack's poetic credo. Systematically built-up relief structures covered with reflecting metal foil become kinetic objects under changing illumination, and their transitory appearances are occasionally recorded in "frottages" (ill. p. 215). Mack's interest in the phenomena of dynamic light pulsation is even more strongly expressed in his "light rotors" — boxes in which different layers of fluted glass are moved in relation to each other by a power source so that the constantly changing play of their structures becomes a dramatic spectacle of fugitive dark-and-light patterns. Similar light modulations are obtained in his "light merry-go-round" of mobile reflecting relief structures and in his "light steles". With these new techniques of his own, Mack seems to be carrying on experiments which Ludwig Hirschfeld-Mack initiated as "reflektorische Lichtspiele" (reflected light displays) at the Weimar Bauhaus in 1922/23 and continued later with others.

The combination of light and smoke, the visualization and dramatization of unstable elements, gaseous and fluid, as plastic media were the concerns of Otto Piene from 1959 onward. While his vibrating light structures are akin to those of Mack, the employment of smoke in conjunction with painting — as a gas or as a visible sediment — points in another direction. Piene's "light ballets" in particular — produced with ever-changing technical devices — are attempts at a new kind of exploration of space. "My preoccupation with light led me to artificial illumination as an easily guided medium for the palpation of space." Of the machines used for his light ballets Piene says: "What these objects created was a motion continuum, without drama, without tragedy, quiet, not exciting, but persisting." It is just this meditative spirit that distinguishes Piene's lumino-kinetic experiments from the optical spectacles of Nicolas Schöffer.

The third member of the Dusseldorf group, Günther Uecker, is a painter whose structurations of impasto pigment led him to relief compositions and, from 1957, to three-dimensional objects. In 1958 he began to drive nails in systematic patterns into plates and bent boards. The edges of his picture were now cancelled out by nails placed in the marginal zones. Rising in serried arrays from the surface of a picture or a three-dimensional object, the metal ranks create an indefinite transition zone between the solid and the impalpable surrounding space. After the end of the fifties Uecker also turned to white serial structures with regular patterns of nails on canvas or boards. In his consistent use of the "non-color" white Uecker is only one of a large group of modern painters and sculptors, some of whom are exploring white as a conscious advance from Malevich's "White square on a white ground", that expression of the "supremacy of pure sensibility". "White in white", a world of emptiness in the sense of Zen Buddhism, was made the subject of a comprehensive international exhibition in the Kunsthalle, Bern, in 1966. As early as 1961 Uecker had stated: "Yves Klein succeeded in making us aware of a zone of empti-

Georg Karl Pfahler: Espan, 1975

ness within an empty space . . . This demonstration had a profound effect on many artists, who saw in white a new idiom in which to communicate their intellectual experience." An analogous experience may be recalled in the work of Lucio Fontana and Piero Manzoni, and there are in fact marked connections between the ideas of the Zero Group in Dusseldorf and those of Italian "Spazialismo".

The "nailing" of objects of everyday use — chairs, television sets, pianos — which Uecker has repeatedly staged as a sort of happening is closely connected to Neo-Dadaist trends in Paris, which demanded a new relationship to material reality and led in 1960 to the founding of "Nouveau Réalisme". The contacts and collaboration of the Zero artists with Jean Tinguely and Daniel Spoerri are particularly close. Yet precisely in Uecker's systematic nail structures — mostly in matt white — a constructive substrate can be recognized, just as it can in Mack's aluminum reliefs. Kinetic light effects are produced by the shadows of the rows of nails that confront the observer like some fakir's bed, at any rate when the relief itself or the light source is moved, so that the nail-shadows veer around and the nail and its shadow become one. Uecker has made fullest use of these possibilities where he has driven his nails into the base not in orthogonal rows but in waves, eddies and spirals (ill. p. 215). The sense of motion is also intensified when the nails are not vertical but rise at a uniform inclination from the base. Such structures—essentially line systems regularly marked by nails—are turned into a billowing surface by the play of light and shade and have much of the appearance of plants swayed by currents in water or fields of grain ruffled by the wind.

Adolf Luther, a member of the older generation who turned from painting to lumino-kinetic objects in the fifties, is also interested in phenomena of light and in changes in visible reality brought about by the manipulation of light. His essential concern is the relationship of light and matter. Systematic assemblages or constructions made of rows of identical lenses, reflecting disks, round convex or concave mirrors are his instrumentarium for the revelation and methodical investigation of a "transoptical" reality.

Herbert Oehm of Ulm, who studied at the Hochschule für Gestaltung there in 1959/60, initially occupied himself with monochrome material structures. Characteristic compositions were his "gold pictures", followed in 1968 by "silver pictures". His works often combine additive color sequences with ribbon forms that produce kinetic surface effects or vibrations (ill. p. 214). A study of curved lines and rhythmically swinging surfaces led in 1968 to three-dimensional compositions, the so-called "Spannplastiken" (tension sculptures). Steel strips are fixed in a base and bent by wires to show a progression of increasing curvature and tension. More than mere elasticity is thus demonstrated. When a straight metal strip is bent in this way until it becomes a bow or spring, it is charged with energy. This energy is "frozen" as long as the pull is exerted. The potential energy imprisoned in these "tension sculptures" gives them the same menacing quality as a taut bowstring.

Raimund Girke emerged as an important exponent of monochrome painting in Germany after 1960. Structure and texture were at first predominant in his work. "White is an extremely sensitive color that calls for very accurate and concentrated treatment. The slightest changes in its coloring result in a fundamental alteration of the complex whole... That is no doubt the decisive point: a new sensibility results from intensive preoccupation with the material white." This sensibility also extends to the organization of the surface by means of subtle, systematic "disturbances". In Girke's work these disturbances are usually based on geometric principles of division (ill. p. 218). The quiet subtlety of these ethereal structures is reminiscent of the controlled, systematically flowing forms of Herbert Oehm's "sand pictures" but goes beyond them in its conceptual implications.

Andreas Brandt was one who in the seventies made effective use of rhythmically spaced vertical bands of color (ill. p. 221). Frank Badur's work has a certain kinship with that of Brandt, but his vertical divisions led rather to color fields that are treated with painterly sensitivity.

Arnulf Letto of Berlin seems at first glance to be satisfied with the rational subdivision of surfaces along clear mathematical principles. The regular division of the square picture area into parallel strips, square planes or slim triangles with apices pointing alternately up and down proves on closer scrutiny to be only a scaffolding for the investigation of continuous gradations of gray. A seemingly plastic articulation of the picture is achieved by taking advantage of a well-known phenomenon: a given shade of gray appears much darker when bordering the next lighter shade than when bordering the next darker shade. Surfaces which are uniform in actual pigmentation consequently appear to differ according to their surroundings. The purposeful application of this perceptual phenomenon permits soothing or disturbing gradations to be created. The two-dimensional paintings evoke the impression of a relief illuminated by a light that seems to fall across ridges and soft hollows.

Research into three-dimensional serial structures which change as the viewer moves in front of them was the theme of Hartmut Böhm's work from 1959. This sculptor from Kassel is one of the most important representatives of both serial and lumino-kinetic art. His systematic work, whose value in the field of information aesthetics has been analysed by the artist himself as well as by other theorists, has become a kind of standard for recent constructive art. "My compositions must be understood as didactic models which are only really present when they are actively absorbed... The relationship of unequivocally determined structure to its visually ambivalent perception provokes an intellectual and sensory reaction. The perceivability of the objects is thus their real subject matter, the aim is the reduction of the distance between artist and observer by an understanding of the operative process." The component parts of Böhm's works are small rods, square or rectangular strips, white on white in the "square reliefs" and "square developments", and of opaque or transparent acrylic in the "relief structures" and the "spatial structures", which are mostly enclosed in cases (ill. p. 216)

Rainer Kallhardt of Munich devoted himself after 1959 to the problems of Concrete Art, particularly in serial form, both in his constructive painting and in his capacities of publicist and exhibition director in Nuremberg. His compositions can be considered as systematic investigations of visual structures. As a rule a given linear system is developed in a square grid. One basic element provides the "key" to a sequence of "multivariable elements" that result from logical manipulatory procedures. In addition to his linear variations in black and white he has produced systematic color variations or "permutations".

Ernst Hermanns: Untitled, VW 200, 1981

220

Andreas Brandt: Black-Gray-Blue, 1974

Sets of concentric squares of the same size are placed next to each other and brought into optical vibration by systematic modification of the color combinations.

Another artist influenced by information aesthetics is Klaus Staudt. This applies particularly to his monochrome reliefs that are built up prismatically from small cubic bodies with alternating orientation of the oblique surfaces. These structural units combine to form an overall texture that is brought to life by incident light. Movement of the light source modifies the effect—a demonstration of the interplay of reality and illusion in relief structures.

Since the early eighties Klaus Staudt has been creating these three-dimensional structures with rectangular white frames forming grids in front of a white ground and producing a surprising shadow play (ill. p. 226).

Some exponents of systematic and constructive art in Germany have established close relations with allied groups in Holland. Among them is Ewerdt Hilgemann, who settled in Gorinchem and made an important contribution to present-day constructive art in Holland (ill. p. 235). Another is Gerhard von Graevenitz, who spent part of his time in Amsterdam. He was one of the founders of the international group "Nouvelle Tendance" in 1962 and investigated the plus-minus relationship in an important series of plaster casts. Small convex and concave hemispheres were combined in systematic arrays so that the diminishing positive form corresponded to a negative form that grew by the same amount. The crescendo and decrescendo of the plastic

mini-shapes produced a surging movement in the white relief field, which was enlivened only by light and shade (ill. p. 217). Later the emphasis moved to mobile reliefs, usually fitted with motors, which gave the kinetic artist the opportunity to study the relation of regularity to irregularity, chance and the laws of probability. Von Graevenitz frequently used slowly rotating micro-elements, white rods or circular disks on a black background. The continuously changing patterns seem never to repeat themselves, for the observer is unable to seize on any given configuration. This "different kind of visual order" comes out clearly in later kinetic reliefs in which slow rotation causes a black ellipse to change both its orientation and its position on a white circular disk (ill. p. 217).

Among constructive sculptors of the younger generation in Germany Eberhard Fiebig attracted attention with his "pneumatic sculptures" and later with constructions of perforated metal plates bolted together. New directions have also come from Erwin Heerich of Dusseldorf, whose constructive cardboard sculptures are so fragile that they amount to a deliberate rejection of the "eternal" materials of traditional sculpture. These stereometric volumes, sometimes simple, sometimes complex, ingeniously constructed from flat boards by box-making methods, reveal the volume as a product of the spatial reshaping of planes (ill. p. 222). Neutral, matt brown cardboard is an ideal medium for demonstrating the relationships of volumes and planes, since it lays no claim to any material value and does not dramatize the play of light and shade.

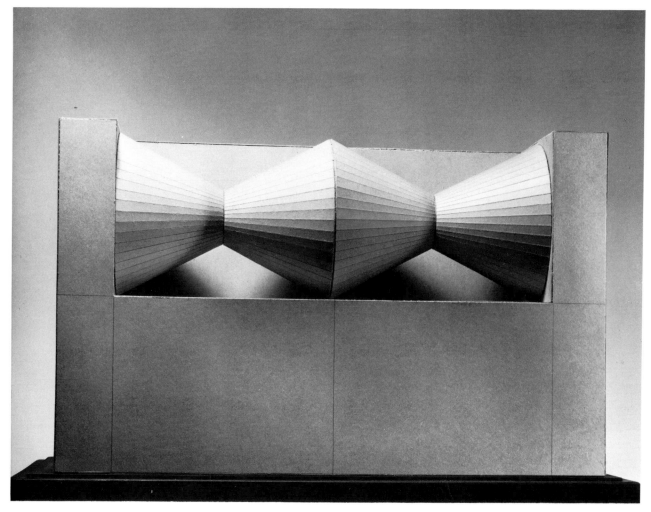

Erwin Heerich: Untitled, 1964

No external beauties veil the fact that these bodies are the result of exact ratiocination based on mathematical laws. "It is crucial to see the proportions and more," Heerich emphasizes. His drawings are particularly useful in showing on what conceptions of shape and space his highly accurate work is based, even if they take "impossible" volumes as their subject. Planimetric and isometric representation is used in these drawings to reveal the pervious frontier between the rational and the irrational.

In 1969 Dietrich Mahlow organized a first Biennale in Nuremberg under the title of "Constructive Art—Elements and Principles". Against the background of the achievements of the pioneer generation, the exhibition presented the principal representatives of recent constructive trends, over 120 artists from Western and Eastern Europe, the United States and South America. Without being really complete, it provided an extremely varied picture of the contributions being made to what was evidently a worldwide and vital art. In particular, the Nuremberg exhibition included a survey of recent German constructive work. Nothing like this had been attempted before, nor has it been since. The exhibition stuck closely to its subject. It did not include work which perhaps lies on the boundary of constructive art or perhaps just beyond

it, but which certainly holds an important place in German postwar art.

Some of this work has been done by painters of the older and younger generations for whom color is more important than—geometric—shapes. Rupprecht Geiger, for instance, is interested in how color affects the human eye. He provokes the radiation of a red circle—typical of his work—as a kind of "ball of fire" on to the surrounding picture area. Gotthard Graubner is a rather different case, he might be regarded as a successor of Abstract Expressionism. He is concerned exclusively with the light space of color and can be compared in this with the representatives of American Colorfield Painting. "The development of my pictorial work can be followed step by step. Color unfolds as an organism; I observe it living its own life, I respect its intrinsic laws. Thus two dimensions were able to condense into a body, the body to dissolve in bodiless condensation in space as a mist... The viewer is involved, he takes possession of the painter's space and enters the painting." Only a minimum of real color is used, especially in Graubner's "cushion pictures", which are wrapped in gauze and suggest a sort of misty space. "Color is made accessible to experience through its nuance."

Erich Hauser: Sculpture, S. 2/71, 1971

Other workers who must be regarded as operating on the margins of constructive art are those who produce Concrete or visual poetry or who explore the domain of "Text—Letter—Picture". This was the title of an exhibition staged in Zurich in 1970 which reflected an international interest in the shapes and the interpretation of letters and numbers, character and figure sequences. The exponents of this art include Peter Roehr (who died young) with his elementary rows of characters and Hanne Darboven with her tabular arrays of figures, both attempts to deal with the problem of sign and language, a problem that belongs to the sphere of non-retinal, conceptual art.

Some particularly interesting work has been done precisely in Germany in these marginal areas of constructive art, most of it by artists born around 1940. They refuse to accept any doctrine, make use of the pictorial means of constructive art in an unorthodox way and are open to impulses and questions from other fields of modern art. Ernst Neukamp of Munich, originally a geologist and interested in landscape, has attempted to combine geometry and organic nature in landscape constructs. Lienhard von Monkiewitsch, working in Brunswick, might be allocated to the new school of Photorealism with his space vistas devoid of all figures and objects, but his illusionary pictures of floors, walls, wainscots and pillars are more than subtle exploitations of the possibilities of perspective construction. His special way of representing items of interior architecture forces the observer to complete the picture in his mind's eye, so that the logic of real space is reestablished. This makes the viewer see things that are actually not shown in the painting. Here use is being made of mechanisms of perceptual experience, of processes which are the concern of perceptual or optical art, of information aesthetics and gestalt psychology. The information reaching the retina is analysed in the central nervous system on the principle of the most sensible possible configuration.

The drawings and paintings of Bodo Baumgarten, a pupil of Gotthard Graubner, must also be understood as perspective projections of simple surface shapes—squares, crosses and arrows (ill. p. 224). When shadows accompany the shapes, the impression of space is emphasized in these sketches, which from a distance remind us of Suprematist works. And space is intended, as his three-dimensional objects show: guide ropes extend across huge rooms in which colorfully painted triangular canvases stretch like sails or awnings in a sort of rigging. These

223

Bodo Baumgarten: Untitled, 1973

spatial cloth constructions of precisely controlled proportions connect up to contemporary trends in painting: it is no longer canvas stretched over a frame that is used as a support for color, but free, color-drenched cloth which hangs in front of a wall or in space. This raises questions of the relation of surface and color such as were discussed at the time in the circles of French Colorfield Painting under the heading of "support-surface". In other words, Baumgarten is moving toward the developments taking place in international Colorfield Painting which Klaus Honnef attempted to analyse in an exhibition entitled "Planned Painting" mounted in Münster in 1974. The German painters included in this survey were Ulrich Erben, Wilfried Gaul, Raimund Girke, Kuno Gonschior, Gotthard Graubner, Edgar Hofschen and Icke Ruden—almost all of them equally interested in simple geometric surface patterns and in monochrome work, and thus answering a worldwide longing for a "Silent Art".

While the scope of constructive surface art was comparatively narrow for its German exponents, sculpture displayed surprising variety. This may be sufficiently explained by the fact that three-dimensional work could be done either in solid volumes, in relief textures or in spatial sculptures. Among the pioneering achievements in this field in Germany are the severe steel sculptures of Ernst Hermanns, for instance the Spartan confrontation of two hemispheres or of a sphere and a cylinder on a common base (ill. p. 220).

One of the initiators of recent volumetric work was the steel sculptor Erich Hauser. Form complexes that often appear irrational, with elements that penetrate each other or grow out of each other, suggest forces that can only be deduced from their disturbing effects: pipes from whose points of collapse other elements ooze forth, or segments of coated disks that seem to be slipping out of their static positions (ill. p. 223). By thus incorporating virtual movement in static sculptures of great technical per-

fection, Hauser creates impressions of instability and irrational dynamism.

Another pioneer was Norbert Kricke. In the fifties, using steel wire and rods as his preferred materials, he produced space constructions that were at first strictly geometric, then emphatically gestural: needles that protrude from nuclear bodies far into space, often aggressively. About 1960 these bundles of lines became straight rays that were increasingly crystalline in character. A reduction process then led to elementary, even minimalist spatial compositions, each consisting of a single, sometimes colored wire or rod bent at right angles, mostly at three points, to enclose or penetrate space—sculptures of an exemplary severity that makes them almost space drawings (ill. p. 225). Not so far removed from them are the imaginary bodies of the sculptor Alf Lechner, which are constructed of square rods or pipes; an example of them is the "Tetrahedron Substraction" of 1976.

Young constructive sculptors devote themselves surprisingly often to the floor sculpture, as a rule of steel. They make wide use of semifinished products: linkages, beams, bars, pipes, and plates are laid down, frequently rising only a little way above the ground. Alf Schuler works in this area, while Joachim Bandau, at least in his more recent work, lays down heavy plates that must be understood as stereometric bodies, or pushes them one above the other. Alf Lechner occasionally applies the same principle when he raises massive diagonally divided squares just above ground level. Layering is the main idea in the sculptures of Thomas Lenk, which are often colored. For each work he uses thin plates of the same dimensions, mostly square but with rounded corners. These plates are heaped one above or one against the other in horizontal, oblique or occasionally vertical positions. In this way bodies are built up out of surfaces, and identical form elements are transformed into corporeal entities whose character is determined in advance by their dimensions.

"Line objects" is the name Leo Erb gives to spatial constructions consisting of identical white square columns. Closely packed but slightly staggered, they form a vertically stepped wall. The ten column verticals are echoed by the parallel, groove-like incisions constituting a horizontal line system, with an additional line on each wall element, so that the tenth falls on the tenth column. The parallel lines thus form sets that grow in regular steps. Other constructive metal sculptors work either with combinations of elementary stereometric volumes or with geometrically cut steel sheets which are set upright in twos or threes to form spatial organizations.

Developments are consequently under way that point in the direction of installations, whether in the open, in city settings or in interiors, and which thus conform to recent international trends in art. These trends are not prejudiced by the Neo-Expressionist currents that emerged in the early eighties; their elementary character ensures their survival and even a renewal of constructive concepts in many countries, including Germany. The work of Diet Sayler is a good example of this (ill. p. 226).

In constructive art it is customary for the order embodied in the picture or sculpture to be determined by a preestablished mathematical program or system. Instead of this

Norbert Kricke: Spatial Sculpture, 1975/VIII

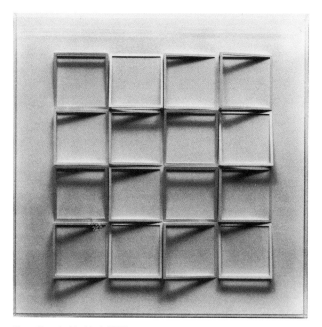

Klaus Staudt: Untitled, 1983

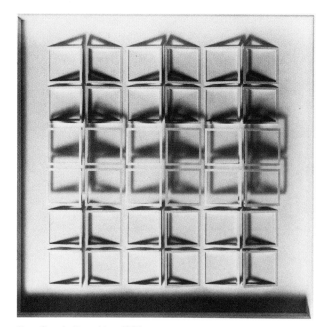

Klaus Staudt: Repetition, 1986

Diet Saylor has developed a method employing "framework rulings" which can also be used by other artists. Although strict conditions are still imposed, they leave room for the unforeseen and thus for free individual decisions. This combination of order and freedom, which has nothing arbitrary about it, offers new scope for work on the surface and in three dimensions. The resulting possibilities are being successfully exploited both in Germany and elsewhere by a younger generation of constructive artists.

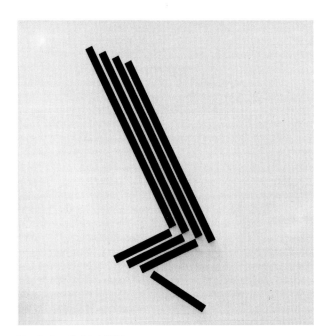

Diet Sayler: Untitled, 1970

Diet Sayler: Untitled, 1983

Calculated Phantasy

The Successors of de Stijl in the Netherlands

Like most other European countries that had been devastated by the war, the Netherlands were faced after 1945 by huge reconstruction problems, complicated by the fact that they had also lost their Indonesian colonies. The need for the speedy reorganization of economic and social life now called forth the inborn faculty of a nation of shipbuilders and seafarers for getting things done with the greatest possible economy of means. A new Dutch style was soon developed that expressed itself in housing and town planning, in industrial plants and in the construction of dams and sluices for the recovery of badly needed land from the sea. A factual but aesthetic approach clearly inspired by the spirit of de Stijl was evident in buildings and engineering schemes. It was not a deliberate revival, but rather a direct and natural continuation of the design principles of de Stijl. In some cases de Stijl architects were still at work, in others a younger generation trained in the same school tackled the immense tasks that awaited them in the spirit of a "reasonable functionalism".

There was also another factor: in the years of the German occupation a powerful resistance had built up in Holland, fomented by the country's intellectual elite. Artists and architects influenced by the Stijl movement, foremost among them the typographer Hendrik Nicolaas Werkman, were among the most active members of the resistance. The Dutch people therefore identified the artistic avant-garde with the national resistance movement, and this greatly aided the application of progressive design ideas during reconstruction. It was not only established architects such as J. H. van den Broek, J. B. Bakema, Aldo van Eyck and the Stijl representative G. T. Rietveld who worked on the building of the new Holland. A younger generation of artists was likewise very active and showed that it took its responsibilities to society seriously. Social commitment was in fact a feature of the new Dutch art.

Some of the impetus of this urbane art movement came from Willem Sandberg, one of the leaders of underground operations during the war, who became director of the Stedelijk Museum in Amsterdam and there deployed a dynamic art policy. Sandberg's exhibitions soon met with keen international interest and set new standards for art institutions all over Europe. Although expressive action painting was in the forefront of developments about 1950 and the Netherlands were involved in it inasmuch as Karel Appel belonged to the "Cobra" group, Sandberg gave vigorous support to constructive art. He extended the museum's de Stijl collection, exhibited the work of the pioneers of Constructivism and of the Swiss representatives of Concrete Art and encouraged the young constructive school in the Netherlands. Further encouragement came from Friedel Vordemberge-Gildewart,

who had lived in Amsterdam since 1938 and only moved to Ulm in 1954. He played a large part in the staging of a comprehensive de Stijl exhibition in Amsterdam in 1951 and had a powerful influence on the younger generation. A still more important event was the purchase of a representative collection of works by Kasimir Malevich for the Museum of Amsterdam. Malevich had left numerous works and manuscripts in Berlin when he had visited that city in 1927. These came to light in Germany in the early fifties. Sandberg was able to buy 51 paintings and drawings which had remained in the West after the big Berlin exhibition of 1927. This collection, covering Malevich's whole career, was shown in numerous exhibitions and helped clarify the idea of his achievement in the Western world.

A salient feature of all the work of the young constructive artists in the Netherlands was a keen interest in the elementary principles of design. Line, surface and volume were carefully investigated in the light of a detailed study of the ideas and accomplishments of de Stijl. These investigations were carried out very systematically, and a few constructive artists developed their own theories of design. Others turned to the laws of structures, which led them on to programming problems and in some cases to the use of the computer for determining possible solutions within a given program. In more recent times random numbers have also been included in the studies in the Netherlands, as in other countries where programming has been taken up. The interest in systematic procedures inspired by the serial principles in Richard Paul Lohse's painting has led to closer contacts with artists in other countries who are working on analogous problems, particularly in Germany and Italy.

Joost Baljeu was one of the first to turn to constructive art under the influence of Vordemberge. This was in 1954. His study of de Stijl initially evoked free geometric compositions embodying surface and color relations, but strictly orthogonal principles—a tribute to Mondrian—soon followed. As a result of contacts with the architect Rietveld, three-dimensional work then began to gain in importance. The relief and the spatial structure were substituted for the surface. Baljeu followed up ideas which Theo van Doesburg had begun to investigate in the twenties in connection with architectural projects. A study of the Cubist theories of Albert Gleizes also brought a confrontation with the time factor. In the late fifties he produced freely suspended three-dimensional structures composed of colored plates engaging with each other at right angles, a development of the isometric space concepts of Van Doesburg. Baljeu later called these works "Synthesist constructions" (ill. p. 228).

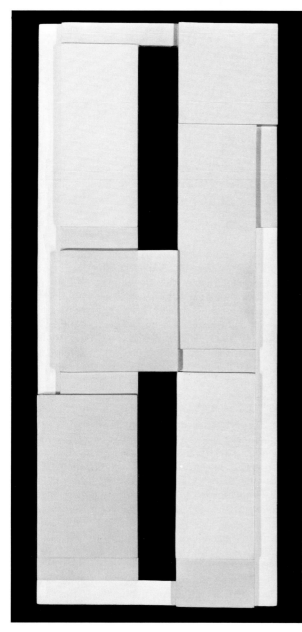

Joost Baljeu: Synthesist construction R 4, 1955

It was almost inevitable that he should get into touch with the American and Canadian Structurists, particularly Charles Biederman. They had much in common and a few points on which they disagreed, as for instance the time factor, which was important to Baljeu but was rejected by Biederman. A common feature of Structurist thought on both sides of the Atlantic is the interest in nature considered as a structural process. Baljeu's theoretical text "Attempt at a theory of synthesist plastic expression" (London 1963) broaches the question of growth and shaping laws in nature. The synthesist theory can be traced back to Jean Gorin, who was occupied from 1930 onward — setting out from Mondrian's Neo-Plasticism — with the borderland between painting and relief, surface and space. The receptacle for synthesist ideas on construc-

tive art was Baljeu's magazine "Structure", which ran from 1958 to 1964. His editorial work brought Baljeu into contact with like-minded artists, for instance with Anthony Hill, Kenneth and Mary Martin, Victor Pasmore and Gillian Wise in England; with Georges Vantongerloo and Jean Gorin in France; with Richard Paul Lohse and Andreas Christen in Switzerland. The outcome of these contacts was the traveling exhibition "Experiments in Surface and Space" which Baljeu mounted with Willem Sandberg in 1962 and which included work by Charles Biederman, Carlos A. Cairoli, John Ernst, Jean Gorin, Anthony Hill and Mary Martin as well as productions of his own. Baljeu outlined his opinions on the new creative principle in the preface to the catalog:

"The new design does not copy and represents no natural forms. It gives expression to universal laws. — The new design uses the rectangle not as a form but as a medium. This medium, in which both the horizontal and the vertical find expression, serves to create spaces which are also rectangular. But at the same time these spaces express bends, curves or angles through their reciprocal relationships. This, leads in the new design to unity in diversity. — The new design represents no material form, geometry or symbols. The representation of universal laws means that it gives expression to relationships: form principles. The new design creates no forms, but plastic relationships. — The new design obtains these relationships from a new conception of reality. It no longer regards reality as a static form, but as a dynamic process, as a process in space-time. — The new design conforms in its conception of reality as a process in space-time to modern science and philosophy ... The new design is rational in the general understanding of reality that it shares with science and philosophy. It has feeling because it is the shaping of a personal, inward relationship of the creative human being to this reality."

Baljeu's later works are to be seen against the background of this credo: translations of his design ideas into spatial compositions of an architectural character. This applies, for instance, to the spatial structures designed as "play constructions" for children in Rotterdam. Since 1970 he has completed numerous other synthesist constructions as environmental constituents of urban complexes, sometimes in collaboration with architects. Art, as represented by Baljeu, "is preparing the complete renewal of our social surroundings: from the dwelling to the town". This is a subject that meets with special interest in the Netherlands.

Baljeu's study of structural problems has been systematically developed by a group of young Dutch and German artists. Their work cannot be fairly judged without a knowledge of what "structure" in this context means: the order of the relationships of the elements in a whole. When this order becomes a self-sufficient subject of artistic investigation, the term "Structurism" can be applied. The Structurist movement in art also has connections with the structural concept in language and philosophy, with Structuralism. The Structurist method in art differs from the methods of Structuralism, developed from anthropology and linguistics, in that it creates structures instead of seeking for them. But if we interpret Structuralism as the "search for unexpected harmonies", as the "discovery of a latent system of relationships present in a

Bob Bonies: Untitled, 1972

series of objects", as Nelson and Tanya Hayes put it, the parallels are clear. In art the creation—and investigation—of structures may go more or less far, and Dutch constructive artists provide good examples of this.

Jan Schoonhoven is perhaps the artist who goes least far, and it is no doubt significant that he comes from "art informel". His monochrome white reliefs show a certain kinship with the reliefs of the Italian successors of Fontana, particularly Bonalumi and Castellani. In both cases interest is concentrated on the effects of light on the relief structures, which in Schoonhoven's work are comparatively simple. Using a papier-mâché technique that leaves plenty of scope for the craftsman's hand, Schoonhoven makes negative, excavated reliefs in which a simple motif—a slim upright or transversal rectangle, a semicylindrical, flute-like depression or a diagonally divided square—is repeated in horizontal and vertical rows (ill. pp. 230, 231). This often creates the impression of regular divisions much like those, say, of a compositor's typecase. It is only the light falling on it that gives the relief its plastic qualities. The intensity of the light and the angle from which it comes therefore determine how strongly the relief is articulated and what tensions are set up between fully illuminated zones and those left in shadow.

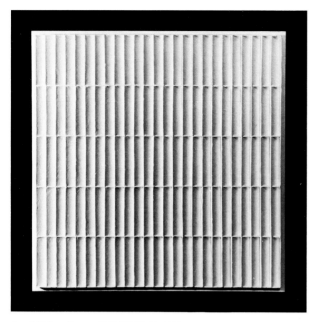

Jan J. Schoonhoven: Relief R-69.46, 1969

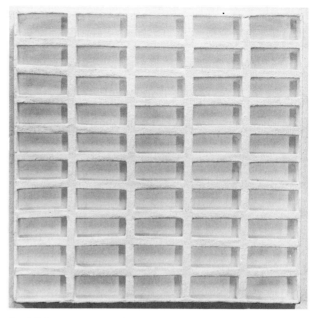

Jan J. Schoonhoven, Relief R-70.28, 1970

Areas of semi-shadow or those brightened somewhat by reflected light enrich the scale of gray tones so much that the illusion of polychromy is created. The simplicity of their structuration, combined with the craftsmanship of their execution, makes these reliefs individual productions in which the viewer may even find an emotional or romantic content.

The painter Bob Bonies chooses an approach not far removed from that of the Swiss Concrete artists. As in the works of Bill, Lohse and Graeser, it is here impossible to separate form and color. Compositions executed in a few basic hues, usually on a white ground, are built up of color-forms ordered in an easily legible system, growing or shrinking proportionally, for instance in a rotary movement from the outside inward (ill. p. 229). Careful attention is paid to the equilibration of these rectangular color-forms, which are arranged in a static horizontal-vertical sequence yet derive an inner dynamism from the progressive or degressive principle they embody. In 1966 the Stedelijk Museum of Amsterdam presented Bonies' work in a wide international context in an exhibition on the subject of "Shapes of Color" that toured many countries. The context extended from Bill and Lohse through Albers to Postpainterly Abstraction and Signal Art. Later Bonies rotated his orthogonal compositions, placing them diagonally in the picture area.

The second Dutch artist to catch the eye in this exhibition of 1966 was Pieter Struycken. While the works on view there, wide-meshed and diagonally distorted lattice structures, suggest experiments in optical effects, his later productions show that he is systematically investigating regular movements or processes. Struycken started out from simple structures which at first owed what complexity they had to a counterdirected color system. As his investigations advanced, however, they confirmed the fact — not in itself new — that as a structure grows more complicated the viewer has more difficulty in recognizing the

rules embodied in it. When the elements of a structure are systematically displaced, this can usually be followed. It is less easy when the relationships are based on a counting system. The rules may be visible in a "closed structure" which is wholly confined to the picture area. An "open structure", by contrast, may extend beyond the edges of the picture, and it then becomes unintelligible for anyone who does not have the key. Many of the lattices used in Islamic architecture embody this principle: the visible part is only a limited — and not necessarily particularly significant — detail extracted from a much larger mathematical line construction.

Struycken has operated with numerical series in his black-and-white pictures built up of small squares, which look like irregular chessboard patterns. Insertion of the individual values in rows produces a positive-negative structure with a constructional principle that is not visually accessible (ill. p. 236). The structures become still more complicated when, as in a series of investigations carried out in 1966–1968, the relationships of tonal values, of the different intensities of color or of combined colors, are represented. Structures embodying numerical series have also confronted Struycken with problems of chance. A computer system with a random variable generator is used to obtain the desired chance structures, for instance the distribution of black and white in the compartments of a square set of nine squares from which a chessboard is built up at random. A similar approach is adopted by Hans van Dyck, whose collages of small colored hexagons are also chance grid structures.

Among the Dutch Structurists the self-taught Herman de Vries holds a special position. He does not regard his productions primarily as models, as Struycken does, but aims at a degree of objectivity that is meant to guarantee a maximum of freedom. In the middle of the fifties he was painting monochrome pictures in action technique. White collages and white paintings followed, and from about

230

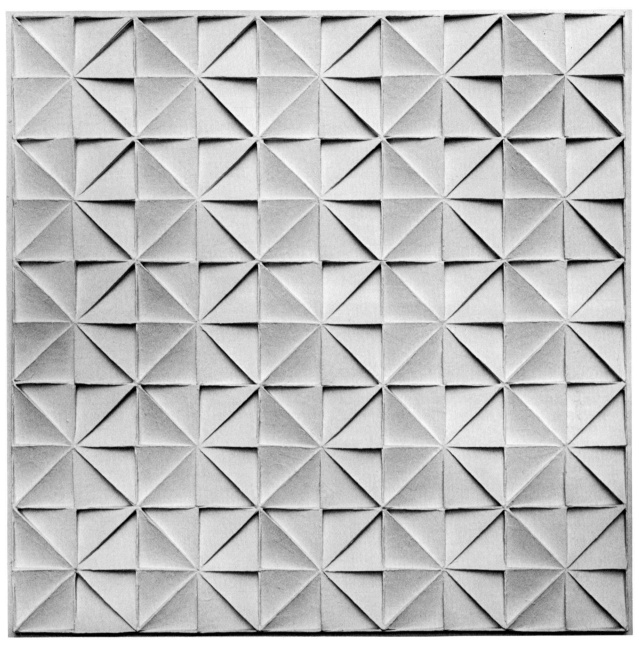

Jan J. Schoonhoven: Relief R-69.3, 1969

1960 white structural reliefs. At this time he was connected, as was Schoonhoven, with the Zero movement. In
1962 he launched out into "random objectivations", a
compositional method that is meant to eliminate subjective influences as far as possible (ill. p. 234). As in
Struycken's work, the principles of chance are applied, a
subject De Vries has studied in theoretical works on sta-
tistics in the natural sciences. In the magazines "0 = nul"
(1961–1964) and "integration" (1965–1973), which he
edited himself, and in "4 + ", of which he is a coeditor, he
has set forth his own theoretical ideas on "chance and
change". His Concrete poems and series of photographs
also bear witness to his individual philosophy of visual
design with the accent on random objectivation.

Another member of the circle of the Dutch Structurists — they are far from forming a compact group — is
the German Ewerdt Hilgemann, who has lived in the Netherlands since 1970. He investigated systematic relief
structures from 1961. After a few years of work along
these lines, he began to produce series of works which
exemplify a structural principle as completely as the material concerned will permit. These series, designated
"systematic structures" by the artist, may consist of monochrome reliefs or of fully three-dimensional bodies. In
the reliefs the starting point is the square, which is split
up by regular horizontal and vertical divisions into smaller
squares. When Hilgemann's reliefs have depth, this principle of division can also be applied three-dimensionally, in

Ad Dekkers: From Square to Circle, 1968

Ad Dekkers: Wood relief with cuts, 1970

deep cuts in which squares and dividing lines have a posi-tive-negative effect. In fully sculptural work Hilgemann sets out from the cube, which is again divided regularly into identical but smaller cubes. The "dialectical relation-ship" of foreground and background in the relief is here represented by the change from open to closed cubes, the alternation of cubic bodies and cubic spaces (ill. pp. 234, 235).

It is part of Hilgemann's concept that all the works in a series are of equal importance. There is accordingly no "best solution". The real essence of each series is the principle it embodies. "My working method is systematic and constructive. I make series, exploring step by step

and accepting all the results produced. In spite of this mine is not a 'logical' art. Systems, programs and num-bers only serve as auxiliaries in making new discoveries. For me true art, whether old or new, is always a combina-tion of intellect and feeling. Art must have an irrational quality, however rational the methods that are used to produce it."

This irrational element in the Structurist approach comes out most clearly in the work of Ad Dekkers. We no doubt have a tendency to overestimate the work of the artist who dies young and to emotionalize the connections between his life and his artistic development. Yet the fact remains that Dekkers' work displays a unique consisten-

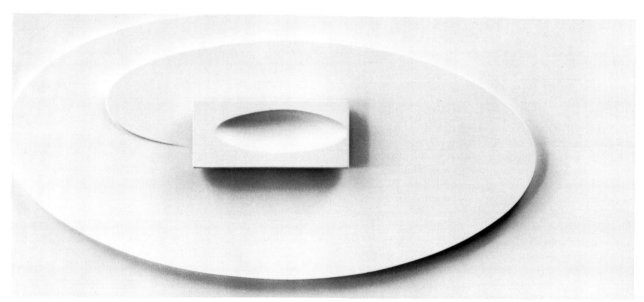

Ad Dekkers: Untitled, 1960

232

Ad Dekkers: First Phase from Circle to Triangle, 1971

Ad Dekkers: First Phase from Circle to Square, 1971

cy and compactness. He differs from his colleagues in that he did not advance from simple questions to ever more complicated ones. He attempted instead to penetrate into fundamentals and to reduce form problems to their elements and their essence.

Setting out from design principles already formulated by Mondrian and by the Swiss Concrete school, Dekkers addressed himself to constructive work after 1960. He moved from the surface color composition to the relief and at first tried to find a correlation between color and relief elements. Light, with its contrasts and transitions from extreme brightness to deepest shadow, soon replaced color: the monochrome white relief took the place of the chromatic composition. Around 1965 staggered geometric forms or the gradual relief development of spirals were central themes. The ground or zero zone now became increasingly important as a basis or starting point. The artist discovered that form-happenings can take place not only on and in front of this base, but in and behind it. Links to the Spatialism of Fontana became apparent. Dekkers now made saw-cuts in his baseplate, and later milled depressions in them. The line had consequently become the main issue (ill. pp. 232, 233).

The surface—which was now usually a square—and the line that appeared on it and destroyed it were henceforward made the subject of systematic investigation. The surface was divided and dissected by horizontal, vertical and diagonal lines. The division might be partial, complete or interrupted, but the simple laws of geometry were always observed. Other series of experiments—Dekkers called them "phases"—dealt with the relationship of square to circle and the transition from the one to the other. The subject of transition in fact increasingly occupied Dekkers' thoughts. But the line remained the principal protagonist. In the reliefs and in drawings on transparent papers (sometimes on both sides) which were then sealed in plastic sleeves the artist demonstrat-

ed that, while the line determines and defines the surface, it also injures and annuls it. This comes out most clearly in works in which the saw-cut line irreparably destroys the immaculate white surface. Dekkers also visualized the transition from one basic geometric shape to another in open reliefs of chromium steel bars. These works in particular—minimal plastic structures—show that Dekkers was always aiming at something palpably real as well as something unreal and imaginary. In one of the texts in which he gave an exact account of his work he referred to this as "the abstract concept of the line".

"In addition to my wood-engravings I started to make drawings: the result was that the two media became mutually influential. Drawing made a lot of things clear to me: it made me more aware of the independent value of line. The recent wood-engravings and drawings on paper are not only equivalent pieces of work, they are also of the same nature . . . The line emerges as an elementary manifestation . . . There are no gradations of tone, the line neither circumscribes a form nor is it a form, and it has no thickness or volume to speak of. It has, really, just one dimension: measure of length and direction of length."

In the meantime other artists have made use of this thinking about the line in their own work. One of them is Carel Balth, who is interested in the phenomena of light. To concretize light, he employs acrylic, on which he makes arrangements of lines and simple geometric patterns. Actual light "draws" additional lines and shapes with shadows and reflections. His relief structures have been called "instruments for the concretization and control of light".

Apart from the Structurists, who maintain close contacts with the Italians working on a similar systematic basis, there are Dutch painters and sculptors of other artistic provenances and interests who have taken up constructive concepts. Foremost among them are the sculptors who are interested in architectural and urbanistic questions and are not content with small individual sculptures

233

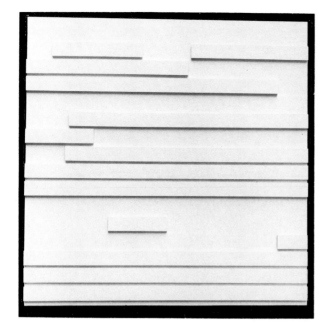

Herman de Vries: Relief V 71-53, 1971

Ewerdt Hilgemann: Relief structure 125, 1971

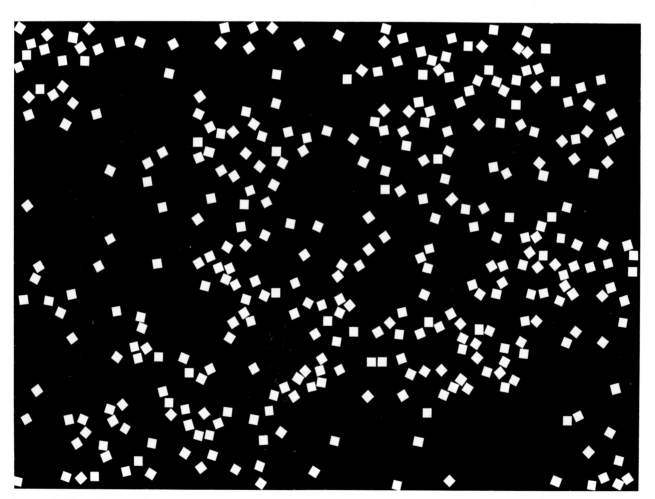

Herman de Vries: Collage V 68-84, 1968

234

Ewerdt Hilgemann: Cube 123 K, 1971

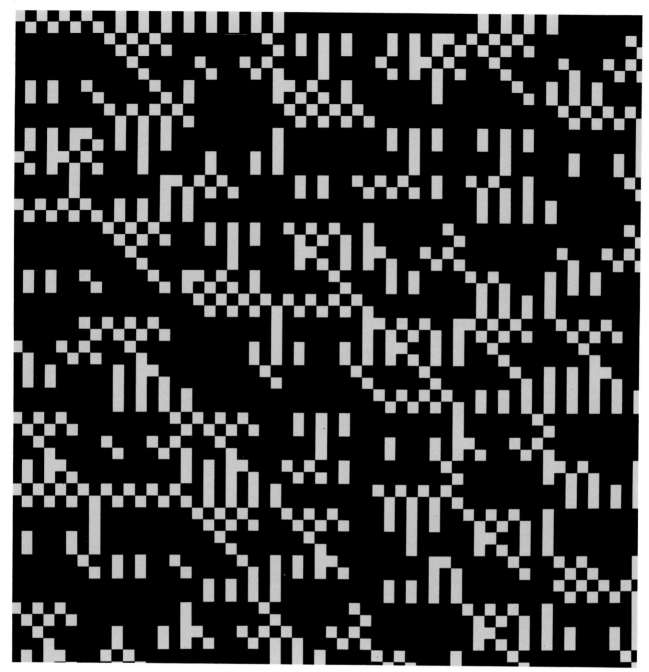

Pieter Struycken: Structure No. 4, 1970/71

but conceive and carry out large-scale environments. Here we must mention first of all the Utopian project "New Babylon" commenced in 1960 by Constant (Nieuwenhuis), a gigantic lattice structure that is less an exploration of form or a sculpture than the visual rendering of a Utopian urbanist idea that has been worked out down to the smallest practical detail. Behind such impulses for the town planners of tomorrow lies the daring urbanist thinking that appeared in the magazine "de stijl" decades ago. While Constant is concerned in his three-dimensional structures with dematerialization, with the reduction of plastic volumes to spatial graphics, Carel Visser remains in close touch with the material of his iron sculptures. He too dissolves the compact sculptural volume into cubic constituents that are stacked on one another or meet each other at right angles, but they are thinned down before our eyes to plates, and even to ribs and rods. Visser has subsequently shown a growing interest in primary structures (ill. p. 237).

Shlomo Koren, an Israeli living in Amsterdam, has other aims. He concentrates on the forces that are contained in a simple stereometric body—a beam, a plate, a round bar. Dynamism and tensions are the subject of his sculptural experiments rather than the statics of bodies (ill.

p. 237). This means that his materials and forms are no longer those of the conventional sculptor, but rather those of the engineer, who subjects the properties of his material to extreme stresses. Koren's works, meant to be monumental but often existing only as drawings and collages or in models, though in some cases realized, utilize seemingly sober technical materials, mostly round or square pipes, rails, sectional iron, steel cables, and the appropriate fittings. The principal objective is not plastic expression but the translation of latent forces or tensions into visible form. The space that is virtually influenced by such constructions plays an important part; Koren's dynamic spatial sculptures really extend far beyond their actual dimensions. They are mostly doomed by their very nature to remain in the plan and model stage, for they can only be turned into full-scale reality in an urban or rural context with the active cooperation of the public authorities. The drafts for them, which often appear fantastic although their technical feasibility has been checked, show that they are the grapplings of a committed artist — sometimes enthusiastic, sometimes critical — with our highly developed technical world and its sociocultural problems. Koren's drawn works are in fact promptings and proposals for the complete integration of art in everyday life. When the artist invokes the projects of the Russian Constructivists, particularly Tatlin, he is thinking perhaps less of the formal and aesthetic aspects than of the social ethos of the Russians.

Siebe Hansma, who has been working in Groningen since the seventies, is also interested in elementary space structures. He has two main themes, in the one case using plates in simple geometric forms such as squares or narrow rectangles that penetrate each other at right angles, in the other steel sheets that are folded at right or acute angles to form simple and perfectly balanced bodies (ill. p. 238). A neutral gray gives these forms the desired anonymous character in space. The works of this young Dutch artist, which follow up the ideas of de Stijl and more particularly of Van Doesburg, may at first glance remind us of the elementary spatial sculptures of the Russian Constructivist Katarzyna Kobro (ill. p. 201), yet such parallels only serve to show how a new generation of constructive artists are enriching their legacy with new ideas and not succumbing to epigonal veneration of the pioneers.

New intellectual impulses are also evident among the Dutch artists who have passed on from painting, sculpture or object art to conceptual work. The problems may well lie in a domain that is related to constructive art, even though the setting-down of the ideas is of a more figurative nature, as for instance in the investigations of Pieter Engels into perspective systems, varying angles of observation and other perceptual phenomena.

Rob van Koningsbruggen, a passionate painter, is interested in the process of painting more than in the product. System and accident are equally represented in his work. A picture consists of two or more sections that are characterized by simple shapes, such as triangles or circles. The composition is smudged by systematically pushing the wet canvases one over the other in the same direction. In this procedure, which takes place in accordance with certain predetermined rules, the precise design looses its rigidity and purity, becoming only the start-

Carel Visser: Piled beams, 1964

ing point of a process. The painter supplies the prerequisites for the process, but the picture makes itself. The result is a form of painting in which construction and gesture are balanced.

In modern Dutch painting and sculpture constructive concepts do not necessarily lead to formal aesthetic products. The central issue is the problem of perception, the interrogation of reality as well as art. The colored felt-pen drawings of Martin Rous, produced in large series, bear witness to this no less than the symmetrical panels of Rudi van de Wint, conceived on the basis of the Golden

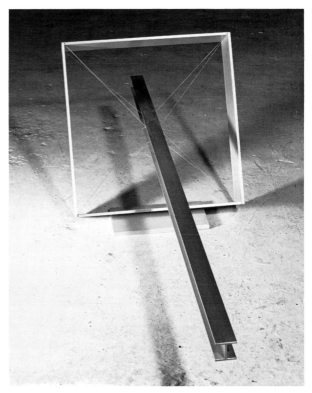

Shlomo Koren: Balance 2: Hovering beam, 1972

Siebe Hansma: P1979.80.16, 1980

Section or Leonardo Fibonacci's numerical series. In Van de Wint's work, too, constructive order is combined with painterly execution.

A constructive spirit is also evinced by the photographic work of Jan Dibbets. He uses color photography for surprising illustrations of the field of vision, restricting or extending the angle of observation, and mounts a series of single views in cyclic sequences. While the phenomena of visual perception are here presented in photographically documented landscape motifs and not by means of geometric forms, the systematic nature of the investigation and its presentation betray the constructive concept. The principles of series and progressions, the variation of the angle from 0 to 360 degrees, a kind of "objectivation of the observation"—all this has as much to do with the domain of constructive art as with Land Art and other forms of conceptual work.

A revival of interest in the present-day productions and the traditions of constructive art is to be observed in the Netherlands, as it is in Switzerland. New, independent groups of constructive artists and sculptors are being formed, and efforts are being made to document and investigate constructive art in its international dimensions and ramifications. This new interest has not been triggered by the recent "Neo-Geometrismus" movement, any more than it has in Switzerland. It is due rather to the realization that the thinking on which geometric constructive art is based can serve as a useful instrument in mastering the sociocultural and ecological problems with which we are today confronted.

From Abstraction to Minimal Art and Colorfield Painting

Constructive Trends in American Art

Twentieth-century American art grows on a cultural soil and in a social climate that differ considerably from those of Europe. The observation of constructive trends in American art leads to different conclusions when it is conducted from a European standpoint and when it is undertaken within America. The European, who thinks of himself as the supplier, the exporter, will ask when, where and how the Americans first took over the ideas of a non-figurative art that employs—whether intuitively or rationally—geometric ordering principles. What tendencies within European constructive art, what personalities have attracted the most attention? What effects have these influences had? Is a process of amalgamation taking place, and are the results different from those reached in Europe? Will the adaptation of European trends remain of marginal significance, or might it lead to something new and without a parallel in Europe? In assessing the role of constructive trends in recent American art the European must of course base his conclusions on the verdicts of American art critics. He is better qualified to judge the influence of American achievements on European developments. For the American observer, the echo at his end is more important than the European sources. What innovations has European constructive art triggered in America, for instance through the intermedium of European artists who have emigrated to the United States? Has it really stimulated developments, or has it been merely an episode without lasting consequences? Have its exponents succeeded in distilling anything specifically American from it? If so, how can the new achievement be defined and compared with European constructive art?

There is a certain risk of continental chauvinism blurring the picture from either viewpoint. Inferiority complexes might have a similar effect, the American observer feeling that his countrymen have yielded to foreign influences, the European that European art lost the lead to America in the fifties. It is just as difficult for some Europeans to confess that they have been beaten at their own game on the other side of the Atlantic as it is for some Americans to admit the borrowings of their own artists.

In reality constructive art has from the first regarded itself as an art of worldwide validity. Internationalism was a password of the pioneers. Constructive art deals with fundamental shaping laws and elementary perceptual processes—in other words with simple and universally understandable principles—and is therefore not a field in which nations or continents should be played off one against the other.

In the late nineteenth century American painters broke away from their local traditions and sought inspiration in Europe, above all in Paris. Thomas Eakins, the leading representative of a locally colored realism, advised his pupils to look for the sources of their art at home instead of going to Europe and picking up a superficial idea of the art of the Old World. They did not take his advice. Nationalistic thinking of this kind was not widespread among American artists at the end of the nineteenth century. American literature, on the other hand, had long achieved independence and could claim a leading role in the world, and this contributed directly and indirectly to the growth of a national identity. Artists, however, still looked to the art metropolis of Paris, where the example set by Manet and the Impressionists was a great aid to them in shaking off provincial realism.

The work shown in a New York exhibition in 1910 by the "Independents" led by Robert Henri—a group that rebelled against the stiff conventions of the National Academy—was an adaptation, twenty or thirty years after the event, of the free, painterly craftsmanship of Manet, plus a choice of everyday themes with which the "Ash Can School" protested against the cult of the idyllic in art. The reaction of the public and the critics was negative. Yet by that time, 1910, the art revolution was already under way. Some American artists had even witnessed the new departure on the spot, in Paris.

At first, a new spirit always percolates almost unnoticed through fine cracks in the fabric of the seemingly solid edifice of traditional art. After a period of infiltration the weakest points begin to give way. In American art the first breaches were visible just after the turn of the century. Perhaps the most significant was due to Alfred Stieglitz. In 1905 he had founded with Edward Steichen, painter and photographer, the "Photo Secession", a group of creative photographers united in their opposition to the prevailing euphemistic photography. In 1907 Stieglitz extended his "Little Gallery" at 291, Fifth Avenue, to include painting and sculpture. Before long "291" was a center from which the latest developments of European art radiated outward to American supporters. The exhibitions in 1908 of Fauvist paintings by Matisse and drawings by Auguste Rodin initiated the acceptance of contemporary European art in New York. By 1911 the gallery was showing Cubist drawings and collages by Picasso. In 1913 Stieglitz met Francis Picabia, who was on a visit to New York. He exhibited Picabia's Futuro-Cubist pictures as well as some Proto-Dadaist works done in New York and inspired by his seeing the modern city, some of them geometric machine constructions incorporating verbal elements. It may be concluded from Picabia's text of 1913, "How New York looks to me—Why New York is the only Cubist city in the world", that this stay marks a turning point in his art. In a "Manifesto of the

Marcel Duchamp: Nude Descending a Staircase, 1912

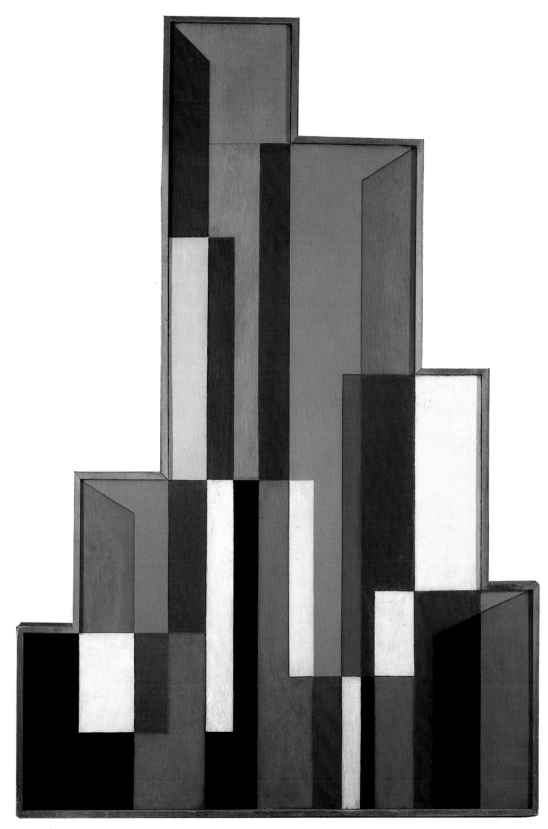

Charles G. Shaw: Plastic Polygon, 1937

Burgoyne Diller: Study, construction, 1937

Amorphist School" which Stieglitz published in his photographic and art magazine "Camera Work" in 1913, Picabia already opposes "form" from a Dadaist standpoint. What he means by "form" is the Cubist academicism that was now beginning to appear. The following year Stieglitz, for the first time in America, exhibited works by Brancusi, in what was no doubt the first showing of "abstract" sculpture in New York. It was the beginning of the great esteem in which Brancusi was later to be held in America. Walter Arensberg and John Quinn at that time laid the foundations of their Brancusi collections.

A second breach in the traditional edifice of American art was made by Gertrude Stein. This unusual woman did more than anyone else, by her attitude to the new departures and by her activity as an intermediary, to prepare the breakthrough of a new conception of art in the first decade of the century. She settled in Paris with her brother Leo in 1903, after she had abandoned her study of medicine and had launched out on a literary career. The house they lived in on the Rue de Fleurus was soon full of contemporary art and became the rallying point of the artistic and literary avant-garde. After buying pictures by Renoir, Gauguin and particularly Cézanne, the Steins took a bold step into modernity with the purchase of the "Femme au Chapeau" by Henri Matisse, which had contributed to the shock effect of Fauvist painting in the "Salon des Indépendants" in 1905. At about the same time the two began to take an interest in the as yet unknown Picasso.

The purchase of works from the Rose Period marked the inception of a friendship between Gertrude Stein and Picasso which was to last over forty years. A portrait of Gertrude Stein painted by Picasso in the winter of 1905/06 is a monument to their relationship. It is the first suggestion of the decisive turning point in Picasso's development. The breakthrough came with the figural composition "Les Demoiselles d'Avignon", which was painted soon after the portrait. Gertrude Stein acquired studies made for this key work. Her Picasso collection continued to expand until the early twenties and was one of the first important collections of this artist's work. Matisse and Picasso were among the regular guests at the Steins' apartment. There they met the two Delaunays and later Juan Gris and the writers André Salmon, Max Jacob and Guillaume Apollinaire, who was to become the spokesman of the Cubists. On Saturday evenings this unusual salon was in fact crowded with painters and poets associated with the Cubists. The Steins also took in many American artists. There were the painters Max Weber and Patrick Henry Bruce, who were pupils of Matisse, Walter Pach, Maurice Sterne and others. These Americans in Paris appreciated this opportunity to make contact with contemporary French art and its protagonists not in a French but in an American ambience, even if it was a somewhat extraordinary one. The example thus set by Gertrude and Leo Stein was later followed by their elder brother Michael and his wife Sarah, who also lived in Paris; they too acquired an important collection. Other friends of the Steins, such as the sisters Etta and Claribel Cone of Baltimore, were also infected by the same enthusiasm. This new attitude toward art, which left its mark on the lively conversations that took place in the Rue de Fleurus, was captured in Gertrude Stein's books and thus continued to influence the American reader.

The third momentous breach in the fabric of the art establishment came with the "Armory Show" of 1913 in New York. It had been preceded by a long period of controversy and preparation. The two principal initiators, Arthur B. Davies and Walter Kuhn, wanted to combine several objectives in their ambitious project. At first the idea had been merely to outdo the much-discussed exhibition of the Independents of 1910 by a more progressive show. A visit to the "Sonderbund" exhibition in Cologne in 1912 then led to a decision to add a general survey of the latest trends in European art to the American section. Walter Pach put the organizers in touch with artists and art dealers in Paris, in particular with the brothers Duchamp. The Armory Show—its name is due to the fact that it was staged in a former armory—was a heterogeneous display of 1600 works, the emphasis being on conventional American art. But the groups of works by the Neo-Impressionists, the Fauves and the Cubists, which represented the latest developments in art, were particularly important. The German Expressionists and the "Blue Rider" movement were unevenly represented. The only work by Kandinsky, his "Improvisation No. 27" of 1912, was bought by Alfred Stieglitz from the exhibition.

The group of Cubist works by Picasso, Braque, Léger, De la Fresnaye and Gleizes encouraged a few American painters who had already been influenced by the developments in Paris. The showing of these Cubist works contributed to the formation of an American Cubist school. Rob-

Burgoyne Diller: Untitled, c. 1944

ert Delaunay was not represented in the Armory Show, as he had withdrawn his work, but in the end his Orphism was to have a more profound effect on American art than analytical Cubism. This is true particularly for Stanton Macdonald-Wright and Morgan Russell, who—setting out from the color theories of the Frenchman Chevreul and the American Ogden N. Rood and from Delaunay's experiments with simultaneous contrast—developed the theory of Synchromism. Their goal was to paint in pure fields of color in simple geometric arrangements, a parallel to the color compositions evolved by Delaunay and Kupka about 1912/13.

The scandal of the Armory Show was Marcel Duchamp's "Nude Descending a Staircase" of 1912 (ill.p.240). This simultaneous representation of several phases of movement, in keeping with Futurist postulates, was more than most of the exhibition visitors could digest. It inspired a small elite—with some reinforcement from Picabia's "Spring Dances", also painted in 1912—to try their own hands at Futuro-Cubist painting. The works of several Americans from this time show that the dynamic approach of Futurism suited the American mentality better than the severity of orthodox Cubism with its restrained coloring. Max Weber, for example, produced dramatic vi-

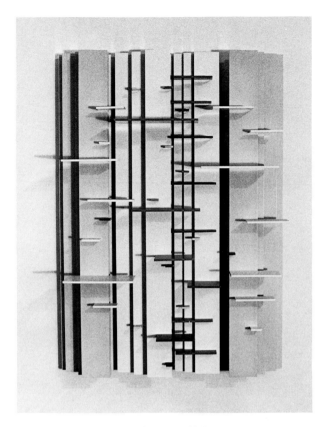

Charles Biederman: Work No. 36, Aix, 1953/72

sions of the city with repetitively staggered forms. Much the same spirit animated Joseph Stella, who turned scenes from Coney Island into wild, amorphous seas of shapes and colors. An instability that is the very antithesis of the studied character of Cubism is evident in the paintings of Marsden Hartley and Arthur Dove. Their work echoes the vital message that the Italian Futurists had tried to convey in their emphatic manifestos. As early as 1910 Arthur Dove produced with his "Extractions", symbolic abstract renderings of motifs from nature, works that were no doubt the first non-objective compositions in American art. But his lyrical temperament was more attracted to the colorful delicacy of Severini and the musicality of Kupka than to the dynamism of Boccioni or Balla. Georgia O'Keefe's painting took a similar line a few years later. Marsden Hartley, who had become acquainted with Cubism on a visit to Paris in 1912, was able to develop the contact in Berlin in 1913: in Herwarth Walden's "Sturm" gallery he saw works of the Italian Futurists and of the "Blue Rider" painters, in whom he found an Expressionist structure and a further development of Delaunay's color rhythms. After a further stay in Berlin in 1914, Hartley produced flat compositions incorporating fragments of flags, heraldic emblems and military insignia. Interpenetrating polychrome ribbon motifs, checkerboard patterns and concentric circles combine to form highly contrasted textured designs which hardly have their like in the painting of the day. The manual treatment of the paint is no less original than the motifs and composition. An impasto color application produces an intentional texture that

anticipates the painting of Alfred Jensen. This bold advance, however, had no lasting consequences. After painting some delicate geometric works that can be allocated to synthetic Cubism, Hartley returned to realistic painting after 1920.

A certain kinship with the floating patterns of Marsden Hartley can be seen in the constructive collages of another artist who was inspired by the Armory Show: Man Ray. He had begun with Fauvist drawings and had picked up some ideas that stimulated his taste for experimentation in Gallery 291. In 1911, he completed "Tapestry", a non-objective cloth montage consisting of identical rectangles of material of differing colors and textures, a work that in its strict horizontal-vertical order and its needlework technique followed the tradition of the patchwork quilt. The Armory Show activated Man Ray's ambitions as a painter. The Cubist landscapes he now painted in the seclusion of Ridgefield gradually became more intense in their coloring and more dynamic in their composition. Rhythmic charcoal drawings also bring out the Futurist tendency.

A Futuro-Cubist portrait of Stieglitz painted in 1913 is no doubt Man Ray's most original work from this period. It is an homage to the great motivator and reminds us that Man Ray owed his most important meeting, that with Marcel Duchamp, to Stieglitz. After the scandal he had caused in the Armory Show, Duchamp moved to the United States in 1914, accepting the invitation of Walter Conrad Arensberg. In 1915 Stieglitz took them both to Ridgefield. Man Ray was at that time shaking off Cubist influences and searching for a "mechanistic" mode of composition. Solutions began to develop when he moved to New York. "Revolving Doors", a sequence of collages of transparent colored papers, dates from 1916. Motifs borrowed from the theater and dance are reduced to predominantly geometric color shapes, sometimes meshing, sometimes superimposed. An oil painting done in 1916, "The Rope Dancer Accompanies Herself with Her Shadows", is the first of a series of hovering, delicately balanced semiconstructive compositions whose irrationally distorted shadows give them the dimensions of a dream. Most of them were executed with a spray gun. This mechanical painting met with disapproval. But the method was to a large extent in keeping with what Duchamp said in 1915 in his first text published in a New York art magazine, "A Complete Reversal of Art Opinions by Marcel Duchamp, Iconoclast". The same "anti-art" ideas were developed in Duchamp's major work which he began about this time, the "Bride Stripped Bare by Her Bachelors, Even". The rebellious element in Duchamp's attitude to art is present in Man Ray's development. After his move to New York he was in active contact with Duchamp and the circle of avant-garde artists, writers, musicians and dancers who met at the house of Walter Arensberg. The atmosphere of this circle, later designated "New York Dada", was expressed in the activities of its initiators, Duchamp and Picabia, and in the work of the Americans Marsden Hartley, Joseph Stella, John Covert, Charles Demuth and Charles Sheeler. In Man Ray's case painting soon took second place to machine-like three-dimensional objects similar to Duchamp's "Ready-mades" and to photographic experiments. In 1921 Man Ray followed his friend Duchamp to Paris. There began the great period of his Dadaist and lat-

Ludwig Sander: Tioga II, 1969

er Surrealist objects and of his "Rayographs", photo-graphs produced without a camera.

A question that was repeatedly posed was whether the intellectual approach of the small group representing New York Dada from 1915 to 1920 included specifically American elements or was only a branch of the European avant-garde. Certainly Duchamp—with his unorthodox thinking about art—and Picabia—with his provocative spontaneity—brought European traits into the New York colony. But the inventive Man Ray also answered with im-pulses of his own, and contributions such as that of Mor-ton Schamberg of Philadelphia, before his premature death, cannot be overlooked. Many of the themes that oc-cupied this group were in the air and were not the pre-serve of any nation: the desire for complete indepen-dence, the indifference toward the established values of

Fritz Glarner: Relational Painting, 1946

society and art, the rebellious, nihilistic and anarchic spirit, the taste for scandal, the use of irony as a weapon, the readiness to accept the workings of chance as well as humor or banality. All this added up to an attitude rather than a style. Art was equated with life and life with art as they had never been before. This was only to be fully appreciated thirty or forty years later, as was Duchamp's "dry", non-retinal art, to which he left a monument in the form of his "Large Glass".

Although the New York Dada group had furnished new impulses, it was never very influential and its works were hardly known to the general public. The same may be said of the small magazines, which must have seemed rather enigmatic to outsiders. Alfred Stieglitz published "291", which as a result of Picabia's collaboration displayed Dadaist traits as early as 1915. Duchamp and Henri Pierre Roché issued two numbers of "The Blind Man" in 1917. The same year saw the publication of Duchamp's "Rongwrong". Some numbers of Picabia's magazine "391" also appeared in New York. In 1921 came the parting shot of this underground press, "New York Dada", published by Duchamp and Man Ray.

In 1920 Duchamp and Man Ray convinced a patroness of the arts, Katherine S. Dreier, of the need to do something courageous. Together they founded "Société Anonyme, Inc., Museum of Modern Art", which was to be their meeting place, exhibition and documentation center and private museum all in one. The ambitious aim was to be,

as Man Ray said, the leaven of the American art world and to keep ahead of the times. The Société Anonyme at first represented Dada only, but on her trips to Europe Katherine S. Dreier also came into direct touch with other groups, with de Stijl, and with Schwitters in Hanover. Americans such as Joseph Stella were welcome in the Société Anonyme, but its attention was concentrated on Europe. This first museum of modern art in the United States was soon presenting Kandinsky, Klee, Léger, Villon, Schwitters, Max Ernst, Miró, Archipenko, Mondrian and even Malevich in group and one-man exhibitions. A highlight came with the "International Exhibition of Modern Art" staged by Katherine S. Dreier at the instigation of Mondrian in the Brooklyn Museum at the end of 1926. Over 300 works provided an overview of the international avant-garde. Many European artists were presented for the first time in America. The collection later went to other cities, and many works were purchased. The selection had been made in accordance with an axiom which the Société Anonyme had derived from a saying of Franz Marc: traditions are fine when you create them yourself but useless when made by others.

But the optimism with which the organizers looked forward to a leavening effect on American art appreciation was as yet premature. Even the art-loving public reacted to the new developments with skepticism or even open hostility. The note of the attacks on modernism that now followed had been struck in 1921 in a pamphlet directed against the John Quinn collection shown in the Metropolitan Museum in New York: "We believe that these forms of so-called art are merely a symptom of a general movement throughout the world having for its object the breaking-down of all law and order and the Revolutionary destruction of our entire social system." Or clearer still: "This 'Modernistic' degenerate cult is simply the Bolshevik philosophy applied to art." Such arguments anticipate almost literally Hitler's objections to every form of modern art. But behind the protest against the new and puzzling, which takes a similar form in all eras and in all places, there was another motive: a subliminal opposition to Europe, in whose disputes the United States had already had to intervene in 1917. All the caprices of art — meaning chiefly Dadaism and later Surrealism — were ascribed to the frivolity of Paris, while "abstractionism", comprising all semi-figurative and non-figurative art, was connected with Germany. And Germany was feared as an outpost of postrevolutionary Bolshevist Russia. The shortsighted equation of Constructivism with Communism stood in the way of any wide acceptance of constructive art by the American public until the late thirties. This does not in any way detract from the pioneering achievements of the Société Anonyme, which donated its collection and documentation to Yale University in 1941.

Many Americans who had adopted abstraction under the influence of Cubism or Futurism or the stimulus of the Armory Show returned to realism in the twenties. Among the more important artists, it was only Arthur Dove, Stuart Davis, Charles G. Shaw (ill. p. 241) and to a certain extent Charles Demuth who were unwilling to drop back into an everyday realistic art.

There were also positive signs in the twenties of a readiness to approach modern art in an unprejudiced spirit. The sixty new museums that were opened in the course

Fritz Glarner: Relational Painting No. 60, 1952

Charmion von Wiegand: Sanctuary of the four directions, 1959

of the decade in the United States bear witness to a belief on the part of the mostly private initiators in the importance of art to modern society. Two of the new ventures were a continuation of the activities of the Société Anonyme in another form. The first was due to A. E. Gallatin, who in December 1927 opened the Museum of Living Art at the University of New York with his own collection augmented by borrowings from private owners. Groups of works by Picasso, Braque, Gris and Léger formed the core of this first public gallery of contemporary art. In the next few years the collection was steadily expanded, with increasing emphasis on works that Gallatin designated as "non-representative". In a catalogue printed in 1933 Jean Hélion outlined the "Development of Abstract Art", beginning with watercolors by Cézanne, as represented in the Museum of Living Art. By this time there were large groups of Concrete and Constructivist works on view — by Arp, Brancusi, Domela, Gabo, Hélion, Lissitzky, Mondrian, Nicholson, Van Doesburg and Vantongerloo as well as by American artists such as Charles G. Shaw, Charles Biederman and Alexander Calder. Four pictures by Mondrian were one of the highlights of the museum. When the Gallatin Collection was donated to the Philadelphia Museum of Art in 1943, it comprised some 170 paintings and sculptures.

The second important venture in support of contemporary art took place soon after the opening of Gallatin's museum. There was something adventurous and even miraculous about it. Three collectors, Abby Aldrich, Lizzie P. Bliss and Mary Quinn Sullivan, had the idea of opening a museum in New York to present regular exhibitions of progressive modern art. In May 1929 they enlisted the support of A. Conger Goodyear as president. He had experience in museum questions and was on friendly terms

with the Société Anonyme and other representatives of new trends. Goodyear won the support of other collectors and sponsors for the scheme and obtained the services of Paul J. Sachs of the Fogg Art Museum in Harvard as an expert. The success of the project now depended entirely on the personality of the future director. Sachs found him in the person of the young art historian Alfred H. Barr Jr., then one of the few young American art historians familiar with modern art. Barr accepted the post in June 1929. In early November the Museum of Modern Art opened its doors, six months after the first discussions and ten days after the big stock exchange crash that was the beginning of the international economic slump.

The founders first made parts of their own collections available for temporary exhibitions. But an application made for recognition as a public institution shows that the organizers were already setting their sights higher. The avowed aim was the operation of a museum of modern art for the purpose of "encouraging and developing the study of modern arts and the application of such arts to manufacture and practical life, and furnishing popular instruction". The scheme thus had an educational aspect from the outset. In his own teaching at various universities and on several trips to Europe, Barr had realized that the endeavors to renew art since the beginning of the century were directed toward a new integration of art and life. A longish trip to Europe in 1927 as part of the preparation of a work on art and the machine had brought Barr into contact with persons and institutions that enabled him to make a closer study of the new relationship between art and life. In Paris he met Le Corbusier, in Holland the architect J. J. P. Oud introduced him to the sociocultural ideas of de Stijl, and finally a trip via Berlin took him to Dessau, where the Bauhaus had just moved into the buildings designed by Walter Gropius.

Here he met the "masters" of the Bauhaus, particularly Feininger and Klee; but even more important was the impression he received of a community of teachers and students who were passionately interested in the interrelations of art and the handicrafts, architecture, industrial design and typography. The Bauhaus, said Barr, had opened a new world. Ten years later he recalled: "It is no wonder, then, that young Americans began to turn their eyes toward the Bauhaus as the one school in the world where modern problems of design were approached realistically in a modern atmosphere." Barr's journey to Europe also included a stay in Russia. He found that Constructivist art had already been removed from the museums as "bourgeois decadence" but its effects became evident to him when he visited art schools. The excitement of Moscow for the American was primarily in the film. He met Sergei Eisenstein and made friends with him.

Alfred H. Barr admired the Bauhaus as the first school of design to be abreast of the times; and it is just as true to say that under his direction the Museum of Modern Art was, a few years later, the first museum to be abreast of the times. His new conception of a modern museum was of course not visible in the opening exhibition — Cézanne, Gauguin, Seurat, Van Gogh — and only became evident gradually in the first few years of activity. The temporary exhibitions, initially consisting of borrowed works, gradually expanded to cover the whole range of contemporary art from its founders to the present. American and Euro-

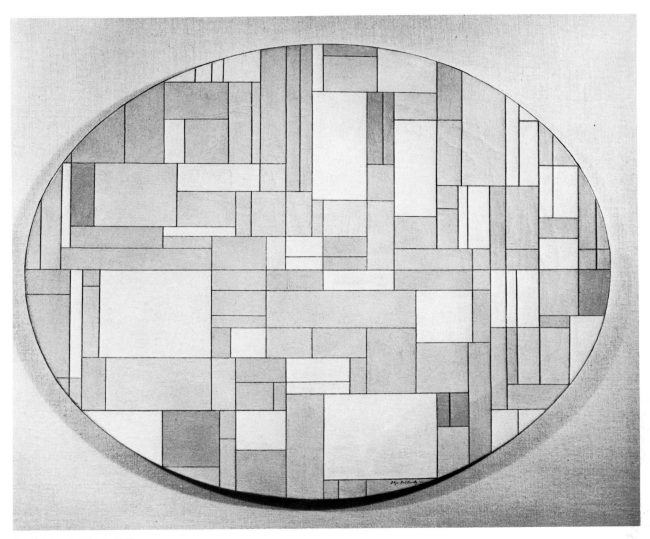

Ilya Bolotowsky: Tondo, 1955

pean art, mainstream productions and marginal developments were included in varying proportions, one-man and group shows alternated with the treatment of individual themes.

The traditional limits of an art museum were exceeded as early as 1932 with an international exhibition of modern architecture which led to the foundation of an architectural department. In the same year photographs first appeared on the walls, again an unorthodox extension of the conception of art at that time. This was the beginning of regular photography exhibitions which were later followed by the opening of a photography department. The first showing of furniture and household articles took place in 1933 and resulted in a new and intense interest in problems of industrial and environmental design. In the same year the Museum of Modern Art began to loan exhibitions to other art institutions. In this way a department for traveling exhibitions developed, an important instrument in the educational mission which Barr had always envisaged. The library, instituted in 1932, was soon a rich source of information and grew to be one of the best existing documentation centers for all areas of modern art and design. The museum's activities in the field of pub-

lishing were soon too wide and varied to be restricted to catalogs. Exhibitions on single artists or subjects invited authoritative publications. At the same time illustrated booklets with straightforward texts were used to introduce modern art to the general public. From the middle of the thirties art education programs were prepared for schools, and children were taken seriously as museum visitors earlier than was the case elsewhere. A film library was added in 1936, making the Museum the first institution able to offer non-commercial art film programs. Lectures and concerts were also organized. These activities were to be copied by museums all over the world.

In the early years, however, the exhibitions were the main concern. A question which was of course asked was whether this was in fact a museum, since a museum normally has a permanent collection. When it was opened, the Museum of Modern Art possessed only a very few paintings, drawings, prints and sculptures donated by its founders. But the core of a museum collection was formed by the bequest of Lizzie P. Bliss in 1931. From then on a sort of magnetism seemed to attract donations and legacies. The trustees set the example for others by their own generous gestures. The connoisseurship dis-

Alexander Calder: The Universe, 1931

David Smith: Three Planes, 1960/61

George Rickey: Two up — one down, 1966

Naum Gabo: Torsion — bronze variation, 1963

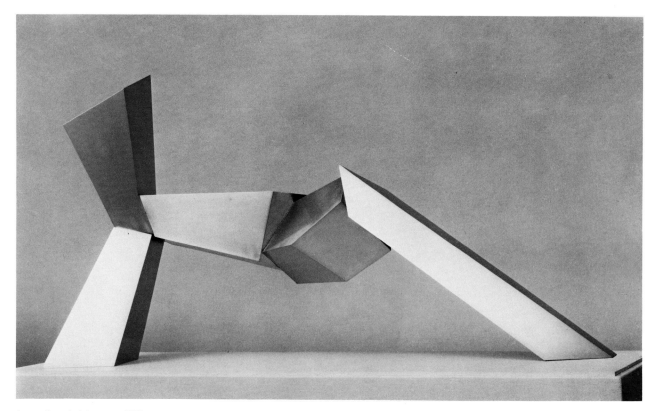

James Rosati: Adversary, 1968

played by Barr and his collaborators, and later by their successors, enabled the gifts to be channeled and enhanced in value by wise additional purchases. Within a few decades the Museum of Modern Art had become the largest and most balanced collection of modern art in existence.

Art was seen here not in its traditional isolation but in the context of all creative endeavor, against the background of art developments in the twentieth century and of socio-cultural conditions generally. By its comprehensive and overlapping activities the Museum demonstrated with exemplary force that modern art and modern life are closely interwoven. Its multifunctional structure had a direct influence on the daily crowds of visitors. It also provoked thought on the organization and activities of other museums. It did a great deal, in fact, to stimulate the crystallization of a new conception of the museum. Its primary objective, however, was to provide a continuous flow of information on the trends, problems and personalities of modern art and on the art aspects of our environment. The information provided was never one-sided and often embraced opposing views reflecting the pluralist character of modern art and design. The Museum of Modern Art has not only practiced a sort of cultural massage over the years, it has also taught tolerance toward the new and different. Katherine Kuh summed this up in the words: "Art has many faces."

The nineteen-thirties were not very kind to artists. They were directly and indirectly affected by the economic slump. The emergency programs of the New Deal, devised to fight the depression, were a help. Minimal monthly allowances from the Federal Art Project, formed by the Works Progress Administration in 1933, assured artists of a bare livelihood. But the repayment in the form of paintings, murals and sculptures, mostly intended for public buildings, was for the most part of no great artistic value. Only a very few of the 16 000 works said to have been produced by over 3500 artists in 1000 cities and towns up to the end of the project in 1943 have survived as art. Still, the WPA can claim to have brought art to the masses, who would otherwise never have come into contact with it. The reasons for the decline in quality really go deeper. Existential anxiety, uncertainty on the part of artists and art consumers alike about their fate and the fate of society in general in these bitter years had led to a turning-away from artistic adventure. People clung to the established values, and that inevitably meant the resumption of realistic representation. The revalorization of tradition, of a world that was still unjeopardized, led to an art that marched under the banner of the "American Scene". The regional trends, in many cases historically colored and all more or less idyllic, were admittedly confronted by harsher, social and realistic movements. Though popular realism at first sight appears to be specifically American, exactly the same backward-looking spirit can be found in some developments in Europe. The committed artists who were aware of the dangers of Fascism opposed the complacent art of the "American Scene", behind which a fear of industrialization and urbanization can also be diagnosed. At the Artists Congress of 1936 Lewis Mumford, sociologist and theoretician of town planning, announced that the time had come for people who loved life and culture to form a united front in order to protect, to watch over and if necessary to defend the human heritage which artists embody.

Connections can be established between these realist trends and Surrealism, which commanded the scene in the thirties in Europe. The representatives of a fantastic realism did not remain on the surface of things with their naturalistic renderings but depicted worlds of obsession, fear, menace, sex and of visionary social criticism. Links with Paris were maintained via the Société Anonyme and Marcel Duchamp. The magazine "Transition", which appeared in Paris, The Hague and New York between 1927 and 1938, and was edited by Eugene Jolas and Elliot Paul, also played an important part. With an open eye and ear for "creative experiment", as indicated in its subtitle, it was the leading magazine of the international artistic and literary avant-garde and the mouthpiece of all schools since Cubism.

The Surrealist currents in New York were strengthened by the exhibition "Fantastic Art, Dada and Surrealism" mounted by the Museum of Modern Art in 1936. This initiated a tendency in American art to mingle suggestions from late Cubism and abstraction with Surrealist elements. Most of the painters who were to establish Abstract Expressionism and Action Painting after World War II passed through a Surrealist phase.

Meanwhile, abstraction, which was still defended by a few American painters, also received new support with the founding of "Abstraction-Création" in Paris in 1931. A logical development leads from Cubism and even from Cézanne to various forms of abstraction and to the constructive art of both Russian Constructivism and the Dutch de Stijl. This was demonstrated in 1936 by the exhibition "Cubism and Abstract Art" in the Museum of Modern Art. It reinforced the position of the open-minded artists who had not succumbed to the blandishments of a popular, "genuine American" art. In the exhibition catalog Alfred H. Barr stated that he had observed a newly awakened interest in abstract art, which had been declared defunct ten years before. If this art — meaning primarily constructive trends — had never quite faded from American awareness, it was because of the Société Anonyme, which owned works by Arp, Baumeister, Brancusi, Buchheister, Cahn, Carlsund, Charchoune, Crotti, Gabo, Glarner, Klee, Kandinsky, Lissitzky, Moholy-Nagy, Malevich, Mondrian, Nebel, Peri, Pevsner, Schwitters, Servranckx, Taeuber-Arp, Torrès-Garcia, Van Doesburg, Villon and others. There was, in addition to Morgan Russell, Stanton Macdonald-Wright and Patrick Henry Bruce of the older generation, a fairly large group of American constructive artists. This is proven by the work collected by the Société Anonyme, which included works by Ilya Bolotowsky, Alexander Calder, Burgoyne Diller, John Covert, Stuart Davis, Arthur Dove, Marsden Hartley, Harry Holtzman, Man Ray, Joseph Stella and Max Weber. Most of these artists belonged to the American Abstract Artists founded by the painter George L. K. Morris in 1936.

A glance at the work of Burgoyne Diller, the first American Constructivist, shows to what an extent constructive art was for years an underground activity in the United States. Setting out from Cézanne and Cubism, Diller first developed an eclectic Cubistic idiom. In 1930 he reduced his compositions to elementary forms. The influences of

Clement Meadmore: Double-up, 1971

Suprematism and Constructivism can be recognized in linear constructions on a white ground. In 1934 he turned to geometric compositions whose horizontal-vertical order reveals that he had come in contact with de Stijl. Later Diller defended himself with tragic tenacity against the charge that his art was merely a derivative of de Stijl. In reality he was the first American to make independent use of the shaping principles of Neo-Plasticism. Diller's sensitivity is fully expressed in his wood reliefs from the thirties. Many of them are small wooden boards with engraved line grids, some of the surfaces being painted while others reveal the structure of the wood (ill. p. 242). Others are relief structures of colored bars and angles, mounted one above the other in several layers, anticipating Structurist compositions.

There were no buyers for such works in the thirties. But Diller got moral support from Hans Hofmann, who had directed an art school in Munich — attended by Americans among others — until 1932, and in 1933 had emigrated to America. As a teacher in New York Hofmann became an influence on the younger painters of the New York school, encouraging his pupils above all to think about color. His theory included the "push-pull" principle, the consciously controlled projection and retraction of color areas in the picture surface. Diller turned his mind to these color problems even before his friend Harry Holtzman brought back information on Mondrian's theories and working methods after a visit to his studio in Paris.

Diller was one of the active nucleus of American Abstract Artists. In 1935 he took over the direction of the murals department in the art program of the Works Progress Ad-

John McLaughlin: Untitled, 1951

ministration. Through him important assignments went to Stuart Davis and to the younger artists Willem de Kooning, Jackson Pollock, Adolph Gottlieb, Ad Reinhardt, Mark Rothko, Philip Guston and Arshile Gorky. Gorky's project for a huge mural in Newark Airport in 1936 —"Aviation: Evolution of Forms under Aerodynamic Limitations"—betrays in its dynamic interpretation the influence of Jean Hélion, at that time living in New York. It was also an echo of the exhibition "Machine Art" of 1934 in which the Museum of Modern Art had illuminated the relations of Cubism, Futurism, Dada and Constructivism to the technical world of the machine.

Diller divided his late work into three main groups. His "First Theme" comprises works in which one or more elements, colored bars or rectangles, are placed on a white ground without any line grid (ill. p. 243). In the "Second Theme" horizontal-vertical screens enclose the colored surface elements; the works are reminiscent of the compositional principles of Neo-Plasticism. In works of the "Third Theme" the white surface is rhythmically divided by black vertical bars, and the black is interrupted by colored transverse stripes. Massive colored cross-beams are laid between the bars like the rungs of a ladder. There is no mistaking the relationship to the late works of Mondrian, the vibrating, optimistic "Boogie-Woogie" compositions. But the syncopation of the color areas is more dynamic in Diller's work than in Mondrian's. In his late years Diller returned to his "First Theme". The white ground on which the elements float in primary colors then gives way to a gray, and later to a black ground. In 1962 the asymmetric orders vanish and a strictly axial arrangement is preferred in compositions that are frequently U-shaped. Their mystic solemnity is reminiscent of Ad Reinhardt's

black cruciform shapes. Diller's late work makes it very clear that the intellectual constructive process in itself does not constitute a picture, and that the visual is something quite different. As Diller said in an interview in 1964, "After all, you can't eliminate this feeling you have for the total thing ... If you are thinking on the one hand of the intellectual resolving of a problem—after all, the visual thing is quite something else. It's certainly not an intellectual process; it only relates to it."

As a result of political developments in Europe, the group of constructive artists in America was reinforced after 1933. Josef Albers was the first to emigrate to the United States in that year, after the closing of the Bauhaus. In 1936 the Swiss Fritz Glarner moved from Paris to New York. Laszlo Moholy-Nagy arrived in Chicago in 1937, coming from London. In 1938 Herbert Bayer settled in Aspen, Colorado. Piet Mondrian, who had moved from Paris to London in 1938, reached New York in 1940. Naum Gabo followed in 1946, having passed the war years in London. Among the exiles of the Bauhaus circle were also the architects Walter Gropius, Marcel Breuer and Ludwig Mies van der Rohe. They and the Viennese Richard Neutra were to make a major contribution to modern architecture in the United States. Their architectural concepts, which aimed at clarity, rationalism and functionalism, but also at humanity, were very close to the design principles of constructive art. The connections were demonstrated in the exhibition "Bauhaus 1919–1928" which Walter Gropius and Herbert Bayer mounted at the invitation of Alfred H. Barr in the Museum of Modern Art in 1938.

Some of these newcomers accepted teaching assignments as Amédée Ozenfant, Alexander Archipenko and Hans Hofmann had done before them. In the "New Bauhaus" in Chicago, Moholy-Nagy tried to adapt the ideas of the Bauhaus to the American mentality. Material difficulties soon made a reorganization under the new name, "School of Design", necessary. In 1944 the school attained college status and from then on was known as the "Institute of Design". It was associated with the Illinois Institute of Technology in 1949. A similar continuation of the Bauhaus was the Graduate School of Design which Walter Gropius organized in 1937 at Harvard University in Cambridge, Massachusetts. The architectural department of the Illinois Institute of Technology did pioneering work in architecture under the direction of Mies van der Rohe. Josef Albers taught painting from 1933 to 1949 at Black Mountain College in North Carolina. Pledged to the philosophy of John Dewey, the college became a leading center of art training as a result of Albers' courses and seminars. It produced painters who were later to play a leading part in American art. Albers was also able to pass on his thinking on the interactions of colors to thousands of students as a regular guest lecturer at Harvard and later at Yale.

Two important events need to be recorded from this era. Hilla Rebay, a pupil and admirer of Wassily Kandinsky, who had now left Germany and settled in Paris, succeeded in assembling a collection of work comprising all phases of the Russian artist's œuvre for Solomon F. Guggenheim, to which were added works by some other nonobjective painters. In 1938 this private collection was transformed into a foundation and opened to the public

John McLaughlin: Painting No. 16-1963, 1963

as the "Museum of Non-Objective Painting". The term "non-objective" derives ultimately from Kandinsky, who wanted to make clear the fundamental difference between "abstract" and "non-objective" along the lines of Van Doesburg's definition of Concrete Art. While the vague general term "abstract" is still in wide use, the word "non-objective" is today often replaced by "non-representational".

The second event was the work of Peggy Guggenheim. A nonconformist by nature, she had opened a gallery of modern art in London in 1937 and had later transferred it to Paris. Marcel Duchamp and Nelly van Doesburg, Theo's widow, were her advisers and put her in touch both with the Surrealists and with their apparent opposites, the exponents of non-objective art. In 1941 Peggy Guggenheim returned to America in the company of Max Ernst. Under the now legendary name "Art of This Century", she opened a museum for her personal collection in New York. It was at the same time a gallery for regularly changing exhibitions. Frederick Kiesler filled the tent-like rooms with unframed works hanging freely in space and illuminated by intermittent lighting. The show was a sensation, partly because of the extravagant lifestyle and social circle of Peggy Guggenheim herself, partly because Surrealist and non-objective art was here presented cheek by jowl. Art of This Century became a center of inspiration much as the Société Anonyme had been some years before. Fantastic and Surrealist works were exhibited as well as Futurist and Constructive ones: Delaunay, Lissitzky, Malevich and Mondrian, Archipenko, Arp, Brancusi, Pevsner and Vantongerloo. Some exhibitions of the American art of the day were also staged. Duchamp and Mondrian acted as jurors together with the critics James Thrall Soby and James Johnson Sweeney. Peggy Guggenheim's greatest merit was that she recognized the significance of the young American artists who were to dominate the scene ten years later: William Baziotes, Adolph Gottlieb, Robert Motherwell, Clyfford Still, Jackson Pollock, Ad Reinhardt, Mark Rothko and others. It was she who really discovered Pollock. In 1947 Peggy Guggenheim returned to Europe and settled in Venice.

Many of the artists who came from Europe to live as immigrants in New York only really found themselves as artists in the New World. This applies to Fritz Glarner, who had painted architectural abstractions in Paris for a time before he moved to New York in 1936 and commenced work in a purely geometric, constructive vein. His basis was not a uniformly strict structure, but rectangular groups made up of wedged elements meshing in ever new modes of interconnection to fill the picture area. Great importance was attached by the artist to patterns of shapes and colors full of character. Attention to this requirement led Glarner to the central subject matter of his "Relational Paintings" (ill. p. 247). In the framework of horizontal, vertical and slightly inclined axes the compositional scaffolding carries the color. This is restricted to yellow, red and blue, but their many nuances and the subtle use of rich shades of gray betray the passionate painter. The personal character of the brushwork is never denied, an anonymous, technically accurate coloring of the polychrome areas never aimed at. Flat as this painting seems at first sight, it can evoke imaginary spaces by the advance or recession of some color planes, darkening or

lightening of gray shades, changing systems of proportion, staggering and interlocking of the surface elements (ill. p. 246). A monumental mural for the Time-Life building in 1958/59 underlines the fact that this painting is meant for the wall. From 1943 on Glarner also produced circular pictures and was one of the few modern painters who have succeeded in giving new meaning to the old tradition of the tondo.

A close friendship linked Glarner to Mondrian in their New York years. The two shared the power to fill a rational picture space with a well-nigh inexplicable lyricism by the force of their personal sensibility. Max Bill once said that Glarner's development began where Mondrian's had had to stop. Glarner found his own idiom by instilling Mondrian's Neo-Plastic method with a new rhythmic and objective, constructive, structural yet subtle and vigorous expression. Just as the vitality of New York inspired a new phase in Mondrian's work, seeing a complex city structure led Glarner to put order into chaos by studying the relations of things to each other.

Mondrian's circle of friends included, in addition to Fritz Glarner, Harry Holtzman, Ilya Bolotowsky and the author and painter Charmion von Wiegand. She published the first essay on Mondrian in an American magazine, the "Journal of Aesthetics", in 1943. As a painter she affected strictly orthogonal compositions under Mondrian's influence, but without restricting herself to the primary colors (ill. p. 248). In her collages she transformed Neo-Plastic arrangements into a poetic and occasionally decorative geometry. Charmion von Wiegand was a member of "Abstraction-Création"; she played an active part in the dissemination of constructive art among the American Abstract Artists, partly in the capacity of a writer.

Ilya Bolotowsky's œuvre — he was a Russian who came to New York in 1923 — is marked by its consistency. He gravitated from figurative abstraction to free non-objectivity about 1933. The decisive influence on his work was exercised by his encounter with the work of Mondrian in Gallatin's Museum of Living Art. With the support of Diller, Bolotowsky was able to purify his style in murals within the art program of the WPA. In 1936 he painted one of the first non-objective murals in America for the Williamsburg estate in New York. He made the personal acquaintance of Mondrian as one of the founders of American Abstract Artists, but a direct influence is only visible after 1945. From that time on Bolotowsky was a constant adherent of Neo-Plasticism. Around 1955 he produced finely organized orthogonal compositions. Into a horizontal-vertical line network transparent areas of color are inserted — a development of Mondrian's style of 1918/19. Many of these pictures are enclosed in a circle or a transverse oval and recall Cubist still lifes (ill. p. 249). After 1960 the compositions become simpler. There are no line grids, but sonorous color planes and bars are combined to create contrasts of shape and color. Related to these works are the colored sculptures, after 1962 mostly triangular columns, in which Bolotowsky transferred his painting principles to the surfaces of a volume in space. Bolotowsky's experience as a painter nourished his teaching activity at Black Mountain College, at the University of Wyoming and other schools.

When the Museum of Modern Art mounted the exhibition "Cubism and Abstract Art" in March 1936, a group of

Josef Albers: Study for Homage to the Square: Light Tenor II, 1961

American artists presented themselves in a gallery as "Concretionists"—a reference to Van Doesburg's definition. They were George L. K. Morris, John Ferren, Charles G. Shaw, Alexander Calder and Charles Biederman. In France about 1930, Jean Gorin had changed flat geometric color areas into three-dimensional sculptural elements, basing his procedure on the theories of Mondrian and Van Doesburg. Van Doesburg's architectural models also provided examples for such reliefs. Biederman investigated these relief structures systematically from 1937 on and formulated theories to explain them, for example

in his book "Art as the Evolution of Visual Knowledge", published in 1949. His reliefs consist of colored rectangular bars, often in the form of lamellae, or projecting perpendicular planes arranged on a baseplate in orthogonal cruciform systems. They may have square or rectangular colored plates added to them, which connect to the bars and seem to hover at various distances above the baseplate (ill. p. 244).

With these reliefs and his accompanying investigations Biederman founded the Structurist movement. Its mouthpiece was the magazine "The Structurist", published in

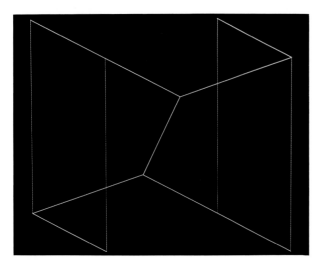

Josef Albers: Structural Constellation, 1954

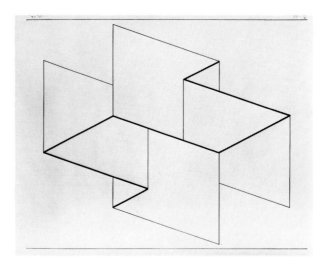

Josef Albers: Structural Constellation, 1956

Canada by Elie Bornstein. The proponents of Structurism were interested in problems of shape and color and their relations, in space and light. They were equally interested in "creative processes in nature". Their work therefore contains an element of natural science and even of philosophy. To appreciate Structurist reliefs, the observer must change his position, but no optical effects are produced as in kinetic art. The younger representatives of Structurism include David Barr, David Geary and Elizabeth Willmott. The group has kindred spirits in England in Pasmore, Mary Martin, Anthony Hill and Gillian Wise, and in the Netherlands in Joost Baljeu, publisher of the magazine "Structure".

Reorientation takes place more slowly in sculpture than in painting. In spite of the impulses from Europe the breakaway from figurative models to cubic or organic abstraction came late in American sculpture. The early Futuro-Cubist experiments of Max Weber and John Storrs had no repercussions. The development was more rapid, though uneven, in the successors of Gaston Lachaise and Elie Nadelman. A specifically American feeling for volume and space now made itself more and more manifest. American sculpture had two prominent representatives in the international movements of the twenties and thirties: Joseph Cornell in Surrealism and Alexander Calder in abstraction. Before them Man Ray had been one of the founders of Dadaist object art.

The first American sculptor to become widely known in Europe was Alexander Calder. He came to the fore in Paris in 1926 with wire figures and his legendary miniature circus. His circle of friends included Miró and Léger, Mondrian and Van Doesburg. As the creator of moving "space drawings" Calder is the founder of a kind of kinetic sculpture, for which Duchamp invented the name "mobile", while Arp called Calder's static metal sculptures "stabiles". Calder soon gave up the use of mechanical drives using cranks or motors. A touch or a breeze set his ingeniously devised wire balances with their leaflike sheet-metal weights in irrational motion — a poetic game played with a delicately balanced equilibrium and with the law of cause and effect (ill. p. 250).

Calder was one of the principal exponents of real-motion kinetic art after he joined "Abstraction-Création" in 1931. If we overlook Duchamp's "Bicycle Wheel" of 1913, he had only two forerunners: Man Ray with his "Lampshade" of 1920 and the Russian Alexander Rodchenko with his "hanging construction" of rings of the same year, to which Tatlin's project for a monumental rotating tower might be added. Calder's inventive œuvre has taught Europe that new impulses are to be expected from America. If there were ever any doubts on this score, they were dispelled by his "Mercury Fountain" which stood directly in front of Picasso's "Guernica" in the Spanish Pavilion at the World Exhibition of 1937 in Paris. In style Calder operated within the organic world of his friend Arp, while in his self-limitation to the primary colors and black and white he followed the example of Mondrian and Van Doesburg.

The immigration of Constructivists from Europe gave a new impetus to the interest of American sculptors in the constructive shaping of volumes and space. Moholy-Nagy, for example, considerably extended his earlier experiments with spatial constructions in the years of his teaching activity in Chicago, 1937–1946. He developed elements of transparent material, the so-called "space modulators". He resumed studies connected with his basic course at the Bauhaus in Weimar by designing weightless sculptures of acrylic and wire. The sculptures of Moholy-Nagy, dematerialized and hanging free in space, yet responding to the light, have led, as did his "Light Space Modulator" or "Light Display Machine" first presented in 1930, to numerous experiments in light painting or "luminism" and to large three-dimensional constructions. His theoretical remarks on the dynamism of vision and on a new understanding of space and time have also stimulated many artists. They appeared in his "The New Vision" of 1930, reprinted in America in 1938, and in the expanded version published posthumously under the title of "Vision in Motion" (1947). Moholy's thoughts on this dynamic space-time vision even had their influence on the development of Abstract Expressionism and Action Painting.

Naum Gabo also concerned himself with problems of space. He settled in the United States in 1946, and his mature work was done there. Unlike the traditional sculptor, for whom space is only what surrounds the plastic mass, Gabo saw sculptural qualities in space itself. "Up to now sculptors have preferred the mass and neglected or paid very little attention to such an important component of mass as space. Space interested them only in so far as it was a spot in which volumes could be placed or projected. It had to surround masses. We consider space from an entirely different point of view. We consider it as an absolute sculptural element, released from any closed volume, and we represent it from inside with all its own specific properties." In his "Realist Manifesto" of 1920 Gabo had already opposed the mass of the conventional sculpted volume, and in his "Kinetic Construction" of 1920, an upright metal rod set in vibration by an electric motor, he had compared the "virtual volume" contained in space with material volumes.

This idea of the plastic-dynamic quality of space is expressed particularly well in the "Linear Constructions in Space" made of acrylic, steel or bronze with line structures of nylon threads or wire. Gabo says: "In our sculpture space has ceased to be for us a logical abstraction or a transcendental idea and has become a malleable material element. It has become a reality of the same sensuous value as velocity or tranquillity and is incorporated in the general family of sculptural emotions where up to date only the weight and the volume of mass have been predominant." Another alternative is to work inward, by pulling space into the sculpture. The projections made visible by engraving on acrylic, by nylon threads or wires are then stretched as if over frames or bows. This applies to the group of works called "Torsion" dating from 1960/64, the variations of which materialized in connection with a project for a fountain (p. 253).

A similar relationship to space, a reaching outward and at the same time an interest in phenomena of motion, characterizes the work of George Rickey. He came to painting by way of studies in history and art history but turned in 1949 to sculpture, which enabled him to indulge his interest in things technical. Kinetic art was his domain from the first. The sculptural volume is reduced to the absolute minimum of material presence needed to manifest movement. Needles or blades of stainless steel pivoting on joints point outward into space. When exposed to air movements, these needles move, outlining imaginary surfaces or virtual hollow bodies of a conical or cylindrical character. They do not touch each other when they move, nor do the circumscribed surfaces and hollow bodies overlap. When at rest, the needles form the sides of a simple shape, a square or triangle set in space, or a regular family of rays (ill. p. 252).

The ingenious technical basis of Rickey's sculpture—the creation of delicately balanced equilibrium by displacing the center of gravity from the point of support to a distant point by means of invisible lead weights—is particularly effective in the reliefs. "Any particular instance of movement takes place in its own span of time and becomes, for the kinetic artist, what color and shape are to a painter. The possible movements are surprisingly few and surprisingly simple. Western music has twelve tones. Kinetic art has scarcely more . . . The movements of oscil-

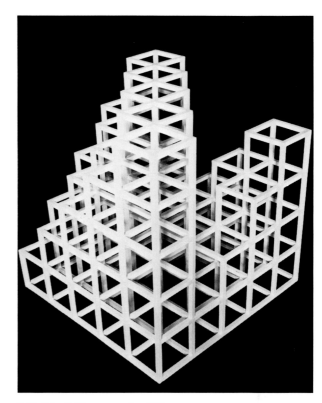

Sol LeWitt: Cubic construction, 1971

lation, rotation, reciprocation, vibration, in addition to passage through space onward or backward, up or down, to the left or to the right, with intensification of these by acceleration or deceleration, are all there are." Rickey's

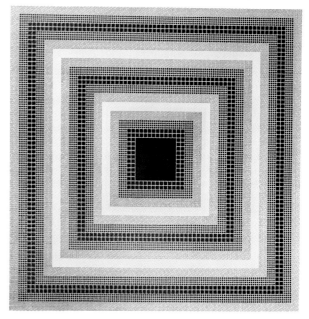

Richard Anuszkiewicz: Sunglow No. 217, 1968

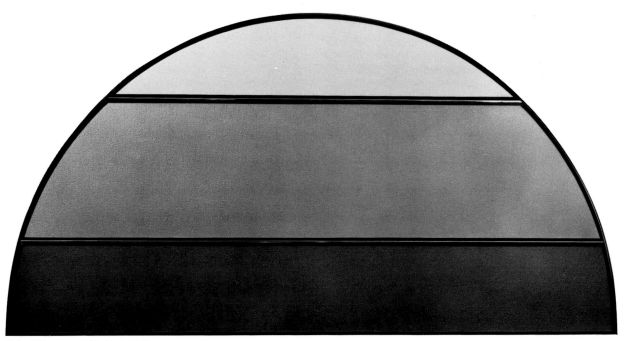

Tadaaki Kuwayama: Untitled, 1972

sculptures are combinations of these possibilities. Their movement is a reaction to air movements. They thus make manifest the Empedoclean element that is only visible in its effects. Rickey's sculptures also reveal, in the way they respond to air currents, the passage of time. "None of my sculptures is in the slightest an attempt to reproduce or copy Nature or to explain or reveal it. I study and make use of the motions which Nature's laws permit — that is within the range of my understanding and technical ability. These motions, and ever-present gravity, are the only Nature that I work with."

Individual talents and training have enabled Rickey to do constructive work that has made people think about aspects of constructive art. One outcome of his reflections has been a publication on the origin and development of Constructivism which appeared in 1967 and soon became, as the first comprehensive account of the subject, an important source of factual information.

The position of David Smith is very different. He became a sculptor in forged metal in the thirties under the influence of the iron sculptures of Picasso and Gonzalez. His open, apparatus-like constructions, often containing witty or ironical allusions to figures or objects, were at first Surrealist in inspiration. It was only after 1960 that he produced, in addition to totem-like iron sculptures, works of a geometric character: the "Zig" series with montages of painted sheet-iron in simple geometric shapes (ill. p. 251) and the "Cubi" series of stainless steel, which relate to more recent developments in American art. The "Zig" series ran parallel with Postpainterly Abstraction and Hard-Edge painting as practiced by Stella and Noland. In his "Cubi" Smith has turned to the elementary form-vocabulary of Minimal Art as exemplified in the primary structures of Tony Smith, Don Judd, Robert Morris, Carl Andre, and Ron Bladen. In the two-dozen-odd "Cubi" Smith piles up bars, cylinders, cubes, and disks of various dimensions into unstable structures. It was less the illogi-

cal handling of stereometric volumes than the elementary force and monumentality of these sculptures that became a model for the younger generation. This generation was well on its way when it made its appearance in the exhibition "Primary Structures" in the Jewish Museum in New York in 1966. With its minimalist goals it guided the sculptural image in the direction of a geometry reduced to its bare essentials.

Stereometric tightening-up of volumes and static or dynamic constructions in space have occupied numerous sculptors since 1960. James Rosati has passed from organic abstractions to free constructions of precisely shaped prismatic bodies (ill. p. 254). While a musical sense of form can be felt in the smaller constructions and brass reliefs — Rosati was initially a musician — the monumental, accessible sculptures in stainless steel are a conscious cubic-dynamic, individual and lyrical response to the functional shapes of high-rise buildings in modern urban architecture. In the work of José de Rivera chrome-steel rods swing in dynamic loops through space, hovering almost weightlessly. Open spatial constructions, made for instance of circular elements, are also found in the work of Alexander Liberman, who does colored steel sculptures alongside his constructive painting. The Australian Clement Meadmore, on the other hand, is interested in specifically three-dimensional problems. Elementary sculptural bodies, often rectangular beams of Corten steel, are used to manifest the enormous energy that is required to transform a static, stationary body into a shape reaching dynamically into space (ill. p. 255). Other forces — mostly tensile or compressive — are portrayed in the works of Kenneth Snelson. He uses round bars or tubes of aluminum in conjunction with steel wires to make spatial structures suggesting bold engineering projects or mathematical models. The stretched wires have, apart from their physical function, the formal purpose of drawing the outlines of imaginary volumes in space, with

Frank Stella: Protractor Variation VI, 1968

the ends of the round bars marking the corners of the po-
lygonal bodies.
Both the "primary structures" of minimalist sculpture and
the geometric space constructions of artists such as Kenneth Snelson and Christopher Wilmarth were seen by
American critics of the time as parallels to the cool steel-
and-glass architecture inspired by Mies van der Rohe.
They were thinking less of the appearance of these sculptures than of the principle on which they were based, the
structure.
In the traveling exhibition "The Art of the Real, USA
1948–1968", mounted for the Museum of Modern Art,
E.C. Goossen attempted in 1969 to present the attitude
behind Minimal Art, both in sculpture and painting. He
stated:
"The gradual divorce of the physical means of art from
expressionistic associations has been accompanied by a
distinct change in attitude toward what art should
attempt. Expressionism, even at its most abstract, continued many aspects of representational art, and constructivism, despite its purist look, was basically nostalgic in
its search for meaning through traditional methods of
composition. The new attitude has been turning art
inside out: instead of perceptual experience being
accepted as the means to an end, it has become the end
in itself. The Renaissance artist labored over perspective
in order to create an illusion of space within which he
could make believable the religious and philosophical
ideals of his time; the contemporary artist labors to make
art itself believable. Consequently the very means of art
have been isolated and exposed, forcing the spectator to
perceive himself in the process of his perception. The
spectator is not given symbols, but facts, to make of
them what he can. They do not direct his mind nor call up
trusted cores of experience, but lead him to the point
where he must evaluate his own peculiar responses.
Thus, what was once concealed within art — the technical

devices employed by the artist — is now overtly revealed;
and what was once the outside — the meaning of its
forms — has been turned inside. The new work of art is
very much like a chunk of nature, a rock, a tree, a cloud,
and possesses much the same 'otherness'. Whether this
kind of confrontation with the actual can be sustained,
whether it can remain vital and satisfying, it is not yet
possible to tell."
In other words, the work of art no longer pointed beyond
itself. It was art about art, or art as art. One might also put
it this way: it was no longer important what the work of
art was, only what effect it had. In this sense we are justified in stating that Minimal Art fundamentally altered our
relationship to space, or at the very least activated it.
Styles do not follow each other in logical succession in
American art any more than in European. They often run
parallel. A great deal depends on the individual personalities involved. Josef Albers, for example, was an influential teacher who helped to shape the outlook of several
generations and schools.
For Josef Albers, as for many other Europeans, the move
to the United States marked the beginning of his mature
work. He already possessed a fund of experience in the
systematic handling of shape and color from the days of
his teaching activity at the Bauhaus. But it was only the
educational and research work he did at Black Mountain
College from 1933 to 1949 that liberated all his creative
potential. The influence of his teaching at this experimental school and later at the Graduate School of Design in
Harvard, at Yale and elsewhere has been powerful. He
also set down in essays the views on art education which
he derived from his own teaching practice.
There are two main accents in Albers' œuvre. The line
takes first place in his drawings and graphic work. Constructions of straight lines reach a first culminating point
in the series of "Tectonic graphics" of 1944. Parallel horizontal and vertical lines in groups of equal emphasis cre-

ate an apparent modulation of space and volume that pruduces a plastic movement. The spatial and volumetric illusions can be interpreted in more ways than one. In the series of "Structural Constellations" begun about 1950 the linear constructions are carried a step further (ill. p. 260). Families of parallel lines appear in these "Transformations", the slanting lines contributing to the formation of parallelograms. Through a kind of ambivalent isometry a spatial impression that confuses the senses is produced, for the space generated by the lines is indefinable. In the book "Despite Straight Lines" (1961) Albers investigated these constructions and the spatial illusions they create. A year before, the theoretical study "Art and Illusion" by E. H. Gombrich had appeared and had placed such phenomena against a more general background. Though limited to a formal minimum, Albers' "Structural Constellations" have contributed more to an understanding of perceptual phenomena than many of the kinetic experiments of Op Art. William C. Seitz drew attention to these problems of surface kinetics in 1965 in the exhibition "The Responsive Eye" at the Museum of Modern Art in New York.

The second emphasis of Albers' work is in the domain of painting. Here problems of shape are subsidiary to those of color. In essentials, Albers studied the problems of the interrelations and interactions of color in two types of paintings, those with two centers and the series "Homage to the Square". A common feature of the two types is the opportunity provided to check the effect of the freely chosen colors within a strict compositional structure, since the surface quantities of the various colors are exactly related to each other, being equal, twice as great or three times as great. Albers set down his thoughts on these color relations in 1963 in his book "Interaction of Color". In connection with the importance of color in his own painting he remarks that the painter would like to express himself in color, but that some regard color as an accompaniment of shape and therefore as subsidiary. For others — today increasing in numbers — color is the principal medium of the painter's language, and here it becomes autonomous. Albers' own pictures represent the latter trend, and he is particularly interested in the psychic effect which — an aesthetic experience — is produced by the interaction of the juxtaposed colors.

These interactions appear at their purest in the "Homage to the Square" series painted from 1949 on (ill. p. 259). An almost neutral formula of surface divisions permits concentrated scrutiny of the colors and their relations. Three or four squares are placed one inside or over the other in a semiconcentric arrangement so that the square forming the nucleus appears in a double or triple frame. The strong vertical axis of the picture stresses its static character. The intervals between the squares are much smaller at the bottom than at the top and sides, so that there is a distinct downward displacement of the center of gravity. The grid is based on a horizontal and a vertical division of the surface into ten units each; half units are also used in both directions, permitting the composition to be carefully balanced. The downward displacement implies additional weight, but also extended movement, says Albers. If the four diagonals are drawn inward through the corners of the squares, a point of intersection common to all squares is obtained and lies well below the center of the picture. This arrangement lifts the squares from two into three dimensions. Color turns the subdivisions into steps. This feature is crucial for the three-dimensional effect of the color combinations, although the factual two-dimensional character of the painting is never denied. The color, opaque and often applied with a palette knife without any ground color or overpainting, is never mixed; Albers uses the paint as it comes from the tube. Every "Homage to the Square" is — in its eccentric grid system, in the choice and sequence of colors — a self-sufficient whole. Pictures using related color schemes can be classed in groups.

Clear as the facts are, the effects of the colors on the observer remain inexplicable. Although these colors create the illusion of space or of relief by their gradations and of movement by their juxtaposition, Albers denies any kinship to the color kinetics of Op Art, though he allows the designation of "perceptual painting". The discrepancy between physical fact and psychic effect encourages closer examination and reflection. Emotional relationships of the observer to a color combination also play their part. Some of the picture titles are allusions to states of mind, to moods inspired by landscapes or times of day, to fundamental phenomena of being. Many embody a mysterious poetry — "Blue Silence" is an example. The titles in this sense confirm Albers' own remark that he has attempted, in his "Homage to the Square", to create something near to modern meditation pictures.

The significance and the sublimation of color in Albers' work distinguish it from that of most constructive painters. While in their compositions the interest of the formal structure or framework is at least equal to that of the color and may even outweight it, the framework in Albers is only a sort of grid within which color enjoys almost complete autonomy. This connects him directly to those American painters who attach primordial or even absolute importance to color. Most of them were originally involved in the Abstract Expressionism of the late forties and early fifties. They had tried to get away from "pure abstraction", organic or geometric non-objectivity, or had even expressly rejected it. Formal and aesthetic categorization was hardly to be reconciled with the requirement of the greatest possible artistic freedom and uninhibited self-expression. Many of them had sought an association with the Surrealists. The Surrealists' automatic writing — "l'écriture automatique" — led to the development of an expressive, gestural pictorial language for which a forerunner has been found in the early Kandinsky. As figuration and composition were discarded, forces were liberated which led to the rise of Abstract Expressionism. Gorky, de Kooning and Pollock embody this development most clearly in their work.

There was a global trend just after the war to an artistic creed of formlessness, or even an animosity to form. But it is still one of the most astonishing phenomena of recent art history that the process of spontaneous self-expression should have led in less than a decade, and from such a small group of artists, to the creation of a new identity in American art. The pride American artists felt at having become independent of Europe led to the realization among Europeans that from now on they would have to reckon with a specifically American art. And the splendid deployment of this art continued up into the eighties.

Frank Stella: Morro Castle, 1958

The concept of "abstract Expressionism" appeared in German art criticism as early as 1920. It was taken up by Alfred H. Barr in 1927 with reference to Kandinsky and was extended to include contemporary American artists in 1947. But the movement then known as Abstract Expressionism divided into several branches about 1950. Gestural abstraction has its parallels in "art informel", in Tachisme and "peinture de geste". Yet in the American version which Harold Rosenberg christened "Action Painting" there is a broader sweep than in the "formless" art practiced in Europe, not only in the bigger dimensions of the pictures but in the freedom, freshness and audacity of the pictorial processes, in the shifting of the accent from the work to the act of painting itself. It was primarily in its approach to space that this work was new to Europeans.

A second tendency can be distinguished from gestural painting. It can be recognized in the work of Robert Motherwell, Clyfford Still and Adolph Gottlieb, although the gestural element is still important here, as it is in Sam Francis. The scripturally inclined painting of Mark Tobey

and of the younger Cy Twombly may also be regarded as lying in this borderland. The true representatives of the tendency, however, are Barnett Newman, Mark Rothko and Ad Reinhardt. The term "Chromatic Abstraction" has been coined for their painting. It is not the action of painting, the emotion-laden process of applying color to the surface, which is here significant, but the color mood which fills or pervades the picture, making it an "environmental painting". The expressive character of the color is now secondary or not in evidence at all; it is hardly possible to distinguish between figure and ground, the whole picture is a single field of color. The term "Colorfield Painting" was therefore put forward to describe a trend which is clearly far removed from the rhetoric of Action Painting. The works of the artists concerned differ in their origins and objectives, but they share a close attention to color and its effects, and a leaning toward a meditative mood.

Since clearly defined forms play no part in this painting, and there are no "tangible facts" on which to get a purchase, American critics of the time had some difficulty in

Al Held: Flemish VII, 1973

coming to terms with this Postexpressionist art. Color-field Painting, said Nicolas Calas in 1971, "tends to become a landscape in which the monotony of continuity is relieved by intervals. Intervals in a continuum are to Field painting what interruptions are to Expressionism. Intervals are planned while interruptions are improvised and must be executed with skill. Intervals reinforce continuity while interruptions threaten structure. Everything about Field painting is of a reassuring tranquility while nothing looks safe in Abstract Expressionism.

Field painting has been called 'nonrelational' on the grounds that the artist is not involved in what 'the motif set in one corner of the canvas does to a specific thing in another section of the surface' (Paul Brach). As Al Held, however, pointed out, the artist has to face the fact that as soon as he puts more than one form in any part of the field, an interrelationship develops inevitably. — Prewar abstract painting visualized geometric forms as structures set against a background, while Field painting stresses expanding effects of color juxtaposition."

Ad Reinhardt never took part in Post-Surrealism, Abstract Expressionism or Action Painting. From 1937 on he painted geometric pictures as part of Burgoyne Diller's art program for the WPA. Intensely chromatic and dynamic abstractions which he described as "baroque-geometric expressionist" followed in the early forties. Then in 1948 came the "archaic color bricks", free geometric organizations of the picture area without any marked color or form accents. From 1950 on Reinhardt restricted himself more and more to monochromy. His picture arrangements become sparer until the type of painting he calls "hieratical red, blue, black, monochrome square-cross-beam symmetries" is attained. Much as in Albers' work, an almost anonymous formal schema had thus been found upon which color modulations could take place. Colors vanish to make way for the monochrome black

pictures of the last twelve years. These are scarcely accessible to the observer, partly because of the matt paint that absorbs almost all the light, but chiefly because of the darkening of the color fields until they approach black. Since Reinhardt made a very close study of the mandala, the circular-polygonal diagram that serves as an aid to meditation in Lamaism, Tantrism and Zen Buddhism, the series of black paintings have been interpreted as modern mandalas. Reinhardt's own description does not bear this out: "... a pure, abstract, nonobjective, impartial picture".

Reinhardt was one of the most striking figures of the New York art world of his time — politically committed, feared as a disputant in matters of art, aggressive and yet enigmatic in his written utterances. He was one of the first Western artists to dip deeply into Eastern art and Zen Buddhism. The Zen axiom "Form is emptiness, emptiness is form" is implicit in many of Reinhardt's statements, as for instance in his "Twelve Rules for a New Academy", which in their negation of everything point to nothingness. His conception of "art as art" has become, over and beyond his personal credo, a starting point for many young American artists. "Art-as-art is a concentration on art's essential nature," declared Reinhardt in 1966. "I am just making the last pictures that can be made at all." A quotation from "I Ging", the Chinese book of transformations, may perhaps be applied to the painter of these black "last" pictures: "He veils his light, and yet he shines."

In Barnett Newman the division of the uniform color field by one or more vertical bands or "zips", as he called them — often vibrating with painterly edges — seems to be the predominant element. But he himself says that instead of using outlines, instead of creating forms and breaking open spaces, his arrangements explain space; instead of working with the remnants of space, he works with the whole of space. Newman's theoretical statements are polemic and directed against European art and its traditions. With an eye on Mondrian, and painting "against" him, he criticizes the "empty world" of a geometric formalism as a pure rhetoric of abstract mathematical relations. Renouncing such an art of relations, Newman aims at an "art of the sublime". He breaks open the frame of the picture, leaves the position of the vertical bands indeterminate. The color of the bands, however, intensifies by contrast the ground color of the picture. As a result of this intensification a connection is established with the surrounding, previously undefined space.

Mark Rothko attained a similar radiant chromatic force by following other objectives. He began with a Surrealist phase of biomorphic and sometimes submarine scenes that recall Miró and Matta. About 1947 a simplification of the composition sets in, the biomorphic elements make way for elementary bar shapes hovering in space. From these his characteristic paintings emerge about 1950: usually two or three horizontal rectangles of color, divided by bands, float in front of the colored ground, which also serves as a frame. The border of these areas, the formal scaffolding, is blurred, the ground and the color fields superimposed on it flow into each other without any clear contours. Unlike Barnett Newman, whose color area forms a single whole, Rothko creates an impression of depth with his floating, vibrant color fields. The il-

Roy Lichtenstein: Modern Painting with Green Segment, 1967

lusion is heightened by a sense of light radiating from the interior of the painting. This chromatic light gives the subtly attuned hues their mysterious luminosity. While Newman enshrouds the observer in a color continuum, Rothko defines the position of the observer in space: drawn by the suggestive power of the colors, which are combined more by affinities than in contrasts, the viewer comes nearer to the picture. As he penetrates into its depths, he finds himself confronted by infinity, by the numinous. Rothko created a meditation chamber for a chapel in Houston in 1965/67 with a cycle of 14 large, dark-

hued panels. These sonorous works were a transition to the somber gray-black panels of his later years. Their composition is even more wall-like than in earlier phases, the extension of the color fields to the edges of the paintings seems to shut in the eye that gazes into the depth. These panels embody the same irrevocable mood of loss and ending that Harold Rosenberg sensed in the black paintings of Ad Reinhardt.

Ludwig Sander has always stressed how much he owes his control of color to his teacher Hans Hofmann. Unlike almost all his friends, however—Gorky, de Kooning,

Kline, Marca-Relli and Reinhardt—he inclined from the first to an undoctrinaire geometry. His picture area was not a stage on which tensions were to be generated by expressive forces, or happenings were to be enacted. He took the view that a painting area is defined by its edges. His solution did not lie in the exact mathematical parallelism of the horizontals and verticals that divide the surface into sectors. His lines, he says, are variants of straight lines; he likes a line to look straight without being straight. Color is more important than the compositional framework. It is a condensation of the color into a harmonious chromatic essence that takes place on the canvas, in a painting process that is at once deliberate and intuitive. Two principles of color composition can be observed: in the one, two contrasting colors are brought into confrontation and reconciled with each other by the intermedium of mixed shades; in the other a single color is modified in the direction of its two neighboring colors (ill. p. 245). The size and proportions of the five to seven color fields in a picture set up a subtle balance between the more radiant and duller colors, the lighter and the darker, the colder and the warmer. His color sensibility makes Sander an important representative of Chromatic Abstraction.

The devaluation of the formal framework in favor of color and the study of its space-forming qualities—characteristics of the work of Newman, Reinhardt and Rothko despite all their individual differences—have fertilized thought about the nature of painting. Chromatic Abstraction developed out of a rejection of gestural subjectivism in the late fifties, when there was also strong opposition to Abstract Expressionism from other quarters.

One of the forms of the opposition was the return to material reality as embodied in the subjects, motifs and techniques of the everyday consumer society. This was the "new realism" represented by Pop Art. If Pop Art, as Robert Rauschenberg once said of his work, operates in the gap between art and life, that implies that the artist is thinking not only about life—whether positively or critically—but also about art. Around 1960 ideas of Marcel Duchamp were refashioned into a theory that was to lead to an "art about art". Much of it was at first ironical, as when Roy Lichtenstein translated characteristic modern classics into his Ben Day technique derived from the comic strip. From the middle of the sixties Lichtenstein systematically explored vulgarizations of constructive art and Art Déco in his "Modern Paintings". His style, he said, already included relations with the aesthetic of the thirties, with Mondrian for example. He was looking for what was common to the architectural forms of this era, the fashions and the paintings of artists such as Van Doesburg. His "Modern Painting with Green Segment" of 1967 is an example of this combination of a stylistic quotation and inventions of his own (ill. p. 267). He went still further in the adaptation of constructive principles around 1970 in his series of "Mirrors", where zones of reflection are transformed into purely structural areas consisting of dot screens. These were followed by "neo-constructive" pictures which consistently pursue the aims of the "Modern Paintings", freed of all objective motifs.

In works of this kind there is an intellectual link with the styles of historical Constructivist art, and principles of ge-

ometric order and of anonymous color application in compact areas are employed. Pictorial techniques of this type are found where Pop artists are concerned with the laconic language of signs and signals, for instance in the "landscapes" of Allan d'Arcangelo, dominated by traffic signs and occasionally turning into constructions pure and simple, or in the letter and number compositions of Robert Indiana. The immediate forerunners of this sign-like painting can be found in the work of Charles Demuth and Stuart Davis, who had still entertained direct relations with European constructive art.

This flat sign-like style that avoids any suggestion of gestural expression through the act of painting is not far removed from the contemporaneous oppositional movement deriving from Abstract Expressionism: Post-painterly Abstraction. This new abstraction, arising around 1960, is not a homogeneous school either in its origins or in its individual preoccupations. The idea of the picture area as a physical picture space and the question of its enclosure or non-enclosure were investigated by Jackson Pollock as well as by Barnett Newman and Morris Louis. The surface was no longer regarded as the support for a painting within whose two-dimensional bounds illusions of color and shape could be generated. The window-like character of the painting, which the exponents of Post-painterly Abstraction criticized in Mondrian, was to be overcome. That was possible only by accepting the autonomy of color and recognizing the picture surface as an autonomous object. In Morris Louis' paintings the paint does not lie on but sinks into the raw canvas, fusing with it. Taking the picture surface seriously in this way attracted attention to the edge of the picture, which was no longer an enclosure but part of the surface. A shape was no longer placed on the surface, and the outline of the picture area itself became a shape.

Frank Stella logically developed this idea of "shape as form" in 1959/60. Adopting a serial method, he produced groups of monochrome panels with patterns of negative white parallel lines, the unpainted raw canvas, which look engraved (ill. p. 265). The size and shape of each painting derives from the internal patterns. The angular or cruciform, hook-, star- or V-shaped picture area is no longer the starting point but the result of the composition. There is a congruence of internal structure and external shape. The attitude manifested here is opposed to that of the European Constructivists. Instead of the elements of shape and color being brought into relation with each other in a given area, the picture is here generated by the system. There are, it is true, certain parallels in the work of the Groupe de Recherches d'Art Visuel in Paris. But whereas their works were regarded as instruments for the acquisition of experience, Stella's painting is based "on the fact that only what can be seen there is there. It really is an object." After 1962 the painted intervals between the lines of the geometrical structure began to turn into stripes of color, first in paintings consisting of concentric squares. In 1965 irregular polygons grew out of the colored stripes and triangles. After 1967 there is a series in which straight stripes and curving stripes developed from arcs interpenetrate on a circular canvas. In the "Protractor Series", the interpenetration of the color stripes takes place in a semicircular area (ill. p. 263), in paintings whose shapes consist of combinations of cir-

Ellsworth Kelly: Two Panels: Yellow-Orange, 1968

cles and squares or in double "color wheels". Stella later broke away from a geometry of form and color in his dynamic painterly reliefs.

A second exponent of Postpainterly Abstraction, Kenneth Noland, put geometric order into the free colorfield paintings of Morris Louis without any new treatment of the problem of the antinomy of figure and ground. This work began in 1960 with concentric bands of color soaked into the raw canvas ground of the picture. These paintings only superficially resemble the "targets" of Jasper Johns from a few years before. Noland's intentions became clearer in the V-shaped "Chevron" compositions of 1963/64, in which he does not divide the transparent acrylic paint, as Stella does, with white lines, but juxtaposes the color areas directly, much as in Albers' work (ill. p. 271). The interdependence of ground and colorfields is

underlined both by the choice of the colors and by "empty zones" of blank canvas between the color bands. Many of the relationships of color and shape explored here are based on thinking such as that formulated by Albers in "Interaction of Color". Noland has stressed the fact that he is aiming at pulsating colors. He fulfilled this intent in 1967 in horizontally striped pictures. The pulsation is generated by the stresses between broad and narrow stripes and their gentle or violent color contrasts. Very narrow marginal bands of intense color can be used to increase the luminosity of the whole colorfield. In 1967 a new American edition of Chevreul's fundamental work on the laws of simultaneous color contrast appeared. In one passage it states that, if we look simultaneously at two stripes of different shades of the same color or equivalent shades of different colors that lie beside each

Alfred Jensen: That is it, 1966

other and are not too broad, the eye perceives certain changes which in the first case influence the intensity of the color and in the second case the optical configuration of the two juxtaposed colors. Even though the painterly element, in the sense of individual brushwork, plays only a subsidiary role in Noland's pictures, the reference to Chevreul reveals that this art depends entirely on the character and effect of its colors. Much the same holds true of other respresentatives of Colorfield Painting.

The exhibition "Toward a New Abstraction" took place in the Jewish Museum in New York in 1963 and, at a time when Pop Art was beginning to monopolize public interest, raised the issue of a more "objective" art. It had been preceded by an exhibition on "Geometric Abstraction in America" in the Whitney Museum. There was then talk of the "New Imagists", by which the younger successors of Newman, Rothko and Reinhardt, Albers and Alfred Jensen were meant, artists who were concerned with an "imago", even if not in the sense of depth psychology.

Alfred Jensen is a special case in this circle. His pictures at first seem to be patterns made up of basic geometric shapes, with the glowing colors applied in an impasto technique (ill. p. 270). The compositions, mostly suggesting rotary movement about a center, sometimes include series of numbers or symbols. A great deal of reflection has gone into these works. They apply theories of Leonardo da Vinci, Goethe's color theory, laws of arithmetic and harmony, numerical symbolism, old popular teachings about the relations of heaven and earth and the laws of growth, including astrological and calendrical systems. Jensen's speculations thus draw on mathematics, astronomy, biology and myth and lead via calculation and study to his paintings. His work might be equally well ascribed to constructive or to conceptual art.

John McLaughlin is, after Burgoyne Diller, the most powerful and independent representative of geometric constructive art in the United States. He lived in Japan in the thirties and steeped himself in Zen Buddhism. Until 1945 he was again in the East, this time in the army, and began to paint when he returned to California in 1946, when he was nearly fifty. Zen was not for him an uncontrolled plunge into esoteric depths for the purpose of spiritual illumination. Western ratio remained for him the key to meditation. He found his inspiration in constructive art, particularly in Mondrian's Neo-Plasticism. McLaughlin's development is a record of the surmounting of these starting points, a constant dumping of ballast, an abandonment of complex color-shape relations. It ends in an oeuvre of the greatest discipline and consistency. Horizontal or vertical bars floating on the background or bands running from edge to edge of the painting, often in gray, white or black, are the outcome of inexorable processes of reduction (ill. pp. 256, 257). In the Zen sense this may be a refinement of simplicity, corresponding in its economy to the concentrated word-patterns of haiku. When McLaughlin made his appearance on the West Coast, his painting was felt to embody "total abstraction". In 1958 Jules Langsner, during the preparations for an exhibition of geometric constructive art in California, coined the term "Hard Edge" with special reference to McLaughlin. Lawrence Alloway and John Coplans seized on it and gave it a more exact definition. McLaughlin was included in the exhibition "The Responsive Eye" in the Museum of Modern Art in 1962, and his work is in the collections of many American museums, but he was not very well known until the 1974 exhibition at the Whitney Museum of American Art in New York. — Leon Polk Smith is another underrated pioneer of postwar geometric art. While others explored the rectangle, he discovered "the physiognomy of the circle and its apparented forms, ovals and rounded squares" (Nicolas Calas).

The heterogeneous circle of the "new abstraction" painters, for whom in 1964 the general designation of "Post-painterly Abstraction" was coined, included — in addition to Stella and Noland — two painters as diametrically different as Al Held and Ellsworth Kelly. Al Held had emerged with free geometric compositions of circles, rectangles, triangles and undulating bands in 1960. The form-vocabulary was reminiscent of Herbin, but Al Held magnified it spontaneously and unhesitantly to gigantic proportions. The geometric shapes were soon replaced by fragments of letters. The viscous, crusted paint, applied in layers that sometimes obliterated parts of the original composition, recalled walls that have continually been painted over and to which remnants of earlier colors still cling. After the middle of the sixties the compositions became more reasoned, the skin of paint smoother and more regular. Ground and figure could now hardly be kept apart. In 1969, however, Al Held gave up this spare flat style, producing black linear constructions on a white ground, and later white ones on a black ground. The principal feature of these works is the destruction of the two-dimensional picture plane: linear projections of bodies materialize, mostly cubes, prisms and irregular hexahedrons, later circular bands (ill. p. 266). The line construction, mostly in parallel perspective, permits two interpretations of the individual body, one receding into the sur-

Kenneth Noland: Blue Veil, 1963

face, the other projecting from it. The impulse for these illusionary line compositions no doubt came from the "Structural Constellations" of Albers (ill. p. 260), whose logic is, however, questioned by Held. The frequency and the self-contradiction of the "reversible figures" throw an ironic light on the principle involved, preventing orientation in the illusionary space. The integral surface character of the picture is discarded, and the picture is no longer an autonomous object but once more a detail seen through a window, an approach which had been declared obsolete by other representatives of Post-painterly Abstraction. In later works Al Held reintroduced color. The mere lineament turned into complicated, illusionary space visions consisting of the unreal interpenetrations of systems of bands.

The development of Ellsworth Kelly took a different course. About 1960 he too had turned his attention to the contradiction of figure and ground. He progressed from biomorphic figures to rectangular shapes on a monochrome ground, but rounded off their corners to get rid of their heraldic character — an instinctive rejection of the constructive design principles of a Diller or McLaughlin. In 1966 Kelly took a decisive step when he placed two rectangular canvases beside or above each other, each completely covered with a flat surface color. In doing so he fulfilled the requirements of a form of painting for which the designation "Hard Edge" had established itself toward 1960. What this meant was extreme formal economy, perfection of the color application and luminosity of the colors. The term was originally used in contradistinction to the geometric school, whose method of composing with interior shapes was rejected. The single-minded inner structure of the work was to be freed of all relations and to become the real subject of art. The principle of the "shaped canvas" underlined the object character of the work. Kelly has varied the principle of combining monochrome color panels in many ways: one panel is placed perpendicular on the wall, the other — in a different color — lies on the floor in front of it; two or three panels of different colors are leaned at intervals against the wall — methods of involving the three dimensions of real space to which the panels are exposed. Different relationships of color, shape and space resulted when, in 1968, Kelly gave up the right angle in order to work with isosceles triangles, trapezoids and parallelograms. The eye sees these shapes as rectangles with their angles distorted by perspective. Spatial illusion and corporeal illusion are created when Kelly shapes two panels so that fitted together they appear as the projection of a cube in parallel perspective (ill. p. 269). The color contrasts take on the function of light and shade. Such projections of bodies on a surface remind us of problems posed by Vasarely and his successors. The essential difference, however, is that in Vasarely the cubic projection forms a microstructure, a "plastic unit", with which a flat kinetic structure is built up, whereas Kelly makes his statement with a minimal use of shape and color. The extension of every color is identical with the bounds of the color panel; every color field has a function in the context of the whole. The boundaries between colors, shapes and functions are created by the joints of the juxtaposed color-shapes. Identity of picture outline and form ("shape as form"), color and form, color and picture outline ("color as shape"), replacement of the interior drawing by the actual outline — these are characteristics of Minimal Art, a conception based on absolute clarity and openness. The term was introduced in America by Richard Wollheim in 1965 to designate an art having as its common attribute "a minimal art-content". This description might also be applied to works of a different kind, for instance Duchamp's "Ready-mades", and it was therefore not entirely satisfactory. At an exhibition in the Guggenheim Museum in New York in 1966 Lawrence Alloway spoke of "Systemic Art", which was also the title of the exhibition. This was meant to emphasize the fact that this art is based on certain systems, plans or concepts. The show contained many works considered today part of the Minimal school. Robert Mangold emerged in the early sixties in the circle of the Hard Edge painters, making his mark with systemic primary structures. His concern is the monochrome picture surface articulated by one or more lines, and his theme the relationship of line to surface, their interdependence, their mutual influence. The line is either a straight one forming a regular or irregular polygon — square, trapezoid, etc. — or an arc in the form of a circle, semicircle or quadrant and occasionally combined with the straight line. Up to 1968 Mangold's primary concern was the relation of the part to the whole. Then he took up the transformation of a given element, usually attacking it in series, for instance by a change in dimensions or in localization or by an interference with its regularity. The frame and perimeter series belong to this phase (ill. p. 272). In the so-called "tangent quadrilateral" a circle is inscribed in an irregular quadrilateral, the points of contact of all tangents lying at the middle of the side concerned. In irregular polygons the inequality of the tangent radii leads to a deformation of the inscribed circle (ill. p. 273). As an analogue to these polygons with distorted internal circle, Mangold has also studied the converse phenomena — the deformations of a square in a circle. As with Kelly, Mangold's works have to do only with what can be seen; they contain no allusions and spark off

Robert Mangold: Perimeter Series, 1969/70

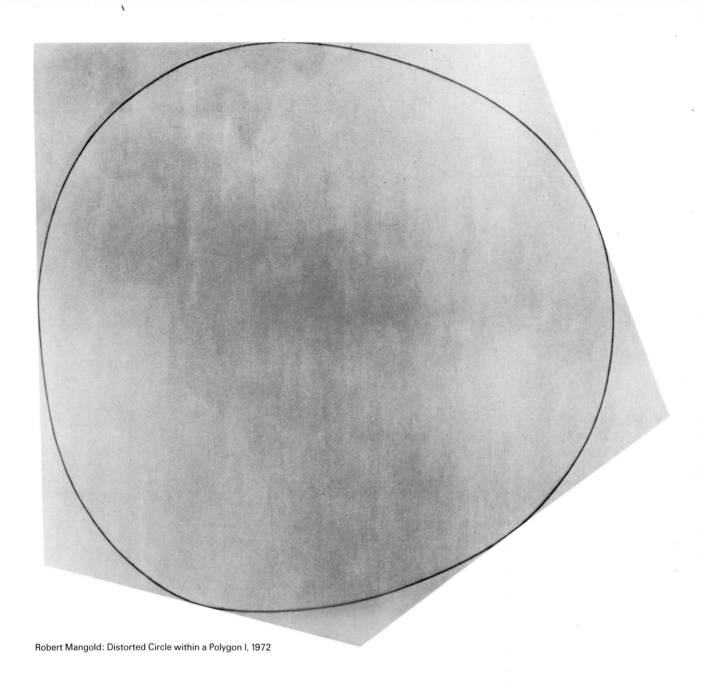

Robert Mangold: Distorted Circle within a Polygon I, 1972

no associations. They are purely intellectual or conceptual in origin; the idea is the work. Yet even so, and in spite of the fact that the color application is anonymous, they are specifically painting inasmuch as the choice of coloring is highly subjective. They are something to be looked at as well as thought about.

Mangold has referred to his painting as a return to an anti-decorative, difficult art. This is entirely in keeping with Lucy R. Lippard's comments when she speaks of an "art of emptiness" and sees Mangold as an exponent of the "Silent Art" which was ushered in by Reinhardt, Newman and Rothko.

Rather than combining areas of color and shape, Tadaaki Kuwayama investigated ways of breaking them down into banal constituent parts. He regarded his works as Minimalist because "ideas, thoughts, philosophy, reasons, meanings, even the humanity of the artist do not enter into my work at all. There is only the art itself. That is all." Kuwayama had attracted attention in the mid-sixties with surface kinetic works that consisted of eye-dazzling concentric circles of color. The circles led to semicircular paintings consisting of three individually framed pictures in different colors and different value gradations (ill. p. 262). As a result of the subdivision of the semicircle, emphasized horizontals are set off against the arcs and inhibit the instinctive search for the center of the circle. The three sectors have a meaning only as a whole, but their color differences and framing stand in the way

Agnes Martin: The River, 1965

of their combination into a semicircle. This is therefore an exemplification of Harold Rosenberg's critical definition of Minimal Art as an "attempt to cut art down to the bare bones of its material elements". Since then, Kuwayama has often combined several identical monochrome elements in larger complexes, which command space when they take the form of screens and therefore stand out from the wall. The muted colors, mostly silver-gray or slate, turn these pictures into quiet mandalas.

The study of optical-kinetic phenomena has been conducted systematically and over long periods only by very few artists in the United States. William C. Seitz collected them in 1965 in the New York exhibition "The Responsive

Edda Renouf: This I, 1973

Eye". The show perhaps had the opposite effect to that envisaged. In any case representatives of Post-painterly Abstraction — Frank Stella, Alexander Liberman, Ellsworth Kelly and others — never went beyond a few optical-kinetic ventures. Only once was a group formed: the "Anonyma Group" founded in Cleveland in 1960 by Ernst Benkert, Francis Hewitt and Edwin Mieczkowski.

Among the painters who are interested in optical and perceptual phenomena Richard Anuszkiewicz has taken a particularly consistent line. After 1960 he presented centered compositions in a square, in which surface kinetic effects are obtained by apparent perspectival expansion or compression of the standard elements. In his serial work, particularly the structural permutations of square fields, Anuszkiewicz proves himself to be a true exponent of the "ars accurata" in which a mathematical system of standardized structures is made visible (ill. p. 261).

Will Insley has made progressive changes to diagonal ray patterns in grid systems. The application of a progression principle within the grid has produced ground plans, isometric representations, projections and cross-sections of imaginary stages and monumental buildings — visions and plans of another world. Fred Sandback, by contrast, constructs his spatial drawings in real, given spaces: stretched colored cords that use the techniques of perspective to describe imaginary cubic or prismatic bodies. Many of these apparent volumes thus isolated from surrounding space are visual paradoxes, since the individual parts belong to different projection systems. Sandback's drawings reveal connections with the "Structural Constellations" of Josef Albers. The drawings of Dorothea Rockburne also have a certain kinship with them, though they are based on numerical series and proportions. The "drawings that make themselves" lead to interesting results: a geometric design is traced through carbon paper, which is then turned over and fixed beside the tracing. The same drawing thus appears mirrored, positive and negative. It is difficult to decide, in this visualization of a process, whether the differences or similarities, transformation or identity, are more important. The conceptual component outweighs the visual, the relationship of cause and effect is more interesting than the morphological evidence.

Serial working methods, the systematic development of specific ideas, are today typical of the work of many artists. Numerical series or other ordering systems often replace the use of geometric figures. In any combinatorial procedure there are two factors involved: simple elements on the one hand, and the rules by which they are combined, varied or permuted on the other. This system of elements and rules, parameters and relations, can reveal variety in uniformity or the endlessness of the possibilities in a given range. Serial work, however, does not aim at a "content", at a special meaning, but only at what it, in fact, is: a simple order. Mel Bochner has pointed out: "For some artists order itself is the work of art. Others manipulate order on different levels, creating both conceptual and perceptual logic."

Jennifer Bartlett first inserted numbers in a regular line grid. She later replaced them by dots of color, so that the number system was turned into a color-shape system. The grouping of the color dots over the grid can only be changed or extended in accordance with a numerical

James Bishop: Central, 1972

principle. The supports are factory-made white-enameled steel sheets to which the square grid is applied by a silk-screen process, creating 2304 miniature compartments. The dots placed in the compartments are made permanent by firing. A complete work consists of a number of such unit sheets embodying a related progression or sequence (ill. p. 276). The colored dots are ordered in characteristic figures according to the chosen "rules of the game". Most of the artists whose three-dimensional work was shown in the exhibition "Primary Structures" in the Jewish Museum in New York in 1966 base their approach on systems of this kind.

This applies particularly to Carl Andre, who employs pre-fabricated standard elements — wooden beams, concrete blocks, square aluminum, copper or steel plates — as modules for his works, adopting an orthogonal order based on an arithmetical principle. His "Floor Sculptures" mostly have a specific relation to the space in which they are placed (ill. p. 280). Much the same applies to Dan Flavin. His basic element, the standardized fluorescent tube, is employed in additive or progressive series. The module of the white or colored strip of light changes the space, clarifying or dimming its limits by its radiation (ill. p. 279). Tony Smith also bases his simple stereometric bodies on modular principles.

The serial arrangement of simple stereometric bodies is also a dominant principle in Don Judd's work. Identical cubic units may be placed at regular intervals or at pro-

275

portionally increasing distances, or else the volumes may increase at the same rate as the intervals are reduced, so that progression and degression take place in equal steps. In more recent works Don Judd often uses hollow, boxlike cubic bodies of colored anodized aluminum that are assembled in rows or groups (ill. p. 277).

Don Judd, an art critic of long standing, has repeatedly emphasized his distance from purely conceptual art. He is interested, he says, in space and in what defines space, in what is visible. "A shape, a volume, a color, a surface is something itself. It shouldn't be concealed as part of a fairly different whole. The shapes and materials shouldn't be altered by their context." In other words, Judd insists, perhaps more than his colleagues, on the autonomy of sculpture. He understands it as a whole with its built-in function. "The thing as a whole, its quality as a whole, is what is interesting."

Sol LeWitt starts out from an open cubic frame in his three-dimensional structures. A multiple of its ground area forms a square grid. The cubic unit is built up on this in the plane and in the vertical direction in accordance with a predetermined numerical system (ill. p. 261). The system permits exhaustive treatment of the possibilities of the three-dimensional square in the square. The situation becomes more complex when a closed cube is used in addition to the open one. A square is likewise used as a module in most of LeWitt's murals. Various linear divisions of the square surface produce a number of basic types which are combined on a predetermined principle. Exactly defined line systems lie one above the other in col-ored ink drawings, so that dense structures result, appearing optically irregular in spite of the logical character of the principle. In their construction the colored pen drawings of John Pearson are similar. Here the direction of a single line or hatching in the square compartment of a grid is progressively diverted, in steps of ten degrees and on a mathematically calculated basis, from the horizontal to the vertical.

In systematic work of this kind the concept is, as Sol LeWitt says, the most important consideration. If an artist practices a conceptual form of art, his plan and all his decisions must be made in advance, so that execution becomes almost automatic. The idea is then the machine that produces the work. Structures that are developed logically to predetermined plans are, if accessible to the perceptive faculties, very near to constructive work. Their form, however, is of little importance as far as the idea is concerned. Ideas can also be conveyed through numbers, photographs, words or in many other ways, as LeWitt points out. This is true of all branches of conceptual art, including its non-retinal forms. Discussing elementary and complex systems in the work of artists such as Sol LeWitt, Walter de Maria and Carl Andre, Nicolas Calas says: "Elaboration of systems for aesthetic purposes leads, oddly enough, to the repudiation of the qualitative aspect of the object. Instead of the work being viewed as an icon, it becomes the exposition of a system. Andre's, LeWitt's and De Maria's predilection for bygone systems, such as the Pythagorean, probably stems from a need to challenge the present by seeking refuge in the order of an irrevocable past."

The exponents of conceptual art often make use of non-pictorial techniques to document the facts, events and processes resulting from their ideas. One of the possibilities is statistical or tabular presentation, the clarity of which is based on ordering principles such as horizontal and vertical columns or coordinate systems. One of the forms used is the diagram, which enables statistical information to be given perhaps less accurately but more memorably than in a table. The diagram serves for the visualization of the functional interdependence of two or more values, for instance a vector in mathematics.

The pluralism of stylistic trends in the past quarter century and the great differences in artists' fields of activity make it difficult to define one school as a reaction to another within a limited period. Conceptual art has been accused of a lack of artistry, since ideas and plans are more important in it than realizations, which are often no more than pieces of evidence, visual or verbal documentation of the real work, which is the idea. If the retinal appeal of conceptual art is slight or entirely absent, the question arises of whether it must not prompt a trend in exactly the opposite direction. The downright visual character of photographic or "radical" realism would thus be an alternative, regardless of the motivations behind such approaches to visible reality. Since many conceptual artists deprecate the autonomy of the individual work of art in their theoretical statements, another form of opposition is also conceivable: an art that leaves plenty of scope for individual skill in its making but raises no morphological problems, i.e. which occupies itself neither with the interpretation of elements of visible reality nor with investigations of form or surface structures in the same sense

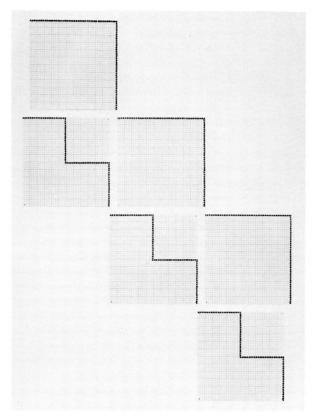

Jennifer Bartlett: Two Step, 1974

Don Judd: Untitled, 1982

as constructive art. This type of painting in fact exists both in America and in Europe.

The representatives of this "new painting" — either celebrated as a return to true painting or criticized as a relapse into it — come from many camps and do not see themselves as a homogeneous group. A common attribute of such painting is a low level of visual appeal, nothing seems to "happen" in the picture. The work, frequently monotonous, is marked by reserve; Lucy R. Lippard coined the term "Silent Art" as early as 1965. The view that the work means no more than what it is in its material reality — a piece of canvas soaked or covered with paint — originates in Minimal Art and Primary Structures. But the fact that there is a rational concept behind this painting, the sober investigation of the painter's media, brings it near to conceptual art. The starting point is again an idea. The work is to be understood as a visible representation of this idea, or else as an objective test of its validity.

As rational as the grounds of such "planned painting" are, in effect it is irrational. Klaus Honnef united several of its exponents in an exhibition titled "Geplante Malerei" (Planned Painting) in Münster in 1974. "The appearance that is achieved by means of planning usually seems irrational or appeals quite simply to receptive faculties that are nourished less from intellectual than from emotional sources. What it inspires is primarily feelings." The visually accessible facts escape conceptual analysis: hardly any significant formal elements such as pictorial form, division of the surface, structures, no clearly definable colors or color contrasts. Where color plays a prominent part, there are close ties to monochrome painting, and where interactions of colors are explored, to Josef Albers. The painterly geometry developed by artists such as

Richard Diebenkorn or Jack Tworkov can be mentioned as an example. Connections with Minimal Art and beyond that with Mondrian can be detected when divisions of the picture area are important. Where structures are placed on the ground or ground textures studied or manipulated, a certain kinship with serial art can be recorded. The exponents of this "new painting" come from various quarters, even from Tachisme and Action Painting, and their development can hardly be reduced to a common denominator.

One of the senior artists of this school is Agnes Martin, from 1960 onward a leading representative of geometric, then kinetic, then systemic, then minimalist art. It is only since the emergence of this silent painting that she has attracted attention as one of its initiators with her symmetrical, uneventful drawings and paintings (ill. p. 274). Brice Marden — of whose pictures it has been said that they offer a lot to look at but very little to talk about — also made his debut in Minimal Art circles. Yet, the subdued multilayer tones of his pictures, originally monochrome, later divided horizontally or vertically into two or three panels of muted color, differ fundamentally from the flat, glowing colors of an Ellsworth Kelly. Robert Ryman often uses an elementary geometric framework, particularly when he combines several panels in a closed series. His handling of his material, however, has a strong element of craftsmanship. He says himself that, while the design is important, the execution has to do mainly with visual reactions and is therefore difficult to describe. This statement is true of the work of most other representatives of this new painting, such as Edda Renouf, whose uneventful compositions are based on the manipulation of the orthogonal system of linen cloth (ill. p. 274).

A characteristic of this school is the preference for tex-

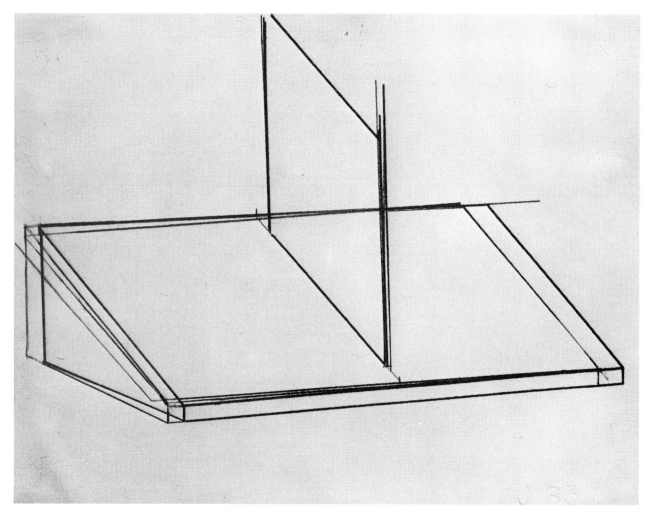

Don Judd: Untitled drawing, 1963

tured, soft, often dull tones both in the near-white range and in the darker range approaching a colored black. The dark, sonorous pictures of James Juszczyk, divided into vertical bands in simple numerical proportions, are an example of this color treatment. A second common feature is the pronounced manual and painterly finish, which is specially conspicuous in Robert Ryman, Brice Marden and Jake Berthot. The stressing of the material nature of the painting is often combined with the third common feature, the gesture. Although some of the artists come from Abstract Expressionism or Action Painting, the gestural element is here of a quite different nature.

Gesture and geometry are also blended in the square pictures of James Bishop. After 1960, following in the wake of the Action Painters, he had covered the picture surface with vigorous, colorful brush-strokes. From 1962 onward an increasingly geometric order led to a rectangular, architectural design. On the bottom edge of the picture, or else at the side, usually in the upper half, there is a beam-like linear construction reminiscent of wooden framing. In later works the square picture is divided horizontally into two halves, and the upper rectangle is then divided

again down the middle. In the two squares thus produced a regular cross is inscribed in a frame (ill. p. 275). This system of division only serves to carry the colors. They are applied as a thin transparent coat on the canvas, which is laid on the floor for the purpose: placed on the edge of the zone to be colored, the paint flows regularly over the surface when the canvas is tipped up. By changing the gradient of tipping, the flow can be accelerated or slowed down and stopped when the desired boundary is reached. The color is thus spread over the planned sections of the picture in all four directions. The surface comes to life because the different amounts of paint used and its acceleration or deceleration produce differences in its adhesion to the ground. The superimposition of several coats heightens the transparency of the color. The real function of the linear framework is to increase the luminescence of the color. The boundary between two color surfaces, differing only slightly, is not an active line and is not even passively marked by the meeting of two autonomous fields of color. Bishop's boundary is an indefinable zone of mutual approximation. In the red-brown pictures this activation of the color is distinctly

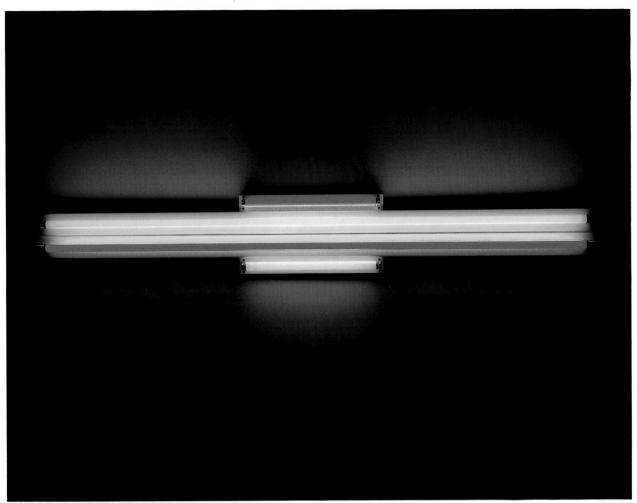

Dan Flavin: Red and Green Alternatives (to Sonja), 1964

evident, in the white pictures, whose coloring consists in a dimming of the pure white in the direction of warmer or cooler shades, it can hardly be discerned. This modulated monochromy brings about a dematerialization of the picture. The color surface becomes a color space, the formal framework makes the color even more impalpable. The dialectic of gesture and geometry is accompanied in Bishop's work by a dialectic of picture materiality, or limitation of the support on the one hand and impalpability or boundlessness of the color on the other.

This new painting — Bishop is only one of its exponents — is as far removed from the self-expressive gesture as it is from the objectivation of geometric laws. But it owes something to both of them. It is perhaps not by accident that Bishop busies his mind with the fundamental concepts of Heinrich Wölfflin — the linear and the painterly, surface and depth, the closed and the open form, multiplicity and singularity, vagueness and clarity.

Concluding his essay in Henry Geldzahler's survey "New York Painting and Sculpture 1940–1970" the art critic Clement Greenberg says:

"As it looks to me, Newman, Rothko, and Still have swung the self-criticism of Modernist painting in a new direction by dint simply of continuing it far enough in its original one. The question now asked in their art is no longer what constitutes art, or the art of painting, as such, but what constitutes good art as such. What is the ultimate source of value or quality in art? And the worked-out answer appears to be: not skill, training, or anything else having to do with execution or performance, but conception alone. Culture or taste may be a necessary condition of conception, but the latter is alone decisive. Conception can be called invention, inspiration, or even intuition (which last is what it was called by Croce, who did anticipate theoretically what practice has just now discovered and confirmed for itself). On the other hand, it is true that skill used to be a vessel of inspiration and do some of the work of conception, but that was when the best pictorial art was, by and large, the most naturalistic. Skill, dexterity, is now revealed as no longer capable of generating quality because it has become too generalized, too accessible, and by the same token too patterned."

279

Carl Andre: Henge (Meditation on the year 1960), 1960

Has Constructive Art a Future?

Thoughts and Perspectives

If we accept a wide definition of constructive art embracing all tendencies in which geometric ordering principles are applied to surfaces and to space, we can now look back on nearly seventy years of it. Works of a constructive character are still being produced, exhibited and diffused all over the globe. What are the prospects for an artistic trend that has lasted as long as this? We can best answer this question by taking a look at the history of art. It reveals to us that there have been innovators at all times, people who were not satisfied with established values, who rejected the tradition of their fathers and in an aggressive spirit of opposition explored and demonstrated the new. Usually overlooked, unrecognized or even cried down, these avant-garde artists have prepared the path for later developments. As a vanguard of the future they have appealed primarily to the younger generation of their day. Something that first appeared hesitantly from the underground, then boldly stepped out into the open, was taken up by a growing band of followers and developed into a fully-fledged style. Historically considered, the new always emerges as a disturbing and even shocking factor flung into the smooth flow of tradition, is then systematically consolidated by its supporters, thereby loses its first aura of sensation and ends by being generally accepted. The adoption of the new has always been a process of establishing a new tradition, with new criteria and new rules. Even in ages when it was not the custom for the champions of the new style to formulate their opinions in manifestos — treatises by artists have been known only since the fifteenth century — new and often exact or even rigorous rules of artistic practice were set up. Rules, however, are always the beginning of academicism in the sense that the new, having been codified, can henceforth be taught and learned. There can be no doubt that today, beside the tradition of authentic constructive art, there is also a worldwide academicism of constructive art.

The foundations of a constructive academicism were laid early by the theoretical writings in which some of the pioneers — such as Malevich, Mondrian and Van Doesburg — attempted to clarify and explain their ideas. Since on the surface at least they were only exploring basic facts of visual design — laws of color and shape, surface, volumetric and spatial relationships — the theories of constructive art were soon being turned into art doctrines and teaching systems. Teaching was often combined with the practice of art, as for instance by Malevich, Klee, Kandinsky, Moholy-Nagy and Albers. But in all the authentic art theories, color and design doctrines, the essential content did not consist in material considerations, so that it could have been divided up into easily grasped precepts. It was concerned instead with mental assumptions leading up to the design approach, it depended and still depends on the visionary power to recognize the possibilities and effects of the new way of seeing, a new kind of pictorial creative thinking in Klee's sense. The artist who merely adheres to rules and recipes derived from constructive concepts will only succeed in producing paraphrases and variations on discoveries others have already made. Constructive academicism is consequently as sterile as any other academicism. Where the creative potency is lacking for an independent advance along the lines adumbrated by earlier workers, for original thought and the development of individual and perhaps different productions out of the common heritage, important impulses can hardly be expected. On the other hand, the initiators of the various phases of constructive art have left so many problems unsolved that there is still plenty of scope for the little master.

Wherever a school or a style tends to become petrified into academicism in Western art, an opposition usually springs up to propose new objectives and encourage the use of new media. In the course of gradual or eruptive substitution processes the new trend then ousts the old, founding a new tradition and again being calcified into academicism. The path from Michelangelo to Roman mannerism, or the school of Leonardo da Vinci in Milan, are striking cases in point. In historical styles, where developments were fairly clearly channeled, a substitution process of this kind usually meant a sweeping change of style. But since the appearance of a simultaneous plurality of styles, which has become ever more complex since its inception about the middle of the nineteenth century, these processes have become much more difficult to follow.

Constructive art has been confronted in several phases of its development by opposing trends and antithetical movements. At the time when Mondrian was producing his purest, most economical horizontal-vertical Neo-Plastic compositions, Surrealism was born, antiformal and overflowing with objective content. Around 1930, when Surrealism commanded the scene with its cult of the unconscious and the fantastic, a neo-constructive reaction produced the "Cercle et Carré" and "Abstraction-Création" groups. They were pushed out on to the periphery by the return to tradition in the prewar and war years. When European countries were looking for a new identity after 1945, a constructive art of simple formal patterns — deriving from Concrete Art in Switzerland — appeared alongside rational tendencies in architecture as a visible sign of the hope for a new order, a rational and human lifestyle. A few years later there was a counter-movement against a formal discipline which was felt to be a constraint on personal freedom. In Tachisme, Abstract Expressionism and Action Painting the emotional was played off against the rational, an uninhibited subjectivism against objectivation and order. When this antiformal art threatened to run down around 1960, the alternatives that presented themselves were the new objectivity and figuration of Nouveau Réalisme and Pop Art, and geometric constructive art, both in its classical form and in the branches concerned with perceptual and dynamic phenomena, viz Op Art and kinetics. In the meantime still other trends have branched off: Structurist, serial, systematic investigations concerned with information theory, cybernetic aesthetics and computer applications, and an antiformalist movement that reduces the relations of colors and shapes, volumes and space to the elements of primary structures. An interest in subtle interactions of color at the expense of formal principles has led to a new painterly sensibility. In its shaping of landscapes Land Art has had recourse to ancient geometrical figures, straight parallels and undulating lines, the pentagram, concentric circles and spirals. Even where the work itself has lost its autonomy in conceptual art and has become only the embodiment of an idea, geometric orders and mathematical laws are utilized, series or progressions such as that of Fibonacci (Leonardo of Pisa). It would be impossible to accumulate primary experience of our environment without arithmetic and geometry.

A glance back into the sixties and seventies shows at what times and places constructive thought and work received new impulses and gave them back to the art of the day. Many pioneers were still active at that time, as some of them are even today. This meant that constructive art was able to react with authentic responses to whatever was going on in the art world. It also meant that a younger generation had the opportunity to measure themselves against or even to challenge the work of the founding fathers. On the other hand, younger constructive artists had to be ready to have their productions judged by the standards of the masters. This applied as much to the question of innovation as to the importance of central art problems and their conscientious solution.

Looking back over the last twenty-five years, however, we also see that in the sixties collectors, galleries, museums and publicists developed a new and lively interest in the history of constructive art and in particular in its impressive early achievements. The "unorthodox" contributions likewise did a great deal to keep constructive concepts alive. Prominent among them was American Minimal Art. Some of its exponents have, it is true, denied any link with the constructive tradition, but in practice, by exploring elementary laws of form and color, they have helped perpetuate constructive thinking.

Parallel to this practice of minimalist art went a discussion of goals and problems among the artists themselves, and of the pros and cons in art criticism. Since primary structures were at issue, the discussion circled around fundamental form, but the question of what art really is also presented itself. It was rightly assumed that art, having been liberated from its contents, motifs, ideologies and history, was now left naked. It was because of this situation that the question could be asked: what is art in reality, when reduced to its basic principle, to its mere skeleton? If structuralist considerations derived from linguistics entered this discussion about the essence of art, that was not just a passing fad. Counsel was sought in the matter of "Sprache und Bedeutung" (Language and Meaning) in the writings of the philosopher Ludwig Wittgenstein. In 1981 Jack Burnham's "Structure of Art" appeared in New York. It proposed a new method of art interpretation based on the structuralist method as developed by Claude Lévi-Strauss. The representatives of Minimal Art and Concept Art who were interested in structural questions were stimulated in their thinking — and writing! — by this analytical structural approach.

This theorizing about basic problems of form and of art itself revealed the affinities of the minimalist, conceptual and constructive approaches. There was no deep division between concepts and ideas on the one hand and practical art on the other. A reading of the numerous, occasionally "Byzantine" texts of artists, such as those of Sol LeWitt, shows how central a role is played there by ideas and how little importance attaches to practice, to the actual making of the work. One is reminded here of the thinking of Mondrian, who expressed the idea that Neo-Plastic art would lead one day to there being no need for art in the normal, traditional sense.

The survival of constructive art cannot be judged merely by the continued production of works of a constructive character. If constructive work is to be more than the routine use of ready-made methods and programs, it must constantly adapt to new situations and developments. It must supply, from its own point of view, impulses, contributions and standards for the solution of the problems that arise.

Minimal Art has abandoned thinking in terms of references. The visible work of art — a systematic series of identical square metal sheets on a rectangular base, the stacking of identical wooden beams by Carl Andre (ill. p. 280), a grid structure built up on a cubic unit by Sol LeWitt (ill. p. 261), or a horizontal or vertical multiplication of identical hollow bodies by Don Judd (ill. p. 277) — no longer refers to any "otherness", nor is it the representation of an idea by artistic means as in the Neo-Plastic Mondrian or the Suprematist Malevich.

In his "Sentences on Conceptual Art" Sol LeWitt makes the following statements: "The concept and idea are different. The former implies a general direction while the latter are the components. Ideas implement the concept. Ideas alone can be works of art; they are in a chain of development that may eventually find some form. All ideas need not be made physical. Since no form is intrinsically superior to another, the artist may use any form ... Successful art changes our understanding of conventions by altering our perceptions. Perception of ideas leads to new ideas."

The elementary stereometric bodies of Minimal Art have led to a new understanding of the space in which such bodies are located. The artist's interest has been diverted from the object to the space in which it is to find its place. This diversion of interest from the thing to the situation has led to the "installation", the creation of special (artificial) space conditions or the transformation of existing space situations. The traditional "exhibition" of works of art as "finished products" has been joined more and

Max Bill: Pavilion Sculpture, Zurich, Bahnhofstrasse, 1983

more often by installations, many of them conceived only for a limited time. These break with the conventional ways of displaying art, whether in the gallery, museum or private house. The "Proun rooms" of El Lissitzky may be regarded as the forerunners of such spatial installations (ill. p. 101). Even in his day it was less the objects used that attracted attention than the spatial effect they produced.

One step beyond these installations lie the interventions of constructive or conceptual artists in the landscape, often on a very large scale. This Land Art usually chooses situations far from civilization, on lonely coasts for instance, or in deserts. The large-scale interventions often take the form of very simple geometry: straight lines marked by stones, stones in rows, circles or spirals, or straight trenches. Art thus returns to the early uses of geometry, to the prehistoric stone deployments of Carnac or Stonehenge. But unlike this prehistoric "Land Art", the works of Richard Long, Robert Smithson, Michael Heizer or Walter de Maria have no religious, astronomical or calendrical function. They are exactly what they are, and only what they are—a dead straight line in the desert, a stone spiral on a beach, a circle filled with fragments of local stone or branches from nearby woods.

The large scale of installations, stone arrangements and earthworks in the landscape has spread to more traditional forms of sculpture. In the last few years exhibitions of sculpture have been staged in extensive parks and in the open landscape in many places in Europe and America. The permanent "sculpture park" has become a desideratum of the cultural authorities of many cities. Since figurative sculpture is unsuitable for extreme monumentalization because of its anthropomorphic character, it is rather constructive volumes and spatial concepts—of wood, stone, or often of steel—that can best fulfill the requirements for the temporary or permanent plastic articulation of open spaces.

Sculpture exhibitions of this kind have once more attracted attention to constructive ideas. When spaces in cities have been placed at the disposal of artists, and when the idea of art in public places has been approached with boldness and liberality, the resulting experience has shown what imposing dimensions are necessary if a work is to hold its own in sometimes chaotic surroundings or in the midst of throbbing traffic. The huge, elementary steel sheet assemblies of Richard Serra, however, are quite capable of overcoming these difficulties.

The concept artist Bernar Venet is also successful when he translates the idea of an acute angle of a fixed number of degrees—relative to the 360 degrees of a full circle— into a mighty steel bar structure over a highway or a big building, or when he places an exactly calculated segment of a circle in the form of a curved steel beam on a piece of grass amidst a Berlin cityscape (ill. p. 287).

Max Bill has also proven with his "Pavilion Sculpture" in Zurich, an architectural structure of identical vertical and horizontal granite slabs (ill. p. 283), that monumental plastic artefacts can hold their own in confined city streets and squares without disrupting the dimensional framework of their setting. Bill has pointed out again and again that the work of art is "an object of mental use". But he has deliberately made this spatial sculpture of practical use to citizens, who can sit on the horizontal slabs, while actions and interactions are possible between the standing columns.

Works of this kind bear witness to the vitality and virility of constructive thought. They carry the chamber-music standards of older constructive art, embodied in the framed picture and the pedestaled sculpture, out into more spacious dimensions. The work done in this field in the last few year opens up new possibilities for Constructivists.

Minimalist works such as Sol LeWitt's "Cube" speak the same language, even if its purpose is not really that of an urban or rural monumental sculpture (ill. p. 285). The point made here is rather that of a confrontation of nature and art, of organic growth and rational concept, reduced to its strictest minimum. Sol LeWitt hardly thought of the ancient idea of the "sacred grove" as a place of meditation or of the apocalyptic vision of the "heavenly Jerusalem" in the shape of an immense cube (Revelation XXI, 16).

Speaking of the cube in 1966, Sol LeWitt said: "The most interesting characteristic of the cube is that it is relatively uninteresting. Compared to any other three-dimensional form, the cube lacks any aggressive force, implies no motion, and is least emotive. Therefore it is the best form to use as a basic unit for any more elaborate function, the grammatical device from which the work may proceed. Because it is standard and universally recognized, no intention is required of the viewer. It is immediately understood that the cube represents the cube, a geometric figure that is uncontestably itself. The use of the cube obviates the necessity of inventing another form . . ."

It is not only exponents of constructive art proper or of Minimal Art who continue to apply their creativity to constructive and geometric compositions. Artists in many countries and in differing stylistic contexts, often members of regional groups, come up with works based on constructive principles which may well be answers to other visual problems. To cite one example, the conceptual artist Rune Mields, who lives in Cologne, has taken up the subject of the "magic square", derived from old Chinese tradition, in its minimal form, the "lo-shu", and has developed from it square panels of nine fields with strict linear vertical and horizontal divisions.

Other phenomena intrigue the German sculptor Ulrich Rückriem. He splits blocks of dolomite horizontally and vertically in accordance with the inherent laws of the material and produces regular cubic fragments which he then fits together again in their original pattern. Drill holes and divisions remain visible in the marble-like bluish-gray stone as traces of human intervention: this is in fact an elementary confrontation of nature and art (ill. p. 289).

Many artists of the "classical" constructive school and of its continuation in kinetics have arrived at new solutions to their problems that sometimes spring from unexpected lines of thinking. François Morellet, always good for innovative conceptual and formal discoveries, has worked with the combination of painted lines and line-like ramifications. Here again art and nature are linked, but so are organic and constructed elements (ill. p. 291). Other recent works by Morellet have the character of spatial installations, for instance the corner sculptures, con-

Sol LeWitt: Cube, 1984, temporary exhibition in Merian Park, Basel

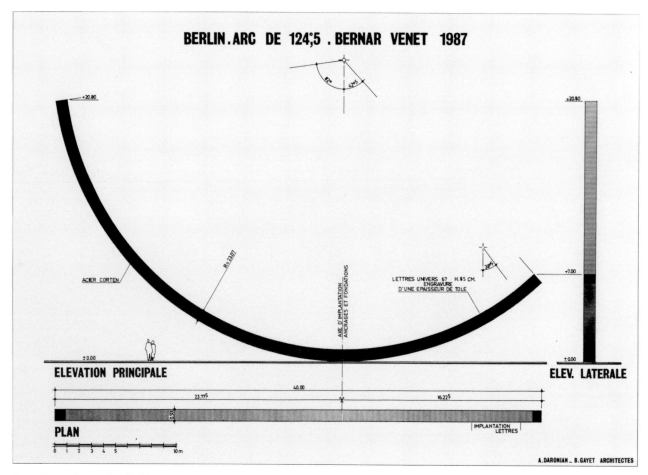

Bernar Venet: Arch of 124.5°, 1987, working drawing

structed with the simplest form media, which take up the idea of Tatlin's "counter-reliefs" (ill. p. 288).

Many young artists, particularly in Germany, the Netherlands and Switzerland, have turned their attention to the numerical relationships of lines, areas and bodies. Sometimes an irregularity is inserted in a regular system as a disturbing factor, which upsets the process of interpretation. Diet Sayler of Nuremberg has used subtle modifications of the direction of lines or the angles they form: "the line as a visible change, as a sensitive energy and transformability potential, as the cancellation of the contradiction between reason and feeling" (ill. p. 226).

Jean Pfaff of Basel has studied the visualization of calendrical problems on the basis of mathematics and color theory. This has led him via monochrome pictures to spatial installations, for which he employs constructive methods. The consideration that the things that happen to regular surfaces when foreshortened by perspective might be taken for truth has led in Pfaff's researches to dynamic form changes of static surfaces and to the transformation of the two-dimensional into an — imaginary — tridimensionality (ill. p. 291).

Florin Granwehr of Zurich also has to do with the three-dimensional, or more precisely with spatial structures. Unlike Sol Lewitt in his grids based on the cube, he devel-

ops structures of considerable mathematical complexity. In two- and three-dimensional investigations that he has pursued systematically for years, Granwehr arrived at seemingly simple but in reality highly complex stereometric structures formed by interpenetrating lines. He calls them "Raumwandler" or "Kreiswandler" ("Space Transformers" or "Circle Transformers"). Some of them have been carried out for public authorities in the form of monumental sculptures constructed of steel beams of square section (ill. p. 292).

There are also young artists, especially in Germany and the Netherlands, who are working with the computer. Manfred Mohr has been doing this since 1970, but unlike other protagonists of programmed art he succeeds in applying his "algorithmic growth programs for cubes" in such a way that black-and-white compositions of great effect and individuality result (ill. p. 290).

In the early eighties constructive art was being pushed into the background by opposing stylistic trends, as it had been from time to time in the preceding decades. A new Expressionism, sometimes abstract but mostly figurative, now swept over the European and American art scenes. In Germany its exponents were known as the "neuen Wilden", and it was in fact seen as a parallel to Fauvism. This new outbreak of a subjective action paint-

Bernar Venet: Arch of 124.5°, 1987, Urania Square Berlin

ing was soon being questioned by a quite different trend: a cool, almost anonymous, often simplistic or even consciously banal or ironic geometry which very quickly suffused through the art world. The strips, ribbons, angles, combs and circles, often in dull, broken colors, seemed surprisingly new. The ribbon structures of a few German and American painters, but above all the strips and environments of Daniel Buren, may have been their models. Some of these "Neo-Geo" painters certainly belong to their circle, for instance the Swiss Olivier Mosset in New York or Niele Toroni, who lives in Paris. The Genevese John Armleder comes from the Fluxus movement, Helmut M. Federle, now living in Vienna, from free action painting. Yet, this new geometry has hardly anything in common with constructive trends or with Minimal Art.

Constructive art can be regarded as the expression of a "new man", as in El Lissitzky's vision; as an attempt to confront outer chaos with an order consisting of pure elements and dynamic or balanced relationships, as the mastering of the inscrutable and incomprehensible in life with concepts that are clear, tangible, understandable. This constructive development of simple formal orders, the execution of logical steps and their recording in visual form would accordingly be a means of holding one's own in the universe. The desire for geometric order can be traced back to man's beginnings, to prehistoric rock paintings that restrict themselves to full or dotted straight lines, to rectangular and circular frame systems. These are the first of the ever renewed attempts to pin down the mystery, unfathomability and menace of the world by elementary pictorial means. Something of all this lives on in the constructive art of our day. It tends to range beyond the formal and aesthetic and to seek signposts and anchorages in science, philosophy and even religion. Both Mondrian and Malevich stated as much from the first and saw their works not as end products but as objects of contemplation, as stepping-stones to something beyond. Max Bill means much the same when he says in connection with mathematical thinking in art that working with rational elements can lead to consequences which defy all explanation. And this was not contradicted by Richard Paul Lohse when he ended an open discussion of the phases of development of his modular and serial orders with the remark that "Only open secrets are effective."

In the programmatic text on Neo-Plasticism written by Piet Mondrian in 1917 for the first number of the magazine "de stijl" we read: "The truly modern artist feels abstraction in a sense of beauty, he is aware that the feeling for beauty is cosmic and general. From this conscious

François Morellet: A square (mirror), 2 angles of 45° with a right angle (band iron) and forming an angle of 67.5° with the floor, 1983

realization we are led to Plasticism, in which man clings only to what is general. Neo-Plasticism therefore cannot take the form of a natural or concrete representation. It cannot boast of things that pick out the particular, for instance natural forms and colors. Instead it must find expression in the abstraction of all form and color, in other words, in the straight line and the exactly determined primary color... Neo-Plasticism consequently means an exactly represented aesthetic relationship. In painting, the artist of today constructs it as a consequence of all the art of the past—and that precisely in painting, since this is the art that is least tied to accident. The whole of modern life can, by a deepening process, be purely mirrored in painting."

Friedrich Vordemberge-Gildewart, one of the founders of constructive art in Germany and a member of the de Stijl group, noted in 1953: "The creative will of the artist expresses itself in order and in the relationship of the individual elements to each other. Even before the Middle Ages use was made of so-called ordering lines based mostly on the Golden Section. These ordering and proportion lines, however, are only auxiliaries whose employ-

ment is in itself no guarantee that a work of art will automatically result. Instead these auxiliaries give us the assurance of an orderly procedure. Whatever mathematical laws are used, the creative element is the essential. Beauty cannot be constructed. Yet, the attempt is made again and again to find new laws of harmony from the experience of the Pythagorean-Platonic tradition, for which the 'Modulor' of Le Corbusier may serve as an example."

Summing up his fight for constructive art Michel Seuphor once said:

"There is no more specifically human task than to build. Everything that is constructed, from the atom to the flower, from the Chinese ideogram to the cathedral, from the prehistoric tool to a Mozart quartet. To be sure, the passive acquiescence in the established order calls forth the reaction of man's vital forces that seek a beyond that is ever new. But there is no more urgent battle today than the about-face needed to push back the disintegration that is everywhere gaining ground. There will always be lies to demolish, diseases to cure by cutting into the living flesh, faults to denounce, hatreds to overcome in our-

Ulrich Rückriem: Dolomite from Anröcht, multicomponent composition, 1986

selves. There will always be the destructive spirit to destroy in ourselves. But it is still by constructing that man destroys best and most surely. This was what the cubist painters did: by building the painting, in spite of the subject, they destroyed the latter and gave pure form the possibility of coming into being. Mondrian at the end of his life said that not enough attention is given, in the realm of art, to the idea of destruction. We know how he meant this. It was a question, for him, of destroying all the traditional images and with them all romanticism, all sentimentality, all tragic sentiment, in order at last to build the bright society and the painting without shadow. "Now, to edify man is to place him out of reach of the assaults of the beast, it is to conceive him otherwise than violent and gregarious, it is to build humanism. Man has always built, against wind and tide, against human and natural catastrophies. He will do so today as he did yesterday.To construct is an ineradicable function of man's deep nature. The word construct expresses his whole manly vocation in the face of nature. Man on the one hand; nature on the other. The notion of constructing is the sign both of the link and the opposition: the bridge and the dam. To construct is always to construct tomorrow, slowly, untiringly, day after day, stone after stone". The pioneers of constructive art and their more independent successors have not thought of themselves as makers of art but as the draftsmen of a new and better global and social order commensurate with our own powers. It is in the most significant achievements of constructive art that the model character is most evident. The observer who mistakes this optimistic or even Utopian trait for a complacent satisfaction with formally and chromatically successful art exercises is likely to accuse constructive artists of an aesthetic and formalistic withdrawal from the real and burning problems of our times. Such a reproach, however, can only be fairly leveled at imitators. The prospects of constructive art are best where it remains what it has really always been throughout its changing history: an instrument of communication directed toward the extension of human awareness.

Like all true art, constructive art can be both: an "organon", which in the Aristotelian sense is a logical tool for the perception of truth, and — to borrow a phrase from Paul Klee's diary — a "parable of the creation".

Manfred Mohr: P-407CC, 1987

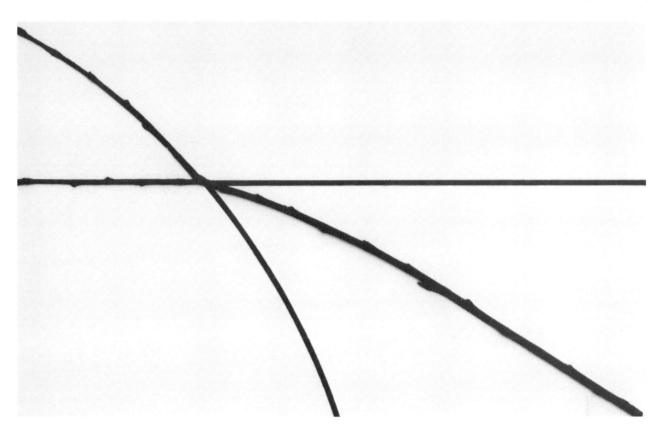

François Morellet: Géométree No. 1, 1983

Jean Pfaff: E.D.2, 1977

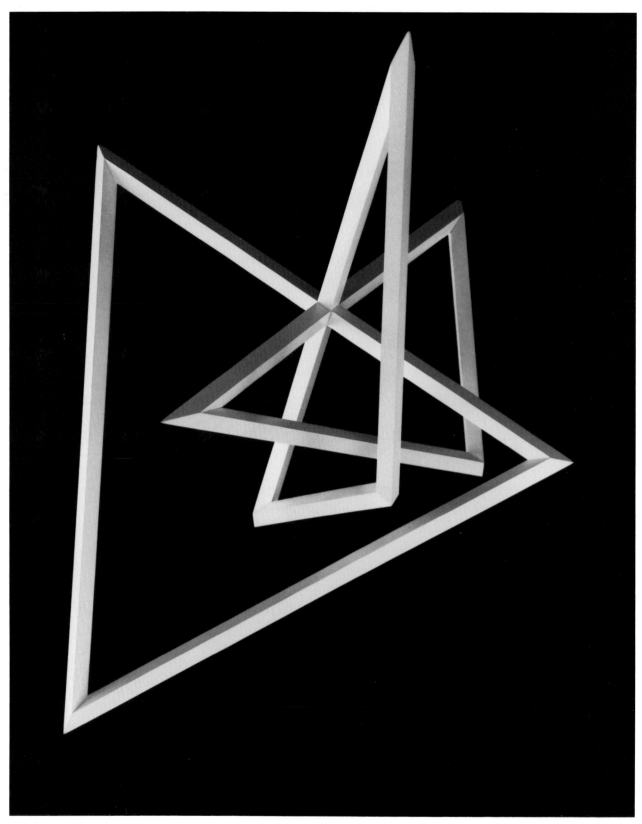

Florin Granwehr: Thing 1: x, 1987

Synoptic Chronology 1907–1970

Arranged by Stefan Paradowski. English version: Karin Rosenberg.

Besides several sourcebooks listed in the bibliography the following publications were consulted:

Magdalena Dabrowski: Contrasts of Form, Geometric Abstract Art, 1910–1980, The Museum of Modern Art, New York 1985.

Willy Rotzler: Constructive Concepts. A History of Constructive Art from Cubism to the Present, Zurich 1977, 1989[2].

Werner Stein: Kulturfahrplan. Die wichtigsten Daten der Kulturgeschichte von Anbeginn bis heute, Berlin 1974[2].

John Willett: The New Sobriety. Art and Politics in the Weimar Period, 1917–1933, London 1978.

Historical Events	Constructive Art
1907 2nd Peace conference in the Hague; constitutes right of neutrality Social unrest in France Offset printing arrives to Europe from the US Maria Montessori opens first house for children	Pablo Picasso paints first painting with cubist components: "Les Demoiselles d'Avignon"
1908 Women get vote in Denmark Austria annexes Bosnia and Herzegowina 73 Russian newspapers and magazines are banned	Pablo Picasso and Georges Braque jointly develop cubism Henri Matisse introduces the term "Cubism" for an image by Georges Braque ("petits cubes")
1909 Disputes in the German centralist party Bakelite (synthetic resin) is produced as one of the first plastic materials	Kasimir Malevich attempts to monumentalize his expressionistic compositions, mainly rural scenes, under the influence of Henri Matisse
1910 Treaty between Germany and Russia: both powers agree to abstain from entering alliances with adversary powers Japan annexes Korea Carnegie-Foundation for peace L. Moss discovers the four blood types	Pablo Picasso achieves a purely geometrical build-up in his paintings (analytical cubism) Robert Delaunay's cubist compositions dissect streetviews into parallel layers Frank Kupka: "pure" painting which lives only through colors and shapes In Amsterdam: constitution of "De Moderne Kunstkring" (including Piet Mondrian) Arthur Dove: "Extractions", presumably the first non-representative paintings in American art
1911 Social unrest in Vienna is brutally quenched Winston Churchill becomes First Lord of the Admiralty Roald Amundsen reaches the south pole for the first time	Frank Kupka from Czechoslovakia paints horizontal-vertical and circular compositions Piet Mondrian in Paris; paints abstractions in series, such as the apple-tree series There is barely a Russian artist who forgoes the opportunity to a sojourn in Paris The paintings of Kasimir Malevich show the influence of some contemporary paintings by Fernand Léger
1912 Renewal of the Triple Alliance between Germany, Austria and Italy Beginning of the Balkan War International Socialist Conference in Basel issues a proclamation against war The luxury liner "Titanic" sinks after colliding with an iceberg First parachuting off an airplane	Pablo Picasso and Georges Braque execute their first paper collages Guillaume Apollinaire introduces the term "Orphism" for the paintings of Robert Delaunay Exhibition of the "Section d'or" in Paris includes most of the cubists The futurists exhibit for the first time in Paris delimiting themselves against the cubists Mikhail Larionov and his companion Natalia Goncharova paint in a "rayonnist" style (overlapping of rays)
1913 President Woodrow Wilson introduces his "New Freedom" program in US internal affairs Under the influence of the UK Tibet declares herself independent from China First broadcasting of music through loudspeakers in the US Niels Bohr develops the theory of the atomic model based on the planetary system	The Russian Vladimir Tatlin creates the first spacial constructions ("Contra-Reliefs") Kasimir Malevich realizes the ideas of suprematism for the first time in his stage decorations for "Victory over the Sun" in St. Petersburg Fernand Léger paints "Color contrasts": three-dimensional elements such as pieces of tubing generate their own dynamic in the picture An ideologically firmly defined group in Russia calls itself "Cubo-Futurists"

Art in General	Publications
Peter Behrens is elected artistic director of AEG in Berlin Constitution of the German Werkbund Alfred Stieglitz develops his gallery at "291", Fifth Avenue in New York into a show-case for avant-garde European art	Oskar Kokoschka: "Mörder, Hoffnung der Frauen", expressionist play Henry van de Velde: "Zum neuen Stil"
	Adolf Loos: "Ornament und Verbrechen" Edward Gordon Craig publishes magazine for stage art "The Mask", until 1929
Wassily Kandinsky and his friends form the "Neue Künstlervereinigung" in Munich Under David W. Griffith Mary Pickford is first movie star	Filippo Tommaso Marinetti's "Manifeste du Futurisme" is published in the Parisian daily "Le Figaro"
Wassily Kandinsky develops "absolute painting", a kind of free painting without reference to the visual world In furniture design the ornamental style of Art Nouveau is replaced by the austere "Neue Sachlichkeit" Igor Stravinsky: ballet "L'Oiseau de Feu"	Umberto Boccioni, Giorgio Severini, Giacomo Balla, and others publish the first manifesto of futurist painting and the "Technical manifesto of futurist painting" Herwarth Walden creates in Berlin the magazine "Der Sturm" (published until 1932)
Wassily Kandinsky and Franz Marc constitute the artists community in Munich, where its first show is seen; the title of the almanac at the same time serves as name for the group: "Der Blaue Reiter" A circle of young artists (Oskar Lüthy and Jean Arp and others) in Switzerland establish the "Moderner Bund" and organize exhibitions in Lucerne featuring Picasso, Matisse, Herbin, and others	Wassily Kandinsky publishes "Über das Geistige in der Kunst" (On the Spiritual in Art)
Herwarth Walden opens the gallery "Der Sturm" in Berlin with an exhibition of the "Blaue Reiter" Wassily Kandinsky paints his first fully abstract "Improvisations" International exhibition of contemporary trends in Cologne, organized by the "Sonderbund westdeutscher Künstler"; has a strong impact on the younger generation	The two painters Albert Gleizes and Jean Metzinger publish the first book on the theory of cubism: "Du Cubisme" Almanac "Der Blaue Reiter" includes the essay "Über die Formfrage" by Wassily Kandinsky Mikhail Larionov: "Manifesto of Rayonnists and Futurists" The manifesto published in Moscow, "A Slap in the Face of Public Taste", is signed a.o. by Vladimir Mayakovsky
Constitution of the Swiss Werkbund In an armory in New York a first exhibition of modern art takes place under the title "Armory Show" Synchromism: sideline of Orphism, created by the Americans Stanton Macdonald-Wright and Morgan Russel (publish manifestoes on occasion of their exhibitions in Paris and Munich) Herwarth Walden shows at the "Erster Deutscher Herbstsalon" in Berlin newest international art	Wassily Kandinsky: "Klänge", poems in prose, with woodcuts The poet Guillaume Apollinaire describes the first cubists in his essay "Les peintres cubistes"

1914	Onset of World War I	Jean Arp and Sophie Taeuber: abstract embroideries and collages
	Conflict between the US and Mexico	
	Mounting socialist opposition in the German Reichstag against war-credits	Piet Mondrian starts his "plus-and-minus" (horizontal-vertical) compositions
	England develops armored cars	The private collections of Ivan Morosov and Sergei Shchukin introduce contemporary French art in Russia
	Opening of the Panama Canal	
		In Paris the Russian Sergei Diaghilev extends his ballet into a "Ballet of Painters" (with Juan Gris, André Derain, Joan Miró, Georges Braque, Pablo Picasso, and others)
		Alfred Stieglitz shows works by Constantin Brancusi, in possibly the first exhibition of "abstract" sculpture in New York
1915	First use of poison gas by Germany on the western front; air raid over Paris; submarine warfare	First futurist exhibition in Petersburg "Tramway W" (Featuring Vladimir Tatlin, Olga Rozanova and others)
	International socialist anti-war conference in Zimmerwald, Switzerland	Giacomo Balla: production of "Feux d'artifice" by Igor Stravinsky, a ballet of geometrical forms and light
	Albert Einstein engages in the development of the theory of relativity	Kasimir Malevich shows his famous painting of the "Null-Form", the "Black square on white background" at the second and "Last futurist exhibition 0.10" in Petersburg.
1916	Heavy fighting at Verdun	Theo van Doesburg brings the evolution of abstraction to its conclusion: free rhythmical composition of geometrical forms
	Karl Liebknecht is sentenced to two years in jail for his fight against war	
1917	International Trade Union Congress demands peace treaty	"De Stijl" movement founded in Holland; includes painters, sculptors and architects
	US declares war on Germany	Anatoly Lunacharsky founds the department for public education. The division for visual arts is headed by Vladimir Tatlin in Moscow; Wassily Kandinsky as well as Kasimir Malevich are involved
	October Revolution in Russia: Bolsheviks proclaim Soviet Republic	
	First Jazz record: Original Dixieland Jazz Band	Vladimir Tatlin and Alexander Rodchenko decorate the "Café Pittoresque" in Moscow
1918	Peace treaty between Germany and the Soviet Union	Jean Arp terms the perspective of inner forms "concretion"
	Hugo Preuss drafts the constitution for the Weimar Republic	The AGIT decorations (street decorations for the May celebrations and the anniversary of the October Revolution) in the Soviet Union are designed according to suprematist principles
	First regular flights between New York/Washington and Berlin/Weimar	Gerrit T. Rietveld designs chairs in the vocabulary of de Stijl
		Piet Mondrian uses orthogonal systems for his compositions (black lines/primary colors)
		In Zurich Sophie Taeuber conceives partly robot-like figures for the abstract puppet theatre "König Hirsch"

Marcel Duchamp exhibits his first "Ready-mades" (industrially produced objects) in New York Wassily Kandinsky must return to Russia Werkbund exhibition in Cologne Marinetti visits Russia David W. Griffith's movie "Birth of a Nation"	"Blast", provocative magazine (2 issues) published by a group of English artists with the same name
"Vorticism" (parallel name to the "Sturm" in Berlin), British movement, combines both futurist and proto-dadaist elements, exhibits regularly at the "Rebel Art Centre" Marcel Duchamp starts on his capital work "La Mariée mise à nu par ses célibataires, même", which will preoccupy him for several years	The New York magazine "291", published by Alfred Stieglitz, displays first dadaist attributes due to the influence of Francis Picabia Heinrich Wölfflin: "Kunstgeschichtliche Grundbegriffe", an attempt to classify artistic forms, exemplified on the transition from Renaissance to Baroque
Hugo Ball, Richard Huelsenbeck, Tristan Tzara, Jean Arp, and others pioneer dadaism in the "Cabaret Voltaire" in Zurich	"Ma" (today), magazine published by the Hungarian circle of avant-garde artists of the same name (published in Budapest, since 1920 exiled in Vienna, until 1927)
Giorgio de Chirico and the former futurist Carlo Carrà call their painting "Pittura metafisica" Guillaume Apollinaire uses the term "Surrealism" for the first time as a subtitle to one of his plays Cubist Ballet "Parade" by Pablo Picasso and Eric Satie in Paris	First issue of "De Stijl" by the Dutch group with the same name (last issue 1932) "The Blind Man" (2 issues) published in New York by Marcel Duchamp and Pierre Roché; "Rongwrong" by Marcel Duchamp
Richard Huelsenbeck in Berlin: founding of the Club Dada Wassily Kandinsky accepts a teaching position at the Swomas, artists workshops; establishes museums in Moscow as well as in the provinces	Amédée Ozenfant and Le Corbusier: "Après le Cubisme", an essay which suggests to rid cubism of ornamental elements (Purism) The first "De-Stijl-Manifest" is published in the magazine "De Stijl"

	Historical Events	Constructive Art
1919	Rosa Luxemburg and Karl Liebknecht assassinated by officers of the extreme right The newly-elected German national assembly congregates in Weimar The peace treaty between the Allies and Germany is signed at Versailles First transatlantic flight Prohibition of alcoholic beverages in the US (until 1933) Spartakus uprising in Berlin	El Lissitzky: "Proun" paintings (from "Pro Unowis" = for a renewal of art) Kurt Schwitters creates his first MERZ paintings in Hanover Vladimir Tatlin: project for a monument to the Third International Hans Richter and Viking Eggeling create abstract films Compulsory first-year course ("Vorkurs") at the Bauhaus (educational concept) Grouping of Swiss and international artists as "Artistes radicaux" in Zurich
1920	Adolf Hitler announces his 25-point program at the Hofbräuhaus in Munich The League of Nations opens in Geneva to safeguard world peace Vladimir I. Lenin designs the distribution network for electrical supply throughout the Soviet Union	Piet Mondrian introduces the term "Neo-Plasticism" for de Stijl painting; later on Theo van Doesburg uses the term "Elementarism" Foundation of Inkhuk, the Institute of artistic culture in Moscow; contacts with artists on international level Kasimir Malevich organizes the group "Pro Unowis" (New forms in art) in Witebsk
1921	Vladimir I. Lenin declares "New Economical Policy"; art is used for political indoctrination of the masses US declines Versailles treaty; sign with Germany separate peace agreement Construction of a streamlined car	In Moscow: group of constructivist artists; Varvara Stepanova uses the term "Constructivism" for the first time Oskar Schlemmer: "Triadisches Ballett" produced in Stuttgart Movement in the Soviet Union against "pure" art; demands for "industrial constructivism" using machine-like conceptions
1922	Germany recognizes the USSR "March towards Rome", fascist coup in Italy; Benito Mussolini elected prime minister World Trade Conference in Genova Telecommunication office in Berlin	First Russian exhibition in Berlin including constructivists Düsseldorf: International Congress of Progressive Artists; an international alignment of constructivism fails The succession of Johannes Itten by Laszlo Moholy-Nagy mirrors a shift at the Bauhaus: the amalgamation of art and craft is replaced by the synopsis of art and technology
1923	France occupies the Ruhr Hitler-Ludendorff coup in Munich; Adolf Hitler is imprisoned, writes "Mein Kampf" Economical crisis in Poland Wireless telegraph between Italy and the US	Oskar Schlemmer integrates the "Triadische Ballet" in an abstract theatre at the Bauhaus Constructivist congress in Weimar, understood by the participants as a farewell to the dadaist movement
1924	The Dawes plan reschedules German reparation payments Great Britain, France and Italy recognize the USSR Parallel cylinder presses allow the printing of newspapers of any size The 10,000,000th Ford car leaves the factory Death of Vladimir I. Lenin	Theo van Doesburg uses compositional structures which base on diagonal lines The slow seizing of power by Stalin strengthens a cultural policy curbing progressive trends in the USSR Gerrit Th. Rietveld designs the villa Schröder in Utrecht in the de Stijl vocabulary Fernand Léger makes an essential contribution to the "Cinéma pur" with his film "Le ballet mécanique"

André Breton and Philippe Soupault discover "écriture automatique" (spontaneous pictorial handwriting)

Dada manifestations in Berlin (including Max Ernst)

The architect Walter Gropius founds the Staatliche Bauhaus in Weimar; in the following years he engages the painters Johannes Itten, Lyonel Feininger, Paul Klee, Oskar Schlemmer, Laszlo Moholy-Nagy, Wassily Kandinsky, Josef Albers, and others as masters

Manifesto of the "November-Gruppe" in Berlin

"Les champs magnétiques" by André Breton and Philippe Soupault is considered the first surrealist publication

Walter Gropius: Manifesto of the Staatliche Bauhaus in Weimar; a woodcut by Lyonel Feininger—later known as the "Cathedral of Socialism"—accompanies the programmatical proclamation

---

Tristan Tzara transfers the provocative demonstrations of Dada from Zurich to Paris

High time of expressive theatre in Germany

Marcel Duchamp, Man Ray and the patron Katherine S. Dreier found the "Société Anonyme Inc., Museum of Modern Art" in New York, an institution exhibiting international avant-garde art

Naum Gabo and Antoine Pevsner: "Realist Manifesto", Moscow

Le Corbusier, Amédée Ozenfant and Paul Dermée found the magazine "L'Esprit Nouveau, Revue d'Esthétique"; 28 issues published until 1925

Wassily Kandinsky leaves his native country with official permission and soon exhibits his compositions again in the West

The department for cultural affairs in Moscow publishes Wassily Kandinsky's lavishly illustrated autobiography, while his educational program for the Inkhuk is rejected

---

André Breton suggests to use the term "surrealism" (invented by Guillaume Apollinaire) to describe certain experiments (e.g. the use of spiritualist methods in his "sleep experiments")

Kasimir Malevich sets out to write a book on suprematism, which is to be published in 1927 under the title "Die gegenstandslose Welt" in the series of the "Bauhausbücher"

El Lissitzky publishes the magazine "Vjeschtsch—Gegenstand—Objekt" in Berlin

---

Piper Verlag in Munich publishes color reproductions of paintings

Kurt Schwitters publishes the first issue of his MERZ bulletin (until 1932)

Le Corbusier's essays published in the magazine "L'Esprit Nouveau" are collected in the anthology "Vers une architecture"; the author envisions a new culture and civilization

---

The office for surrealist research in Paris becomes accessible to the public

Joan Miró makes the transition from representative to abstract-surrealist painting

Abstract period in Pablo Picasso's painting

André Breton: first "Manifeste du Surréalisme"

El Lissitzky, Jean Arp: "Die Kunst-Ismen"

Foundation of the magazine "La Révolution Surrealiste"

Historical Events	Constructive Art
1925 Agreement of Geneva against the use of chemical and bacteriological warfare Adolf Hitler reestablishes the NSDAP First compact camera "Leica" for commercial film	Exhibition "Neue Sachlichkeit" at the Städtische Kunsthalle in Mannheim Piet Mondrian leaves the de Stijl movement in disagreement with Theo van Doesburg Synthesis of the arts: Le Corbusier's "Pavillon de l'Esprit Nouveau" at the "Exposition Internationale des Arts Décoratifs" in Paris
1926 The German SPD opposes the Reichswehr Organization of the Hitler-Jugend Nonaggression and neutrality agreement between Germany and the USSR Electrical sound-recording technology	The Warsovian group "BLOK" becomes the "Praesens" association and exhibits for the first time El Lissitzky conceives a "Room for abstract art" for the international exhibition at Dessau
1927 World Trade Conference in Geneva The USSR decide on the first five-year plan First successful sound movie in the US	An international team of renown architects works on the exemplary Weissenhof-Siedlung in Stuttgart; the Swiss Camille Graeser (later a representative of conrete art) appoints apartments in house designed by Mies van der Rohe 56 paintings by Kasimir Malevich are shown at the Grosse Berliner Kunstausstellung
1928 The League of Nations recognizes the unconditional neutrality of Switzerland Berliner Funkausstellung: Demonstration of wireless television Walt Disney: first Mickey Mouse cartoons	The collaboration of the leading architects in the Weissenhof project gives the impulse for the founding of CIAM (Congrès International d'Architecture Moderne), held at La Sarraz in the French part of Switzerland
1929 Crash of the New York stock exchange triggers financial crisis worldwide Revolution in Mexico fails First television broadcasting in Berlin Erich Maria Remarque: "Nothing new on the western front"; one of the first books on World War I	Kasimir Malevich for the last time shows suprematist paintings; returns to figurative painting Piet Mondrian reaches extreme containment in form and color composition in some of his paintings Exhibition of the Bauhaus masters at the Kunsthalle in Basel
1930 Clearing of the Rhineland France builds the Maginot line Unrest in Brazil 250 million moviegoers per week worldwide Permanent wave in hairdressing	Theo van Doesburg uses the term "concrete art" for the first time in a manifesto Michel Seuphor founds the artists group "Cercle et Carré"; the name serves as a program and heading for an international exhibition of constructivist art as well
1931 After his speech, the German industrials pledge their support to Adolf Hitler	Foundation of the association "Abstraction-Création, Art non-figuratif" joining the representatives of constructive art in Paris, at times over 400 members, as compensating movement to surrealism
1932 Adolf Hitler obtains German citizenship Antonio Oliveira Salazar, Prime Minister of Portugal, establishes the fascist corporative state Severe famine in the USSR 8-mm movie camera by Kodak Highway Bonn-Cologne Wernher von Braun starts developing rockets	Constructivism is deemed decadent in the Soviet Union; the proclamation of "Socialist Realism" by Joseph Stalin deals a final blow to constructivism The participation of many Polish artists in "Abstraction-Création" is one of the reasons for the creation of the "International collection of modern art" at the museum in Lodz.

Art in General	Publications
The Bauhaus is transferred to Dessau Max Ernst invents the technique of "Frottage" (generation of an image through rubbing the paper on rough surface) New strong atonal style in Jazz in Chicago Sergei Eisenstein's movie "Potemkin"	Paul Klee: "Pädagogisches Skizzenbuch", published in the series "Bauhausbücher" 14 of 50 planned "Bauhausbücher" are published between 1925 and 1931
Installation of the "Aubette" restaurant in Strasbourg by Jean Arp, Sophie Taeuber and Theo van Doesburg (until 1928) "Blaue Vier", association of abstract painters (Klee, Kandinsky, Jawlensky, Feininger)	"Bauhaus. Zeitschrift für Gestaltung", Dessau, published until 1929 Wassily Kandinsky: "Punkt und Linie zu Fläche", published in the series of the "Bauhausbücher"
Scandal around the competition for the League of Nations building in Geneva Walter Gropius: "Total Theatre" project for Erwin Piscator	"Transition", a "creative experiment", published until 1938, international organ for all trends in art and literature since cubism
The political extremism forces Walter Gropius to resign from the Bauhaus; the Swiss Hannes Meyer becomes his successor (until 1930) Laszlo Moholy-Nagy resigns as Bauhaus master First performance of the "Dreigroschenoper" by Bert Brecht and Kurt Weill in Berlin	Amédée Ozenfant: "Art", important publication on the essentials of modern art
Werkbund exhibition "Wohnung und Werkraum" in Breslau Foundation of the Museum of Modern Art New York with the goal to organize regularly exhibitions of progressive artists	Publication of the "Second manifesto of Surrealism" in Paris
Riot during the first release of "Age d'Or" by Luis Bunuel and Salvador Dalí; interdiction of the movie After Hannes Meyer's resigning Mies van der Rohe becomes director of the Bauhaus	Publication of "Cercle et Carré" in Paris Publication of the Manifesto on concrete art in the only issue of the magazine "Art Concret"; constitution of an association "Abstraction-Création" in the following year
Le Corbusier's project for the Soviet Palace in Moscow is rejected René Clair's movie "A nous la Liberté" Charles Chaplin: "City Lights"	Publication of Jacov Tchernikhov's paper on "Construction of architectural and mechanical forms"
The Bauhaus is moved to Berlin The Museum of Modern Art in New York presents regularly photographic exhibitions as an extension of the traditional notion of art	"Abstraction-Création", publication by the association of the same name in Paris, 5 issues

Constructive Art

1933	Adolf Hitler becomes chancellor of Germany	British group "Unit One", with Ben Nicholson and Henry Moore participating amongst others

1933 — Adolf Hitler becomes chancellor of Germany
Burning of the Reichstag
"Law for the prevention of congenital infirmity" passed in Germany
Establishment of NS concentration camps
All parties except the SPD vote for the enabling act in favor of the Hitler regime; end of the Weimar Republic

British group "Unit One", with Ben Nicholson and Henry Moore participating amongst others
The "Galleria del Milione" in Milan becomes the meeting point of constructivists, with the painter Gino Ghiringhelli as its director; a "geometria-sentimento" develops at the same time in Como
Josef Albers starts teaching at the Black Mountain College

1934 — Meeting of Hitler and Mussolini in Venice
Adolf Hitler proclaims himself "Führer and Reichskanzler"
Balkan treaty for the protection of the Balkan frontiers

"Machine Art" exhibition at the Museum of Modern Art in New York illustrates the relation between cubism, futurism, dadaism, and constructivism and the technological world of machines and apparatus

1935 — So-called "Blood-protection laws" (anti-Semite "Nuremberg Laws") passed in Germany
Italy invades Abyssinia
World Congress of the Comintern in Moscow
Magnetic tapes register sound

Constructivists in Milan call themselves "artisti astratti"
"These, Synthese, Antithese" exhibition at the Kunstmuseum in Lucerne with the goal "to obtain the components for a new art through a synthetical approach"
First group-show of abstract Italian art in Torino (with manifesto)

1936 — Invasion of the demilitarized Rhineland by German troops
German-Italian agreement; Benito Mussolini speaks of the "Axis Berlin-Rome"
Outbreak of a military uprising in Spanish Morocco under General Franco starts Spanish civil war
BBC sets up official television broadcasting

"Cubism and Abstract Art" exhibition at the Museum of Modern Art in New York
The painter George L.K. Morris creates the group of "American Abstract Artists"
Referring to Theo van Doesburg's concept of concrete art, a New York Gallery presents a group-show of American artists under the heading of "Concretionists"

1937 — State visit of Mussolini in Germany (Hitler reciprocates in 1938)
Italy withdraws from the League of Nations
Culmination of Stalin's purging of Russia
Violent strikes and unrest in the US
Nonagression pact between China and the USSR
Television broadcasting with regular programs in Berlin

The Nazis declare constructivist art and other trends in modern art as unpatriotic and subversive and organize the travelling exhibition of "Entartete Kunst" (degenerate art)
Founding of the "Allianz" in Switzerland as affiliation of modern painters and sculptors; the association was the start of what developed later on into the group known as "Schweizer Konkrete" with its center in Zurich
"Konstruktivisten", international exhibition at the Kunsthalle Basel

1938 — Austria is incorporated into the German Reich
Officially organized persecution of the Jews in Germany ("Reichskristallnacht")
Small radio receivers set up in Germany for a more thorough indoctrination of the population ("Volksempfänger")

"Bauhaus 1919–1928", exhibition at the Museum of Modern Art in New York curated by Walter Gropius and Herbert Bayer

Initiation of "Gruppe 33" in Basel; not the artistic expression, rather the attitude is relevant

Paul Nash: Manifesto of the British group "Unit One"

Museum of Modern Art in New York: an exhibition of furniture and household objects leads to in-depth reflection on industrial and environmental design

In the US the "Federal Arts Project" by the "Works Progress Administration" guarantees a minimal monthly allowance for artists (until 1943)

The Bauhaus in Berlin is closed down by the nazis

Museum of Modern Art in New York includes film making as a valid art form

The surrealists of Paris condemn the Moscow trials

Max Bill: "Konkrete Gestaltung", in: "Zeitprobleme der Schweizer Malerei und Plastik", exhibition catalogue, Kunsthaus Zurich

"Deutscher Künstlerbund" banned

German ministry of propaganda prohibits art criticism, admits only positive "art description"

"Modern Times", movie by and with Charles Chaplin

Laszlo Moholy-Nagy establishes the "New Bauhaus" in Chicago (since 1944 the "Institute of Design" which in 1949 becomes part of the "Illinois Institute of Technology")

Publication of the British periodical "Circle", an international survey of constructivist art. Co-editor is Ben Nicholson, with contributions by Le Corbusier, etc.

Walter Gropius establishes with the "Graduate School of Design" at Harvard University in Cambridge, Mass. another descendant of the Bauhaus

"Plastique", trilingual magazine published by Sophie Taeuber-Arp, 5 issues until 1939

Pablo Picasso paints "Guernica" for the world fair in Paris in memory of the bombings of the Spanish town by fascist troops

Le Corbusier: "Quand les Cathédrales étaient blanches"

"Three Centuries of American Art", exhibition in Paris

Max Bill: "Quinze variations sur un même thème", 15 graphics in portfolio, trilingual edition

Documentary film of the Berlin Olympics 1936

High time of Jazz-Swing music with Benny Goodman

1939	Adolf Hitler starts World War II by invading Poland	
	Great Britain and France declare war against Germany	
	Unsuccessful bomb attack on Hitler	
	3065 km of highways completed in Germany	
1940	Triple alliance between Germany, Italy and Japan	Piet Mondrian paints a series of "Boogie Woogie" compositions in New York (vibrating nets of small rectangular color fields in band-like structures)
	First German air raids on London and Malta	
	Extermination of the mentally ill in Germany	
1941	Hitler attacks Russia, successfully at first; the Soviet army stops German tanks before Moscow in the winter battle	Mondrian gives a lecture in New York on "A New Realism"
	First British jet plane	
1942	Extermination of millions of Jews in the German gas chambers starts	Peggy Guggenheim opens premises in New York called "Art of this Century" where exhibitions of modern European and young American art is shown (later she in fact discovered Jackson Pollock)
	The Japanese defeat in the sea battle near the Midway Islands marks the turning point of the war in the Far East	
	Allies attempt landing near Dieppe	
1943	Hitler orders the policy of "Burnt Earth" in retreating from Russia	Richard Paul Lohse: first serial and modular structures based on orthogonal color shapes
	Uprising against the Nazis in the Ghetto of Warsaw	The Swiss artist Fritz Glarner, living in New York since 1936, paints circular paintings; he gives new meaning to the old shape of the Tondo
1944	Landing of the Allies on the coast of Normandy at unprecedented technological expense	Opening of the Denise René Gallery in Paris showing mostly abstract geometrical art
	Employment of the German V1 and V2 missiles against Britain	"Konkrete Kunst", exhibition at the Kunsthalle in Basel
1945	Adolf Hitler commits suicide in the shelter of the State Chancery in Berlin	During the post-war years the development in Italy runs between the extremes of "poetic geometry" and the stern "arte concreta"
	On May 9, at 1 a.m., the general surrender of Germany becomes effective	"Art Concret" exhibition in Paris
1946	League of Nations is dissolved	First "Salon des Réalités Nouvelles" in Paris: annual exhibition of primarily geometrical abstract art
	Nuremberg trials of war criminals	
	First general assembly of the United Nations	
1947	Partition of Palestine into a Jewish and an Arab state	
	Marshall Plan for economic aid to Europe	
	India and Pakistan become independent states	
1948	The USSR announces the final release of German prisoners of war	A group of artists found the "movimento per l'arte concreta" ("mac") in Milan
	Israel is proclaimed independent Jewish state in Palestine	"Tendances de l'Art abstrait", international exhibition of the group around the Denise René Gallery in Paris

Art in General	Publications
Auctioning off of paintings confiscated in 1936/37 in German museums at the Fischer Gallery in Lucerne; Georg Schmidt is one of the few who purchases works for the public collections in Basel, as well as the Musée des Beaux-Arts in Lüttich and the Kunstmuseum in Berne	
The political drawings against Hitler by the British cartoonist David Low generate wide response "The Great Dictator", a satirical portrait of Hitler, movie by and with Charles Chaplin	"Almanach neuer Kunst in der Schweiz"; includes almost all the names of those who still represent the constructivist movement in Switzerland today; published by "Allianz"
Henry Moore makes his "Shelter Drawings" in London's underground tunnels during German air raids	Special issue on the surrealists of the American magazine "View" Ben Nicholson: "Notes on abstract art", in: "Horizon" Max Horkheimer: "Art and Mass Culture"
The collection of the "Société Anonyme" is shown for the first time at Yale University	
"Abstract Expressionism": general term for the emerging New York school	The American painter Charmion von Wiegand publishes the first paper on Piet Mondrian in an American magazine, the "Journal of Aesthetics"
"American Buildings 1932–44", exhibition at the Museum of Modern Art in New York	Max Bill, theoretician and representative of concrete art, creates "abstrakt-konkret", a periodical published for the Zurich Gallery "Des Eaux Vives", 12 issues until 1945
Jean Dubuffet and Jean Fautrier exhibit for the first time paintings of "art informel" in Paris	
The restoration of Rembrandt's "Vigil" produces relevant changes in light and content of the image	Lucio Fontana solicits in his "Manifesto blanco" a new dynamic art, a spacial dimension in painting
The American painter Jackson Pollock completes a series of "Drip-paintings" which initiate "action painting" An extensive exhibition at the Art Institute in Chicago focusses on surrealist and abstract painting	Willi Baumeister: "Das Unbekannte in der Kunst" (important publication for German art of the post-war era) Richard Paul Lohse: "Die Entwicklung der Gestaltungsgrundlagen der Konkreten Kunst", in: "Allianz", exhibition catalogue, Kunsthaus Zurich Alexander Dorner: "The Way beyond Art"
COBRA (COpenhagen-BRuxelles-Amsterdam): organization of mainly Danish, Dutch and Belgian artists in Paris (art informel)	Hans Sedlmayr: "Verlust der Mitte" (reactionary art criticism) Sigfried Giedion: "Mechanization takes command" Thomas Stearn Eliot: "Notes towards the Definition of Culture"

	Historical Events	Constructive Art
1949	Federal Republic in Western Germany proclaimed with provisory constitution and capital Bonn; Theodor Heuss (FDP) is first president Council of Europe in Strasbourg: attempt of a West European parliament Constitution of the North Atlantic Pact	The Italian artist Lucio Fontana discovers the "concetti spaziali" in Milan (perforated, slit paintings, "Spazialismo") Josef Albers starts his series "Homage to the Square"
1950	Federal Minister of Commerce Ludwig Erhard sets up a largely free market policy for Western Germany Troops of Soviet-influenced North Korea trespass the 38th degree of latitude into South Korea Import of the American "Blue Jeans" in Europe 1.5 million television sets in the US	The "Geschwister-Scholl-Stiftung" commissions Max Bill to design a building for the "Hochschule für Gestaltung" in Ulm, realized according to his program In the US so-called Colorfield Painting, a kind of "chromatic abstraction", evolves in parallel to Abstract Expressionism
1951	Peace treaty between Japan and the US and 47 other nations, excluding the USSR Interdiction of communist ideologies in the US First color television in the US	
1952	Agreement on reparation payments between the Federal Republic of Germany and Israel The Democratic Republic of Eastern Germany announces the formation of national forces	
1953	Soviet tanks crash an uprising of East German workers International committee supervises the armistice in Korea	
1954	Paris Agreements provide for a rearmament of the Federal Republic of West Germany Revolt in Algeria against the French France loses Dien Bien Phu during the war in Indochina	
1955	Official visits of Konrad Adenauer in Moscow and in Washington NATO manoeuvres in German air space Otto Hahn, "Cobalt 80, Gefahr oder Segen für die Menschheit?", stresses the absurdity of nuclear war Successful attempt to fight polio on a large scale in the US The problem of teenage neglect is discussed openly in media and public	Yves Klein: first exhibiton of monochrome paintings Exhibition "Le Mouvement" in Paris with manifesto (better known as "Yellow manifesto") organized by the Denise René Gallery. The term "kinetic art" is frequently used
1956	First divisons of the German army Immediate stand-by of planes with nuclear warheads in the US and in Russia Switzerland suggests international conference to avoid the imminent confrontation	

Oskar Kokoschka exhibits at the Museum of Modern Art in New York	Jean Arp: "Onze Peintres vus par Arp"
At the occasion of the exhibition "L'Imaginaire" in Paris Georges Mathieu introduces the term "tachisme"	Michel Seuphor publishes a paper titled after the exhibition "L'Art abstrait, ses origines, ses premiers maîtres" in Paris Charles Estienne: "L'Art abstrait, est-il un académisme?" (against a dogmatically geometric art)
Michel Tapié organizes an exhibition "Signifiants de l'Informel" at Facchetti in Paris; creates the term "informel" for action painting Le Corbusier designs the government city of Chandigarh in India	
Le Corbusier: "Unité d'habitation" in Nantes-Rézé (apartment buildings designed according to the "modulor", measuring unit based on the human body)	The Parisian art critic Michel Tapié publishes "L'Art autre" which becomes the seminal book for tachist painting; exhibition with the same title
Frank Lloyd Wright designs the Guggenheim Museum in New York "40,000 years of Modern Art", exhibition of prehistoric and primitive painting in Paris, 1955 in Cologne	"Spirale", international magazine for young art in Berne, 9 issues until 1964
André Breton and Charles Estienne champion and defend tachism against their common enemy, the "cold abstraction"	Theodor W. Adorno: "Essays zur Kulturkritik und Gesellschaft" Werner Haftmann: "Malerei im 20. Jahrhundert. Eine Entwicklungsgeschichte"
"documenta": art of the 20th century; international exhibition at the Museum Fridericianum in Kassel; creates a link between Germany and contemporary art "The Family of Man", photo exhibition at the Museum of Modern Art in New York Inauguration of the buildings for the "Hochschule für Gestaltung" in Ulm; faculties include product design, architecture, urban design, visual communication, information; first headmaster: Max Bill	Wassily Kandinsky: "Essays über Kunst und Künstler", edited by Max Bill
The British art critic Lawrence Alloway introduces the term "Pop Art" Excavation of the palace of Diocletianus in Split, Yugoslavia	Paul Klee: "Das bildnerische Denken", edited by J. Spiller, a publication on the theory of form and design; becomes a seminal work in the discussion of the pictorial means of expression

Historical Events	Constructive Art
1957 Great Britain tests her first hydrogen bomb; thus becomes the third nuclear power Birth control is widely discussed and publicized	The Italian artist Piero Manzoni begins with "Achromes" (white folded or sewn canvasses)
1958 Constitution of the European Parliament in Strasbourg within the framework of the European Economic Community Civil war in Lebanon, US intervention First US satellite "Explorer I" launched	Kinetic light-structures and problems are the concerns of the group "Zero" in Düsseldorf Jules Langsner introduces the term "Hard Edge" while preparing an exhibition of geometric-abstract painters in California ("total Abstraction", paintings of a high degree of discipline and formal reduction)
1959 Cuban revolution under Fidel Castro Turning point in the French policy toward Algeria: Charles de Gaulle concedes to Algeria her sovereign right Nikita Khrushchev calls for complete disarmament within four years at the general assembly of the UN in New York	The British artist Bridget Riley explores with exemplary perseverance and method the possibilities of kinetic design Frank Stella works according to the principle of "shape as form": dimension and shape of his paintings result from their inner structure
1960 John F. Kennedy elected President of the US Surplus of nuclear power ("overkilling"): leads to an "atomic stalemate" A satellite of the USSR returns safely with plants and animals after 17 orbits	Exhibition "Konkrete Kunst—50 Jahre Entwicklung" at the Helmhaus in Zurich, curated by Max Bill and Margit Staber Founding of the "Groupe de Recherche d'Art Visuel" (including François Morellet and Victor Vasarely); Parisian group dedicated to kinetic research
1961 Democratic Republic of East Germany erects the wall separating West Berlin from East Berlin U Tant is unanimously voted General Secretary of the UN Albania detaches herself politically from the USSR and strengthens ties to China Close to 50% of all children worldwide do not receive primary education	Begin of the "Postpainterly Abstraction" (no personal mark in the brushwork or gestural application of paint, Morris Louis, Kenneth Noland) First integral exhibition of kinetic art in Amsterdam entitled "Bewogen Beweging" (Moving movement) Founding of "Nouveau Réalisme"; Jean Tinguely, Daniel Spoerri and others bestow new aesthetic qualities upon their "objets trouvés", objects found in a civilisation of consumerism
1962 US blockade of Cuba because of the Soviet nuclear bases "The Beatles" emerge in Liverpool	
1963 France and Germany sign mutual cooperation treaty John F. Kennedy assassinated in Dallas "Shopping Centers" following US examples built in Europe	Groups such as "Equipo 57" in Paris, "Gruppo N" in Padova, "Gruppo T" in Milan, "Nul" in the Netherlands and "Zero" in Düsseldorf together form the international association "Nouvelle Tendance" with the goal to research the field of optical kinetic art
1964 Yassir Arafat takes over the command of the "Fatah" (Arabic movement for the expulsion of Israel from Palestine) Atomic power plants become economically competitive to the conventional power plants in the US	Victor Vasarely speaks of "surface kinetics" in referring to seemingly pulsating images. Time Magazine suggests the more successful term "Op Art" (optical art) in analogy to "Pop Art" "Postpainterly Abstraction" gains acceptance in the US; heterogenous circle of artists

Art in General	Publications
"Interbau Berlin": international architectural exhibition situated in the newly-designed Hansa district Jasper John's "Flag on an Orange Field" becomes seminal work for Pop Art	"Tagebücher von Paul Klee 1898–1918", edited by Klee's son Felix
	"Neue Grafik", international magazine for graphics and related fields, 18 issues until 1965 "Zero", publication of the artists association with the same name in Germany, 3 issues The sociologist/psychologist Abraham A. Moles publishes "Informationstheorie und ästhetische Wahrnehmung"
"18 Happenings in 6 Parts" in New York, an event by Allan Kaprov who is considered the originator of the happening Discovery of rock paintings in the Kalahari desert in the south of Africa; considered evidence that prehistoric painting moved from the south northwards 2nd Documenta in Kassel, concentrates on post-war art between 1945 and 1955	Lucio Fontana publishes the manifesto of "Spazialismo"
Jean Tinguely: "Homage to New York", a self-destructive machine The new capital of Brazil, Brasilia, is being built according to the plans of the architect Lucio Costa; Oscar Niemeyer designed the public buildings	So-called "Declaration of the 121" comments on the war in Algeria and is published in cooperation with the surrealists "The Structurist", magazine published by Elie Bornstein in Canada
First exhibiton of the "Pop artists" including Roy Lichtenstein, Claes Oldenburg and Andy Warhol, in New York Half-life of the radio-active carbon 14 newly established at 5770 + 60 years; relevant for determination of age in archaeology Guidelines issued by the arch-diocese Paderborn against certain trends in contemporary sacral architecture such as the design of the chapel at Ronchamp by Le Corbusier	Josef Albers: "Trotz der Geraden" Georg Muche: "Blickpunkt. Sturm — Dada — Bauhaus — Gegenwart"
Exhibition "Entartete Kunst" in Munich as belated criticism of national-socialist conception of art	Camilla Gray: "The Great Experiment: Russian Art 1863–1922" renews interest for Russian art
Progressive artists in the USSR are denounced as "bourgeois formalists"	Josef Albers: "Interaction of Color", basic theory on the perspective of seeing
"Lincoln Center" becomes new cultural center in New York Acrylic paint replaces oil as paint medium 3rd Documenta in Kassel, presents survey over the last five years establishing a link to the contemporary scene	Otto Stelzer: "Die Vorgeschichte der abstrakten Kunst. Denkmodelle und Vor-Bilder"

Historical Events	Constructive Art
1965 Bombing of North Vietnam by American forces; spurs protests in East and West	Exhibition "The Responsive Eye" at the Museum of Modern Art in New York, broad survey of artistic works dealing with optical and kinetic phenomena
Soviet astronaut is first human to leave spaceship in orbit	The term "Minimal Art" emerges in the US describing works with minimal expressive content; Ellsworth Kelly principal representative
"Peace March" of black and white civil rights activists under the leadership of Martin Luther King in the US	Lucy R. Lippard introduces the term "Silent Art" for "eventless" monochrome art, such as the paintings by Robert Mangold and Agnes Martin in the US, which derives from Minimal Art and primary structures
1966 Indira Gandhi (daughter of Jawaharlal Nehru) becomes Prime Minister of India	The exhibition "Formen der Farbe" in Amsterdam, Stuttgart and Berlin brings the representatives of American "Postpainterly Abstraction" for the first time together with the European constructivists
Mao Tse-Tung mobilizes China's youth through his "Cultural Revolution"	Exhibition "10" at the Virginia Dwan Gallery in New York presents Minimal Art
At the convention of the SPD party Willy Brandt calls for an "orderly side-by-side" (Geordnetes Nebeneinander) of the two German states; elected Chairman of the SPD	Dutch structurists, such as Jan Schoonhoven and Ad Dekker, produce interconnecting systems in white reliefs, or work, as Pieter Struycken, with numerical series or random latices
Soft landing of Russian, later of American spacecapsula on the surface of the moon	
Miniskirts become popular, mainly in England	
1967 Official visit by the Shah of Persia in the Federal Republic of Western Germany; leads to violent opposition in the streets of Berlin in the course of which B. Ohnesorg, a student, is killed	"Lumière et mouvement", exhibition of kinetic art in Paris
Racial unrest in Detroit	"Avantgarde Osteuropa 1910–1930", exhibition West Berlin
1968 Student revolts produce great unrest in Paris	"Kunst aus dem Computer", exhibition during the convention "Der Computer in der Universität" at the Technische Universität Berlin
Troops of the Warsow pact invade Czechoslovakia	"50 Jahre Bauhaus", exhibition in Stuttgart
Robert Kennedy and Martin Luther King are assassinated in the US	
1969 Sweden as first western nation recognizes North Vietnam	"Konstruktive Kunst: Elemente und Prinzipien", international exhibition in Nürnberg, represents all major representatives of new constructivist tendencies from East and West
Civil war between Nigeria and Biafra	
Neil Armstrong sets foot on the moon	
1970 Continuation of the Viennese talks between the US and the USSR on the limitation of the use of strategic arms (SALT)	Mario Nigro and artists around him in Italy develop a method of working with computer technology, known as "arte programmata"
Court cases against the members of the Baader-Meinhof gang	Representatives of "Concept Art" frequently use non-pictorial means; the underlying idea is often deemed more relevant than the manifestation of the work itself
The need for effective protection of the environment is publicly acknowledged	Celia Ascher assembles the first comprehensive collection of constructivist art for the McCrory Corporation; it is donated in 1985 to the Museum of Modern Art, the Louisiana Museum Humlebaek and the Tel Aviv Museum
Salvador Allende is elected president of Chile by democratic vote	

Pop Art originating from England is internationally accepted	Jürgen Becker, Wolf Vostell: "Happenings, Fluxus, Pop Art, Neuer Realismus", collection of statements, events and theories
Discovery of a large number of previously unknown paintings by Piet Mondrian "Signale" exhibition at the Kunsthalle in Basel	Max Bense explores the "Programmierung des Schönen" (Computer aesthetics) in "Aesthetica" Werner Hofmann: "Grundlagen der modernen Kunst. Eine Einführung in ihre symbolischen Formen"
"Synchromism and Related American Color Painting", exhibition at the Museum of Modern Art in New York	"Constructivism, Origins and Evolution", first complete investigation into constructive art published by the sculptor George Rickey in New York Frank Popper publishes the seminal work "L'Art cinétique" (Op Art)
Christo: "Verpackte Luft", air-filled plastic bags (70 m high), landmark of the 4th Documenta in Kassel Kunstmuseum in Basel purchases Picasso paintings for 8 million Swiss Francs (credit spoken by popular vote) Closing of the Hochschule für Gestaltung in Ulm	
	"Le quatrième chant" in "Le Monde" proclaims the end of surrealism as "organized movement in France"
27 caves with ice-age paintings are discovered since 1950 in France, Spain, Portugal, Italy, and the USSR; in total 131 caves are known	Theodor W. Adorno: "Ästhetische Theorie" Konrad Farner: "Der Aufstand der Abstrakt-Konkreten"

Select Bibliography

Compiled by Stefan Paradowski

General Studies on Artists and Movements

Bann, Stephen (Ed.):
The Tradition of Constructivism.
Selected Bibliography
by Bernard Karpel
New York 1974

Dabrowski, Magdalena:
Contrasts of Form.
Geometric Abstract Art 1910–1980.
From the Collection of The Museum
of Modern Art.
Selected Bibliography by Clive Phillpot
New York 1985

Osborne, Harold (Ed.):
The Oxford Companion to
Twentieth-Century Art
Oxford/New York 1981

Theory/History of Art

Adorno, Theodor W.:
Ästhetische Theorie
Frankfurt am Main 1970

Bergson, Henri:
Matière et mémoire
Paris 1896
dt., ders.:
Materie und Gedächtnis
Jena 1919

Bergson, Henri:
L'évolution créatrice
Paris 1907
dt., ders.:
Schöpferische Entwicklung
Jena 1912

Bergson, Henri:
La pensée et le mouvant
Paris 1934
dt., ders.:
Denken und schöpferisches Werden.
Aufsätze und Vorträge
Meisenheim am Glan 1948

Bill, Max:
Vom Sinn der Begriffe in der neuen
Kunst, in:
Konkrete Kunst – 50 Jahre
Entwicklung, Katalog, Helmhaus
Zürich 1960

Bürger, Peter:
Theorie der Avantgarde
Frankfurt am Main 1974

Burnham, Jack:
Structure of Art
New York 1971
dt., ders.:
Kunst und Strukturalismus
Köln 1973

Chipp, Herschel B.:
Theories of Modern Art.
A Source Book by Artists and Critics
Berkeley / Los Angeles / London 1968

Davis, Douglas:
Vom Experiment zur Idee. Die Kunst des
20. Jahrhunderts im Zeichen von
Wissenschaft und Technologie
Köln 1975

Frascina, Francis;
Harrison, Charles (Hg.):
Modern Art and Modernism.
An Anthology of Critical Texts from
Manet to Pollock
New York 1983

Fry, Roger:
Vision and Design
London 1920

Gehlen, Arnold:
Zeit-Bilder. Zur Soziologie und Ästhetik
der modernen Malerei
Frankfurt 1960

Giedion-Welcker, Carola:
Plastik des XX. Jahrhunderts,
Volumen- und Raumgestaltung
Stuttgart/Zürich 1955

Goodman, Nelson:
Sprachen der Kunst. Ein Ansatz zu einer
Symboltheorie
Frankfurt 1973

Grautoff, Otto:
Formzertrümmerung und Formaufbau
in der bildenden Kunst. Ein Versuch
zur Deutung der Kunst unserer Zeit
Berlin 1919

Haftmann, Werner:
Malerei im 20. Jahrhundert.
Eine Entwicklungsgeschichte
München 1979[6]
(Erstausgabe 1954)

Haftmann, Werner:
Malerei im 20. Jahrhundert.
Eine Bildenzyklopädie
München 1980[3]
(Erstausgabe 1965)

Heinrich, Dieter; Isler, Wolfgang (Hg.):
Theorien der Kunst
Frankfurt am Main 1982

Hermand, Jost:
Stile, Ismen, Etiketten.
Zur Periodisierung der modernen Kunst
Wiesbaden 1978

Hofmann, Werner:
Grundlagen der modernen Kunst.
Eine Einführung in ihre symbolischen
Formen
Stuttgart 1966

Imdahl, Max:
Bildautonomie und Wirklichkeit.
Zur theoretischen Begründung
moderner Malerei
Mittenwald 1981

Koch-Hillebrecht, Manfred:
Die moderne Kunst. Psychologie einer
revolutionären Bewegung
Köln 1983

Kultermann, Udo:
Neue Dimensionen der Plastik
Tübingen 1968

Kultermann, Udo:
Neue Formen des Bildes
Tübingen 1969

Lucie-Smith, Edward; Hunter, Sam;
Vogt, Adolf Max:
Kunst der Gegenwart.
Propyläen Kunstgeschichte
Frankfurt a.M./Berlin/Wien 1978

Neue Sammlung München:
Die verborgene Vernunft. Funktionelle
Gestaltung im 19. Jahrhundert, Katalog
München 1971

Read, Herbert:
Art Now
London 1933,1968[6]

Read, Herbert:
The Grass Roots of Art
London 1946

Rowell, Margit (Hg.):
Skulptur im 20. Jahrhundert
München 1986

Richter, Horst:
Geschichte der Malerei im
20. Jahrhundert. Stile und Künstler
Köln 1974

Sartre, J.P. u.a.:
Abstrakte Kunst.
Tendenzen und Theorien
Baden-Baden 1951

Schmied, Wieland:
Wegbereiter zur modernen Kunst.
50 Jahre Kestner-Gesellschaft
Hannover 1966

Schoenmaekers, Jan:
Het Nieuwe Wereldbeeld
(New view of life)
Bussum 1915

Schoenmaekers, Jan:
Beginselen der Beeldenden Wiskunde
(Foundations of the arts)
Bussum 1916

Semper, Gottfried:
Der Stil in den technischen und
tektonischen Künsten oder praktische
Ästhetik, 2 Bde.
Frankfurt am Main 1860/München 1963

Stelzer, Otto:
Die Vorgeschichte der abstrakten
Kunst. Denkmodelle und Vor-Bilder
München 1964

Thomas, Karin:
Bis Heute. Stilgeschichte der bildenden
Kunst im 20. Jahrhundert
Köln 1971

White, Lancelot Law:
Aspects of Form. A Symposium on
Form in Nature und Art
London 1951

Wittgenstein, Ludwig:
Remarks on the Foundations of
Mathematics
Oxford 1956

Worringer, Wilhelm:
Abstraktion und Einfühlung
München 1959
(Erstausgabe: München 1906)

Worringer, Wilhelm:
Abstraction and Empathy
London 1953

Wölfflin, Heinrich:
Kunstgeschichtliche Grundbegriffe
München 1915, Basel 1960[12]

Ballo, Guido (Hg.):
Origini dell'astrattismo, Verso altri
orizzonti del reale, 1885–1919, Catalogo
Milano 1979

Constructive Art in General

Bann, Stephen (Ed.):
The Tradition of Constructivism
New York 1974

Blass, Brigit; Koella, Rudolf:
Eine Pioniersammlung moderner Kunst.
Das Legat Clara und Emil
Friedrich-Jezler im Kunstmuseum
Winterthur
Zürich 1985

Blok, Cor:
Die Geschichte der abstrakten Kunst
1900–1960
Köln 1975

Brion, Marcel:
Art abstrait
Paris 1956
dt., ders.:
Geschichte der abstrakten Kunst
Köln 1961[2]

Dabrowska, Magdalena;
Elderfield, John (Introduction):
Contrasts of Form. Geometric Abstract
Art 1910–1980, From the Collection of
The Museum of Modern Art
New York 1985

Degand, Léon:
Langage et signification de la peinture
en figuration et en abstraction
Paris 1956

Farner, Konrad:
Der Aufstand der Abstrakt-Konkreten
Neuwied/Berlin 1970

Frauen Museum Bonn:
Die Rationale: rationale Konzepte von
Künstlerinnen 1915–1985, Katalog
Bonn 1985

Kunsthaus Zürich:
Aspekte konstruktiver Kunst.
Sammlung McCrory Corporation,
New York, Katalog
Zürich 1977

Musée d'art moderne de la ville de
Paris:
Aspects historiques du constructivisme
et de l'art concret, Catalogue
Paris 1977

Rathke, Ewald (Hg.):
Konstruktive Malerei 1915–1930
Frankfurt a.M. 1967

Rickey, George:
Constructivism. Origins and Evolution
New York 1967

Rotzler, Willy (Essay):
Constructivism and the Geometric
Tradition. Selections from the McCrory
Corporation Collection, Catalogue
Denver 1982

Rotzler, Willy;
Weinberg-Staber, Margit (Einführung):
Konstruktive Form. Aspekte der
geometrischen Kunst, Katalog,
Ausstellung des Schweizerischen
Bankvereins
Basel 1985

Sandler, Irving:
Concepts in Constructions 1910–1980,
Catalogue, Independent Curators Inc.
New York 1982

Seuphor, Michel:
L'Art abstrait
1: 1910–1918 Origines et premiers
maîtres
Paris 1971

2: 1918–1938
Paris 1972
3: 1939–1970 en Europe
Paris 1973

Tavel, Hans Christoph von (Einleitung):
Die Sprache der Geometrie.
Suprematismus, De Stijl und Umkreis –
Heute, Katalog, Kunstmuseum
Bern 1984

Vergine, Lea:
L'altra metà dell'avanguardia,
1910–1940
Pittrici e scultrici nei movimenti delle
avanguardie storiche
Milano 1980

Cubism

Apollinaire, Guillaume:
Les Peintres cubistes
Paris 1913
dt., ders.:
Die Maler des Kubismus
Zürich 1956

Cabanne, Pierre:
Le Cubisme
Paris 1982

Cooper, Douglas; Tinterow, Gary:
The Essential Cubism 1907–1920.
Braque, Picasso and their Friends
London 1983

Fauchereau, Serge:
La Révolution cubiste
Paris 1982

Fry, Edward:
Der Kubismus
Köln 1966

Gamwell, Lynn:
Cubist criticism
New York 1981

Gleizes, Albert;
Metzinger, Jean:
Du Cubisme
Paris 1912

Gomez de la Serna, R.:
Die Wahrheit über Picasso und den
Kubismus
Wiesbaden 1961

Jeanneau, Guillaume:
L'Art cubiste. Theories et réalisations.
Etude critique
Paris 1929

Kahnweiler, Daniel-Henry:
Der Weg zum Kubismus
Stuttgart 1958[2]

Rosenblum, Robert:
Der Kubismus und die Kunst des
20. Jahrhunderts
Stuttgart 1960

Roskill, Mark:
Cubism: An Interpretation
Cranbury 1984

Teuber, Marianne; Steinberg, Leo;
Hohl, Reinhold u.a.:
Kubismus. Künstler, Themen, Werke
1907–1920, Katalog
Köln 1982

Futurism

Appolonio, Umbro:
Der Futurismus. Manifeste und
Dokumente einer künstlerischen
Revolution 1909–1918
Köln 1972

Baumgarth, Christa:
Geschichte des Futurismus
Reinbek bei Hamburg 1966

Calvesi, Maurizio:
Il Futurismo
Milano 1970

Clough, Rosa Trillo:
Futurism. The Theory of a Modern Art
Movement. A New Appraisal
New York 1969

Markov, Vladimir:
Russian Futurism. A History
Berkeley/Los Angeles 1968

Martin, Marianne W.:
Futurist Art and Theory 1909–1915
Oxford 1968

Nautilus-Moderne
(Gemeinschaftsproduktion):
Eine Ohrfeige für den öffentlichen
Geschmack. Russische Futuristen
Hamburg 1988

Pinottini, Marzio:
L'Estetica del futurismo.
Revisioni storiografiche
Roma 1979

Rathke, Ewald:
Futurismus – Italien 1905–1925.
Futurismus und Pittura metafisica,
Katalog, Kunstverein
Hamburg 1963

Städtische Kunsthalle Düsseldorf:
Wir setzen den Betrachter ins Bild.
Futurismus 1909–1917, Katalog
Düsseldorf 1974

Taylor, Christina J.:
Futurism. Politics, Painting and
Performance
Ann Arbor 1979

Constructivism

Akademie der Künste Berlin:
Sieg über die Sonne. Aspekte
russischer Kunst zu Beginn des
20. Jahrhunderts, Katalog
Berlin 1983

Annely Juda Fine Art London:
The Non-Objective World 1914–1924,
Catalogue
London 1970

The Non-Objective World 1914–1955,
Catalogue
London 1973
The Non-Objective World. Twenty-Five
Years, 1914–1939, Catalogue
London 1978

Annely Juda Fine Art London:
Configuration 1910–1940 and Seven
Tatlin Reconstructions
London 1981

Arvatov, Boris:
Kunst und Produktion. Entwurf einer
proletarisch-avantgardistischen
Ästhetik
München 1972

Bowlt, John:
Russian Art of the Avant-Garde.
Theory and Criticism 1910–1934
New York 1975, 1977

County Museum of Art Los Angeles:
The Avant-Garde in Russia 1910–1930.
New Perspectives, Catalogue
Los Angeles 1980

Deutsche Gesellschaft für Bildende
Kunst; Akademie der Künste Berlin:
Avantgarde Osteuropa 1910–1930,
Katalog
Berlin 1967

Galerie Bargera Köln:
Russische Avantgarde 1910–1930.
Bilder, Konstruktionen, Katalog
Köln 1978

Galerie Chalette, New York:
Construction and Geometry in Painting
from Malevitch to Tomorrow, Catalogue
New York 1960

Galerie Gmurzynska Köln:
Konstruktivismus. Entwicklungen und
Tendenzen seit 1913, Katalog
Köln 1972

Galerie Gmurzynska Köln:
Von der Fläche zum Raum. Russland
1916–24, Katalog
Köln 1974

Galerie Gmurzynska Köln:
Die Kunst-Ismen in Russland. The Isms
of Art in Russia 1907–30, Katalog
Köln 1977

Galerie Gmurzynska Köln:
Künstlerinnen der russischen
Avantgarde 1910–1930, Katalog
Köln 1979

Galerie Gmurzynska Köln:
Von der Malerei zum Design. Russische
konstruktivistische Kunst der zwanziger
Jahre, Katalog
Köln 1981

Galerie im Taxispalais Innsbruck:
Klassiker der Avantgarde. Die
ungarischen Konstruktivisten, Katalog
Innsbruck 1983

Gray, Camilla:
The Russian Experiment in Art

1863–1922
London 1962

Grübel, Rainer Georg:
Russischer Konstruktivismus.
Künstlerische Konzeptionen,
literarische Theorie und kultureller
Kontext
Wiesbaden 1981

Hayward Gallery London:
Art in Revolution: Sovjet Art and Design
since 1917, Catalogue
London 1971

Lodder, Christina:
Russian Constructivism
New Haven 1983

Lunatscharski, Anatoli:
Die Revolution und die Kunst. Essays,
Reden, Notizen (includes "Letters from
Paris", 1913)
Dresden 1974[2]

Moderne Galerie Bottrop:
Osteuropäischer Konstruktivismus,
Katalog
Bottrop 1976

Musée d'Art contemporain Montréal:
Constructivisme et Avant-garde russe,
Catalogue
Montréal 1982

Nakow, Andrei:
Russische Avantgarde
Genf 1984

Österreichisches Museum für
angewandte Kunst Wien:
Kunst und Revolution. Russische und
Sowjetische Kunst 1910–1932. Art and
Revolution. Russian and Soviet Art
1910–1932, Katalog
Wien 1988

Rowell, Margit;
Zander-Rudenstine, Angelica:
Art of the Avant-Garde in Russia.
Selections from the George Costakis
Collection, Catalogue
New York 1981
dt., Zander-Rudenstine, Angelica:
Russische Avantgarde-Kunst.
Die Sammlung George Costakis
Köln 1982

Salmon, André:
Art russe moderne
Paris 1928

Schneede, Uwe M.:
Die zwanziger Jahre. Manifeste und
Dokumente deutscher Künstler
Köln 1979

Shadowa, Larissa A.:
Suche und Experiment. Russische und
sowjetische Kunst 1910 bis 1930.
Leben und Wirken Kasimir Malewitschs
Dresden 1979

Stanislawski, Ryszard:
Constructivism in Poland 1923–1936,
Catalogue
Essen/Otterlo 1973

Tate Gallery London:
Abstraction. Towards a New Art –
Painting 1910–1920, Catalogue
London 1980

Umanskij, Konstantin:
Neue Kunst in Russland 1914–1919
Potsdam 1920

Weiss, Evelyn (Hg./Einführung):
Russische Avantgarde 1910–1930.
Sammlung Ludwig Köln,
Bestandeskatalog
München 1986

De Stijl

Bulhof, Francis;
Nijhoff, Ostaijen van (Ed.):
De Stijl. Modernism in the Netherlands
and Belgium in the first Quarter of the
20th Century. Six essays
The Hague 1976

Blotkamp, Carel; Esser, Hans u.a.:
De beginjaren van De Stijl 1917–1922
Utrecht 1982

De-Stijl-Manifest, in:
De Stijl, 2. Jg. 1918/19, Nr. 1, abgedruckt
in: Konkrete Kunst –
50 Jahre Entwicklung, Katalog,
Helmhaus
Zürich 1960

Galerie Gmurzynska Köln:
De Stijl. Cercle et Carré. Entwicklung
des Konstruktivismus in Europa ab
1917, Katalog
Köln 1974

Jaffé, H.L.C.:
De Stijl 1917–1931.
Der niederländische Beitrag zur
modernen Kunst
Frankfurt am Main 1965

Jaffé, H.L.C.:
Mondrian und De Stijl
Köln 1967

Jaffé, H.L.C.; Welsh, Robert P. u.a.:
De Stijl 1917–1931. Visions of Utopia,
Catalogue
Chicago 1982

Lemoine, Serge:
Mondrian et de Stijl
Paris 1987

Bauhaus

Bayer, Herbert; Gropius, Walter:
Bauhaus 1919–1928,
Museum of Modern Art
New York 1938
dt., Bayer, Herbert; Gropius, Walter;
Gropius, Ise (Hg.):
Bauhaus 1919–1928
Teufen 1955³

Clemens, Roman:
Bauhaus, eine Ausstellung von Idee und
Arbeit, von Geist und Leben am

Bauhaus von 1919–1928 und –1933, in:
Lebendiges Darmstadt, Nr. 25/26
Darmstadt 1961

Franciscono, Marcel:
Walter Gropius and the Creation of the
Bauhaus at Weimar
Illinois 1971

Hahn, Peter (Einführung):
Künstler des Bauhauses. Arbeiten von
26 Meistern und Schülern aus der Zeit
von 1919 bis 1983, Katalog
Weingarten 1983

Hüter, Karl-Heinz:
Das Bauhaus in Weimar. Studie zur
gesellschaftspolitischen Geschichte
einer deutschen Kunstschule
Berlin 1982³

Itten, Johannes:
Mein Vorkurs am Bauhaus
Ravensburg 1963

Kröll, F.:
Das Bauhaus 1919–1933
Düsseldorf 1974

Neumann, Eckhard (Hg.):
Bauhaus und Bauhäusler.
Bekenntnisse und Erinnerungen
Bern 1971

Neuy, Heinrich:
Bauhaus – der Weg zur abstrakten
Malerei
Köln 1984

Scheidig, Walther:
Bauhaus. Weimar 1914–1924.
Wekstattarbeiten
Leipzig 1966

Schreyer, Lothar:
Erinnerungen an Sturm und Bauhaus
München 1956

Wick, Rainer:
Bauhaus Pädagogik
Köln 1982

Wingler, Hans M.:
Das Bauhaus. 1919–1933 Weimar
Dessau Berlin und die Nachfolge in
Chicago seit 1937
Bramsche 1975³

Wingler, Hans M.:
Kleine Bauhaus-Fibel. Geschichte und
Wirken des Bauhauses 1919–1933.
Berlin 1979²

Wingler, Hans M.; Mai, Ekkehard;
Shadowa, Larissa u.a.:
Bauhaus. Archiv-Museum.
Sammlungs-Katalog (Auswahl).
Architektur, Design, Malerei, Graphik,
Kunstpädagogik
Berlin 1981

Wolfe, Tom:
Mit dem Bauhaus leben.
«From Bauhouse to our house»
Königstein/Ts. 1982

Württembergischer Kunstverein
Stuttgart:

50 Jahre Bauhaus, Katalog
Stuttgart 1968

Concrete Art

Arp, Hans:
Konkrete Kunst, in: ders.,
Unsern täglichen Traum . . .
Zürich 1955
(Text reprinted from the French
introduction to: Konkrete Kunst,
Katalog, Kunsthalle
Basel 1944)

Berswordt-Wallrabe, H.L.A. von (Hg.):
Neue Konkrete Kunst.
Konkrete Kunst – Realer Raum
Bochum o.J.

Bill, Max:
Konkrete Gestaltung, in: Zeitprobleme
in der Schweizer Malerei und Plastik,
Katalog, Kunsthaus
Zürich 1936
(Revidierter Text unter dem Titel
«Konkrete Kunst» als Einleitung, in:
Zürcher Konkrete Kunst, Katalog zur
Wanderausstellung 1949 in
Deutschland)

Claus, Jürgen:
Das Energiefeld der Farbe, Max Bill.
Konkrete Kunst und Funktionsbegriff,
in: ders., Kunst heute. Personen,
Analysen, Dokumente
Reinbek bei Hamburg 1965

Doesburg, Theo van (Ed.):
art concret
Paris 1930
Magazine, one issue only, with
Manifesto of Concrete Art, reprinted in:
Konkrete Kunst – 50 Jahre
Entwicklung, Katalog, Helmhaus
Zürich 1960

Helmhaus Zürich:
Konkrete Kunst – 50 Jahre
Entwicklung, Katalog
Zürich 1960

Hofmann, Werner:
Über den Begriff der Konkreten Kunst,
in: Deutsche Vierteljahresschrift
für Literaturwissenschaft und
Geistesgeschichte, S. 57–75, 1955

Kandinsky, Wassily:
Abstrakt oder konkret, in:
ders., Essays über Kunst und Künstler,
hg. von Max Bill
Stuttgart 1955

Lohse, Richard Paul:
Die Entwicklung der
Gestaltungsgrundlagen der konkreten
Kunst, in: Allianz, Katalog, Kunsthaus
Zürich 1947

Musée des Beaux-Arts Dijon:
Art concret suisse. Mémoire et progrès,
Catalogue
Dijon 1982

Staber, Margit:
Konkrete Kunst, in: Gesammelte
Manifeste. Serielle Manifeste 66
St. Gallen 1966

Staber, Margit:
Konkrete Kunst als strukturelle Malerei,
in: G. Kepes (Hg.), Struktur in Kunst und
Wissenschaft
Brüssel 1967

University of Art Museum Austin:
Swiss Concrete Art in Graphics,
Catalogue
Austin 1975

Constructive Art before 1950

Bell, Clive:
Art
London 1923

Biederman, Charles:
Art as the Evolution of Visual
Knowledge
Minnesota 1948

Bill, Max; Le Corbusier; Leuppi, Leo u.a.:
Almanach neuer Kunst in der Schweiz,
hg. von der Allianz, Vereinigung
moderner Schweizer Künstler
Zürich 1940

Degand, Léon:
Défence de l'art abstrait, in:
Les Lettres françaises
2. August 1946

Degand, Léon:
Témoignage pour l'art abstrait
Boulogne 1952

Dorival, Bernard:
Le Salon des Réalités Nouvelles, in:
Les Nouvelles Littéraires
Paris, 7 août 1947

Georgel, Pierre:
Art Abstrait 1910/1940, Dessins,
Catalogue, Musée National d'Art
Moderne
Paris 1975

Giedion, S. (Einführung):
These. Antithese. Synthese. Katalog,
Kunstmuseum
Luzern 1935

Henderson, Linda D.:
The Fourth Dimension and
Non-Euclidean Geometry in Modern Art
Princeton 1983

Herzogenrath, Wulf; Fath, Manfred, u.a.:
Malewitsch – Mondrian und ihre Kreise
Aus der Sammlung Wilhelm Hack
Köln-Ludwigshafen 1976

Hess, Thomas B.:
Abstract Painting, Background and
American Phase
New York 1951

Ivins (Jr.), William M.:
Art & Geometry. A Study in Space
Intuitions
Harvard 1946/New York 1964

Kettle's Yard Gallery Cambridge:
Constructivism in Poland 1923–36,
Catalogue
Cambridge 1984

Koella, Rudolf:
Allianz. Vereinigung moderner
Schweizer Künstler 1937–1954, Katalog
Köln 1981

Kunstmuseum Düsseldorf:
Die reine Form. Von Malewitsch bis
Albers, Katalog (McCrory Collection)
Düsseldorf 1976

Kunstmuseum Winterthur:
Dreissiger Jahre Schweiz. Konstruktive
Kunst 1915–45, Katalog
Winterthur 1981

Kunstverein Hannover:
Malewitsch-Mondrian. Konstruktion als
Konzept. Alexander Dorner gewidmet,
Katalog
Hannover 1977

Kunstverein St. Gallen:
Konstruktive Kunst und
Goldschmiedekunst 1916–1948, Katalog
St. Gallen 1982

Léger, Fernand:
Fonctions de la Peinture,
édité par Roger Garaudy
Paris 1965
dt., ders.:
Mensch, Maschine, Malerei, übersetzt
und eingeleitet von Robert Füglister
Bern 1971

Mansbach, Steven A.:
Visions of Totality. László Moholy-Nagy,
Theo van Doesburg and El Lissitzky
Ann Arbor 1980

Musée d'Art Moderne de la Ville de
Paris:
Abstraction-Création 1931–1936,
Catalogue
Paris 1978

Nash, J.M.:
Cubism, Futurism and Constructivism
London 1974
dt., ders.:
Kubismus, Futurismus und
Konstruktivismus
München/Zürich 1975

Palazzo Exreale Milano:
Arte astratta e concreta, Catalogo
Milano 1947

Rathke, Ewald:
Konstruktive Malerei 1915–1930 (mit
einem Beitrag von Eckhard Neumann)
Hanau 1967

Seuphor, Michel:
L'art abstrait, ses origines, ses premiers
maîtres
Paris 1950

Seuphor, Michel:
Ein halbes Jahrhundert abstrakte
Malerei
München 1962

Seuphor, Michel:
La peinture abstraite. Sa genèse.
Son expansion
Paris 1964

Seuphor, Michel:
Cercle et Carré
Paris 1971
(New edition of the texts of 1930)

Staatliche Kunstsammlung Dresden:
Von Malewitsch bis Mondrian. Graphik
und Zeichnungen des Konstruktivismus
aus den Jahren 1913 bis 1930
Dresden 1982

Staber, Margit:
The Non-Objective World 1914–1955
Die gegenstandslose Welt 1914–1955
Bromley Kent 1973

Städtisches Museum
Mönchengladbach:
Rationale Spekulationen.
Konstruktivistische Tendenzen in der
europäischen Kunst zwischen 1915 und
1930. Ausgewählt aus deutschen
Privatsammlungen, Katalog
Mönchengladbach 1972

Vantongerloo, Georges;
Florsheim, Lilian u.a.:
Belgien 1915–1960. Pioniere der
abstrakten Kunst: De Boeck, Joostens,
Servranckx, Vantongerloo
Köln 1976

Westfälisches Landesmuseum
Münster:
abstraction-création 1931–1936, Katalog
Münster 1978

Walden, Herwarth:
Einblick in Kunst. Expressionismus,
Futurismus, Kubismus
Berlin 1917

Recent Constructive Tendencies

Bann, Stephen:
Experimental Painting. Construction,
Abstraction, Destruction, Reduction
New York 1970

Claus, Jürgen:
Kunst heute. Personen, Analysen,
Dokumente
Reinbek bei Hamburg 1965

Drian Galleries London:
Construction. England 1950–1960,
Catalogue
London 1961

Exakte Tendenzen, Verein für
konstruktive Gestaltung, Arbeitskreis
für systematisch konstruktive Kunst
(Hg.):
Theorie und Praxis zur konstruktiven
Kunst heute, Katalog
Wien 1979

Gerstner, Karl:
Kalte Kunst? Zum Standort der heutigen
Malerei
Teufen 1957

Gesellschaft für Kunst und Gestaltung
Bonn:
Eck-Punkte. Positionen
konkret-konstruktiver Kunst heute,
Katalog
Bonn 1987

Hayward Gallery London:
Pier + Ocean. Construction in the Art of
the Seventies, Catalogue
London 1980

Honnef, Klaus (Vorwort):
Geplante Malerei, Katalog
Münster 1974

Institut für Moderne Kunst Nürnberg:
Konstruktive Kunst, Elemente +
Prinzipien. Biennale 1969 Nürnberg,
Katalog, 2 Bde.
Nürnberg 1969

Jewish Museum New York:
Toward a New Abstraction, Catalogue
New York 1963

Modern Art Galerie Wien:
Exakte Tendenzen 82, Aspekte
konstruktiver Kunst in Österreich,
Katalog
Wien 1982

Moderna Museet Stockholm/Amos
Andersons Konstmuseum Helsinki:
Konstruktivisme 1974, Konstruktiivinen
1974, Katalog
Stockholm 1974

Riese, Hans-Peter:
Konstruktive Tendenzen in der BRD,
Katalog, Werkkunstschule
Offenbach 1970

Rotzler, Willy (Bearbeitung):
Konstruktion und Geste: Schweizer
Kunst der 50er Jahre. Katalog, Städt.
Galerie im Prinz-Max-Palais Karlsruhe
u.a.
Karlsruhe 1986

Whitney Museum of American Art:
Generations of Geometry, Abstract
Painting in America since 1930,
Catalogue
New York 1987

Constructive Trends in the USA

Alloway, Lawrence; Seuphor, Michel;
Brunius, Teddy:
Hard-Edge, Catalogue
Paris 1964

Alloway, Lawrence:
Topics in American Art since 1945
New York/London 1975

Battcock, Gregory:
Minimal Art. A Critical Anthology
Dutton/New York 1968

Battcock, Gregory:
Constructivism and Minimal Art. Some
Critical, Theoretical and Aesthetic
Correlations (Dissertation)
New York 1979

Galerie Denise René Paris:
Hard-Edge, Catalogue
Paris 1964

Geldzahler, Henry:
New York Painting and Sculpture:
1940–1970
(with Essay «After Abstract
Expressionism» by Clement Greenberg)
New York 1969

Gemeentemuseum Den Haag:
Minimal Art, Katalog
Den Haag 1968

Lippard, Lucy R.; Develing, Enno:
Minimal Art, Katalog
Düsseldorf 1969

Los Angeles County Museum of Art:
Post Painterly Abstraction, Catalogue
Los Angeles 1964

Lowe Art Museum, University of Miami:
Less is More. The Influence of the
Bauhaus on American Art, Catalogue
Miami 1974

Withney Museum of American Art
New York:
Geometric Abstraction in America,
Catalogue
New York 1962

Kinetic Art/Op Art

Barrett, Cyril:
An introduction to Optical Art
London 1971

Hultén, Pontus; Bordier, Roger;
Vasarely, Victor:
Le Mouvement, Catalogue
Paris 1955

Hultén, Pontus:
The Machine as Seen at the End of the
Mechanical Age. Introduction to:
The Machine, Catalogue, Museum of
Modern Art
New York 1968

Kunsthalle Bern:
Licht und Bewegung. Kinetische Kunst,
Katalog
Bern 1965

Kunst- und Museumsverein Wuppertal:
Optical Art, Katalog
Wuppertal 1969

Museum of Modern Art New York:
The Responsive Eye, Catalogue
New York 1965

Popper, Frank:
Origins and Development of Kinetic Art
London 1968

Stedelijk Museum Amsterdam:
Bewogen Beweging, Katalog
Amsterdam 1961

**Structure/Series/Computer/
Cybernetics/Mathematics**

Arts Council Gallery Cambridge:
Unit, Series, Progression. An Exhibition
of Constructions, Catalogue
Cambridge 1967

Baljeu, Joost:
Aspects of a Theory of Synthesist
Plastic Expression
London 1963

Bense, Max:
Konturen einer Geistesgeschichte der
Mathematik. Die Mathematik in der
Kunst, Bd. 2
Hamburg 1949

Bense, Max:
Aesthetica
Baden-Baden 1966

Bill, Max:
Die mathematische Denkweise in der
Kunst unserer Zeit, in: Werk, Nr. 3, 1949

Bill, Max:
Struktur als Kunst? Kunst als Struktur?
u.a. in: Eduard Hüttinger, Max Bill
Zürich 1977

Bauleau, Charles:
La géométrie secrète des peintres
s.l. 1963

Coplans, John:
Serial Imagery, Catalogue
Pasadena 1968

Franke, Herbert W.; Jäger, Gottfried:
Apparative Kunst. Vom Kaleidoskop
zum Computer
Köln 1973

Guderian, Dietmar:
Mathematik in der Kunst der letzten
dreissig Jahre. Von der magischen Zahl
über das endlose Band zum
Computerprogramm, Katalog,
Wilhelm-Hack-Museum
Ludwigshafen 1987

Kästner, Erhart; Osten, Gert van der;
Keller, Horst u.a.:
Ars multiplicata. Vervielfältigte Kunst
seit 1945, Katalog, Kunsthalle
Köln 1968

Kepes, Gyorgy (Hg.):
Struktur in Kunst und Wissenschaft
Brüssel 1976

Kepes, Gyorgy (Hg.):
Modul, Proportion, Symmetrie,
Rhythmus
Brüssel 1969

Kepes, Gyorgy:
Sprache des Sehens
Mainz/Berlin 1970

Landespavillon Stuttgart:
System + Zufall, Katalog
Stuttgart 1978

Menninger, Karl:
Mathematik und Kunst
Göttingen 1959

Moles, Abraham A.:
Art et Ordinateur
Tournai 1971
dt., ders.:
Kunst und Computer,
hg. von Hans Ronge
Köln 1973

Pfeiffer, Günter:
Kunst und Kommunikation.
Grundlegung einer kybernetischen
Ästhetik
Köln 1972

Sykora, Katherian:
Das Phänomen des Seriellen in der
Kunst. Aspekte einer künstlerischen
Methode von Monet bis zur
amerikanischen Pop Art
Würzburg 1983

Westfälischer Kunstverein Münster:
Tendenzen strukturaler Kunst, Katalog
Münster 1966

Wiener, Norbert:
Cybernetics, or Control and
Communication in the Animal and the
Machine
New York 1948
dt., ders.:
Kybernetik. Regelung und
Nachrichtenübertragung im Lebewesen
und in der Maschine
Düsseldorf 1963

Artists' Writings/Manifestoes

Albers, Josef:
Trotz der Geraden
Bern 1961

Apollinaire, Guillaume:
Chroniques d'art 1902–1918.
Textes réunis avec préface et notes par
L.-C. Breunig
Paris 1960

Apollonio, Umbro (Hg.);
Richter, Horst (Essay):
Der Futurismus. Manifeste und
Dokumente einer künstlerischen
Revolution 1909–1918
Köln 1972

Arp, Hans:
Onze peintres vus par Arp
Zürich 1949

Baumeister, Willi:
Das Unbekannte in der Kunst
Stuttgart 1947

Bächler, Hagen; Letsch, Herbert (Hg.):
De-Stijl-Schriften und -Manifeste zu
einem theoretischen Konzept
ästhetischer Umweltgestaltung
Leipzig/Weimar 1984

Bense, Max; Gomringer, Eugen;
Artaud, Antonin u.a.:
Gesammelte Manifeste.
Serielle Manifeste 66
St. Gallen 1966

Bill, Max:
Quinze variations sur un même thème.
15 Tafeln, Textheft 3sprachig, in Mappe
Paris 1938

Bill, Max:
System mit fünf vierfarbigen Zentren.
Anleitung zum Betrachten eines Bildes
Zumikon/Zürich 1972

Bill, Max:
Konkrete Kunst/Die mathematische
Denkweise in der Kunst unserer
Zeit/Feststellungen 1974–76, in:
Eduard Hüttinger, Max Bill
Zürich 1977

Braque, Georges:
La peinture et nous, recueillis par Dora
Vallier, in: Propos de l'artiste recueillis,
Cahiers d'art,
Paris 1954
dt., ders.:
Vom Geheimnis in der Kunst.
Gesammelte Schriften und von Dora
Vallier aufgezeichnete Erinnerungen
und Gespräche (darunter auch «Mein
Weg»)
Zürich 1958

Claus, Jürgen:
Theorien zeitgenössischer Malerei in
Selbstzeugnissen
Reinbek bei Hamburg 1963

Delaunay, Robert:
Zur Malerei der reinen Farbe. Schriften
1912–1940, hg. von Hajo Düchting
München 1983

Doesburg, Theo van:
Grundbegriffe der neuen gestaltenden
Kunst
Bd. 6 der «Bauhausbücher»
München 1925
Reprint Reihe «Neue Bauhausbücher»,
hg. von Hans M. Wingler
Mainz/Berlin 1966

Gleizes, Albert:
Kubismus
Bd. 13 der «Bauhausbücher»
Reprint Reihe «Neue Bauhausbücher»,
hg. von Hans M. Wingler
Mainz/Berlin 1980

Herbin, Auguste:
L'art non-figuratif non-objectif
Paris 1949

Hinterreiter, Hans:
Geometrische Schönheit
Celle 1958

I Manifesti del Futurismo. Prima Serie
Firenze 1914

Kandinsky, Wassily; Marc, Franz (Hg.):
Der Blaue Reiter. Almanach
München 1912
Dokumentarische Neuausgabe von
Klaus Lankheit
München 1965

Kandinsky, Wassily:
Klänge. Gedichte in Prosa mit

schwarz-weissen und farbigen
Holzschnitten vom Stock gedruckt
München 1913

Kandinsky, Wassily:
Punkt und Linie zu Fläche. Beitrag zur
Analyse der malerischen Elemente
Bd. 9 der «Bauhausbücher»
München 1926

Kandinsky, Wassily:
Über das Geistige in der Kunst,
hg. von Max Bill
Bern 1973[10]
(Erstveröffentlichung 1912 im Almanach
«Der Blaue Reiter»)

Kandinsky, Wassily:
Essays über Kunst und Künstler,
hg. von Max Bill
Bern 1963[2]

Klee, Felix (Hg.):
Tagebücher von Paul Klee 1898–1918
Köln 1957

Glaesemer, Jürgen;
Kersten, Wolfgang (Hg.):
Paul Klee, Tagebücher
Stuttgart/Teufen 1988

Klee, Paul:
Pädagogisches Skizzenbuch
Bd. 2 der «Bauhausbücher»
München 1925

Klee, Paul:
Das bildnerische Denken,
hg. von Jürg Spiller
Basel 1956
(based on Klee's teaching at the
Bauhaus)

Klee, Paul:
Beiträge zur bildnerischen Formlehre,
hg. von Jürgen Glaesemer
Basel 1979
(Faksimilierte Ausgabe des
Originalmanuskripts zum ersten
Vortragszyklus am Staatlichen
Bauhaus Weimar 1921/22)

Léger, Fernand:
L'esthétique de la machine, in:
Bulletin de l'Effort Moderne, Nos 1/2
Paris 1924
dt., ders.:
Maschinenästhetik, in:
Fernand Léger. Mensch, Maschine,
Malerei
Bern 1971

Lissitzky, El; Arp, Hans (Hg.):
Die Kunst-Ismen. Les Ismes de l'Art.
The Isms of Art
Erlenbach 1925

Lissitzky, El:
Proun und Wolkenbügel.
Schriften, Briefe, Dokumente
Dresden 1977

Lohse, Richard Paul:
Entwicklungslinien 1945–1975, in:
R.P. Lohse, Modulare und serielle
Malerei, Katalog, Kunsthaus
Zürich 1976

Lynton, Rob. (Vorwort):
Worte und Gedanken von
Ben Nicholson, Katalog, Galerie Beyeler
Basel 1968

Malewitsch, Kasimir:
Die gegenstandslose Welt
Reihe «Bauhausbücher»
München 1927

Malewitsch, Kasimir:
Suprematismus –
Die gegenstandslose Welt
Köln 1962

Malevitch, K.S.:
Essays on Arts, ed. by T. Andersen
London 1969

Marinetti, F.T.:
Manifest des Futurismus, in:
Die Futuristen, Katalog,
Galerie «Der Sturm»
Berlin 1912

Moholy-Nagy, László:
Malerei, Photographie, Film
Bd. 8 der «Bauhausbücher»
München 1925

Moholy-Nagy, László:
Vision in Motion
Chicago 1947

Moholy-Nagy, László; Kassák, Ludwig:
Buch neuer Künstler. Nachdruck mit
einem Nachwort von Eva Körner
Budapest 1977
(Erstdruck in der Zeitschrift
«Ma» (Heute), Wien 1922)

Mondrian, Piet:
Neue Gestaltung. Neoplastizismus.
Nieuwe Beelding.
Bd. 5 der «Bauhausbücher»
München 1925
Reprint Reihe «Neue Bauhausbücher»,
hg. von Hans M. Wingler
Mainz/Berlin 1974

Muche, Georg:
Blickpunkt.
Sturm DADA Bauhaus Gegenwart
München 1961

Nicholson, Ben:
Notes on Abstract Art, in:
Horizon
London, October 1941

Ozenfant, Amédée:
Art
Paris 1928
dt., ders.:
Leben und Gestaltung.
I: Bilanz des 20. Jahrhunderts,
II: Aufbau eines neuen Geistes,
hg. und übersetzt von
Gertrud Grohmann
Potsdam 1931

Pörtner, Paul (Hg.):
Literaturrevolution 1910–1925.
Dokumente, Manifeste, Programme,
2 Bde.
Neuwied u.a. 1960

Rotzler, Willy (Hg.):
Johannes Itten. Werke und Schriften
Zürich 1972, 1978[2]

Schlemmer, Oskar; Moholy-Nagy,
László; Molnár, Farkas:
Die Bühne im Bauhaus
Bd. 4 der «Bauhausbücher»
München 1925

Schmidt, Dieter:
Manifeste 1905 bis 1933
Dresden o.J.

Vasarely, Victor:
Notes pour un manifeste, in:
Le mouvement, Catalogue
Paris 1955

Velde, Henry van de:
Vom neuen Stil
Leipzig 1907

Vitt, Walter:
Von strengen Gestaltern.
Texte, Reden, Interviews und Briefe zur
konstruktiven und konkreten Kunst
Köln 1982

Vries, Gert de (Hg.):
Über Kunst. Künstlertexte zum
veränderten Künstlerverständnis
nach 1965
Köln 1974

Periodicals

ABC, Beiträge zum Bauen, hg. von
Hans Schmidt, Emil Roth, Mart Stam
Zürich 1924–28

abstraction-création, Art non-figurativ,
5 Nos
Paris 1932–36

abstrakt–konkret, hg. von Max Bill für
die Galerie «Des Eaux Vives», 12 Nrn.
Zürich 1944/45

art concret, hg. von Theo van Doesburg,
1 No.
Paris, April 1930

Bauhaus, Zeitschrift für Gestaltung
Dessau 1926–29

Blast, Review of the Great
English Vortex, 2 Nos.
London 1914/15

The Blind Man, ed. by Marcel Duchamp
and Henri Pierre Roché,
2 Nos.
New York 1917

Blok, Czasopismo awangardy
artystycznej, 11 Nrn.
Warszawa 1923–26

Casabella-Continuità, Rivista
internazionale di architettura
Milano, ab 1923

Cercle et Carré, hg. von Michel Seuphor,
3 Nos.
Paris 1930

Circle, International Survey of
Constructive Art, hg. von J.L. Martin,
Ben Nicholson, Naum Gabo
London 1937

De Stijl, gegründet von Piet Mondrian
und Theo van Doesburg
1917–37
De Stijl. Complete Reprint, 1917–1932,
2 Bde.
Amsterdam 1968

Domus, hg. von Gio Ponti
Milano, ab 1928

G, Zeitschrift für elementare Gestaltung,
hg. von Hans Richter, Werner Graeff,
El Lissitzky
Berlin 1923–25, Reprint München 1987

Integration, Zeitschrift für eine neue
Konzeption der Kunst und Kultur,
Eschenau 1965–73/0+Nul, 1961–64/4p,
hg. von Herman de Vries
(bei «4p» Mitherausgeber)

L'Esprit Nouveau, éd. par Le Corbusier,
Amédée Ozenfant, Paul Dermée,
28 Nos.
Paris 1920–25

Ma (Heute), Hg. von Lajos Kassák,
Budapest 1916–20,
im Exil in Wien 1920–27

Merz, hg. von Kurt Schwitters
Hannover 1923–32

Neue Grafik. New Graphic Design.
Graphisme Actuel. Internationale
Zeitschrift für Grafik und verwandte
Gebiete, 18 Nrn.
Olten 1958–65

Plastique, hg. von Sophie Taeuber-Arp,
3sprachig, 5 Nrn.
Meudon bei Paris 1937–39

Spirale, Internationale Zeitschrift für
junge Kunst, hg. von Eugen Gomringer,
Dieter Roth, Marcel Wyss, 9 Nrn.
Bern 1953–64

Praesens, Awartalnik Modernistow
Warszawa 1926–30

Structure, hg. von Joost Baljeu
Amsterdam 1958–64

The Structurist, ed. by Elie Bornstein
Saskatoon (Kanada), ab 1960

Supremus
(nie erschienene Zeitschrift des
russischen Supremistenzirkels,
1916 an der Planung
beteiligt u.a. Ljublow Popowa,
Olga Rozanowa)

Transition
Paris/Den Haag/New York 1927–38

Vjeschtsch-Gegenstand-Objekt,
hg. von El Lissitzky, Ilja Ehrenburg
Berlin 1922

Zero, hg. von Otto Piene, Heinz Mack,
3 Nrn.
Düsseldorf 1,2: 1958, 3: 1961

Germany between the Wars

Billeter, Erika (Redaktion):
Deutschland 1930–1939.
Verbot-Anpassung-Exil.
Zusatz zum Ausstellungskatalog:
Die dreissiger Jahre – Schauplatz
Deutschland, Kunsthaus
Zürich 1977

Haus der Kunst München/Kunsthaus
Zürich:
Die dreissiger Jahre – Schauplatz
Deutschland, Katalog
München 1977

Hinz, Berthold:
Die Malerei im deutschen Faschismus.
Kunst und Konterrevolution
Frankfurt am Main 1977

Kaiser, Fritz (Redaktion):
Entartete Kunst. Führer durch die
Ausstellung, Haus der Deutschen Kunst
München 1937, Nachdruck
München 1969

Neue Gesellschaft für bildende Kunst
Berlin:
Wem gehört die Welt? Kunst und
Gesellschaft in der Weimarer Republik,
Katalog
Berlin 1977

Neue Nationalgalerie Berlin u.a.:
Tendenzen der zwanziger Jahre.
15. Europäische Kunstausstellung,
Katalog
Berlin 1977

Willett, John:
The New Sobriety, Art and Politics in
the Weimar Period 1917–1933
London 1978
dt., ders.:
Explosion der Mitte.
Kunst und Politik 1917–1933
München 1981

Color/Perception

Albers, Josef:
Interaction of Color
New Haven 1963
dt., ders.:
Interaction of Color. Grundlegung einer
Didaktik des Sehens
Köln 1970

Albrecht, Hans J.:
Farbe als Sprache. Robert Delaunay,
Josef Albers, Richard Paul Lohse
Köln 1974

Grignani, Franco:
Una metodologia della visione.
A Methodology of Vision.
Eine Methode des Sehens, Katalog
Milano 1975

Itten, Johannes:
Kunst der Farbe. Subjektives Erleben
und objektives Erkennen als Wege
der Kunst
Ravensburg 1961[4]

Kunsthalle Bern:
Formen der Farbe, Katalog
Bern 1967

Merleau-Ponty, Maurice:
Phénoménologie de la perception
Paris 1947
dt., ders.:
Phänomenologie der Wahrnehmung,
Übersetzung und Einführung
von Rudolf Boehm
Berlin 1966

Moles, Abraham A.:
Informationstheorie und ästhetische
Wahrnehmung
Köln 1971

Pawlik, Johannes:
Goethe, Farbenlehre. Textauswahl mit
einer Einführung und neuen Farbtafeln
Köln 1980[3]

Architecture

Behne, Adolf:
Der moderne Zweckbau
München 1926

Conrads, Ulrich (Hg.):
Programme und Manifeste zur
Architektur des 20. Jahrhunderts, in:
Bauwelt Fundamente, Bd. 1
Berlin 1964

Giedion, Sigfried:
Space, Time and Architecture.
The Growth of a New Tradition
Cambridge 1941
dt., ders.:
Raum, Zeit, Architektur.
Die Entstehung einer neuen Tradition
Ravensburg 1965

Le Corbusier:
Vers une Architecture
Paris 1923
(Collection of articles from the
magazine «L'Esprit Nouveau»)
dt., ders.:
Kommende Baukunst, übersetzt von
Hans Hildebrandt
Berlin/Leipzig 1926
dt., ders.:
Ausblick auf eine Architektur,
Hans Hildebrandts Übersetzung
neu überarbeitet von Eva Gärtner
Berlin/Frankfurt am Main/Wien 1963

Persico, Edoardo:
Profezia dell'architettura
Milano 1945

Persico, Edoardo:
Scritti d'architettura 1927–1935
Firenze 1968

Roth, Alfred:
Die Neue Architektur
Erlenbach–Zürich 1948

Sartoris, Alberto:
Gli elementi dell'architettura funzionale.
Sintesi panoramica dell'architettura
moderna
Milano 1932

Sartoris, Alberto: Encyclopédie de
l'architecture moderne
Milan 1948

Gropius, Walter:
Internationale Architektur
Bd. 1 der «Bauhausbücher»
Passau 1925
Reprint Reihe «Neue Bauhausbücher»,
hg. von Hans M. Wingler
Mainz/Berlin 1981

Photo/Cinema/Montage

Die Fotomontage. Geschichte und
Wesen einer Kunstform
Ingolstadt o.J.

Jürgens-Kirchhoff, Annegret:
Technik und Tendenz der Montage in
der Bildenden Kunst des
20. Jahrhunderts
Lahn-Giessen 1978

Lach, Friedhelm:
Der Merzkünstler Kurt Schwitters
Köln 1971

Leyda, Jay:
Kino
New York/London 1960

Lusk, Irene Charlotte:
Montagen ins Blaue. László
Moholy-Nagy:
Fotomontagen und -collagen
1922–1943, Werkbund-Archiv 5
Giessen 1980

Roh, Franz; Tschichold, Jan:
foto-auge, œil et photo, photo eye
Stuttgart 1929

Siepmann, Eckhard:
Montage: John Heartfield. Vom Club
DADA zur Arbeiter-Illustrierten Zeitung
Berlin 1977

Wescher, Herta:
Die Collage. Geschichte eines
künstlerischen Ausdrucksmittels
Köln 1968

Württembergischer Kunstverein
Stuttgart:
Film und Foto der 20er Jahre, Katalog
Stuttgart 1979

Special Aspects

Becker, Jürgen; Vostell, Wolf:
Happenings, Fluxus, Pop Art,
Nouveau Réalisme
Hamburg 1965

Busoni, Ferruccio:
Entwurf einer neuen Ästhetik der
Tonkunst
Leipzig 1916[2]
ders.:
Entwurf einer neuen Tonkunst. Mit
Anmerkungen von Arnold Schönberg
und einem Nachwort von H.H.
Stuckenschmidt
Frankfurt am Main 1974

Claus, Jürgen:
Expansion der Kunst. Beiträge zu
Theorie und Praxis öffentlicher Kunst.
Action, Environment, Kybernetik,
Technik, Urbanistik
Hamburg 1970

Dienst, Rolf Gunter:
Pop Art. Eine kritische Information
Wiesbaden 1965

Giedion, Sigfried:
Mechanization takes command
New York 1948
dt., ders.:
Die Herrschaft der Mechanisierung.
Ein Beitrag zur anonymen Geschichte
Frankfurt am Main 1982

Gombrich, E.H.:
Art and Illusion. A Study in the
psychology of pictorial representation
New York 1960
dt., ders.:
Kunst und Illusion. Zur Psychologie der
bildenden Darstellung, übertragen von
Lisbeth Gombrich
Köln 1967[2]

Gombrich, E.G.:
The Sense of Order. A study in the
psychology of decorative art
Oxford 1979
dt., ders.:
Ornament und Kunst. Schmuckbetrieb
und Ordnungssinn in der Psychologie
des dekorativen Schaffens
Stuttgart 1982

Honnef, Klaus:
Concept Art
Köln 1971

Krauss, Rosalind E.:
Passages in Modern Sculpture
New York 1977

Lambert, Jean-Clarence:
COBRA – un art libre
Paris 1983
dt., ders.:
COBRA
Königstein im Taurus 1985

Maenz, Paul:
Art Déco 1920–1940.
Formen zwischen zwei Kriegen
Köln 1974

Mahlow, Dietrich (Hg.):
Was die Schönheit sei, das weiss ich
nicht, Künstler – Theorie – Werk,
Katalog
Nürnberg-Köln 1971

Musée National d'Art Moderne,
Centre Georges Pompidou Paris:
Paris–New York, Catalogue
Paris 1977

Musée National d'Art Moderne,
Centre Georges Pompidou Paris:
Paris – Berlin 1900–1933. Rapports et
contrastes France–Allemagne,
Catalogue

Paris 1978
dt.: Paris – Berlin 1900–1933.
Übereinstimmungen und Gegensätze
Frankreich–Deutschland, Katalog
München 1979

Musée National d'Art Moderne,
Centre Georges Pompidou Paris:
Paris – Moscou, Catalogue
Paris 1979

Musée National d'Art Moderne,
Centre Georges Pompidou, Paris
Les Années Cinquante, Catalogue
Paris 1988

Müller-Brockmann, Josef und Shizuko:
Geschichte des Plakats
Zürich 1971

Nelson, E.; Hayes, Tanya:
Claude Lévi-Strauss. The Anthropologist
as Hero
Cambridge 1970

Piene, Otto; Mack, Heinz (Hg.):
Zero
Köln 1973

Rose, Barbara:
Amerikas Weg zur Modernen Kunst.
Von der Mülltonnenschule
zur Minimal Art
Köln 1969

Rotzler, Willy:
Objekt-Kunst von Duchamp bis Kienholz
Köln 1972, 1981[3]

Rublowsky, J.; Heyman, K.:
Pop Art. Images of the American Dream
New York 1965

Schneckenburger, Manfred:
Deutsche Bildhauer der Gegenwart,
Katalog, Kunstverein
Augsburg 1983

Tairoff, Alexander:
Das entfesselte Theater
Potsdam 1923

Trier, Eduard (Einführung):
Dreidimensional. Aktuelle Kunst aus der
Bundesrepublik Deutschland, Katalog
Stuttgart 1983

Tschichold, Jan:
Die neue Typographie
Berlin 1928
Neuausgabe: Berlin 1988

Monographs

Agam, Yaacov

Agam, Yaacov:
Textes de l'artiste
Neuchâtel 1962

Albers, Josef

Gomringer, Eugen:
Josef Albers. Das Werk des Malers und
Baumeisters als Beitrag zur visuellen
Gestaltung im 20. Jahrhundert
Starnberg 1968

Spies, Werner:
Josef Albers
Teufen 1970

Archipenko, Alexander

Karshan, Donald:
Alexander Archipenko.
The Sculpture and Graphic Art
Tübingen 1974

Arp, Jean

Seuphor, Michel:
Arp – Mission Spirituelle de l'Art.
A propos de l'œuvre de Sophie
Taeuber-Arp et de Jean Arp
Paris 1953

Giedion-Welcker, Carola:
Hans Arp
Teufen 1957

Bill, Max

Staber, Margit:
Max Bill
St. Gallen 1971

Hüttinger, Eduard:
Max Bill
Zürich 1977, 1987[2]

Anker, Valentina:
Max Bill ou la recherche d'un art logique
Lausanne 1979

Rotzler, Willy; Honisch, Dieter u.a.:
Max Bill. Zur Ausstellung anlässlich
seines 75. Geburtstages, Katalog,
Helmhaus
Zürich 1983

Calder, Alexander

Caradente, Giovanni:
Alexander Calder, Catalogo
Torino 1983

Marter, Joan:
Alexander Calder
New York 1984

Caro, Anthony

Whelan, Richard:
Anthony Caro
Oxford 1974

Rubin, William:
Anthony Caro
New York 1979

Delaunay, Robert and Sonja

Vriesen, Gustav; Imdahl, Max:
Robert Delaunay, Licht und Farbe
Köln 1967

Cohen, Arthur A.:
Sonia Delaunay
New York 1975

Doesburg, Theo van

Jaffé, Hans L.C.:
Theo van Doesburg
Amsterdam 1983

Doig, Allan:
Theo van Doesburg
Painting into Architecture,
Theory into Practice
Cambridge 1986

Feininger, Lyonel

Hess, Hans:
Lyonel Feininger
Stuttgart 1959

Haus der Kunst München:
Lyonel Feininger, Katalog
München 1973

Fleischmann, Adolf

Wedewer, Rolf:
Adolf Fleischmann
Stuttgart 1977

Fontana, Lucio

Schulz-Hoffmann, Carla:
Lucio Fontana, Katalog
München 1983

Fruhtrunk, Günter

Imdahl, Max; Besset, Maurice:
Günter Fruhtrunk, Bilder 1952–1972
München/Karlsruhe 1972

Gabo, Naum

Read, Herbert; Martin, Leslie:
Naum Gabo. Bauten, Skulpturen,
Malerei, Zeichnungen, Grafik
Neuenburg 1961

Nash, Steven A.; Merkert, Jörn (Hg.):
Naum Gabo. Sechzig Jahre
Konstruktivismus. Mit Œuvre-Katalog
der Konstruktionen und Skulpturen
München 1986

Glarner, Fritz

Staber, Margit:
Fritz Glarner
Zürich 1976

Gorin, Jean

Pomere, Marianne Le:
Jean Gorin. Ein führender Vertreter
des Neo-Plastizismus in Europa
Zürich 1986

Graeser, Camille

Müller, F. (Hg.);
Gomringer, E. (Einführung):
Camille Graeser
Teufen 1968

Rotzler, Willy:
Camille Graeser. Lebensweg und
Lebenswerk eines konstruktiven
Künstlers
Zürich 1979

Hauser, Erich

Bott, Gerhard (Hg.):
Erich Hauser. Werkverzeichnis
Nürnberg 1970

Herbin, Auguste

Massat, René:
Auguste Herbin
Paris 1953

Hinterreiter, Hans

Albrecht, Hans J.; Koella, Rudolf:
Hans Hinterreiter, ein Schweizer
Vertreter der konstruktiven Kunst,
hg. von István Schlégl
Buchs-Zürich 1982

Honegger, Gottfried

Lemoine, Serge:
Gottfried Honegger. Sculptures
1953–1983
Paris/Zürich 1983

Lemoine, Serge:
Gottfried Honegger. Tableaux-Reliefs,
Skulpturen 1970–1983
Buchs–Zürich 1983

Itten, Johannes

Rotzler, Willy; Itten, Anneliese (Hg.):
Johannes Itten, Werke und Schriften
Zürich 1972, 1978[2]

Westfälisches Landesmuseum
Münster:
Johannes Itten, Katalog
Münster 1980

Jawlensky, Alexej

Zweite, Armin:
Alexej Jawlensky 1864–1941, Katalog
München 1983

Judd, Donald

Smith, Brydon; Smith, Roberta a.o.:
Donald Judd. Catalogue Raisonnée of
Paintings, Objects and Wood-blocks
1960–1974, Catalogue
Ottawa 1975

Kandinsky, Wassily

Grohmann, Will:
Wassily Kandinsky. Leben und Werk
Köln 1958

Roethel, Hans Konrad:
Kandinsky
München 1982

Messer, Th.M.; Poling, V.:
Wassily Kandinsky. Russian and
Bauhaus Years, 1915–1933, Catalogue
New York 1983

Baumann, Felix; Poling, Clark V.:
Kandinsky in Russland und am Bauhaus,
Katalog
Zürich 1984

Kassák, Lajos

Štraus, T.:
Kassák. Ein ungarischer Beitrag zum
Konstruktivismus
Köln 1975

Kelly, Ellsworth

Staatliche Kunsthalle Baden-Baden:
Ellsworth Kelly. Gemälde und
Skulpturen 1966–1979, Katalog
Baden-Baden 1980

Klee, Paul

Grohmann, Will:
Der Maler Paul Klee
Köln 1966

Geelhaar, Christian:
Paul Klee und das Bauhaus
Köln 1972

Schmalenbach, Werner:
Paul Klee. Die Düsseldorfer Sammlung
München 1986

Klein, Yves

Wember, Paul:
Yves Klein
Köln, 1969

Kovács, Attila

Gomringer, Eugen; Scotti, Roland:
Attila Kovács. Bezugssysteme –
Metalinien, Katalog
Ludwigshafen 1987

Kupka, Frank

Vachtova, Ludmila:
Frank Kupka
London 1968

Salomon R. Guggenheim Museum
New York:
František Kupka, Catalogue
New York 1975

Vachtova, Ludmila;
Mladek, Meda; Rowell, Margit:
Frank Kupka, Catalogue
New York 1975, Zürich 1976

Leck, Bart van der

Institut Néerlandais Paris:
Bart van der Leck 1876–1958.
A la recherche de l'image des
temps modernes, Catalogue
Paris 1980

Le Corbusier

Badovici, Jean (Avant-Propos):
Le Corbusier. Œuvre plastique.
Peintures et dessins, Architecture
Paris 1938

Léger, Fernand

Golding, John u.a.:
Léger and Purist Paris, Catalogue
London 1970

Green, Christopher:
Léger and the Avant-Garde
New Haven 1976

Staatliche Kunsthalle Berlin:
Fernand Léger 1881–1955, Katalog
Berlin 1980

Musée National d'Art Moderne Paris:
Léger et l'esprit moderne, Catalogue
Paris 1982

Leuppi, Leo

Helmhaus Zürich:
Leo Leuppi, Katalog
Zürich 1980

LeWitt, Sol

Museum of Modern Art New York:
Sol LeWitt, Catalogue
New York 1978

Lissitzky, El

Richter, Horst:
El Lissitzky. Sieg über die Sonne.
Zur Kunst des Konstruktivismus
Köln 1958

Lissitzky-Küppers, Sophie:
El Lissitzky. Maler, Architekt. Typograf.
Erinnerungen, Briefe, Schriften
Dresden 1976

Grohn, Christian; Hemken, Kai-Uwe;
Nobis, Beatrix u.a.:
El Lissitzky, 1890–1914, Retrospektive,
Katalog
Hannover 1988

Loewensberg, Verena

Kappeler, Susanne:
Verena Loewensberg. Betrachtungen
zum Werk einer konstruktiven Malerin
Zürich 1980

Lohse, Richard Paul

Gomringer, Eugen; Holz, Hans H. u.a.:
Richard Paul Lohse. Modulare und
serielle Ordnungen
Köln 1973

Matheson, J.; Albrecht, H.J.; Billeter, F.;
Ammann, J.Ch.:
Richard Paul Lohse.
Modulare und serielle Ordnungen,
Katalog, Kunsthaus Zürich
Zürich 1976

Albrecht, Hans J.; Fuchs, Rudi;
Holz, Hans H. u.a.:
Richard Paul Lohse. Modulare und
serielle Ordnungen 1943–84
Zürich 1984

Malevich, Kasimir

Andersen, Troels:
Malevitch, Katalog
Amsterdam 1970

Martin, Jean-Hubert:
Casimir Malévitch, Œuvres
Paris 1980

Kowtun, Jewgeni; Shadowa, Larissa:
Kasimir Malewitsch 1878–1935.
Werke aus sowjetischen Sammlungen,
Katalog
Düsseldorf 1980

Shadowa, Larissa A.:
Kasimir Malewitsch und sein Kreis
München 1982

Mavignier, Almir

Kunstgewerbemuseum Zürich:
Almir Mavignier. Serielle
Farbprogressionen, Katalog
Zürich 1975

Moholy-Nagy, László

Kostelanetz, Richard (Ed.):
László Moholy-Nagy
New York/Washington 1970

Moholy-Nagy, Sibyl:
László Moholy-Nagy. Experiment in
Totality
Cambridge 1950/1969
dt., dies.:
László Moholy-Nagy.
Ein Totalexperiment, mit einem Vorwort
von Walter Gropius
Mainz 1972

Weitemeier, Hannah (Hg.):
László Moholy-Nagy
Stuttgart 1974

Passuth, Krisztina:
László Moholy-Nagy
Weingarten 1986

Mondrian, Piet

Seuphor, Michel:
Piet Mondrian. Leben und Werk
Köln 1956

Wijsenbeek, L.J.F.:
Piet Mondrian
Recklinghausen 1968

Wismer, Beat:
Mondrians ästhetische Utopie
Baden 1985

Jaffé, Hans L.C.:
Piet Mondrian
New York 1985

Morellet, François

Lemoine, Serge;
Staber, Margit (Vorwort):
François Morellet
Zürich 1986

Nicholson, Ben

Russell, John (Introduction):
Ben Nicholson. Drawings, Paintings and
Reliefs 1911–1968
London 1969

Noland, Kenneth

Moffett, Kenworth:
Kenneth Noland
New York 1977

Pevsner, Antoine

Peissi, Pierre; Giedion-Welcker, Carola;
Salles, Georges:
Antoine Pevsner
Neuenburg 1961

Puni, Iwan

Berninger, Herman; Cartier, Jean A.:
Jean Pougny (Iwan Puni) 1892–1956,
Catalogue de l'œuvre
Tübingen 1972

Richter, Hans

Kunsthaus Zürich:
Hans Richter 1888–1976.
Dadaist, Filmpionier, Maler, Theoretiker.
Katalog
Zürich 1982

Rickey, George

Rosenthal, Nan:
George Rickey
New York 1977

Riley, Bridget

Ruhrberg, Karl; Schmied, Wieland;
Robertson, Bryan:
Bridget Riley, Katalog, Städtische
Kunsthalle
Düsseldorf 1971

Rodchenko, Alexander

Rodtschenko, W. (Hg.):
Alexander Rodtschenko. Maler,
Konstrukteur, Fotograf
Dresden 1984

Khan-Magomedov, Selim O.:
Rodchenko, The Complete Work
London 1986

Schlemmer, Oskar

Hildebrandt, Hans
Oskar Schlemmer
München 1952

Grohmann, Will (Hg.):
Oskar Schlemmer. Zeichnungen und
Graphik, Œuvre-Katalog
Stuttgart 1965

Maur, Karin von:
Oskar Schlemmer. Der Maler,
der Wandgestalter, der Plastiker,
der Zeichner, der Graphiker,
der Bühnengestalter, der Lehrer
München 1982

Schoonhoven, Jan

Gemeentemuseum Den Haag:
Jan Schoonhoven, Retrospectief,
Katalog
Den Haag 1984

Strasser, George; Lemoine, Serge:
Jan Schoonhoven. Rétrospective.
Katalog
Paris/Grenoble 1988

Smith, David

McCoy, Garnett:
David Smith
London 1973

Soto, Jesus Rafael

Joray, Marcel:
Jesus Rafael Soto
Neuenburg 1984

Stella, Frank

Kunsthalle Bielefeld:
Frank Stella. Werke 1958–1976, Katalog
Bielefeld 1977

Rubin, William:
Frank Stella, Catalogue
New York 1982

Rubin, William:
Frank Stella, 1970–1987. Catalogue
New York 1987

Taeuber-Arp, Sophie

Schmidt, Georg (Hg.):
Sophie Taeuber-Arp. Werkverzeichnis
1916–1942
Basel 1948

Staber, Margit:
Sophie Taeuber-Arp
Lausanne 1970

Lanchner, Carolyn:
Sophie Taeuber-Arp
New York 1981

Thomas Jankowski, Angela:
Sophie Taeuber-Arp. 1889–1943
Ascona 1983

Tatlin, Vladimir

Andersen, Troels:
Vladimir Tatlin, Catalogue
Stockholm 1968

Shadowa, Larissa A.:
Tatlin
Weingarten 1987

Vantongerloo, Georges

Bill, Max (Introduction):
Georges Vantongerloo, Catalogue,
Marlborough Fine Art Ltd.
London 1962

Baumann, Felix; Bill, Max:
Georges Vantongerloo, Katalog
Zürich 1981

Vasarely, Victor

Joray, Marcel:
Victor Vasarely
Bde. I–III
Neuchâtel 1965–74

Spies, Werner:
Victor Vasarely
Köln 1971

Vivarelli, Carlo

Kappeler, Susanne:
Carlo Vivarelli. Malerei – Plastik –
Gebrauchsgrafik
Zürich 1988

Vordemberge-Gildewart, Friedrich

Jaffé, Hans L. C.:
Friedrich Vordemberge-Gildewart.
Mensch und Werk
Köln 1971

Rotzler, Willy:
Vordemberge-Gildewart
St. Gallen 1979

Index of Illustrations

All works stated to be owned by the Museum of Modern Art, New York, by the Louisiana Museum, Humlebaek-Copenhagen or by the Tel Aviv Museum are part of the donations of the Riklis Collection of McCrory Corporation, New York.

326

Index of names

(Numbers in italics refer to illustrations)